Economy and Ecosystems in Change

ADVANCES IN ECOLOGICAL ECONOMICS

General Editor: Robert Costanza, *Director, University of Maryland Institute for Ecological Economics and Professor, Center for Environmental and Estuarine Studies and Zoology Department, US*

This important new series is designed to make a significant contribution to the development of the principles and practices of ecological economics. As this field has expanded dramatically in recent years, the series will provide an invaluable forum for the publication of high quality work and show how ecological economic analysis can make a contribution to understanding and resolving important problems.

The main emphasis of the series is on the development and application of new original ideas in ecological economics. International in its approach, it will include some of the best theoretical and empirical work in the field with contributions to fundamental principles, rigorous evaluations of existing concepts, historical surveys and future visions. It will seek to address some of the most important theoretical questions and give policy solutions for the ecological problems confronting the global village as we move into the twenty-first century.

Economy and Ecosystems in Change
Analytical and Historical Approaches
Edited by Jeroen C.J.M. van den Bergh and Jan van der Straaten

Transition to a Sustainable Society
A Backcasting Approach to Modelling Energy and Ecology
Henk A.J. Mulder and Wouter Biesiot

Economy and Ecosystems in Change

Analytical and Historical Approaches

Edited by

Jeroen C. J. M. van den Bergh
Department of Spatial Economics, Free University,
Amsterdam, The Netherlands

Jan van der Straaten
European Centre for Nature Conservation and Department
of Leisure Studies, Tilburg University, Tilburg,
The Netherlands

Technical Editor: Paula Hill Jasinski

ADVANCES IN ECOLOGICAL ECONOMICS

Edward Elgar
Cheltenham, UK • Lyme, US

Published by
Edward Elgar Publishing Limited
8 Lansdown Place
Cheltenham
Glos GL50 2HU
UK

Edward Elgar Publishing, Inc.
1 Pinnacle Hill Road
Lyme
NH 03768
US

A catalogue record for this book
is available from the British Library

Library of Congress Cataloguing in Publication Data

Economy and ecosystems in change : analytical and historical
   approaches / edited by Jeroen van den Bergh, Jan van der Straaten ;
   in association with the International Society for Ecological
   economics.
         (Advances in ecological economics)
   Papers presented at the third meeting of the International Society
   for Ecological Economics, held in San José, Costa Rica from October
   24–28, 1994.
   Includes index.
     1. Environmental economics. 2. Ecology—Economic aspects.
   3. Sustainable development. 4. Environmental policy—Economic
   aspects. I. Bergh, Jeroen C.J.M. van den, 1965–   .
   II. Straaten, Jan van der. III. International Society for
   Ecological economics. Meeting (3rd : 1994 : San José, Costa Rica)
   IV. Series.
   HC79.E5E286 1997
   333.7—dc21   97–23111
                                                       CIP

Printed and bound in Great Britain by Hartnolls Limited, Bodmin, Cornwall

ISBN 1 85898 647 8

CONTENTS

FIGURES

TABLES

CONTRIBUTORS

Jaap Arntzen	Department of Environmental Science, University of Botswana, Gaborone, Botswana
Sander de Bruyn	Department of Spatial Economics, Free University, Amsterdam, The Netherlands
Sam Cole	Department of Geography and Planning, Center for Regional Studies, State University of New York at Buffalo, New York
Sylvie Faucheux	Centre d'Economie et d'Ethique pour l'Environnement et le Développement (C3ED), Université de Versailles, Guyancourt, France
Carl Folke	Beijer Institute for Ecological Economics, The Royal Swedish Academy of Sciences, and Department of Ecology, Stockholm University, Stockholm, Sweden
Géraldine Froger	Centre d'Economie et d'Ethique pour l'Environnement et le Développement (C3ED), Université de Versailles, Guyancourt, France
Silvio Funtowicz	EC—Joint Research Centre ISEInformatics, Ispra (VA), Italy
John Gowdy	Department of Economics, School of Humanities and Social Sciences, Rensselaer Polytechnic Institute, Troy, New York
Nico Heerink	Department of Development Economics, Agricultural University of Wageningen, Wageningen, The Netherlands
Friedrich Hinterberger	Division for Material Flows and Structural Change, Wuppertal Institute for Climate, Environment, and Energy, Wuppertal, Germany
Susan Kask	Department of Economics and Finance, Western Carolina University, Cullowhee, North Carolina
Henk Kox	Department of Development and Agricultural Economics, Free University, Amsterdam, The Netherlands
Arie Kuyvenhoven	Department of Development Economics, Agricultural University of Wageningen, Wageningen, The Netherlands
Glenn-Marie Lange	Institute for Economic Analysis, New York University, New York, New York
Pete Morton	Department of Biological Sciences, University of Denver, Denver, Colorado
Giuseppe Munda	Department d'Economia i d'Història Econòmica, Universitat Autònoma Bellaterra, Barcelona, Spain
Martin O'Connor	Université de Versailles Saint-Quentin-en-Yvelines, Guyancourt, France
Hans Opschoor	Institute of Social Studies, The Hague, The Netherlands
Charles Perrings	Department of Environmental Economics and Environmental Management, University of York, York, United Kingdom
Futian Qu	College of Land Management, Nanjing Agricultural University, China

Jerry Ravetz   RMC Ltd., London, United Kingdom

Jason Shogren   Department of Economics and Finance, University of Wyoming, Laramie, Wyoming

Kerry Turner   CSERGE, University of East Anglia, Norwich, United Kingdom

Cees van Beers   Department of Economics, Faculty of Law, Leiden University, Leiden, The Netherlands

Jeroen van den Bergh   Department of Spatial Economics, Free University, Amsterdam, The Netherlands

Teunis van Rheenen   Department of Development Economics, Agricultural University of Wageningen, Wageningen, The Netherlands

Jan van der Straaten   European Centre for Nature Conservation and Department of Leisure Studies, Tilburg University, Tilburg, The Netherlands

Gerhard Wegner   Faculty of Economics, University of Witten, Herdecke, Germany

Carlos Frickmann Young   Department of Economics, University College London, London, United Kingdom

PREFACE

The interaction between economies and ecosystems is a topic that has received increasing attention in the last few years. Environmental economics has dealt with natural resources, but has generally not gone further than a very abstract level of analyzing exploitation of renewable resources. This means that issues related to ecosystem structure and functions, multiple use and assessment of use and non-use values have received little attention. However, as this book shows, much attention has recently been focused on dealing with such problems, using both analytical-theoretical, empirical-statistical, and historical–descriptive approaches. On a macro- or regional level economy–ecosystem relationships are more varied and heterogeneous than on a very micro-level, and as a result it will be very difficult to deal analytically with impacts such as ecosystem stress on national economies. However, as is also shown in this book, statistical evaluation and historical analysis may contribute to a better understanding of the intricate links between socioeconomic and environmental–ecological systems on such a scale. In the last part of the book the perspective is further broadened to specifically address policy and institutional issues.

With the exception of one, all the papers in this book were presented at the third meeting of the International Society for Ecological Economics (ISEE), titled "Down to Earth: Practical Applications of Ecological Economics," held in San Jose, Costa Rica from October 24–28, 1994. Since there were many paper presentations at the conference, it was possible to compose an interesting collection of original contributions that represent many of the important research directions within the area of ecological economics. Chapter 2 is additional, and is regarded as a useful contribution as it compares ecological and (traditional) environmental economics. Consequently, it serves as an introduction to ecological economics as well as a background to many of the discussions in other chapters of this book.

Based on detailed comments, several contributions have been substantially revised and improved. The final product has been realized thanks to technical editorial support by the ISEE, which we gratefully acknowledge. We hope that this book stimulates discussion among scientists from natural and social sciences, and contributes to integrated economic and environmental policy making.

Jeroen van den Bergh
Jan van der Straaten

ABOUT ISEE

Ecological economics is concerned with extending and integrating the study and management of nature's household (*ecology*) with humanity's household (*economy*). Ecological economics acknowledges that, in the end, a healthy economy can only exist in symbiosis with a healthy ecology. Ecological economics is the name that has been given to the effort to transcend traditional disciplinary boundaries in order to address the interrelationship between ecological and economic systems in a broad and comprehensive way. Ecological economics takes a holistic worldview with human beings representing one component (albeit a very important one) in the overall system. Moreover, human beings play a unique role in the overall system because they can consciously understand their role in the larger system and manage it for sustainability. Ecological economics seeks to constitute a true marriage of ecology and economics so as to give meaning and substance to the idea of sustainable development. Mechanisms for achieving sustainable development will enable modern societies to develop and prosper within a natural world that is safeguarded from ecological destruction.

The International Society for Ecological Economics (ISEE) is a not-for-profit organization with more than 1,600 members in over 60 countries. Regional chapters have been established in Russia, Brazil, Canada, Europe, and Australia–New Zealand. A chapter is currently being formed in Meso-America, and there are efforts underway to organize chapters in China, Africa, Japan, South America, India, and Southeast Asia. ISEE promotes the integration of ecology and economics by providing information through its membership journal, *Ecological Economics,* and the Ecological Economics Bulletin, and encourages the exchange of ideas by supporting major international conferences and smaller regional meetings on topics of interest to members, as well as research and training programs in ecological economics.

1 ECOLOGICAL ECONOMICS BETWEEN THEORY AND POLICY

Jeroen van den Bergh
Department of Spatial Economics
Free University, De Boelelaan 1105
1081 HV Amsterdam, The Netherlands

Jan van der Straaten
European Centre for Nature Conservation and
Department of Leisure Studies
Tilburg University, P.O. Box 1352
5004 BJ Tilburg, The Netherlands

INTRODUCTION

Natural and social scientists are aiding the social decision-making processes surrounding environmental management and degradation. These scientists are collecting and classifying information, developing indicators and frameworks, and perfecting and applying methods for historical inquiry, forecasting, and scenario analysis for the support of environmental policies and the management of ecosystems. Multidisciplinary information and cooperation are generally accepted as essential. This involves a number of activities which can be classified, for instance, in the following way.

- Selection of basic frameworks and concepts
- Assessment of basic causes of environmental and ecosystem degradation
- Classification of ecosystem functions and value categories
- Selection of performance indicators
- Choice of management and policy instruments
- Modeling of multi-actor, dynamic or spatial processes on various spatial and temporal scales
- Statistical evaluation of historical patterns of economic and environmental indicators, as well as the relationship between them
- Description and analysis of impacts of policy, management and institutional arrangements
- Evaluation of policy scenarios using a broad set of criteria

1

This book aims to give an illustration of different approaches and applications that contribute to the above list of options. In this process, various methods and problem areas will be indicated. The book is divided into four main parts. The first part addresses basic issues in ecological economics approaches. This includes a comparison of perspectives in environmental and ecological economics, in which special attention is given to issues of uncertainty, information, complexity, and evaluation. The macro-analysis scale is the topic of the second part of the book, where attention is given to macroeconomic sustainability analysis, statistical analysis of industrial transformation, theories of trade and environment, historical analyses of the trade–equity–sustainability interface on a regional scale, and the relationship between sustainable agriculture and rural development. The third part of the book deals with the ecosystem scale. This covers a historical island study, theory and empirical issues related to management of communal rangelands, and a new holistic perspective on valuing ecosystems by means of experimental economics methods. The last part of the book addresses institutional policy and management options. Here expositions are included on national planning based on natural resource accounts, on the need for practical policy objectives based on the precautionary principle, and on a combination of theoretical and empirical aspects of policies related to Lower Developing Countries' (LDC) primary exports. This chapter offers some general background discussions about these four sections, along with brief summaries of the various chapters.

RESOURCE, ENVIRONMENTAL, AND ECOSYSTEM ECONOMICS

Establishing the relationship between ecosystems and economic activities has been a low priority in conventional environmental economics. Ecosystems have generally not been considered very important to economic production and consumption processes. Environmental economics, and in particular resource economics, has focused its attention on nonrenewable resources (Dasgupta and Heal 1979; Howe 1979) and to some extent on renewable resources (see Clark 1976, 1985; Wilen 1985) or the interaction between them (Swallow 1990). The renewable resource concept may be regarded as a very simple ecosystem approach (see also Chapter 2). However, most models of regeneration processes are restricted to population dynamics, and do not address wider ecosystem issues.

Environmental economics, excluding specific resource-related issues, ignores explicit treatment of natural processes and impacts of economic decisions and activities on environmental indicators and processes. This is circumvented by adopting the externality framework, in which only impacts are considered that go from one economic actor to another, usually analyzed in a static context. The external effect can occur directly and locally (congestion) or indirectly via air (noise and pollution affecting health), water (quantity and quality), and soil (degradation), or very indirectly via global processes (climate change). In some of these cases, external effects occur via changes in the performance or presence of ecosystem functions, or in the structure of ecosystems (e.g., species extinction, loss of functions). It is possible to extend or adapt the externality framework to include ecosystem functions explicitly (Crocker and Tschirhart 1992; Crocker 1995). This more or less completes the theoretically possible perspectives on static and dynamic economics of ecosystems, which also include dynamic optimal control of ecosystems, price analogues in ecosystems, and input–output ecosystem accounting (Hannon 1976, 1986, 1991). This then provides for a theoretical framework for studying the economic use of ecosystems.

In addition, the understanding of multiple functions and multiple uses of ecosystems is necessary for a successful management of ecosystems. This has, among others, been addressed via dynamic simulation models (e.g., Braat 1992). Using such models, dynamic externalities between various uses can be made explicit, so that the trade-off can be studied between different uses of ecosystems under specific external and management scenarios. Generally, simulation approaches allow for more complexity than the analytical approaches of theoretical environmental economics, and may in addition be based on ecosystem models with stress factors (Braat and van Lierop 1987; Latour, Reiling, and Wiertz 1994). They can be linked to different perspectives on ecosystem analysis and management (Watt 1968; Holling 1978; Walters 1986; Costanza, Norton, and Haskell 1992). In addition to studying single, isolated ecosystems, many researchers have proposed to study ecosystems in a context of regional and economic processes. For this approach, it is essential that all systems on all levels are open, so that interactions between the various systems are as important as their internal dynamics (Zuchetto and Jansson 1985; Hannon and Ruth 1994; Clark, Perez-Trejo, and Allen 1995; van den Bergh 1996).

Besides analytical approaches (e.g., those based on energy flows and mechanistic processes), inclusion of evolutionary dynamics in modeling may be a fruitful area for future research. To a large extent, the evolutionary approach has been formulated as a criticism of conventional or neoclassical economic approaches. In evolutionary dynamics nonmechanistic, nonaverage and nondeterministic characteristics prevail. In the context of modeling, the difference between mechanistic and evolutionary modeling is sometimes defined as having less of a distinction between parameters and variables. This view raises some problems, however, as the respective distinction in a concrete model is not always perfectly clear. This may be one reason why there is some separation between formalized and informal (historical–descriptive) approaches in the area of evolutionary economics (see also Faber and Proops 1990; Vromen 1995).

Economic systems may be regarded as the most evolutionary of all systems we know (physical, biological, and social), which implies that short-term dynamics should really be considered in the context of long-run evolution. Of course, much the same holds for interactions between economic and environmental systems, which have been considered under the notion of coevolution (Boulding 1978; Norgaard 1984). A new element is that in addition to such a temporal hierarchy, interaction between different spatial levels of systems should also be taken into consideration (i.e., allowing for interactions between the levels of local degradation of ecosystems, land use, and regional activity) (Clark, Perez-Trejo, and Allen 1995).

In addition to such modeling, many ecological economists are applying valuation methods to transform functions and structure of ecosystems, via revealed and expressed preferences, into use and nonuse values. In the future, researchers may focus more on the interaction between economic valuation techniques and ecological biophysical/energy, ecological and hydroecological modeling (e.g., Costanza, Farber, and Maxwell 1989; Turner and Jones 1991; Barendregt, Stam, and Wassen 1992; Claessen et al. 1994; Gren et al. 1994).

Increasingly, researchers are categorizing values on the basis of criteria such as use versus nonuse values, direct and indirect use values, present and future values, option and quasi-option future values, and anthropocentric and nonanthropocentric nonuse values. The values of future generations can be distinguished as either bequest (internalized by the present generation) or independent of the present generation, where the latter may include values related to flood protection and more general life support functions (Gren et al. 1994), which cannot easily be monetized. The total net value can now be defined as the sum of various specific values, less the total (concrete and opportunity) costs of management, restoration, or construction of the ecosystem. Opportunity costs may be regarded as forgone benefits (shadow values), such as those of upstream pollution and use of canals and rivers as economic infrastructure. The total net value can be useful for the evaluation (cost–benefit analysis) of projects and decision making about management instruments. The objective of the latter may be to design taxation schemes, for instance, to regulate the scale of recreation, land use, or pollution. In this case marginal rather than average values may be required. These may be nonexistent or unlimited at thresholds.

Some concrete policy questions in this context focus on which ecosystems society would like to protect or develop, which locations should be chosen for maintaining or developing ecosystems, what the implications to resource use, environmental targets, and specific nature conservation measures are, and what costs and benefits are associated with ecological engineering and nature conservation (see van Ierland and de Man 1993). Clearly a combination of economic and ecological information is required to answer such questions.

PERSPECTIVES, INFORMATION, AND UNCERTAINTY IN ECOLOGICAL ECONOMICS

The purpose of the first part of this book is to clarify new elements and fundamental notions in ecological economics, from the perspective of economists, ecologists, philosophers, and decision theorists. However, this group is not in unanimous agreement as to how ecological economics should be evaluated. Some contributors believe that ecological economics may offer mainly an extended research agenda, while others regard it as essential in terms of striving to be interdisciplinary and to have a more realistic perspective on the complexity of environmental problems and policy. To begin with, in Chapter 2, Turner, Perrings, and Folke present an introductory overview of ecological economics by examining whether ecological economics offers an alternative and competing paradigm to that represented by conventional environmental economics. The authors argue that the mild acceptance of ecological economics-oriented research in various mainstream journals implies that ecological economics is a fruitful field of interdisciplinary cooperation rather than an alternative paradigm. If there is a fundamental difference, it is related to the distinction between (static) externality theory and dynamic resource theory, as indicated in the previous section. The focal points of ecological economics are discussed and illustrated within a historical perspective on environmental economics. Core concepts including sustainability, scale, thresholds and valuation are examined. Next, policy implications are considered, with specific attention to safe minimum standards, environmental assurance bonds, international trade including institutional aspects related to the GATT/WTO, and environmental indicators.

Other chapters in Part I emphasize uncertainty as an element to be given special attention in ecological economics. Risk and uncertainty are conventional topics in economics and decision theory. Approaches to risk analysis in economics have focused on state-preference theory (focusing on the allocation of resources under uncertainty) and statistical-parameter-preference approaches (focusing on the allocation of risks). On the macro-level uncertainty has a different dimension. The most important incentive to considering uncertainty on this level was developed by the founding father Keynes, which has given rise to different interpretations and implementations in terms of methodological approaches (Blaug 1992). On the micro-level forms of uncertainty are normally dealt with, through market uncertainty and technological (event) uncertainty (Hirschleifer and Riley 1979). The first concept reflects that individuals are uncertain about the actions of other economic agents. At the microeconomic level, search processes dominate, while at a macro- or meso-level market disequilibrium and price dynamics are essential. Market uncertainty concerns the endogenous variables of the economic system and may be considered as institutionally induced. Event uncertainty on the other hand deals with exogenous data, usually as resource endowments and production possibilities, and may be useful in the context of ecological economics issues. In the case of exhaustible resources, it is linked with issues such as size and quality of resource reserves, costs of extraction, discovery of new reserves and invention of substitute products.

Given that uncertainty prevails, decision makers can take either terminal actions or informational actions. The first actions (passive) will allow individuals to adapt to uncertainty, while by means of the second (active) type individuals can overcome uncertainty. Within the class of terminal actions, we can distinguish between the trade, sharing, or modification of risk. In addition, information may also emerge autonomously with the mere passage of time. For example, a special informational activity, relevant in a context of sustainable development, is waiting, in order to benefit from the so-called quasi-option (or flexibility) value (Fisher and Krutilla 1985; Graham-Tomasi 1995). This value is defined as the gain from being able to learn about future benefits, that would be precluded by some development, if one does not initially develop (preservation). Therefore, quasi-option value is a conditional value of information and exceeds (or equals) the unconditional value of information. An alternative approach to valuation under uncertainty about demand for and supply of a resource is to define an option value as an additional value over the expected value of a good's consumption, and derived from its future certain availability (Ready 1995).

Uncertainty can also be dealt with on a more fundamental level. When it is taken for granted that economic decisions are always made under differing psychological conditions, one may assume a fundamental uncertainty and unpredictability in the decisions made by economic agents. Also, when the degree of complexity is high, formation of expectations and forecasting may be impossible. This will be dealt with later in Part I. Many researchers argue that current environmental issues have different conceptual frameworks of uncertainty. When we try, for example, to assess the chain of effects of our behavior in terms of emissions, concentrations, combinations of ecological stress factors, changes in ecosystem functioning and structure on different scales, and impacts on anthropogenic production and consumption processes, it will be clear that we are faced with an extreme amount of uncertainty. We know, for instance, that forest ecosystems are threatened by acid precipitation, but we have little information about the regenerating capacities of these ecosystems if acid deposits are reduced to an acceptable level. The same types of uncertainty can be identified in the case of global climate change, where the spatial and temporal complexity is immense. We can therefore never be sure to what extent possible global climate change, currently and in the future, is caused by anthropogenic influences. This does not mean, however, that we should not address such issues from a social science perspective.

In Chapter 3, Faucheux, Froger, and Munda argue that traditional probability theories, relying on Bayesian theory, deny any distinction between different kinds of uncertainty from the point of view of normative theory. As a result, the application of these theories in environmental economics does not seem particularly useful. In cases where indeterminacy, irreversibility, and complexity prevail, it is too often assumed that the socioeconomic processes resulting from ecological changes can be predicted: agents make decisions based on a substantive rationality. Different modalities of uncertainty require decision-making theories based on different axioms. The traditional probability theories work rather well in the case of weak uncertainty, but they seem inapplicable in the case of strong uncertainty and near ignorance. This situation requires other kinds of decision-making approaches based on a broader hypothesis of rationality called procedural rationality. Although a rigorous normative theory of decision making in the face of complexity, irreversibility, and uncertainty is not available, there are fragments of an analytical approach which may help us to clarify some important issues, such as the value of intertemporal flexibility. Some sort of procedural norm is necessary if a decision rule has to be formulated. The appropriate way to apply a procedural rationality when both decision stakes and uncertainties are high should be investigated. If complexity and uncertainty are significant, as is the case with many environmental problems, the subgoals in the decision-making process are difficult to formulate and may often conflict with each other. Multi-criteria analysis can perform a useful function in this respect. This makes it an appropriate instrument for framing the decisions and assisting in negotiation, thereby taking into account the various conflictual subgoals.

In Chapter 4, Funtowicz, O'Connor, and Ravetz address the complex feedback relationship between scientific theories and scientific understanding of ecosystem change. In this context, specific attention is devoted to the evolution of social institutions and cultural habits, including those thoughts and norms related to the natural environment. One characteristic of analytical complexity is related to the role of scientific inputs to policy design. This role has currently become more complex to define than, for instance, in the industrial age, as there is more interconnectedness in terms of actors and spatial levels. There are major scientific uncertainties with regard to risks and possible benefits when important decisions have to be made. The demise of simple beliefs in material and moral progress means that there is no longer confidence in technical expertise alone providing solutions. Dealing with environmental problems therefore requires opening the analytical and decision-making processes to broader categories of facts and actors than those traditionally recognized as legitimate. In a sense, when facing an environmental problem, all stakeholders are experts: in different ways, from different points of view, and with regard to different aspects of the problem. Many environmental problems are so complex and diffuse that they are difficult to grasp, let alone to be managed effectively. Very often, for instance, different definitions of the problem exist as well as alternative ways of selecting and conceiving its relevant aspects, and multiple formulations of the goal. The authors argue that a post-normal science is needed. The study of emergent complex systems necessarily transcends traditional scholarly disciplines. It is impossible to have an effective process to investigate such problems while remaining within the confines of a particular paradigm which restricts the focus of research to a subset within the whole system. Thus the principle of dialogue, expressed via post-normal science in relation to the policy stakeholders in an issue, applies now also to the disciplinary stakeholders. With its means of effective management of uncertainty and value commitments, it is argued that post-normal science provides a viable mode of practice for ecological economics.

Munda, in Chapter 5, discusses the extent to which cost–benefit analysis can contribute to welfare measurement when environmental issues are at stake. He argues that traditional economic theory is based on optimizing principles to find precise and best solutions. The starting point of cost–benefit analysis is characterized by strong commensurability and strong comparability. In order to find an optimum, a complete pre-order structure is needed. Essential in this approach is the quality of the final decision and not the quality of the decision process. Complete compensability and commensurability implies the inseparability of efficiency, equity, and environmental issues. Consequently, no objective, value-free optimization of a monocriterion type can be done. A weak sustainability concept is always implied since substitution between man-made and natural capital is a direct consequence of the compensation concept. From an intragenerational point of view, the compensation model presents strong distributive aspects, as the monetary value of a negative externality depends on social institutions and distributional conflicts. Thus, the value society attaches to natural resources and the environment is likely to deviate from individual values because the simple aggregation of individual preferences may imply the extinction of species and ecosystems. Munda argues that ecological economics explicitly recognizes that economy–environment interactions are also characterized by significant institutional, political, cultural, and social factors. Therefore the use of a multidimensional approach seems desirable. This implies that in the framework of ecological economics, the strong commensurability and strong comparability premises of traditional economics have to be changed. As multi-criteria evaluation techniques are based on a constructive rationality and take into account conflictual, multidimensional, incommensurable, and uncertain effects of decisions, they seem to offer a promising assessment framework for ecological economics.

THE MACRO-SCALE

In Part II of this book studies on a macro-scale are presented. The first question to be answered therefore is what the macro-level precisely supposes or implies. A negative answer may be that it excludes all that falls within the microeconomic approach which makes up the larger part of traditional environmental economics. A positive answer is that it covers national to global processes and issues, or, more specifically, that it focuses on relationships on an aggregate level, where aggregation takes place over economic actors and assets such as commodities, services capital goods, labor, money, and wealth. This also involves the aggregation of primitive parameters of taste and technology. Economics has generally used averaging approaches here, in contrast to the evolutionary perspective mentioned above.

Aggregation typically leads to a loss of information. For instance, the low-level behavioral and technical relationships and especially the associated low-level interactions between these are lost. As a result, the macro-level aggregation supposes that these interactions are somehow fixed or that their changes are of minor importance to the behavior of the macrosystem. Economists have tried to provide for a consistent linkage between micro- and macrorelationships, dominated by discussions about measurement of man-made capital, the interpretation of the aggregate production function, and the role of rational expectations in formulating behavior-based macro-models (Scarth 1988). Daly (1991) has strongly argued that macroeconomics cannot offer a good perspective on environmental problems as long as it does not deal with the issue of optimal scale of the economy. This would require that a macroeconomic equivalent of carrying capacity is included in macroeconomic theories.

Economic–environment interactions differ conceptually over micro- to global geographical levels. One human being may interact with one plant, for instance, by eating it. A type of interaction between the world population and the global population of birds is less evident, and, in any case, multidimensional and indirect. One must deal with mutually consistent boundaries, spatial and temporal scales, and physical and other units. Although sometimes suggested, a holistic approach cannot be entirely satisfactory, since data can only be based on some disaggregation choice. Instead, disaggregation in terms of description seems essential to arrive at macro-conclusions which can be checked against assumptions made. This is necessary, independent of whether bottom-up or top-down approaches are adopted, as long as empirical applications are pursued. Another important issue is whether it is possible and useful to deal with ecology on a macro- or even global scale. Of course, even before

Lovelock's Gaia and public awareness of global environmental issues, the science of the biosphere had been developed. Recently, it seems that this field is making swift progress, also in an empirical direction using modern techniques such as remote sensing of land use and vegetation cover (e.g., Rotmans 1990). Notably in the context of climate change research many disaggregate models from different disciplines are presently combined and integrated (e.g., IPCC 1995). These latter issues, interesting though they may be, are not specifically addressed in Part II of the book. Instead, the studies presented here show more modest approaches focusing on country and regional scales.

In Chapter 6, Young's starting point is that the sustainability concept is not given sufficient attention in terms of a complete macroeconomic perspective. The environmental economics literature concerning economic growth usually follows the standard neoclassical approach, which does not consider the problem of effective demand. The emphasis is instead on the long-term problem of sustainability at a certain level of economic activity (i.e., supply-side oriented). On the other hand, standard Keynesian macroeconomics focuses on the demand side and unemployment problem, but does not address the sustainability issue. The intertemporal linkages between current production and the long-term effects of man-made capital accumulation are generally analyzed in the multiplier–acceleration interaction models. Young's objective is to link both modeling traditions in the context of a developing country undergoing a structural adjustment program. The determination of the aggregate level of production is the short-term problem to be considered. The maintenance of a nondecreasing total stock of assets, which is the weakest definition of sustainability, is studied to address the long-term problem. The dual nature of resource depletion is emphasized (i.e., the influence on both effective demand and environmental sustainability). In the short term, natural asset depletion will have a positive impact on employment because it represents addition to effective demand. However, natural resource depletion reduces the total asset stock, compromising future economic activity. The solution to this apparent contradiction rests on combining higher investment levels with lower resource depletion, because investment in man-made capital has the advantage of increasing effective demand and the asset stock simultaneously. However, private investment is not fully controlled by policy-makers, and the ideal solution is not easily achieved by developing countries. This problem is especially relevant during structural adjustment programs, when the economy is under pressure to achieve short-term objectives.

Van Beers and van den Bergh present a critical overview of formal analyses of the relationship between environmental quality, international trade, and environmental and trade policies in Chapter 7. Relatively little attention was given to this issue until the end of the 1980s. Indeed, the bulk of work in environmental economics seems to have concentrated on environmental policies in closed economies. However, an increasing number of studies have been devoted to environment and trade in the last few years. Important questions in the context of open economies relate to the environmental or welfare effects of trade and trade policies, the impact of environmental deterioration on welfare and trade in the open economy, and the influence of environmental policy on international competitiveness. The approaches considered include traditional trade theory, standard partial equilibrium analysis, modern trade theory, and general equilibrium analysis. The main assumptions and results are discussed, as well as the range of issues considered by each particular approach. In addition, intertemporal trade analysis in the context of environmental sustainability as well as spatial approaches are discussed. Finally, some main points of criticism on the formal approaches are examined

In Chapter 8, Gowdy discusses whether or not regional sustainability will be strengthened by reducing international trade, which often indirectly leads to deterioration of nature and the environment. Many environmentalists advocate regional-based economies and call for restrictions on international trade. Although there are many good environmental arguments for local production, evidence from the past shows that autarkic regional economies have not always been environmentally sustainable. The problem of environmental sustainability involves more than physical production and consumption. It is intimately connected with power relationships and the distribution of economic surpluses. The importance of social structure for trade and sustainability can be seen in a comparison of the role of trade in hunting and gathering as opposed to agricultural societies. Among hunter–gatherers, trade did not adversely effect environmental quality, nor did it have a negative impact on the generally egalitarian social structure of these societies. With the widespread adoption of agriculture came social stratification and the concentration of decisions involving production and consumption in a few hands. Among early agriculturalists, there are numerous examples of trade leading to increased social stratification. Social stratification, and the control of economic surpluses by political or religious elites, can be linked to the environmental degradation and eventual collapse of many ancient civilizations. Examining the positive and negative roles of trade in preindustrial societies can be useful in developing criteria for evaluating the environmental and social desirability of trade in modern economies. Questions that arise from such an examination concern the effect of trade on distribution, the role of trade in promoting efficiency and economic growth, and the effect of trade on local environments and indigenous cultures.

Qu, Kuyvenhoven, Heerink, and van Rheenen, in Chapter 9, discuss rural development and sustainable agriculture as implemented in China. Sustainable agriculture in China differs in a number of respects from sustainable agricultural practices in developed countries. These differences arise from China's different physical and socioeconomic conditions, such as the high population pressure, the long history of farming, the primary phase of agricultural development, and the household management of very small-scale land units. Important characteristics of sustainable agriculture in China are the high importance attached to the goals of food security and income generation, the diversified structure of agro-ecosystems, the integration of different agricultural sectors and agro-processing industry at the farm and village level, the intensive external input use, and the instigation and intervention by the government. Thus, the authors argue, sustainable agriculture in China may be considered as close to the concept of sustainable agriculture and rural development proposed by the FAO, and may thus serve as an interesting example of its implementation. During the last few decades, the upsurge of sustainable agriculture has resulted in some important achievements with respect to the agricultural environment and rural development in China. Sustainable agriculture has become the main strategy of agriculture and rural transformation. The agricultural structure has been transformed accordingly. An integrated system of techniques in sustainable agriculture has resulted in innovation and application of new techniques. Ecological product markets, such as the market for "green label" products, has emerged in more developed areas. The more intensive use of labor in sustainable agriculture has to some extent alleviated employment pressure caused by increasing population in the rural areas. In most sustainable agriculture programs, output and farmers' incomes have increased while simultaneously improving and maintaining the resource base and environmental quality.

In Chapter 10, de Bruyn, van den Bergh, and Opschoor deal with the problem of the ecological restructuring of industrial economies. Special attention is devoted to the materials use side of this adjustment process. It is argued that preventive environmental policy may be aimed at stimulating structural change in the consumption of materials by industrial activities. By reducing the resource input of production, less emissions and waste that have a negative impact on the natural environment will be produced. Several authors have tried to show that structural change in modern economies has led to a de-linking of materials consumption and economic growth. The concept of structural change is explored by presenting an overview of the relevant contributions to this field and by investigating whether de-linking, enforced by structural change, has actually occurred in developed economies. Empirical estimations are discussed by considering cross-section, time series, and decomposition analysis. These different approaches do not confirm de-linking unambiguously. Especially in the 1980s, structural change turned out to be quite insignificant. But, even if de-linking is found, one should be very careful in interpreting it as more than a partial result, (i.e., applying merely to particular countries, to certain periods of time, and most importantly to specific classes of resources or pollutants).

THE ECOSYSTEM SCALE

Underlying Part III of this book is the basic question of whether ecosystems and economies can be treated independently. The integration of both systems is, of course, a step forward in addressing the complex relationship and inter-dependencies over time between human activities and natural processes on all levels. Especially when considering issues related to sustainability, typically characterized by feedback between local and global systems, a monodisciplinary approach can only generate incomplete, partial insights, and will therefore provide insufficient information for environmental and resource management, as well as more general policies oriented toward sustainable development. Crocker (1995) argues that a monodisciplinary approach can only be advocated if production and consumption decisions are independent of each other and, additionally, when humans are absent on a large scale. Both conditions are hard to fulfil in the context of sustainability oriented research. In that case, production and consumption will be interactively determined; furthermore, they will be linked over time via impacts and dependence on natural systems. The condition of the absence of humans may be satisfied in the short run, in which case the ecosystem can attain a natural equilibrium or go through a series of equilibria. However, as times passes, the openness of local ecosystems makes it virtually impossible for a specific ecosystem to develop in isolation from ecosystems affected by human activities. This implies that ecosystems and economic systems cannot be discussed separately from each other, and that economics and ecology should react to this in an appropriate sense. In this part of the book some examples of such reactions are shown, covering different perspectives formalized via input–output, dynamic systems and valuation approaches.

In Chapter 11, Cole highlights the complex relationship in space and over time between economic culture and ecology in Aruba, a small Caribbean island. Like all other islands of the Caribbean, Aruba passed through a succession of distinctive global epochs, mainly driven by sweeping political, technological, and economic changes. Through each historical era, external actors sought specific environmental resources such as natural harbors, mineral and agricultural products, and today, primarily sun, sand, and sea (i.e., the raw materials used by modern tourism). These influences from abroad have shaped the economic and ecological development of the island. This wider context is used to produce an extended input–output approach to quantify specific links between the island's economic cultures and key components of the island's environmental support system, notably energy and water, and selected policy-relevant environmental indicators like land use and emissions. The resulting matrix, called an ecological cultural accounting matrix, is developed at varying levels of aggregation, including individual processes and firms, groups engaging in the same type of activities and lifestyle, and public activities. The aim is to use the matrix to explore the implications of continued economic growth and changing lifestyles as well as to study the tension between the traditional and the modern views on the island's future. Linked to these, the relationship between the physical and economic carrying capacity of the island and the related possibilities for sustainable development can be investigated.

Arntzen, in Chapter 12, examines crucial problems in the everyday life of farmers in Botswana, namely the degradation of rangelands and their sustainable use and management. The causes and characteristics of degradation are investigated, and it is argued that the concept of sustainable development may offer a suitable analytical framework, because it does justice to the complexities of interresource and intersectoral dynamics governing rangelands. The definition of desertification plays a significant role when defining sustainable development. It is necessary to separate physical and human causes of degradation in the context of desertification. The author makes clear that current theories of rangeland management do not adequately address the issue of sustainable rangeland management. Communal rangelands, such as in southern Africa, are used for at least three purposes, namely raising livestock, wildlife, and gathering, where each of these provide a range of products. Although a new rangeland theory can address more adequately the rangeland dynamics and complexities, it may fail to look beyond the boundaries of the livestock sector. In this respect, the theory strengthens the livestock bias in government policies as a trade-off between livestock on the one hand, and wildlife utilization and gathering on the other hand. Key issues for sustainable rangeland management include comparative ecological and socioeconomic advantages, opportunities for multiple rangelands, and popular participation. The author recommends that government policies and research adopt a wider starting point, incorporating the various rangeland uses and the key resources.

In Chapter 13, Kask, Shogren, and Morton discuss the problem of valuing ecosystems, particularly ecosystems which are changing. The valuation of an ecosystem versus the valuation of its parts—such as timber, genetic resources, and recreational activities—is becoming increasingly important. As resource management agencies move to a more holistic management approach, they also require information about relative and marginal valuation. In addition, the resulting valuation estimates can allow for including environmental resources in national income accounts. This suggests the need for a more holistic valuation approach than is presently found in the literature. The authors present a theoretical framework for analyzing consumer ecosystem values, discuss the issues related to measurement, and present a valuation approach that may address these issues. They argue that such an approach must account for the varied and wide-ranging flow of direct and indirect services to economic systems provided by ecosystems. Both the theoretical basis and the measurement of ecosystem values pose challenges for economists. In this respect issues like familiarity with the good, definition of the good, embedding, and surrogate valuation are relevant. In addition, problems with measurement procedures occur, such as those associated with using the hypothetical market approach, the difficulty of defining the good, or the definition of a private proxy. Further development of the theoretical foundation of consumer valuation of ecosystems may provide useful insights for addressing these problems. Moreover, further development of the tools available may address some of the measurement problems. The proposed approach (CVM-X) combines a laboratory procedure with a hypothetical market approach to capture the best aspects of both, a broad base and laboratory learning.

THE INSTITUTIONAL SCALE

In Part IV of this book, the institutional scale is addressed. Ecosystems are often subject to one or more economic uses, be it for recreational purposes, as a source of drinking water, or as a stabilizing factor in water management. Public policy creates the institutional conditions for all types of appropriate uses, as most larger and important ecosystems are not privately owned. Experiences in many countries demonstrate that public policy often supports an unsustainable use of these resources. Although conventional resource economics offers suggestions for measures to realize intertemporally efficient resource allocation, it pays relatively little attention to important issues related to implementation of instruments and monitoring of actors. Observing resource and nature policies in many countries, one can observe many differences in terms of institutional design. This can be partly explained by the fact that policies are linked in distinctive ways to different levels of policy-making, such as on national, regional, or urban scales, as well as to different institutions or organizations, focusing on agriculture, economics, environment, nature, land use, or transport.

In some countries relevant stakeholders can influence public policy, in which case conflicts and trade-offs can become clear in early stages of policy preparation. In this respect, legislation, as a relevant part of the institutional framework, is crucial. In several European countries, for example, current legislation allows environmental pressure groups to be stakeholders. In many other countries, they do not have the right to be informed about, for instance, the conditions under which pollution licenses are granted to industries. It can then be very difficult to use legal means to influence or change the policy outcomes.

Usually, the owner of a property affected by a certain public decision is in a good position to start a legal case against this decision. When there is no private property right it may still be possible to effectively utilize existing legislation as long as common property rights are to some extent recognized by society. In terms of value categories, this means that one may benefit from presenting estimates of intrinsic values as indications of social interest in specific common property resources. This is just one example of linking the use of valuation methods to policy, institutions, and legislation. Whereas in Part II and Part III of this book policy issues are somewhat peripheral, in Part IV they are very much at the forefront, linking them to theoretical, methodological, and empirical issues.

In Chapter 14, Lange discusses strategic planning for sustainable development, linked to a method that may become part of the institutional framework, namely natural resource accounting (NRA). How an NRA system is constructed will depend on the conditions and assumptions that are accepted beforehand when defining economic development. The author claims that too often economic development and natural resource conservation have been viewed as separate objectives, if not objectives of economic development and natural resource conservation by linking economic activities with their use of the natural resource base. NRAs are constructed initially in physical units as stock and flow accounts which, in the framework proposed by the United Nations for NRA, are a set of satellite accounts to the System of National Accounts, which may also be compiled totally or in part in monetary terms through the application of valuation techniques to the physical accounts. The primary advantage of NRA is the comprehensive framework it provides for integrating environmental and resource concerns with economic accounts. This makes NRAs especially useful for understanding the environmental implications of economic activities where complex trade-offs need to be evaluated from an economic perspective. Determined in large part by the framework and concepts of economic accounts, NRAs are less satisfactory for portraying complex ecological processes and feedback loops which ecologists and environmental scientists need for environmental management. NRA was applied in Indonesia, and from the policy perspective the results of the case study can be used by planners in Indonesia. Some important issues that should be explored further are the costs and benefits and income effects of natural resource policies, the environmental impacts in different regions of Indonesia, and the impact of trade policies.

Hinterberger and Wegner, in Chapter 15, discuss the problem of policy-making in the context of environmental systems and problems for which knowledge is limited. This applies to ecological processes, human impacts on these, and consequences of ecological changes for economic production and welfare. The authors argue that limited knowledge is not a reason for refraining from intervention, but should mean careful regulation—adopting a precautionary principle. To this end an overview of different perspectives on environmental policy is offered, with much attention to the German liberal school. It is concluded that interventions in markets are often characterized by short-term revisions, which can result in destabilization of market allocation, as economic agents may speculate on political decisions. As an alternative, Eucken's principle of a constant economic policy is suggested, representing a focus on stabilizing expectations of economic agents. In addition, Hayek is mentioned as having strongly argued that evolutionary processes fail to meet the criteria of welfare economics. Instead of a precise steering of socioeconomic developments towards some sort of optimum, a general guideline is discussed in this chapter, namely to reduce the material input to all economic activities. The Wuppertal Institute has proposed that on a global scale material inputs should be reduced by about 50% over the next 50 years. As compared with the developing countries, the industrialized countries should take a high share of this, which has resulted in a proposal of a factor 10 reduction. This has, since it was first suggested, often been mentioned by nongovernmental organizations (NGOs), governments and private enterprises. The implication is that the material productivity of economies would have to be improved, for example, via resource efficient processes, use of alternative materials, less use of compound materials, redesigning of products, longer usage of products, and dematerialized services to satisfy needs previously met by material products. In order to realize such changes, technical, organizational, and social innovations are required. The authors argue that general rules of conduct allow for a greater variety of potential innovation than traditionally suggested environmental regulation based on fine-tuned command and control.

In the final chapter of the book, Kox pays attention to the particular problem that many developing countries face, namely that their economies are often largely dependent on the export of a small number of export products to Western countries. Against this background, the author examines how to deal with internalizing the environmental costs associated with the production of the respective products. Without a significant change in the institutional framework, these countries are not able to tackle this problem. The 1992 United Nations Conference on the Environment and Development (UNCED) summit in Rio de Janeiro called for a worldwide application of the Polluter Pays Principle as a central guideline for the internalization of environmental costs. Kox argues that developing countries will not readily follow this recommendation for their major source of foreign exchange earnings, the export of primary products. Given the virtual impossibility of most countries to influence world commodity prices, unilateral internalization measures work out as a tax on exports. The resulting income and foreign exchange effects create a difficult trade-off between domestic environmental quality and export earnings. Without a cooperative international approach, it is unlikely that international commodity prices will ever reflect the real natural resource costs of their production. The presence of recurrent transborder externalities, adjustment costs and international capital market imperfections render the resulting international production allocation inefficient. Exporting countries stand to gain from a joint approach to suppress free rider behavior with regard to each other's internalization attempts. The presence of transboundary externalities and the existence of feedback loops between environmental quality and commodity prices makes participation by the importing countries a matter of self-enlightened self-interest. Kox describes the potential of a new type of international environmental agreement, namely the international Commodity-Related Environmental Agreements, to deal with the issues. These institutions may enable the governments of less developed countries to implement the necessary environmental policies now, rather than in the distant future.

PROSPECTS

Collectively, the various contributions in the four parts of this book provide a reasonably good overview of the manner of thinking and types of approaches in ecological economics. However, it is clear that some topics receive much attention while others receive relatively little. Particularly, the economics of ecosystems seem to be an area where much linking of resource allocation theory, ecological theory, and economic valuation can be done. This would, of course, also entail application to various types of ecosystems, notably tropical and temperate wetlands. Coevolutionary theories can also add some new dimensions to the study of long-term interdependence between economic and ecosystem processes, both in a theoretical and applied sense. Specifically, the management of evolutionary natural systems should receive more attention on a policy-relevant level, addressing mechanisms, goals, and incentives. This may be done in such a way as to integrate the economic and ecological theoretical insights, rather than coming up with an alternative ad hoc approach. On an applied level, the selection of performance indicators remains an issue which is often pursued without much consistency between studies. Furthermore, on a macro-level it is important to decide what set of aggregate indicators is useful to monitor sustainable development. There is a lot of literature on this subject, but it still contains rather divergent perspectives. This area is also important in bringing the debate on de-coupling and dematerialization to a successful conclusion, where there is a need to integrate models of economic behavior and materials flows. Another important issue is the openness of systems. Although sustainability is mentioned consistently in publications on ecological economics, and environment and trade conflicts are a hot item as well, the issues of spatial and regional sustainability have, so far, received relatively little attention. This is somewhat strange, as such sustainability concepts, relating specifically to open systems, are relevant on the level of ecosystems, cities, regions, and nations. Research in this context may focus, among other things, on the interface between trade and growth, the spatial organization or location of firms and presence of sensitive natural areas, and the role of infrastructure and transport in disruption of spatial environmental processes. Next, more attention may be given to historical and statistical evaluation of past patterns of economic and environmental indicators and their relationship. This can be useful for more prospective exercises as well, in order to link them with the mentioned evolutionary approach. Finally, in the evaluation of projects and policies more attention can be given to the potential and areas of application of multidimensional evaluation, including multi-criteria and conflict analysis. Many of these suggestions reappear in the various chapters in this book.

REFERENCES

Barendregt, A., S. M. E. Stam, and M. J. Wassen. 1992. Restoration of fen ecosystems in the Vech River plain: Cost–benefit analysis of hydrological alternatives. In *Restoration and Recovery of Shallow Eutrophic Lake Ecosystems in the Netherlands,* eds. L. van Liere and R. D. Gulati. Dordrecht: Kluwer Academic Publishers.

Blaug, M. 1992. *The Methodology of Economics: Or How Economists Explain.* 2nd ed. Cambridge: Cambridge University Press

Boulding, K. E. 1978. *Ecodynamics: A New Theory of Societal Evolution.* Beverly Hills: Sage Publications.

Braat, L. C. 1992. Sustainable Multiple Use of Forest Ecosystems: An Economic Ecological Analysis for Forest Management in the Netherlands. Ph.D. dissertation, Free University, Amsterdam.

Braat, L. C. and W. F. J. van Lierop, eds. 1987. *Economic Ecological Modelling.* Amsterdam:North-Holland.

Claessen, F. A. M., F. Klijn, J. P. M. Witte, and J. G. Nienhuis. 1994. Ecosystems Classification and Hydroecological Modelling for National Water Management. In *Ecosystem Classification for Environmental Management,* ed. F. Klijn. Dordrecht: Kluwer Academic Publishers.

Clark, C. W. 1976. *Mathematical Bioeconomics: The Optimal Management of Renewable Resources.* New York: Wiley-Interscience.

Clark, C. W. 1985. *Bioeconomic Modelling and Fisheries Management.* New York: Wiley-Interscience.

Clark, N., F. Perez-Trejo, and P. Allen. 1995. *Evolutionary Dynamics and Sustainable Development: A Systems Approach,* Edward Elgar, Aldershot.

Costanza, R., C. S. Farber, and J. Maxwell. 1989. Valuation and management of wetland ecosystems. *Ecological Economics* 1:335–361.

Costanza, R., B. G. Norton, and B. D. Haskell. eds. 1992. *Ecosystem Health: New Goals for Environmental Management.* Washington DC: Island Press.

Crocker, T. D. 1995. Ecosystem functions, economics and the ability to function. In *Integrating Economic and Ecological Indicators: Practical Methods for Environmental Policy Analysis,* eds. J. W. Milon and J. F. Shogren. Westport, Connecticut: Praeger.

Crocker, T. D. and J. Tschirhart. 1992. Ecosystems, externalities and economics. *Environmental and Resource Economics* 2:551–567.

Daly, H. E. 1991. Elements of an environmental macroeconomics. In *Ecological Economics: The Science and Management of Sustainability,* ed. R. Costanza. New York: Columbia University Press.

Dasgupta, P. S. and G. M. Heal. 1979. *Economic Theory and Exhaustible Resources.* Cambridge: Cambridge University Press.

Faber, M. and J. L. R. Proops. 1990. *Evolution, Time, Production and the Environment.* Heidelberg: Springer Verlag.

Fisher, A. C. and J. Krutilla. 1985. Economics of nature preservation. In 1985/1993. *Handbook of Natural Resource and Energy Economics, Vol. 1.* eds. A. V. Kneese and J. L. Sweeney. Amsterdam: North-Holland.

Graham-Tomasi. 1995. Quasi-option value. In *The Handbook of Environmental Economics,* ed. Bromley. Oxford: Blackwell.

Gren, I. G., C. Folke, K. Turner, and I. Batemen. 1994. Primary and secondary values of wetland ecosystems. *Environmental and Resource Economics* 4:55–74.

Hannon, B. 1976. Marginal product pricing in the ecosystem. *Journal of Theoretical Biology* 56:253–267.

Hannon, B. 1986. Ecosystem control theory. *Journal of Theoretical Biology* 121:417–437.

Hannon, B. 1991. Accounting in ecological systems. In *Ecological Economics: The Science and Management of Sustainability,* ed. R. Costanza. New York: Columbia University Press.

Hannon, B. and M. Ruth. 1994. *Dynamic Modeling.* Berlin: Springer-Verlag.

Hirschleifer, J. and J. G. Riley. 1979. The analytics of uncertainty and information: An expository survey. *Journal of Economic Literature* 17:1375–1421.

Holling, C. S. ed. 1978. *Adaptive Environmental Assessment and Management.* Wiley, International Series on Applied Systems Analysis, Vol. 3. New York: Wiley.

Howe, C. W. 1979. *Natural Resource Economics: Issues, Analysis and Policy.* New York: Wiley.

Intergovernmental Panel on Climate Change (IPCC). 1995. *Climate Change 1994: Radiative Forcing of Climate Change and An Evaluation of the IPCC IS92 Emission Scenarios.* Cambridge: Cambridge University Press.

Latour, J. B., R. Reiling, and J. Wiertz. 1994. A flexible multiple stress model. In *Ecosystem Classification for Environmental Management,* ed. F. Klijn. Dordrecht: Kluwer Academic Publishers.

Norgaard, R. B. 1984. Coevolutionary development potential. *Land Economics* 60:160–173.

Ready, R. C. 1995. Environmental valuation under uncertainty. In *The Handbook of Environmental Economics,* ed. Bromley. Oxford: Blackwell.

Rotmans, J. 1990. *Image: An Integrated Model to Assess the Greenhouse Effect.* Dordrecht: Kluwer Academic Publishers.

Scarth, W. M. 1988. *Macroeconomics: An Introduction to Advanced Methods.* Toronto: Harcourt Brace Jovanovich.

Swallow, S. K. 1990. Depletion of the environmental basis for renewable resources: The economics of interdependent renewable and nonrenewable resources. *Journal of Environmental Economics and Management* 19:281–296.

Turner, R. K. and T. Jones. eds. 1991. *Wetlands, Market and Intervention Failures.* London: Earthscan.

van den Bergh, C. J. M. 1996. *Ecological Economics and Sustainable Development: Theory, Methods and Applications.* Edward Elgar, Aldershot.

van Ierland, E.C. and N. Y. H. de Man. 1993. *Sustainability of Ecosystems: Economic Analysis.* RMNO Internal Report, Rijswijk, the Netherlands.

Vromen, J. J. 1995. *Economic Evolution: An Enquiry into the Foundations of New Institutional Economics.* London: Routledge.

Walters, C. 1986. *Adaptive Management of Renewable Resources.* New York: MacMillan.

Watt, K. E. F. 1968. *Ecology and Resource Management: A Quantitative Approach.* New York: McGraw-Hill.

Wilen, J. E. 1985. Bioeconomics of renewable resource use. In 1985/1993. *Handbook of Natural Resource and Energy Economics,* eds. A. V. Kneese and J. L. Sweeney. Vol. 1. Amsterdam: North-Holland.

Zuchetto, J. and A. M. Jansson. 1985. *Resources and Society: A Systems Ecology Study of the Island of Gotland, Sweden.* New York: Springer-Verlag.

PART I

ECONOMICS, ECOSYSTEMS,
AND
UNCERTAINTY

2 ECOLOGICAL ECONOMICS: PARADIGM OR PERSPECTIVE

Kerry Turner
CSERGE
University of East Anglia
Norwich NR4 7T
United Kingdom

Charles Perrings
Department of Environmental Economics
and Environmental Management
University of York
York, United Kingdom

Carl Folke
Beijer Institute for Ecological Economics
The Royal Swedish Academy of Sciences, and
Department of Ecology, Stockholm University
Stockholm, Sweden

INTRODUCTION

What is ecological economics? In institutional terms, the International Society for Ecological Economics was formed and launched its journal, *Ecological Economics,* in 1989. A number of ecological economics research institutes have also been established. Both governmental and nongovernmental organizations have begun to make appointments in the field, and environmental authorities are increasingly asking for an ecological economics perspective. Ecological economics is clearly something of a phenomenon. Moreover, it looks as though it is here to stay – at least for a while. Yet the intellectual content of this development remains unclear to most economists. Indeed, most do not get beyond an identification of who is involved. The question "what is ecological economics?" is preempted by the question "who does ecological economics?" Given that many contributors to *Ecological Economics* have no background in economics, and that many of them argue that ecological economics offers nothing less than a new paradigm, most economists have been persuaded that they

25

need to know no more. One contribution to the journal claimed that foundational disagreements exist between environmental and ecological economists (Norton 1995).

This chapter examines the proposition that ecological economics offers an alternative and competing paradigm to that represented by environmental economics. To this end, we take environmental economics to be characterized by the application of a standard economic tool kit and assumptions to the problem of environmental externality. We take the issues addressed by environmental economics, at least in the U.S. literature, to be those surveyed in Cropper and Oates (1992). There are no analogous surveys of ecological economics, and we do not offer one here. To test the competing paradigms hypothesis, though, we do offer a guide to its intellectual motivation, concepts, methods, and policy implications as these appear to us at the moment. The emphasis on policy implications derives from the fact that if ecological economics did offer a competing paradigm, then we would expect to find not only an alternative view of economy–environment interactions, but also a different set of implications for environmental policy.

There are certainly differences of emphasis within environmental economics, but the diversity of viewpoints within ecological economics is much more pronounced. The notion that ecological economics offers a new paradigm is easiest to understand if the minority extremes of both views are compared. Thus the economic growth-oriented technological optimism of environmental economics may be contrasted with the steady-state oriented technological pessimism of ecological economics, the latter position implying the need for some new environmental ethic to guide individual action and public policy.

Growth optimists contend that over the long run, economic growth, trade expansion, and environmental protection are not just mutually consistent, but are highly correlated. Some recent empirical work on long-run economy–environment interactions seems to offer support for this view. The so-called Kuznets curve models indicate an inverted U-shaped relationship between the emission of some pollutants and income per capita. They draw the inference that increasing income per capita will, over the long term, reduce an individual's environmental damage impact (Selden and Song 1994; Beckerman 1992). Growth pessimists, on the other hand, argue that continuous economic growth is neither a feasible nor a desirable option. They hold that technological innovation is less important than the capacity of ecological processes to adapt, and that the focus of policy should be technological and institutional measures to reduce the throughput of matter and energy from the environment into the economy and back out into the environment. If such switches are not made then they argue that nature itself will force such changes via an under-supply of food, energy, or materials and an increasingly polluted and unstable environment (Daly 1973, 1991). Extreme growth pessimists argue that public policy should be dominated by a "no-growth" objective, since they argue that the carrying capacity of the planet has already been exceeded (Ehrlich 1989).

It seems to us that neither of these polar viewpoints are strongly supported by the bulk of published natural sciences findings. Nor do they adequately characterize either environmental economics or ecological economics. Rather we see signs of an emerging consensus around a new substantive research agenda which straddles environmental, resource, and ecological economics. Resource economics has, for example, over many years sought to address the problems posed by the dynamic nature of natural systems. Bioeconomics (i.e., an approach to the exploitation of biological resources which depends on the specification of the control problem in terms of the dynamics of the populations being utilized), is also an important foundation of ecological economics. What we do argue is that the distinctive contribution of ecological economics has been to champion this research agenda.

The most striking evidence that ecological economics is raising questions of fundamental importance is found in the fact that both the questions and the approaches are increasingly being taken up by economists in related fields who remain dismissive of the journal *Ecological Economics*. Papers in ecological economics, in the sense that we use the term in this chapter, are now appearing not just in the specialist environmental and resource economics journals, but also in the mainstream generalist journals. To anticipate our conclusions, we do not therefore see ecological economics as an alternative paradigm, but a potentially very fruitful field of joint interdisciplinary inquiry.

In this chapter we address three separate questions. We summarize the historical development of ecological economics, paying particular attention to developments in ecology that have prompted ecological economists to take a different, or put more emphasis on, a particular line of attack on a number of issues. Next, we present a stylized comparison of environmental and ecological economics approaches to these issues. Then we address the policy implications of these differences. Finally, we present our conclusions on the validity of the alternative paradigms proposition and on the place of ecological economics in the evolution of economic analysis of environmental issues.

FOUNDATIONS OF ECOLOGICAL ECONOMICS

Ecological economics is, in some ways, closer to renewable resource economics than environmental economics. Historically, both ecological and resource economics have been strongly influenced by developments in science, and especially by developments in population biology and community ecology. This is because resource economics and ecological economics have, at different times, been motivated by a common research problem. Both have explored the dynamics of the natural systems with which the economy interacts in order to understand optimal rates of resource use. Where the ecological and environmental economics approaches diverge is in the fact that ecological economists look to understand the dynamics of the natural system in order to understand the dynamics of external effects. Externalities are not an incidental add-on to the optimizations problem. As in environmental economics, ecological economics treats externality as a pervasive characteristic of the system. Unlike some work in environmental economics, however, ecological economists look to the dynamics of the natural system to characterize and value externalities. Some environmental economics focuses on static consumer valuation of externality (in which natural system dynamics are of peripheral interest), ecological economics focuses on real effects (in which natural system dynamics are crucial).

Nevertheless, environmental economics also encompasses dynamic resource/ growth models which include intertemporal externalities via the impacts of resource dynamics on economic values. It further provides a clear decision rule for decision makers. Ecological economics has yet to formulate rigorous alternative rules. Determining the real effects is an input to the decision process, not itself the basis for a decision.

Ecological economics, like environmental economics, hypothesizes that externalities mediated by a common environment are pervasive. The notion that material growth in the economic system necessarily increases both the extraction of environmental resources and the volume of waste deposited in the environment was highlighted in the mass-balance general equilibrium models of Ayres and Kneese (1969) and Mäler (1974). These models, following earlier insights by Georgescu-Roegen (1966), Leontief (1966), Daly (1968), and Marshall (1970), yielded important insights into pollution (waste) externalities, and helped in the development of pollution control instruments. But they did not become a focus for further extensive work in environmental economics. Indeed, such work as was done on both mass-balance and entropy models was out of the mainstream. The so-called "regional environmental quality models" of the 1970s, for example, never really gained full entry into the core of standard economics; and Georgescu-Roegen's (1971) work on entropy-based models was very definitely on the fringe. Environmental economists would counter that materials balance constraints thinking has influenced work on marketable permits schemes and their practical implementation, as well as underpinning recent integrated modeling research in the context of, for example, climate change. The mass-balance work remains, however, one of the intellectual foundations of ecological economics. Indeed, two basic conclusions drawn from this literature are now taken as axiomatic by most ecological economists. First, since perfect recycling of resources is precluded on thermodynamic grounds, the potential growth of physical output is finite. Second, since the waste generated in the process of production is seldom inert, higher rates of physical growth imply higher rates of change in the processes of the environment (Perrings 1987).

The focus on ecological processes is important, since these are the basis of the ecological services on which most economic activity relies. Ecological services include maintenance of the composition of the atmosphere, amelioration of climate, operation of the hydrological cycle including flood controls and drinking water supply, waste assimilation, recycling of nutrients, generation of soils, pollination of crops, and provision of food, as well as the maintenance of particular species and landscapes (de Groot 1992). For example, timber harvest can obviously affect the hydrology on which timber production depends and this is sometimes taken into account in forestry models, but there are many other less obvious feedbacks that are not taken into account. This is also the case with marine systems where the sensitivity of fish populations to the level of harvest due to interactions between components of the food web has not been adequately addressed in bioeconomic models.

Ecological economics is, in part, an outcome of recent developments in community and systems ecology which seek to explain the dynamics of ecological processes. Here, recent research on scale, complexity, stability, and resilience is beginning to influence the analysis of ecological economic systems. Work on dryland systems, for example, has shown how stressed systems can flip from one state to another. For example, grazing pressure beyond some critical threshold has been shown, in some cases, to induce an irreversible switch in vegetation type that changes the central characteristics of the system (Perrings and Walker 1995).

The ecological origins of the ecological economics approach to systems with these properties lie in the "four box" model developed by Holling (1973, 1986) in which the dynamics of ecosystems is described in terms of the sequential interaction between four system functions. These are exploitation (processes responsible for rapid colonization of disturbed ecosystems); conservation (the accumulation of energy and biomass); creative destruction (abrupt change caused by external disturbance which releases energy and matter); and reorganization (mobilization of matter for the next exploitive phase). Reorganization may be associated with a new cycle involving the same structure, or a switch to a completely different structure. Joint ecological economic systems are seen as having similar dynamics (Norgaard 1984).

The general point here is that complex nonlinearity is now widely accepted as a useful way of approaching the description of real phenomena in the natural sciences. Since this is especially true of epidemiology, population biology, and ecology it is not surprising that it should be a feature of ecological economics. The particular characteristics of complex nonlinear systems that is important in ecological economics is resilience: the ability of a system to maintain itself in the face of stress and shock. Again we hint at our conclusion that ecological economics need not necessarily be considered as an alternative paradigm, but rather as a different perspective which has highlighted potentially substantive new research issues and agendas.

THE COMPETING PARADIGM HYPOTHESIS

To address the differences between ecological economics on the one side and environmental and resource economics on the other, it is useful to take the major issues addressed by ecological economists and to consider how the approach to these issues differs. Four main issues have dominated the ecological economics literature: sustainability and the substitution between produced and "natural" capital; the scale of economic activity and the "de-coupling" of economic and ecological systems; threshold effects at the species, habitat and ecosystem scale; and the valuation of environmental resources. We consider these issues in turn.

Sustainability

Sustainable economic development may be characterized as a process of change in an economy that ensures that welfare is nondeclining over the long-term (Pearce, Barbier, and Markandya 1990). It is nevertheless the case that the concept is often difficult to pin down in operational terms. The dominant view among both environmental and ecological economists is based on capital theory, and defines sustainable development in terms of the maintenance of the value of a capital stock over time. The definition of capital used encompasses natural capital (the functions, goods, and services provided by the environment), and manufactured, human and institutional capital (with the latter taken to include ethical or moral capital and cultural capital) (Berkes and Folke 1992).

While the capital theory approach itself is criticized by some ecological economists, who identify problems in aggregating natural and produced capital, the main difference between environmental and ecological economics concerns the problem of the substitutability of produced and natural capital. The ecological economic concepts of weak and strong sustainability are, for example, defined in terms of the degree to which various capital stocks may be substituted for each other (Pearce, Barbier, and Markandya 1990; Turner 1993). Weak sustainability assumes perfect substitutability between natural and other forms of capital. Under weak sustainability, the maintenance of an aggregate capital stock over time is both a necessary and a sufficient condition for sustainable economic development. Economic growth can continue indefinitely according to this perspective, as long as the "Hartwick Rule" is observed (i.e., that the economic rents derived from the exploitation of exhaustible natural resources, such as fossil fuels, are invested in other forms of capital capable of yielding an equivalent stream of income in the future) (Hartwick 1978).

Strong sustainability assumes well-defined limits to substitution. Under strong sustainability a minimum necessary condition for sustainability is that separate stocks of aggregate natural capital and aggregate "other" capital must be maintained. Keeping the natural capital base intact over time has been interpreted to mean conserving all "critical natural" capital (e.g., life-support functions and services and supporting environmental attributes) which by definition is subject to irreversible loss. This could be achieved via the imposition of environmental standards or regulations mandating lower bounds on appropriate natural capital stocks, including the environment's waste assimilation capacity.

The ecological economics approach to sustainability may be described as a strong sustainability approach with a tendency among some of its advocates to view man-made and natural capital as complements and not just poor substitutes. In part, it is motivated by high levels of uncertainty about the nature of ecological processes and functions. There is some concern that the capital theory approach to sustainability may serve to delude policy-makers into thinking that there are "simple" rules linked to "simple" indicators that can guarantee progress along a sustainable path. Many researchers believe that "true" sustainability conditions and indicators can only be derived from a model that adequately characterizes the limits to long-run substitutability of produced and natural capital, and we currently lack such models.

It is unclear that there is a well-defined environmental economics view on this. Many might argue that putting positive prices on environmental resources on the basis of current market conditions and current preference environmental resources is still better than having zero prices. But, given uncertainty about ecological processes and functions, reliance on preference-based valuation might well mean that aesthetically attractive rather than "life-supporting" resources get assigned relatively higher prices, thus threatening sustainability. Critical natural capital would therefore be best protected via standards and regulations rather than by in situ valuation. Even if it were possible to assign meaningful monetary valuations to all environmental resources, it may not be prudent to do so if sustainability is the overriding policy goal. We will return to the valuation question later.

Scale

A second point of difference between environmental and ecological economics concerns the issue of scale, and the related issue of the de-coupling of economic and environmental systems. Ecological economics accepts the principle of separating scale and allocation decisions in environmental policy (Daly

1991). One of the most frequently cited ecological economic arguments is that current levels of economic activity are such that further growth threatens to overwhelm the carrying capacity of the environment (both as a source of natural resources and in particular as a sink for wastes), and that this could result in environmental collapse. The argument is easily misconstrued as a resurrection of the "limits to growth" arguments of the 1970s. It is more subtle than that. A number of ecological economists would accept the feasibility and desirability of growth. This process may well result in permanent reductions in natural resource stocks, but provided that compensating investments are made in re-produced capital and technical progress then there is no inconsistency with the sustainability objective. They would, therefore, stress the need to de-couple economic growth, wherever practicable, from materials and energy usage in order to safeguard environmental functions and processes in the interests of sustainability. Indeed, this is belatedly coming to be seen as the central issue in the debate about the environmental implications of growth (Arrow et al. 1995).

Strong sustainability supporters would be concerned that defining what is practicable in terms of de-coupling is shrouded by uncertainty. The "right" level of compensatory investment is very difficult to define given the sharp limits on human knowledge and analytical capability. Better then to err on the side of caution and conserve natural capital in order to maintain the options of future generations (Howarth 1995).

Ecological economists recognize much more complex limits than those naively specified in the earlier 1970s literature. The more recently appreciated limits include total human claims on global primary productivity. The key concept here is net primary product (NPP), which is the energy fixed by photosynthesis minus that required by plants themselves for their life processes. NPP is equivalent to the total supply of food to all living organisms on Earth, including humans. The concern lies in the fact that humans currently consume, divert, or forgo around 40% of global NPP. Other potential limiting processes include the erosion of biological diversity, interference in overall temperature control systems, and other regulatory systems such as the ozone layer. In all cases these limits are binding or potentially binding constraints that have to be addressed if economic growth is to continue.

Relieving these constraints depends on the extent to which it is possible to de-couple growing economic systems from their underpinning ecological foundations. The ecological economics view is that the economy and the environment are jointly determined systems and that the scale of economic activity is such that this matters (the carrying and assimilative capacity of many ecological systems are binding constraints). However, ecological economists also take the view that there is scope for reducing the environmental impact of economic activity. Some environmental economists similarly recognize the jointness of the economic–ecological system and the binding nature of many environmental constraints. They may be more optimistic about the mitigating power of technological progress and the resilience of ecological and economic systems. But on this issue there does not appear to be a fundamental difference.

So why should scale be an issue? Particularly as the biophysical carrying and assimilative capacity of ecological systems are not static but vary with the preferences and technology of the user, as well as with changes in the nature of the ecosystem itself.[1] The answer to this appears to lie in the phenomenon of dynamic feedback effects. Ecosystems do not always clearly signal when some carrying or assimilative capacity has been breached, and the feedback effects of so doing are often very indirect and long delayed. They may also be irreversible. In the absence of private indicators of the scarcity of environmental resources – the externality and problems – there is no reason to believe that private resource users will recognize such effects on the global commons. Hence, there is no reason to believe that resource users will respect the constraints imposed by carrying and assimilative capacity of the environment. The level of economic activity is currently regulated by reference to a very short-run set of indicators, mainly the stability of market prices. It is argued that it is necessary to take account of the longer-term environmental consequences of current levels of activity precisely because it has important consequences for the future growth potential of the system.

Threshold Effects

This is related to a third issue. Ecological economists argue that a characteristic feature of the ecological economic system is that its dynamics are discontinuous around critical threshold values for species and their habitats and for ecosystem processes and functions (just as they are around economic and institutional thresholds). Such thresholds are the boundaries between locally stable equilibria (Common and Perrings 1992).

The closer the system is to a threshold, the smaller the perturbation needed to dislodge it. There already exist numerous examples of discontinuous change as a result of a gradual buildup of economic pressure. In many such cases large-scale modifications of ecosystems are the result of many local and disconnected activities (the tyranny of small decisions). The widespread destruction of mangroves in South East Asia and South America for shrimp farming is an example. In this case, the incremental destruction of mangrove systems has had a nonincremental affect on the ability of these systems to provide spawning and nursery grounds for fish and shellfish (Folke, Holling, and Perrings 1994). In Honduras, the incremental transformation of the landscape has induced the outbreak of new diseases by shifting the pattern and abundance of insects (Alemendares et al. 1993). Similarly, in some coastal waters, an incre-

mental buildup of pollutants has changed the structure of plankton communities causing an increase in toxic algal blooms, an incidental effect of which has
been the outbreak of infectious diseases including cholera (Epstein, Ford, and
Colwell 1993).

One consequence of discontinuous change is the novelty of many effects,
and this is related to the scale issue. Current rates of human population growth
and consequential rates of growth in the demand for environmental resources
has increased the interconnectedness of ecological and economic systems in
time and space. This is not just a problem for the de-coupling of the economy
from its environment. It has also moved societies and ecosystems into such
novel and unfamiliar territory that the future evolution of both has become
more unpredictable. We consider the policy implications of an ecological economics approach to this later. But to anticipate, lack of information about thresholds and the precise consequences of breaching them lead ecological economics to advocate a precautionary approach (in preference to a cost–benefit approach). This favors conservation and environmental protection measures,
unless the social opportunity costs are unacceptably large. More importantly,
it favors protection of the resilience of the joint system.

In principle, the problem posed by threshold effects is the same in ecological and environmental economics. In both cases the problem lies in the fact
that market prices do not indicate whether a system is approaching the limits
of system resilience. This is partly due to the structure of property rights and
other institutions, partly to our lack of understanding of ecosystem dynamics,
and partly to the public good nature of many environmental resources. The
difference between ecological and environmental economics in this case lies
wholly in the extent and significance accorded to thresholds effects. A number
of models in environmental economics still assume that environmental damage functions are smooth and continuous.

Valuation of Environmental Resources

The problem of valuation forms a fourth debating arena. In environmental
economics, a preference-based value system operates in which the benefits of
environmental gain (or the damages) are measured by social opportunity cost
or total economic value. Within this approach distinctions are made between
use values (direct and indirect use values), option value and quasi-option value
and nonuse values (bequest and existence value) (recently reviewed by Cropper
and Oates 1992). While the meaning of use value (direct and indirect) is straightforward, option and nonuse values are somewhat more obscure in both litera-
tures. Option value is essentially the willingness of an individual to pay for an
"insurance premium" to safeguard future resource use and appreciation opportunities. Quasi-option value is a reflection of the conditional expected value of

information and is not commensurate with other value components. Bequest value is motivated by a desire to ensure opportunities are kept available for future generations. Existence value covers a number of motivations individuals might hold not in the context of resource use, but relating to the mere knowledge that certain resources are conserved and will continue to be so.

Debate continues over the precise boundaries between these different components of economic value, but the conventionally accepted approach to the valuation of environmental resources is based on the assumption that households maximize utility deriving from these different sources of value subject to an income constraint; and that their private willingness-to-pay (WTP) is a function of prices, income, and household tastes (including environmental attitudes), together with conditioning variables such as household size and so on. The social value of environmental resources committed to some use is then simply the aggregation of private values.

Ecological economics also uses these value categories. But emphasis on the limiting role of ecological processes and the importance of ecological resilience means that it places much greater emphasis on the health of overall systems and life support functions served by ecological processes and biogeochemical cycles. From this perspective, the aggregation of private values does not adequately capture the "true" social value of ecosystems and their interrelationships. One formulation of this argument is that total economic value captures only "secondary" values (associated with useful functions and/or services of an ecosystem) but not "primary" values (the value of an overall healthy and evolving ecosystem, necessary to support the continuing provision of a range of secondary values) (Turner and Pearce 1993; Gren et al. 1994). A shorthand description of the differences between an ecological economics and an environmental economics approach to the valuation question would be that environmental economists are inclined to deploy estimates of aggregate private WTP to test the efficiency of resource allocation. Ecological economists, on the hand, are less confident that private valuations arrived at in present market conditions can be expected to take account of all external costs. Ecological economists are also more inclined to ensure that conservation of system integrity is a high priority, in order to ensure species diversity and complexity of relationships. This position reflects a view that some ecological assets have an elasticity of substitution of zero, or close to zero. Environmental standards (known as safe minimum standards or sustainability constraints) would be advocated and would be deployed in order to conserve critical environmental resources before cost–benefit analysis was carried out (reducing this analysis to a cost-effectiveness exercise).

Two other differences in emphasis follow. One is that some positions within ecological economics give greater emphasis to intrinsic values, or values *in* things compared to purely instrumental values, or values *of* things. This has led to questions being raised about the nature of the conventional distinction between use and nonuse value and therefore whether there is such a thing as environmental existence value that can be measured. There are variations in the extent to which such wider values are encompassed, partly depending on the practicality of entering intrinsic values into decision making and the problems of choosing a meta-ethical principle that enables trade-offs between intrinsic and instrumental values.

The other is due to the emphasis in ecological economics on sustainability, and is due to the prominence it gives to intergenerational criteria. Many ecological economists, for example, support a Rawlsian rather than a utilitarian approach to intergenerational equity. Those economists see sustainable development as a condition imposed on the present generation in order to satisfy some notion of intergenerational equity. The present generation can assure the welfare of future generations by underwriting the health, diversity, resilience, and productivity of natural systems. A widely held view in ecological economics is that the requirements of the system sometimes outweigh those of its individual components. This view contradicts the principle of consumer sovereignty by recognizing the bounds within which sovereignty may be exercised. It also lies behind arguments for a new environmental ethic or morality.[2]

The environmental economics valuation literature has addressed the interests of future generations via an investigation of irreversible choices (development versus conservation) and the contradictions between discounting and obligations to the distant future. How societies value the environment is part and parcel of the sustainability question. But incorporating environmental values into decision making will not in itself guarantee sustainability values each generation is committed to transferring to the next sufficient reproducible and natural capital to make development sustainable (Howarth and Norgaard 1992). Howarth (1995) has recently shown that a Kantian approach to intergenerational equity requires the prior imposition of sustainability criteria as a moral constraint on the maximization of social preferences concerning the distribution of welfare between generations. Such an approach precludes actions that yield present benefits but impose the risk of irreversible future losses when scientific research would permit the effective resolution of uncertainty over generational time.

The partial substitution of a collectivist perspective in place of an individualistic perspective also lies behind the so-called "social limits to growth" position. This is a set of arguments that were given prominence in the 1960s and 1970s by orthodox economic writers such as Scitovsky, Hirsch, Mishan, and Thurow, which questioned the social desirability of the economic growth society (the "zero-sum society") and put forward an array of more and less radical policies to restructure the market economy along more egalitarian lines. Some ecological economists empathized strongly with this line of thought and have sought to encapsulate it as a reinforcing argument for their own versions of "steady-state" and "bioeconomic" economic and social systems.

POLICY IMPLICATIONS

In so far as ecological economics identifies the same underlying forces of environmental change as environmental economics, it supports the same set of economic instruments. There are, however, some differences both in emphasis and in kind. In what follows, we consider only those policies and instruments that appear to be treated in a distinctive manner by ecological economics, and that derive from an ecological economics perspective on the underlying physical system.

We begin at a general level by considering the way in which equity and efficiency considerations are addressed in the policy problem. One of the main results in ecological economics is that intertemporal efficiency in the allocation of resources is neither a necessary nor a sufficient condition for the sustainability of resource use. Indeed, sustainability is widely viewed as an equity (intergenerational and intragenerational) rather than an efficiency category. At the same time, the ecological economics treatment of the valuation of environmental resources implies that much environmental degradation is a consequence of the discrepancy between private WTP for and social opportunity cost of environmental goods and services.

The specific problems to be addressed by policy derive from the fact that no signals currently exist as to the long-term consequences of a wide range of environmental effects, including the loss of ecological resilience. This is partly because ecosystems typically continue to function in the short-term even as resilience declines. Indeed, they often signal loss of resilience only at the point at which external shocks at previously sustainable levels flip those systems into some new state and level of operation. The principal policy challenge is not just to correct the institutional biases in the price signals that constitute the main measure of system performance, but to design institutions to accommodate the difficult-to-discern sources of ecosystem instability (and the uncertainty they engender).

While the ecological–economic system may be neither observable (through the set of prices) nor controllable (through any set of incentives based on those prices), it may still be "stabilizable." That is, it may still be possible to protect the resilience of the joint system providing that the uncontrolled, unobserved, processes of the environment are stable. Stabilization of the joint system requires that economic activity be constrained so as not to destabilize essential ecosystem processes and structures. Indeed, this is a necessary condition for the sustainability of the joint system. Analytically, the problem is very similar to the problem of economic stabilization discussed in the 1960s (Perrings 1991).

There are therefore three characteristics of ecological–economic systems that call for distinctive policies: the existence of threshold effects; the existence of fundamental uncertainty, including potentially catastrophic environmental risks associated with economic activity which has become endogenous in the sense that the risks are affected by the activity, and correlative in the sense of not being statistically independent (e.g., greenhouse gases emissions and ozone layer depletion emissions); and the congestible but public good nature of many ecological functions. So far, the policies indicated by an ecological economics approach to these three characteristics tend to be more precautionary than those deriving from a standard approach. The first indicates policies that safeguard the range of options open to future generations by protecting thresholds of resilience. The second indicates policies that minimize the fundamental uncertainty associated with economic activity either by restricting the level of activity to preserve a degree of system predictability or by ensuring the risks associated with innovative activities/experiments that test the resilience of the system are bounded.

The first two characteristics indicate the same microeconomic instruments as those analyzed in environmental economics. The second also involves an adaptive approach to environmental management. Adaptive environmental management treats innovative resource-based development as an experiment, one output of which is an improved understanding of the perturbed system. To ensure that the results of such experiments are bounded, their scale must similarly be bounded (Walters 1986). The third characteristic indicates policies to ensure that environmental effects are taken into account in the international trade and transfer regime. It involves institutions and instruments that operate at the international level.

Safe Minimum Standards

Policies that safeguard the range of future options by protecting thresholds of resilience are generally conceptualized as sustainability constraints. The aim of such constraints is to assure that the joint ecological–economic system adapts to changes that take place in environmental conditions (including not only changes in climatic and other natural conditions, but also changes in political, social, and market conditions). Sustainability requires each generation to maintain the systems that provide the context and the opportunities for human activity. The best example of the instruments associated with sustainability constraints are safe minimum standards and their associated penalties. The rationale for safe minimum standards (or other precautionary instruments) in ecological–economic systems is clear. The existence of threshold effects involving irreversible loss of potential productivity, and the failure of markets to signal the nearness of such thresholds, both imply the need for instruments that maintain economic activity within appropriate bounds. The problem here is that the component of value least likely to be picked up in market transactions involving threshold effects, is user cost (e.g., excessive waste disposal pollution in an enclosed sea, or resource depletion and pollution impacts which interfere with vital environmental processes such as nutrient cycling and climate stabilization). This omission constitutes an unsystematic source of error in market indicators. The tendency for ecosystems to experience catastrophic and irreversible change when stressed beyond some threshold level is a problem that becomes more acute the more distant the effects, which is why forward markets for environmental resource-based products are so poorly developed.

Safe minimum standards are generally conceptualized as quantitative restrictions. Indeed, the class of instruments to which safe minimum standards belong – including harvesting quota and limits, hunting seasons, emission permits, and ambient standards – is generally conceptualized in the same way. Since such restrictions have force only to the extent that they are backed up by penalties, the instruments of the policy are the penalties corresponding to the standards. Such instruments are market based, and like others of their kind (taxes, subsidies, user fees), their standards and corresponding penalties work by changing the private cost of resource use. What makes safe minimum standards appropriate in ecological economics is not that they involve quantitative restrictions, but that they involve discontinuous private cost functions that more closely mirror the discontinuities in social costs associated with ecological threshold effects.

Sustainability constraints have also been justified on uncertainty grounds. Uncertainty about system boundaries and the effects of scale and thresholds indicates a precautionary approach, and many sustainability instruments are precautionary in nature. The degree of scientific uncertainty is such that it is not, for example, possible to specify minimum viable populations and minimum habitat sizes for the survival of many species. A precautionary approach would protect such species by setting standards involving a significant (though uncertain) margin for error. The implication is that for many ecosystems conservation decisions will necessarily be influenced by ethical, cultural, or political considerations. Indeed, it may be that society may choose to adopt the safe minimum standard not because it results from a rigorous model of social choice, but simply because individuals in the society feel intuitively that the safe minimum standard is the right thing to do, given all the trade-offs involved (Bishop 1978).

Environmental Assurance Bonds

A second set of instruments, environmental assurance bonds, prompted by the pervasive uncertainty of innovative economic activity, involves a variant of the long-established deposit-refund systems. The development of environmental assurance bonds in ecological economics has focused on the private incentives they can offer to research the environmental effects of economic activity in a way that both bounds the potential harm inflicted on society and insures society against such harm. Agents undertaking activities for which no precedents exist are required to post a bond with the environmental authority equal to the expected worst case losses. This indicates the value placed by the environmental authority on allowing the activity to proceed given the current state of knowledge about its wider and longer-term effects. To accommodate the results of research, the bond may be revised in line with experimental or historical data available on the user or external costs of the activity.

Wherever the range and probability distribution of the future environmental effects of present activity is known, it is sufficient to require resource users to take out commercial insurance against environmental costs. In other words, bonds should be required of resource users only where the future environmental costs of present activities are commercially uninsurable because the actuarial risks cannot be calculated from historical data. However, since innovative use of environmental resources in a dynamic and evolving system means that fundamental uncertainty is endemic, one would expect that the class of activities for which bonds might be required in a growing economy would be very large, for example wetland conservation and restoration, hazardous waste disposal, and recycling.

It is argued that environmental assurance bonds with these characteristics indemnify society against the potential environmental costs of unprecedented activities, and provide an incentive to both the environmental authority and the resource user to commit additional resources to research activity in proportion to the authority's best estimate of the worst case losses arising out of the use of the resource. The bond is a precautionary instrument in the sense that it imposes the cost of anticipated environmental damage on the resource user in advance. Doubts have, however, been raised about the effectiveness of the indemnity component of environmental assurance bonds based on the experience of performance bonds on the labor market. A closer common analogue of the indemnity component of the bond would be the housing rental market, but so far this has not been investigated. While use of the bond for the protection of environmental assets continues to grow, the research incentives it provides have not yet been tested in practical applications. The point about environmental assurance bonds is that they change the private cost of resource use in a way that may or may not align it with the social cost, but which protects the social interest. The reference point in setting the penalty is not social opportunity cost but the marginal net private benefit of resource use (Costanza and Perrings 1990).

International Trade

In the mid-1980s, many argued forcefully that the liberalization of agricultural product markets would have beneficial environmental effects. More recently, the focus of attention has switched to the environmental implications of the liberalization of trade in general, and the more exaggerated expectations of the effects of liberalization have been tempered in the process. This is partly in anticipation of the fact that environmental issues are expected to be a significant element in the next round of negotiations over world trade. The main point at issue concerns the potentially contradictory implications of environmental and trade policy.

Considered as an allocation problem, the problem of environmental degradation lies in the existence of environmental externalities, and the point of much ecological economic research is to identify where dependence on ecosystem functions generates externality. In ecological economics, as well as environmental economics, the externality cannot be, in practice, internalized by the appropriate allocation of property rights. Therefore the solution lies in the correction of market prices through the use of taxes, charges, fees, regulations together with supporting penalties, and so on. That is, the solution lies in intervention in the price system. The liberalization of trade policy, on the other hand, implies the removal of barriers to the effective working of markets, including the elimination of taxes, subsidies, and protective measures. Driven by the potential efficiency gains from free exchange in competitive markets, the liberalization of national and international markets alike is, in a sense, blind to externalities.

The potential contradiction between the two shows up in the implications that trade policy is thought to have for the environment, and that environmental policy is thought to have for trade. There are two levels to the debate. At the theoretical level, it is possible to identify a number of potentially contradictory effects of the liberalization of trade and the internalization of environmental externalities, giving rise to competing (testable) hypotheses. At the institutional level, the context within which national and international environmental policy is being developed is a pre-existing set of arrangements governing international trade – especially the GATT/WTO. Part of the current debate concerns the environmental implications of the GATT as it is currently structured, and the extent to which the internalization of environmental externalities depends on reform of the GATT.

There are two issues raised by the fact that trade liberalization is independent of the internalization of environmental externality, and that the impact of trade liberalization on incomes is somewhat ambiguous. First, as trade policy directly affects both the volume and location of productive activities, if liberalization of trade stimulates demand for the products of environmentally damaging activities, then it follows that it will increase environmental damage. Moreover, if the (external) environmental costs of these activities increase by more than the gains to be had from liberalization, there will be a net welfare loss. Even if these losses are not net welfare losses, the resultant pattern of trade will be distorted, for the reason that trade liberalization does not address the inefficiency due to environmental externalities. Ecological economists argue that the extent of environmental externalities is such that the specialization induced by trade liberalization is not just inefficient (a perception shared by environmental economics), but that it threatens the resilience of many of the systems on which global society depends. In addition, it is claimed that any increase in the overall volume of trade involves an increase in the transportation of commodities. To the extent that transportation is associated with environmental externalities, trade liberalization will increase environmental damage irrespective of the pattern of specialization (Folke, Ekins, and Costanza 1994).

A second point concerns the positive impact of trade on welfare (under the compensation principle), providing that the gainers are able to compensate the losers to the point that the latter are better off than they would be under autarky. Indeed, trade liberalization is generally held to be environmentally beneficial precisely because it raises incomes and, given that environmental protection is in the nature of a luxury good, environmental protection expenditures. On this point, ecological economists argue that many countries have become locked into a pattern of specialization in export-oriented activities, and that the compensation that might make such a pattern of specialization worthwhile has not been forthcoming. In these cases, it is argued that the income effects of trade on the environment may be perverse (Røpke 1994). When countries specialize in products for which the terms of trade decline then, in order to maintain foreign exchange earnings, they tend to increase exports through expansion at the extensive margin – bringing increasingly economically marginal, environmentally sensitive resources into exploitation (Pearce and Warford 1993).

To the extent that the GATT exaggerates such effects, ecological economists have argued for its reform on environmental grounds. While it is clear that environmental and safety regulations have been used to protect local industries against foreign competition where more conventional trade restrictions are outlawed by agreement, there is also evidence that governments tend to impose an excessively lax regime of pollution control in order to enhance the market competitiveness of local industries. Such "ecological dumping" can induce competitors to impose countervailing tariffs equal to the difference in emission abatement or environmental protection costs between the two countries. The position taken by ecological economists on this is that such countervailing tariffs may be optimal and hence allowable under the GATT. There are two areas in which the GATT as currently structured is argued to compromise attempts to protect the environment:

- First, the GATT is argued to institutionalize the presumption that the environmental costs of trade liberalization will be outweighed by the benefits of increased trade. In part, this is argued because the GATT does not recognize an important class of externalities. The GATT artificially distinguishes between externality in production (welfare loss caused during the production of a good) and externality in consumption (welfare loss caused by the consumption of that good), and allows only the latter as an exception (Pearce and Warford 1993).

- Second, the GATT prohibits subsidies that make export prices lower than domestic prices, and where a subsidy does exist in contravention to the terms of the Subsidies Code, it allows countervailing duties to be imposed. The implication of this is that the GATT does not recognize the right of countries to impose countervailing duties on countries which implicitly subsidize their exports by overexploiting the environment. The effect of this is that a country is permitted under the GATT rules to protect its own environment, but denied the right to protect its producers against countries that choose not to protect their environment (Daly and Goodland 1994).

There appears to be a consensus that in order to realize the potential gains from trade without incurring environmental costs, environmental externalities should be addressed directly. That is, there is a consensus that trade restrictions are not the best way of addressing environmental externalities. There is, however, no consensus as to the value of proceeding with trade liberalization independently of environmental policy reform. The GATT position is that environmental concerns should not be a reason to slow the reform of trade policy, and that trade policy should eschew environmental objectives. However, given that trade liberalization may lead to the exacerbation of environmental change, it is unhelpful to take such a position.

The point made by ecological economists is that the degradation of environmental resources reflects market failure—whether due to economic policy, institutional rigidities, or uncertainty—and is socially inefficient. Where it threatens life support systems such inefficiency is also dangerous. The promotion of trade at current market prices irrespective of the external effects of such trade ignores this problem. If environmental effects cannot be addressed directly, a more rational procedure would be to evaluate the welfare gains and losses from trade liberalization taking environmental and other external costs into account, and to liberalize only if there are indeed net gains in welfare. The treatment of environmental effects as an entirely separate issue from trade liberalization is not only theoretically unsustainable, it is also potentially harmful to the interest of producers and consumers alike. The question of whether any environmental costs of trade liberalization will be outweighed by the gains is an empirical one, and should not be assumed away.

Environmentally Adjusted Performance Indicators

Ecological economists have been in the forefront of a movement to improve the information based, so-called environmentally adjusted performance indicators, on which policy and enabling instruments must rely, if ecological–economic systems are to be stabilized. Chapter 8 of Agenda 21, approved at the Rio Earth Summit in June 1992, calls on governments to "expand existing systems of national economic accounts in order to integrate environment and social dimensions in the accounting framework, including at least satellite systems of natural resources in all member States."

Two general approaches towards the development of environment–economic performance indicators have emerged: environmental satellite accounts (in natural resource accounts, pollution emissions accounts, and environmental protection expenditure accounts), which are annually produced in addition to conventional gross national product (GNP) accounts; and adjusted GNP or extended magnetized accounts.

A range of motivations seems to lie beneath this research to which mainstream, environmental, and ecological economists have all contributed. There is the concern, first investigated and judged insignificant in the early 1970s by the work of Nordhaus and Tobin (1972) regarding the links between measures of income and measures of welfare. This led to the development of adjusted GNP measures of economic welfare, as well as to estimates of the costs of meeting a range of predetermined sustainability norms.

Other economists have used a capital approach, combined with Hicksian measures of income, to formulate sustainability indicators and estimates of sustainable national income (Pearce and Atkinson 1993). A number of unresolved theoretical issues and one methodological issue have been debated in this literature. Ecological economists have sought to include the "critical natural capital" concept and "constant capital" rule in the indicators debate. Sustainability threshold levels for critical natural capital use, for example, would in effect require a range of supplementary indicators for sustainability. Critics of this approach have either focused on the inapplicability of a "capital intact" rule (e.g., technical progress can guarantee sustainable welfare in the presence of declining total capital stock); exaggerated the significance of natural capital and its lack of substitutability; or focused on the unacceptable welfare effects imposed on the current generation in order to fulfill obligations to future generations. The ecological economics riposte is, as we pointed out earlier, not to deny the human capacity for invention and innovation but to stress the potential problems that natural systems may face when forced to adapt to changes in demand induced by the technological switches.

More fundamentally, ecological economists argue that none of these environmental economic indicators are proper measures of indicators of sustainable national income or sustainable development. All of these environmentally adjusted economic indicators only serve to indicate the *cost* of achieving sustainability vis-à-vis the current development path with its existing configuration of capital stocks and assumptions about substitution possibilities. The corrected national income measure is therefore based on measure of income in current prices, and of opportunity costs associated with preserving capital stocks also valued in current prices or shadow prices linked to the status quo situation. The corrections give us an indication of the distance from sustainability that current economic–ecological systems are characterized by, in terms of cost adjustment. They do not, however, tell us much about the magnitude of the sustainable national income associated with potential sustainable development paths (based on appropriate capital values and prices) if policy-makers actually choose such a path.

So the question becomes what utility, if any, do such indicators possess. Some ecological economists have concluded that such numbers could obscure rather than clarify issues relevant to the pursuit of sustainability. As they see it, more extensive physical accounts and indicators based on existing data sources are required. These should link human welfare and ecosystem changes in a relatively straightforward manner given the availability of scientific knowledge. Some environmental economists have come to more positive conclusions based on a survey of several developed and developing countries' practical experiences. They have concluded that satellite accounting techniques, especially construction of pollution emissions accounts, and to a lesser extent, resource flow and environmental expenditure accounts, do have real policy relevance. On the other hand, direct policy use of adjusted national accounts aggregates is more limited, even more so as long as the methodological disputes remain unresolved (Common and Norton 1994).

CONCLUSIONS

The treatment of both technology and consumption preferences as endogenous to the economic growth process is a fundamental change that brings economics much closer to ecology. Economics can no longer be seen as the science of the allocation of an arbitrary set of resources among the competing uses given by a fixed institutional structure (the subject matter of politics, anthropology, and sociology); technology (the subject matter of engineering, physics, and chemistry); and preference (the subject matter of psychology); within an unchanging environment (the subject matter of ecology, geology, hydrology, and climatology). The constraining set within which economists have traditionally analyzed the allocation of resources has become part of the system dynamics.

Both environmental and ecological economists would, we think, accept the general validity of this perception, though they might differ over details of the economic policy implications and analysis, as well as over appropriate response options. The emergence of ecological economics represents a recognition of the profound importance of understanding the dynamics of physical systems on which economic activity depends. It challenges many of the assumptions conventionally made about the nature of production and preference sets, but it also involves a substantive change in the method of analysis. Ecological economics has resulted in a more thorough analysis of the underlying physical processes that has been common in environmental economics, and has harnessed the skills of those specializing in the dynamics of ecological systems. The result is an interdisciplinary perspective that has the potential to improve the capacity of both economics and ecology to deal with the interdependence of ecological and economic systems. A new potentially very fruitful joint field of inquiry has emerged with a research agenda derived from ongoing multidisciplinary research.

The ecological economics research agenda continues to be less focused than that in more established fields. It is however, dominated by questions raised by properties of the underlying physical system, and the need to model economic and ecological systems simultaneously. These questions include the implications of the nonlinearity of the system: path dependence, discontinuity, far-from-equilibrium behavior, and uncertainty. There are two classes of research questions prompted by these properties of ecological, as well as economic systems. The first concerns the formulation of a coherent development theory for ecological–economic systems based on an axiomatic structure that respects the properties of ecological as well as economic systems. The second centers on problems of the valuation of ecosystem services, and the development of enabling institutions and instruments. The latter agenda is not, of course, exclusive to ecological economics. However, the perception of the underlying physical system is exclusive to this field, and as more environmental economists are persuaded of the relevance of this perception, there are signs that the research agenda is being adopted by economists and ecologists. The intellectual content of the approach may be gaining ground independently of the institutional structures that are ecological economics' most visible sign.

ACKNOWLEDGMENTS

CSERGE is a designated research center of the UK Economic and Social Research Council.

We are grateful to J. van den Bergh, B. T. Brown, M. S. Common, H. Daly and D. W. Pearce for helpful comments on an earlier draft of this chapter, the usual disclaimer however applies.

FOOTNOTES

1. Assimilative capacity is the ability of the environment to neutralize or recycle wastes into nutrients, organic matter, and so on. This makes such matter available for the production of ecological resources.
2. Various candidate ethical codes have been put forward in the "bioethics" literature, ranging from human-centered stewardship through to "deep ecology." The latter case ascribes interests and rights to nonhuman species and even inanimate objects (Ralston 1988; Turner 1988).

REFERENCES

Almendares, J., M. Sierra, P. M. Andersson, and P. R. Epstein. 1993. Critical Regions, A Profile of Honduras. *The Lancet* 342:1400–1402.

Arrow, K., B. Bolin, R. Costanza, P. Dasgupta, C. Folke, C. S. Holling, B.-O. Jansson, S. Levin, K.-G. Mäler, C. Perrings, and D. Pimentel. 1995. Economic growth, carrying capacity and the environment. *Science* 268:520–521.

Ayres, R. U. and A. V Kneese. 1969. Production, consumption and externalities. *American Economic Review* 59:282–297.

Beckerman, W. 1992. Economic growth and the environment: Whose growth? Whose environment? *World Development* 20:481–496.

Berkes, F. and C. Folke. 1992. A systems perspective on the interrelations between natural, human-made and cultural capital. *Ecological Economics* 5:1–8.

Bishop, R. C. 1978. Economics of a safe minimum standard. *American Journal of Agricultural Economics* 57:10–18.

Common, M. S. and T. W. Norton. 1994. Biodiversity, natural resource accounting and ecological monitoring. *Environmental and Resource Economics* 4:29–54.

Common, M. S. and C. Perrings. 1992. Towards an ecological economics of sustainability. *Ecological Economics* 6:7–34.

Costanza, R. and C. Perrings. 1990. A flexible assurance bonding system for improved environmental management. *Ecological Economics* 2(1):57–76.

Cropper, M. L. and W. E. Oates. 1992. Environmental economics: A survey. *Journal of Economic Literature* 30:675–740.

Daly, H. E. 1968. On economics as a life science. *Journal of Political Economy* 76:392–406.

Daly, H. E. 1973. The steady state economy: Toward a political economy of biophysical equilibrium and moral growth. In *Toward a Steady State Economy,* ed. H. E. Daly. San Francisco: W. H. Freeman.

Daly, H. E. 1991. Ecological economics and sustainable development: From concept to policy, Environment Department Divisional Working Paper 1991–24. Washington DC: World Bank Environment Department.

Daly, H. E. and R. Goodland. 1994. An ecological–economic assessment of deregulation of international commerce under GATT. *Ecological Economics* 9(1):73–92.

de Groot, R. S. 1992. *Functions of Nature.* Amsterdam: Wolters Noordhoff.

Ehrlich, P. R. 1989. The limits to substitution: Meta-response depletion and a new economic–ecological paradigm. *Ecological Economics* 1:9–16.

Epstein, P. R., T. E. Ford, and R. R. Colwell. 1993. Cholera-algae connections. *The Lancet* 342:14–17.

Folke, C., P. Ekins, and R. Costanza. eds. 1994. Trade and environment. Special issue of *Ecological Economics* 10:1–98.

Folke, C., C. S. Holling, and C. Perrings. 1994. *Biological Diversity, Ecosystems and Human Welfare.* Beijer Institute, Stockholm, mimeo.

Georgescu-Roegen, N. 1966. *Analytical Economics.* Cambridge, MA: Harvard University Press.

Georgescu-Roegen, N. 1971. *The Entropy Law and the Economic Process.* Cambridge, MA: Harvard University Press.

Gren, I-M., C. Folke, R. K. Turner, and I. Bateman. 1994. Primary and secondary values of wetland ecosystems. *Environmental and Resources Economics* 4:55–74.

Hartwick, J. M. 1978. Substitution among exhaustible resources and intergenerational equity. *Review of Economic Studies* 45(2):347–354.

Holling, C. S. 1973. Resilience and stability of ecological systems. *Annual Review of Ecology and Systematics* 4:1–23.

Holling, C. S. 1986. The resilience of terrestrial ecosystems: Local surprise and global change, In *Sustainable Development of the Biosphere,* eds. W. C. Clark and R. E. Munn. Cambridge: Cambridge University Press.

Howarth, R. B. 1995, Sustainability under uncertainty: A deontological approach. *Land Economics* 71:417–27.

Howarth, R. B. and R. B. Norgaard. 1992. Environmental Valuation Under Sustainable Development. *American Economic Review* 82:473–477.

Leontief, W. 1966. *Input–Output Economics.* New York: Oxford University Press.

Marshall, A. 1970. *Principles of Economics.* Macmillan: London.

Mäler, K.-G. 1974. *Environmental Economics: A Theoretical Enquiry.* Baltimore, MD: John Hopkins University Press.

Nordhaus, D. and J. Tobin. 1972. Is growth obsolete? In *Economic Growth.* New York: National Bureau of Economic Research.

Norgaard, R. B. 1984. Coevolutionary agricultural development. *Economic Development and Cultural Change* 32(3):525–546.

Norton, G. 1995. Evaluating ecosystems states: Two competing paradigms. *Ecological Economics* 14:113–127.

Pearce, D. W. and G. Atkinson. 1993. Capital theory and the measurement of weak sustainability: A comment. *Ecological Economics* 8:103–108.

Pearce, D. W., E. B. Barbier, and A. Markandya. 1990. *Sustainable Development.* London: Earthscan.

Pearce, D. W. and J. Warford. 1993. *World Without End: Economics, Environment and Sustainable Development.* Oxford: OUP for the World Bank.

Perrings, C. 1987. *Economy and Environment: A Theoretical Essay on the Interdependence of Economic and Environmental Systems.* Cambridge: Cambridge University Press.

Perrings, C. 1991. Ecological sustainability and environmental control. *Structural Change and Economic Dynamics* 2:275–295.

Perrings, C. and B. Walker. 1995. Biodiversity and the economics of discontinuous change in semi-arid rangelands. In *Biological Diversity: Economic and Ecological Issues,* eds. Perrings et al. Cambridge: Cambridge University Press.

Ralston, H. 1988. *Environmental Ethics.* Philadelphia: Templeton University Press.

Røpke, I. 1994. Trade, development and sustainability: A critical assessment of the "free trade dogma." *Ecological Economics* 9(1):13–22.

Selden, T. M. and D. Song. 1994. Environmental quality and development: Is there a Kuznets curve for air pollution emissions? *Journal of Environmental Economics and Management* 27:147–162.

Turner, R. K. 1988. Wetland conservation: Economics and Ethics. In *Economics, Growth and Sustainable Development,* eds. D. Collard, D. W. Pearce, and D. Ulph. London: Macmillan.

Turner, R. K. 1993. Sustainability: Principles and practice. In *Sustainable Environmental Economics and Management: Principles and Practice,* ed. R. K. Turner. London: Belhaven Press.

Turner, R. K. and D. W. Pearce. 1993. Sustainable economic development: Economic and ethical principles. In *Economics and Ecology,* ed. E. B. Barbier. London: Chapman and Hall.

Walters, C. 1986. *Adaptive Management of Renewable Resources.* New York: Macmillan.

3 TOWARD AN INTEGRATION OF UNCERTAINTY, IRREVERSIBILITY, AND COMPLEXITY IN ENVIRONMENTAL DECISION MAKING[1]

Sylvie Faucheux
Géraldine Froger
Centre d'Economie et d'Ethique pour l'Environnement et le Développement (C3ED), Université de Versailles
47 boulevard Vauban, 78280
Guyancourt, France

Giuseppe Munda
Department d'Economia i d'Història Econòmica
Universitat Autònoma Bellaterra
08193 Bellaterra
Barcelona, Spain

INTRODUCTION

Recent works relating to environmental issues support the implementation of a "precautionary principle." Such a principle implies the safeguarding of environmental resources against the potentially catastrophic outcomes of some decisions. These are decisions taken in situations such that the probability distribution of future outcomes cannot be known with confidence. Given that environmental effects of economic activities are, in important respects, unknown and unknowable in advance, it would appear that a theory of decision making linking precautionary considerations with a structured appraisal of uncertainty is urgently called for.

This chapter is mainly concerned with decision-making models for environmental issues and with the hypotheses of rationality underlying such decision-making models. Following Simon's assertion (1964, 1972), a distinction may be made between the general notion of rationality as an adaptation of available means to ends, and the various theories and models based on a particular rationality which can be either substantive or procedural. This terminology can be used to distinguish between the rationality of a decision considered independently of the manner in which it is made (substantive rationality) and the rationality of a decision in terms of the manner in which it is made (procedural rationality). In the case of substantive rationality, the rationality hypothesis refers exclusively to the results of the choice, whereas in the case of procedural rationality, the rationality hypothesis refers to the decision-making process itself.

The thesis supported here is that most environmental problems, such as the increase of the greenhouse effect, the reduction of the ozone layer or the loss of biodiversity, are simultaneously indeterminate, irreversible, and complex. In this chapter, we explain why stressing the role of indeterminacy, irreversibility, and complexity implies a change of the traditional attitude toward decision making in environmental economics. Our discussion is in two parts. The first part concerns the justification of procedural rationality in a decision-making framework for environmental issues. The second part concerns the outlining of one way to implement procedural rationality in a context of sustainable development, namely the use of analytical multi-criteria decision aid (MCDA) in a manner that is consistent with procedural rationality and that can take account of the interactions between indeterminacy, irreversibility and complexity.

WHY A PROCEDURAL RATIONALITY IN ENVIRONMENTAL DECISION MAKING?

Contrary to the opinion of some exponents of the Bayesian theory like de Finetti (1937) and Savage (1954), different modalities of uncertainty may require theories of decision making based on different axioms (the same opinion is expressed in Machina 1987). The application of traditional probability theory or expected value approach does not seem very useful in environmental economics. In cases of indeterminacy, as that involved in many global environmental problems and sustainability issues, decision analysis consistent with a substantive rationality hypothesis supposes, in effect, that socioecological interactions are *predictable*. Such a perspective is ill-suited to deal with long-term environmental problems, or those of complexity. Therefore it is necessary to work out a more general and satisfactory criterion, which we call procedural rationality, for studying the interactions between economic activities and natural environment.

From Weak to Strong Uncertainty: Implications for the Nature of Environmental Uncertainty

According to Knight (1921) and Keynes (1971[1921]) a distinction can be made between two kinds of uncertainty: a weak variety called "risk" and a strong one called "uncertainty." In decisions under risk, the analysis specifies each possible decision, not in terms of a unique certain outcome, but in terms of a known and quantified probability distribution of potential outcomes. In decisions under uncertainty, a person lacks information about relevant states of the world, and so cannot even assign definite probabilities to the various possible outcomes of the possible actions. Uncertainty in its fundamental sense is an absence of knowledge about what may occur in the future.

In the debate among economists, asserting the presence of "uncertainty" as opposed to "risk" has been generally taken to mean the nonexistence of a probability distribution. The notion of complexity (Stengers 1986, 1987) is that the incompleteness of human knowledge is due not only to our ignorance (lack of information), but also stems from inherent indeterminacies in social–ecological processes. Indeterminacy should then be considered as a significative feature of social life and action. Following O'Connor (1990, 1994a), the postulate of indeterminacy has two meanings: (1) radical or ontological indeterminacy, which means that one can never have, even in principle, a complete and truly reliable description of what is (indeterminacy can be stated as a feature of a reality or of a situation); and (2) time indeterminacy, which refers to the dimension of unpredictability about the future. The postulate of indeterminacy is essentially a rejection of historical and ontological determinism, and as such, the question of a possible *complete* specification or prediction of reality. Yet, from a Bayesian point of view, a decision maker can nonetheless use his belief to generate subjective probability distributions regarding relevant states of the world and outcomes of available actions. Therefore a subjective probability can always be formulated as the equivalent of a bet on a certain event. The only requirement is conformity with a few consistency conditions (de Finetti 1980; Savage 1954).

Uncertainty should then be related not to the absence of a probability distribution, but only to its unreliability. It becomes necessary to make a distinction between the probability of an event and its degree of reliability. The concept of reliability of probability can be linked to the concept of "weight of argument" as formulated by Keynes (1971[1921]). In this case, "risk refers to probability distributions based on a reliable classification of possible events and uncertainty refers to events whose probability distribution is not fully definable for lack of reliable classification criteria" (Vercelli 1991). Following Vercelli (1995), we can thus establish the following hierarchy.

1. Situations of certainty, said to exist when a unique, wholly reliable probability distribution reduces to just one value.
2. Weak uncertainty, where contingencies are defined by a unique probability distribution; additive, and fully reliable.

3.   Strong uncertainty described by a distribution of nonadditive probabilities and/or by a plurality of probability distributions that are not fully reliable.
4.   Ignorance (Shackle 1955, 1969), as the upper limiting case of strong uncertainty, when none of the conceivable probability distributions are reliable.

What attracts our attention here is the strong uncertainty and its upper limit (ignorance) because it is a commonplace occurrence in interactions between the economic system and the biophysical environment. In some cases, we are well-informed about the effects of air pollution and water pollution. We know, for example, that cars have negative effects on the ecological situations in oligotrophic areas and forests. We know what the emissions are, how they are distributed and approximately where the damage will take place. This corresponds to situations of weak uncertainty, if complications such as cumulative effects of tree disease and ecosystem change are put aside. On the other hand, we are not well informed about the effects of global environmental problems such as the global climate change and the loss of biodiversity. There are great uncertainties, not about the basic mechanisms of the greenhouse effect, but about the severity of the changes in weather patterns that could result from current emissions trends, especially on the scale of water supply, flooding, biodiversity, food production, and building security in different regions of the world. Scientific knowledge and hypotheses on these matters are beset with controversy. Furthermore, the global environmental problems do not have historical precedents. Since there is no data bank of reliable observations of the historical environmental effects of contemporary economic activities, there is no statistical basis on which to estimate their possible consequences or to construct reliable probability distributions for those effects. This means that the information on which decisions have to be made is most often of a nonprobabilistic kind. The consequences of the choices are partly unknown, and the probabilities of those contingencies that lend themselves to treatment in statistical terms are unreliable.

Much of the uncertainty emerges from unforeseeable qualitative changes in economic and biological systems, which are not due to stochastic variability but to integral shifts in behavioral patterns including changes in policy institutions. In such cases the interactions between the economy and the natural environment cannot be defined as a system's optimal trajectory within a given (stochastic) parameter space, but (preserving the vocabulary of optimization) as a set of sequential, optimality regimes governed by sometimes dissipative structures (van den Bergh and Nijkamp 1991). The decision problems get much more complex since the option set can change endogenously, due to the effects of past decisions and as a consequence of complex interactions between the economy and the environment.

We take the view that, for major environmental issues, uncertainty is endogenous and is renewed recursively by economic (and ecological) actions which have both collective and individual components and which moreover concern processes that may be irreversible.

The changes in the natural environment caused by human activities may be irreversible to a degree unmatched by manufactured capital. For example, buildings can be constructed and later demolished. However, once an oil deposit has been depleted and the oil burned for energy, or once an area of wilderness has been developed, it is effectively impossible to recreate these components of the natural environment (Krutilla 1967; Victor 1991). The intertemporal analysis of decisions in the face of uncertainty therefore must give weight to an important new dimension – the degree of irreversibility that characterizes the consequences of sequential decisions. Combinations of environmental events with a small likelihood of occurrence and a significant long-term impact are therefore to be considered seriously. The choices of the present generation may, through such contingencies as accidents and biodiversity reduction, influence in an irreversible way the options available to future generations. The presence of uncertainty and irreversibility together comprises a strong argument to justify the maintenance of natural capital stocks to ensure broadly equal access by different generations.

From Substantive to Procedural Rationality: The Implications for Environmental Decision Making

Some environmental economists (Mäler 1989a, 1989b; Asheim and Brekke 1993) have adopted an expected value analysis based on Bayesian theory for dealing with uncertainty, irreversibility, and complexity. They point out that we do not know the long-term environmental consequences associated with economic activities, nor do we know what value environmental systems may have for future generations. From these considerations, however, they foreclose the framework to that of individual decision making under risk. The probability of occurrence for each possible outcome is specified—each possible action is associated with a known distribution of potential outcome. The choices of an individual are analyzed by assuming that he maximizes his preferences represented by a Von Neumann–Morgenstern expected utility function.

In fact, this analysis maximizes a unique criterion. It assumes individuals will create an exhaustive list of all possible decisions, their corresponding probability (Von Neumann and Morgenstern 1947; Savage 1954). In the simplest case, the individual is assumed to know the distribution of probability of the outcomes. In a relaxation of this assumption, the individual is assumed to initially have a subjective estimate of probabilities that may differ from the objective ones, introducing the possibility of learning following Bayesian decision rules. It means that the agents may, over time, learn more about the opportunity costs associated with use of the environment, for example whether or not a particular exploitation or damage is reversible. This may be a basis for caution decision making.

The intuitive meaningfulness of this last result – a probabilistically derived principle of prudence – is not in question. One may doubt, however, the adequacy of this approach to the major problems involving environmental uncertainty. Generally speaking, the orthodox decision theory in environmental economics employs the analytical tools rooted in the paradigm of substantive rationality. Here the emphasis is placed on finding the best outcomes through constrained optimization. In this framework, individual or collective rationality is identified with constrained maximization of an objective function. As an extension to situations of risk and of uncertainty, the same choice paradigm may be elaborated in terms of constrained maximization of expected values of outcomes based on application of probability theory. The agents are assumed to possess perfect information on which to base their decisions, or they act *as if* they may have perfect, or complete probabilistic, information at the outset.

This assumption is very demanding in the context of environmental issues as it requires, for instance, that the decision makers have fully reliable information about distributions of future environmental damages. The attempts to apply Bayesian theory to learning are not convincing. Representation of choices *as if* they involve expected utility maximization amounts to imposing a form of representation of decision-making rationality primarily conceived for situations of certainty, and postulating it as equally applicable in situations of strong uncertainty. As Binmore (1986) has remarked, Bayesian theory applies only to "closed universe" problems (i.e., problems in which all potential surprises can be discounted in advance). Existing decision theories, based on substantive rationality, are consistent with the Laplacian view of science. This view considers all events as being predictable in the sense that the set of outcomes and the corresponding probability distributions can be defined in principle, even if not in practice (Stengers 1986; O'Connor 1994a). Nonetheless, decision making in face of strong uncertainty, implies the possibility of ex-post mistakes whose consequences cannot be reliably evaluated in advance by stochastic analysis and may be virtually boundless. This is particularly acute when damages to ecological systems are both more harmful and harder to reverse than economic production changes because of the complexity in spatial scale and slower time of adaptation in these systems.

Loomes and Sugden (1982) argue that expected value analysis represents a restrictive notion of rationality that does not take account of the notion of regret. The absence of systematic ex-post mistakes, which is the distinctive feature of a validated substantive rationality, is only plausible whenever the decision maker faces a stationary stochastic process that has persisted long enough to allow the decision maker to fully adjust to it (Lucas 1986). The interactions between economic development and the natural environment are characterized by strong forms of uncertainty and irreversibility which are inconsistent with the stationality of the socioecological processes involved. Whenever the features of irreversibility are coupled with uncertainty, the socioecological process is not stationary and there is no way to transform this nonstationary process into an equivalent stationary one.

Decision theories, based on substantive rationality, have limited value for dealing with environmental decision situations characterized by a high degree of uncertainty about nature, incidence and/or timing of possible environmental costs (e.g., situations where the effects may be catastrophic for future generations). This exposes future generations to extreme risks on the basis of arbitrary calculations. Examples of such practices are cost–benefit analyses of new technologies making use of supposed statistical estimates of probabilities of serious accidents as with nuclear reactors or radioactive waste disposal, or with genetically modified organisms. Funtowicz and Ravetz (1994) and Wills (1994) discuss the incalculable character of such events and their consequences. If indeterminacy is postulated, the concepts of expected value and probability are not appropriate for description of the interrelations between the economy and the environment because we are not dealing with a stationary state being discovered; rather the ecological–social–economic histories are being made and understood in time.

Only for environmental questions characterized by an analytical context where the scientific knowledge is stable and the reversal of the impacts of economic activities on the environment is possible, can decision making make a convincing appeal to a rationality of a substantive nature. But, for current environmental problems such as the global climate change, which is characterized by strong uncertainty and great irreversibility both on the level of consequences as well as that of probabilities of occurrence, such a hypothesis seems to be too limited. A criterion of rationality that goes beyond the structures of the traditional economic criterion of substantive rationality is required.

We suggest that some sort of procedural norm is necessary if a decision rule is to be formulated in such a context (see also Delorme 1995). As Simon (1976) has suggested, "behavior is substantively rational when it is appropriate to the achievement of given goals within the limits imposed by given conditions and constraints .... Behavior is procedurally rational when it is the outcome of appropriate deliberation. Its procedural rationality depends on the process that generated it." Procedural rationality may be expected in situations that are not "sufficiently simple as to be transparent to [the] mind." Then "we must expect that the mind will use such imperfect information as it has, will simplify and represent the situation as it can, and will make such calculations as are within its powers" (Simon ibid.).

When indeterminacy or complexity prevail, decision making embodies deliberation and search, and is sensitive to the forms of representation the decision makers know about or prefer. A solution is then constructed through a heuristic process in which it is reasonable to retain "an alternative that meets or exceeds specified criteria, but that is not guaranteed to be either unique or in any sense the best." This defines a "satisfying" solution adequate to some aspiration level, which is the essence of procedural rationality. It is no longer possible to get rid of deliberation when there is indeterminacy or complexity. The formation of human perceptions and preferences should be considered as part of the problem of decision. Decision making is influenced by the decision-maker's mind: "A body of theory for procedural rationality is consistent with a world in which human beings continue to think and continue to invent: a theory of substantive rationality is not" (Simon 1976). In this case, learning and changes in ways of understanding are acknowledged.

The comparison between the features of procedural and substantive rationality is made in Table 3.1.

Table 3.1. Comparison Between Procedural and Substantive Rationality

Procedural rationality	Substantive rationality
Deliberation	Computation
Satisfying	Optimization
Heuristics	Algorithmics
Decision-making aids	Decision making
Process of decision	Results

The items in each column illustrate what is the main concern in each principle of rationality. Substantive and procedural rationalities both contain procedure and result of decision making but they differ in the weight and the priority given to them. Procedural rationality is primarily concerned with deliberation and with conventions for practice relating to the definition and pursuit of some aspiration level or procedure. Since it supposes a purposeful behavior of the decision maker it is evidently aimed at obtaining some result. In other words, while procedural rationality puts forward the notion of process of decision, it does not exclude the subsequent consideration of the result. But the relationship between procedure and outcome is not analytically precise. Substantive rationality is, on the contrary, primarily concerned with obtaining some predefined type of result designated analytically by some criterion such as optimization. The consideration of procedure in the sense of a method of calculation is not excluded, but the way it is practiced is guided by the reference to a predefined type of end state and a selection criterion which relies on an assumption of exclusion of strong uncertainty, irreversibility, and complexity. It cannot be said that substantive rationality rules out the depiction of the process through which computation, optimization and decision are arrived at. It does rule out what makes procedural rationality specific, namely changeable preferences, learning and the plurality of a priori admissible representations, criteria and conducts (e.g., what permits to deal with indeterminacy).

Delorme (1995) has distinguished different modalities of rationality.

1. Strong substantive rationality, which corresponds to global optimizing rationality;
2. Weak substantive rationality, which means recourse to routines, to algorithms that can be changed, and second best optimization;
3. Weak procedural rationality, which means recourse to heuristics, to pre-established reasoning, and to dealings permitting deliberation, whose convergence is not established, but that are satisfying; and
4. Strong procedural rationality, where there is no available satisfying heuristic and where a complete deliberation is needed in order to conceive a heuristic.

There is a link between these different rationalities and the different modalities of uncertainty we have distinguished before. A behavior of strong substantive rationality is dealing with situations of certainty; a behavior of weak substantive rationality is suitable for dealing with situations of weak uncertainty; a behavior of weak procedural rationality is suitable for dealing with situations of strong uncertainty; and finally a behavior of strong procedural rationality is suitable for dealing with situations of ignorance. As we are interested in situations of strong uncertainty and ignorance, we retain the hypothesis of procedural rationality, in either the weak or strong sense, for dealing with environmental decision making.

TOWARD A PROCEDURAL RATIONALITY FRAMEWORK FOR SUSTAINABLE DEVELOPMENT ISSUES

Though we do not have a rigorous normative theory of decision making in the face of indeterminacy, irreversibility and complexity, we may have a discussion of the appropriate way of applying a procedural rationality in situations where decisions stakes are high and uncertainties very large (e.g., for issues of sustainability). The relationship between studying sustainable development and dealing with uncertainties is mainly related to the long-term horizon and the ecological–economic interactions that are complex and irreversible. Because of uncertainties, complexity of ecosystem functions and the long-term scale involved, scientific analyses are not sufficient to determine sustainability requirements without ambiguity. Therefore, decision making in a context of sustainable development requires a criterion of procedural rationality aimed to design a project of harmonic interaction between economic development and natural environment and able to specify a strategy for its implementation. This project should guarantee future generations a degree of freedom not inferior to that enjoyed by the current generation. This requires a plan for conservation of exhaustible resources, the control of pollution and the protection of biodiversity. A straightforward procedure responding to these preoccupations may be described in the following terms.

1. *Principle of subgoals.* The implementation of procedural rationality proceeds through the replacement of a global nonmeasurable objective with intermediate objectives or subgoals whose achievement can be observed and measured. A first step is to identify a set of these intermediate subgoals together with appropriate means of measuring them. Generally speaking, these subgoals are irreducible, so that they define multiple decision criteria which must be considered simultaneously.

2. *Satisfying principle.* Because of the uncertainties involved, the decision makers are not in position to solve the decision problem in the sense of an optimal choice. Rather they must arbitrate between the different subgoals and choose a course of action they feel to be satisfactory taking into account several imperatives. This corresponds to Simon's "satisfying principle." Indeed Simon puts great emphasis on the method that he defines as "satisfactory choices" rather than "optimal choices." The aim of an analysis under procedural rationality is to help to provide more insight into the nature of the conflicts underlying the determination of a satisfactory choice.

Illustrations of the Principle of Subgoals: Some Indicators of Sustainability

Sustainability, now widely proclaimed as an objective of public policy worldwide, evokes a diversity of objectives, or possible subgoals, that are more or less unreconciled with each other (Norgaard 1994). It has become commonplace to consider concerns for sustainability under the three broad headings of economic, social, and ecological. According to Passet (1979), these three dimensions are at root inseparable; the economic is a part of the social and the social category may be considered to include perceptions of the natural world.

Each of these goals, ecological, social, and economic sustainability, may be broken down into several subgoals, which may take the form of standards or norms. A large variety of such subgoals may be proposed. However they are not fixed immutably. Rather they represent reference points to be worked with in an ongoing collective decision-making process. In seeking to operationalize sustainability, as an objective, we have to search for measures and indicators of sustainability, as subgoals.

For example, for ecological sustainability we have to determine norms or indicators that are established in physical terms. We propose to illustrate our methodology by choosing three ecological subgoals.

The first one is a very simple indicator of biodiversity based on the number of species (biodiversity). The other two use energy-based valuation techniques to resolve the problem of the aggregation of heterogenous physical units (Faucheux and O'Connor 1996; Peet 1992). They are defined as follows:

1. *National eMergy Surplus (NES).* The environmental sources of energy may be considered a category of "critical natural capital" in the sense defined by Daly (1994) and others. It is crucial to consider the spatial distribution of energy availability as well as the temporal dimensions of depletion and renewal (Victor 1997). Embodied energy analysis is one method for aggregating different types of energy in a coherent way. If we use solar energy equivalents for embodied energy (that is, Odum's eMergy analysis conventions; see Faucheux and Pillet 1994), for a national economy we can define an ecological intermediate subgoal called the National eMergy Surplus (NES). The NES, for a given period of time, is defined, for a nation, as the difference between the amount of eMergy produced with natural resources within the country and the amount of eMergy consumed by this country's economy. If the concern is for natural resource self-sufficiency, then a criterion for national sustainability (ecologically sustainable development) is that NES ≥ 0, that is extraction rates for primary energy resources (measured in eMergy terms) are never higher than the overall renewal rate for energy natural resources.

2. *Entropy degree (Ne-Nm).* Some aggregated indicators may be constructed by using the total enthalpy, exergy, or entropy flux, associated with a given level and type of economic activity, that are discharged into the environment (Ayres and Martinas 1995). For a national economy, we can define an indicator relating to the objective of reducing pollution impact called the entropy degree defined as the difference between the actual entropy increase resulting from economic activity that is discharged into the natural environment (Ne) and the minimum entropy production technologically possible while achieving the same production (Nm). The

greater the difference between Ne and Nm (Ne − Nm —> +∞), the less sustainable the development is. Minimization of this difference (Ne − Nm —> 0) may then constitute a minimization of pollution subgoal because it signals a lessening of pollution impact through waste discharges. We note that is a crude indicator, since the cumulative impacts of pollutants in ecological processes are not something that can, in general, be expressed in aggregate by well-behaved functions of a few variables, in this case entropy increase. O'Connor (1994b) discusses this issue in detail.

For the socioeconomic sustainability we discuss three possible subgoals: the unemployment rate, the variation of gross national product (GNP), and the National Exergy Surplus. The first two are well-known economic performance indicators, and we will not discuss their merits and limitations here. The last one gives a measure of the technical efficiency of production. The question is whether a given output level might be achievable with less energy inputs, through technological changes or production efficiency improvements. The exergy valuation procedure can be used to define the indicator of the energy efficiency of an economic system, the National Exergy Surplus (NRS). The NRS is defined, for a given time period, as the difference between the exergy value (free content) of the inputs available for economic production, and the amount of exergy dissipated in a production or consumption process (or national economic system as a whole). For a time-trajectory of development to remain physically feasible, it is necessary to have NRS > 0, meaning that the economic system has a surplus of exergy (free energy) which may be used to undertake further development. Relative to a constraint on per period energy resource input availability, technical improvements in energy use will mean a higher NRS and thus a better growth and long-term economic sustainability prospect.

It is emphasized that the indicators we have selected are merely illustrative of our procedural rationality method; we do not suggest that these are the best sustainability criteria. Moreover, while scientific inputs are essential for the determination of appropriate environmental standards, there are irreducible social and political dimensions as well (O'Connor et al. 1995; Wills 1994). This is also the case for the determination of economic performance standards. The aim of procedural rationality methodology is to provide insight into the nature of the conflicts and the choices that implicitly or explicitly will have to be resolved through time. This can help the process of negotiated compromise situations, so increasing the transparency of the decision-making process (Froger and Zyla 1997). The point is no longer to choose an optimal solution but to identify a satisfactory action from the various possible options deriving from consideration of different criteria of sustainability.

The Satisfying Principle and Multi-criteria Decision Aid: Toward an Analysis of Conflictual Situations

During the last two decades, much support has emerged for the view that welfare is a multidimensional concept, thus the conventional complete commensurability principle underlying cost–benefit analysis can be questioned. As a consequence one of the key problems a systemic approach must tackle is complexity. The limits inherent in conventional decision theory methodologies and the necessity of analyzing conflicts between policy objectives have led to many calls for more appropriate analytical tools for strategic evaluation. This is the classic aim of multi-criteria evaluation. Furthermore multi-criteria evaluation offers some ways to cope with fundamental uncertainty, for example by means of fuzzy set theory. As such, multi-criteria decision aid does not itself provide a unique criterion for choice, rather it helps to frame the problem of arriving at a political compromise (see Munda, Chapter 5). The multi-criteria procedure for assessing sustainable development trajectories aims to bring together the multiple considerations represented by the subgoals and their associated measures. To clarify the meaning of the results provided by our multi-criteria procedure, an illustrative example will also be discussed here.

Some Conceptual Aspects

Fuzzy uncertainty (Zadeh 1965) focuses on the ambiguity of information in the sense that uncertainty does not concern the occurrence of an event but the event itself, which cannot be described unambiguously. In fact it corresponds to what we call strong uncertainty, and is a sort of mathematical expression of indeterminacy identified in socioecological processes, seen above. Fuzzy set theory is therefore a mathematical theory useful for modeling situations of such a sort. As formulated by Zadeh, fuzzy sets are based on the simple idea of introducing a degree of membership of an element with respect to some sets. Fuzzy nominal information is the basis of fuzzy set theory, since it considers all cases between 0 (nonmembership or unsustainability) and 1 (complete membership or sustainability), and it is represented by means of the membership functions which indicates the grade of membership of an element (or the degree of sustainability and/or unsustainability).

Unlike the analysis in which indicators are handled in a sequential lexicographic structure (thus no compensation between different indicators is possible), all the indicators are evaluated simultaneously; our fuzzy approach will allow for trade-offs (since the intensity of preference is taken into account) between different indicators to exist. However, one has to note that a hypothesis of complete compensability would imply the acceptance of the assumption of complete substitution between manufactured capital and natural capital. Therefore, an important requirement for the procedure to be used is the one of partial compensability.

Given the nature of the problem we want to tackle, it is not possible to apply an existing multi-criteria method, but there is a need for the development of a particular procedure responding to a number of requirements. The model can be formalized as follows:

> **a** is a particular nation to be evaluated according to a finite number (m) of different points of view or indicators g_i (i = 1, 2, ... , m) considered relevant, where g_i: A –> R, $\forall$ (i = 1, 2, ... , m) is a real valued function representing the i-th indicator according to a nondecreasing preference (i.e., the higher the better).

All the indicator scores are supposed to be measured on an interval or ratio scale (quantitative information). The assumption of equal weighting of the different indicators is made as well. Finally, because time is not considered the analysis is static in nature.

Definitions of Goals in the Form of Standards to be Attained

For each indicator (g_i) it is necessary to establish a standard (S_i) to be met; formally this can be considered as a desired level. At the same time it is necessary to establish a veto threshold (V_i). The veto threshold indicates a minimum level on each indicator below which even if all the other indicators have good performances, the country has to be declared to be in an unsustainable situation. The veto threshold indicates at which level a compensation between satisfactory and unsatisfactory indicators is not possible any more (Roy 1985). Since the intensity of preference is taken into account, compensability is allowed in the model, but because of the veto threshold, only into certain ranges. Thus the model can be classified as a partial compensatory one. Roughly speaking, because the lower the veto threshold the less important the indicator, in a somewhat arbitrary and incomplete way the notion of importance is taken into consideration.

The presence of both the veto threshold (V_i) and the standard (or subgoal, S_i) on each indicator creates a typical case of fuzziness.

1. If the veto threshold (V_i) is not satisfied, the country under study can be classified as unsustainable, thus it is possible to attribute the value of membership 0.
2. If the standard (S_i) is completely met, the value 1 can be attributed. In the case of the veto threshold, a zero value on a single indicator is sufficient for implying unsustainability; on the other hand a value 1 on an indicator does not imply any overall judgement. A country can be evaluated as sustainable only if it presents the value 1 on all the indicators considered.
3. In all cases in which the values of one or more indicators are between the

veto threshold and the standard, it is necessary to verify if this value is closer to 1 or 0 (i.e., to compute a "membership degree," this can be done by means of the notion of a "fuzzy relation").

We define standard and veto threshold for all selected indicators of sustainability (e.g., the percentage of annual variation of GNP, the unemployment rate, an indicator for biodiversity and the two energy indicators discussed before). For NES and NRS pure numbers between 0 and 1 are considered, 1 meaning achievement of the standards (NRS ≥ 0, NES ≥ 0) and 0 the achievement of the veto threshold (a negative difference too strong). For (Ne - Nm) the values are ranging between 0 and 1, where 1 means a complete achievement of the standard (Ne - Nm $\rightarrow 0$) and 0 a too strong positive difference (veto threshold). For biodiversity also a (0, 1) scale is considered (where 1 means achievement of the standards and 0 the veto thresholds). For GNP, it might be proposed to use the percentage of annual variation, where 3% is the goal to be achieved (S_i) and zero-growth is the veto threshold (V_i). For the unemployment rate, let us propose 5% represents the goal (S_i) and 10% the veto threshold (V_i).

The values of any or all of the indicators may be situated between (S_i) and (V_i). For example, we can examine the following configuration.

1. NES = 0.2 (since this value is close to 0, it is possible to conclude that this indicator depicts a bad situation);
2. Ne - Nm = 0.15 (this indicates a bad situation); biodiversity = 0.2 (a value close to zero is present, the biodiversity indicator shows a bad performance of the country);
3. NRS = 0.57 (the socioeconomic situation is moderately good);
4. ΔGNP = 2.5% (this value is close to the predefined standard, this indicator shows a good performance of the economy);
5. Unemployment rate = 6.3% (also the socioeconomic situation can be evaluated as good).

We now have to compute a membership degree (e.g., to evaluate how *distant* the values of these indicators are from the standard (S_i)).

Establishing Fuzzy Relations for Each Indicator

By using fuzzy relations, a formal analysis of imprecise linguistic relations such as: "distance x is much longer than distance y," or "x is similar to y," is allowed. In our model, by means of fuzzy relations it is possible to evaluate linguistically how distant the values of an indicator are from its standard.

In the proposed procedure, the following fuzzy relations are taken into consideration (the reference point is the standard to be met).

- very close
- close
- intermediate
- distant
- very distant

These fuzzy relations are "soft" measures of the distance of a current measurement on a given indicator from its predefined standard. By means of the membership functions of the various fuzzy relations, all the measurements are transformed in a "normalized" scale ranging from zero to one. For measurements not far from the standard, the fuzzy relations *close* and *very close* assume high values. The further away the measurements are from the standard, the lower the values of the fuzzy relations *close* and *very close,* but the higher the values of the fuzzy relations *distant* and *very distant.* When measurements in a middle positions are present, the fuzzy relation with the highest values is *intermediate.* Analytically, these fuzzy relations can expressed by the following equations.

$$\mu \text{ (very close)}_i = \begin{cases} [e^{-k_1 ((x_i - S_i)/S_i)^2}]^2 & \text{if } x_i \in [V_i \ S_i] \\ 0 & \text{if } x_i = V_i \end{cases} \quad (3.1)$$

$$\mu \text{ (close)}_i = \begin{cases} e^{-k_2 ((x_i - S_i)/S_i)^2} & \text{if } x_i \in [V_i \ S_i] \\ 0 & \text{if } x_i = V_i \end{cases} \quad (3.2)$$

$$\mu \text{ (intermediate)}_i = \begin{cases} e^{-k_3 (x_i - \gamma_i)^2} \end{cases} \quad (3.3)$$

$$m \text{ (distant)}_i = \begin{cases} 1 - e^{-k_4 ((x_i - S_i)/S_i)^2} & \text{if } x_i \in [V_i , S_i] \\ 1 & \text{if } x_i = V_i \end{cases} \quad (3.4)$$

$$m \text{ (very distant)}_i = \begin{cases} 1 - [e^{-k_5 ((x_i - S_i)/S_i)^2}]^2 & \text{if } x_i \in [V_i , S_i] \\ 1 & \text{if } x_i = V_i \end{cases} \quad (3.5)$$

where:

x_i (with $x_i \in [V_i, S_i]$) is the value according to the indicator i,

S_i is the standard defined on the i-th indicator,

V_i is the veto threshold,

γ_i is the middle value between V_i and S_i and

k_j, $j = 1, 2, ..., 5$ (with $k_j \in R+$) is the scaling factor.

$x_i < V_i \Rightarrow$ overall unsustainability (i representing a single indicator)

$x_i \geq S_i \; \forall \; i =1, 2,..., m \Rightarrow$ overall sustainability

The choice of the membership functions of the different relations as well as of the different parameters needed in the model is a subjective and somewhat arbitrary process. In a constructive decision aid framework this is not necessarily a bad characteristic; on the contrary since interaction with decision makers is required, it may be a desirable feature. However, a subjective component may be easily be transformed into subjectivism. The role of the analyst for balancing this process is very important (see Munda 1995 and Chapter 5, this volume).

For example, Table 3.2 illustrates some values of the fuzzy relations measuring the distance of the specified values of the different indicators with respect to their respective standards or goals. The computations are made by using equations 3.1 to 3.5 and these fuzzy relations are obtained starting from the hypothetical set of measurements of the various indicators already presented: NES = 0.2, Ne – Nm = 0.15, biodiversity = 0.2, NRS = 0.57, ΔGNP = 2.5%, unemployment rate = 6.3%. To make these easier to understand, we show all the details relative to the computations of the first indicator (NES), in the first column. These are:

$$\mu \text{ (very close)}_i = [e^{-1.25 \, (0.2)^2}]^2 = 0.2$$

$$\mu \text{ (close)}_i = e^{-1.88 \, (0.2)^2} = 0.3$$

$$\mu \text{ (intermediate)}_i = e^{-10 \, (-0.3)^2} = 0.4$$

$$\mu \text{ (distant)}_i = 1 - e^{-2.51 \, (0.2)^2} = 0.8$$

$$\mu \text{ (very distant)}_i = 1 - [e^{-0.9 \, (0.2)^2}]^2 = 0.7$$

The values presented in Table 3.2 show a clear situation of conflict between economic (NRS, ΔGNP, and unemployment rate) and ecological (NES, Ne - Nm, and biodiversity) indicators.

We can see that for NES, Ne - Nm, and biodiversity the fuzzy relations *close* and *very close* have low values; whereas the fuzzy relations *distant* and *very distant* have high values. This means that ecological indicators are far away from the standard or have bad performance. By contrast, for ΔGNP and the unemployment rate, the fuzzy relations *very close* and *close* have high

Table 3.2. *Fuzzy Relations*

	NES	Ne - Nm	Biodiversity	NRS	ΔGNP	Unemployment rate
Very close	0.2	0.1	0.1	0.6	0.85	0.7
Close	0.3	0.1	0.1	0.65	0.9	0.8
Intermediate	0.4	0.3	0.2	0.5	0.3	0.4
Distant	0.8	0.9	0.9	0.4	0.1	0.2
Very distant	0.7	0.85	0.9	0.3	0.1	0.15

values, as is the case for NRS to a lesser extent. This means that economic indicators show relatively good performance of the country, though still not up to full sustainability standards.

Aggregation of the Different Fuzzy Relations

Given the above information on the performance of the alternatives according to each single indicator, it is necessary to aggregate these evaluations in order to take all criteria into account simultaneously. For this purpose, some results obtained in the field of decision theory can be useful (Munda 1995). The simplest way of aggregating such individual values is the following.

$$\mu \ (\bullet) = \frac{1}{T} \sum_{i=1}^{T} \mu \ (\bullet)i$$

where $\mu \ (\bullet)_i$ indicates the evaluation of a given fuzzy relation according to the i-th criterion or indicator. A disadvantage of this approach is that the diversity among the assessments of single fuzzy relations is not considered (since the preference intensities completely compensate one another).

Another approach can be found in the use of an α-level nonfuzzy preference relation; this is defined by:

$$r_{ij} \ (\alpha) = \begin{cases} 1 & \text{if } r_{ij} \\ 0 & \text{if } r_{ij} < \alpha \end{cases}$$

However, the application of this rule in our problem would imply the loss of any information of the $\mu \ (\bullet)_i$ on the intensity of preference.

Therefore, in the framework of the NAIADE method (Munda 1995), the use of the following equation was proposed.

$$\mu \ (\bullet) = \frac{\sum_{i=1}^{T} \max \ (\mu \ (\bullet)_i -\alpha, 0)}{\sum_{i=1}^{T} \max | \mu \ (\bullet)_i -\alpha|} \tag{3.6}$$

where α is a minimum requirement imposed on each fuzzy relation, $\mu(\bullet)_i$ is a value of a given fuzzy relation indicating the distance from the standard and $\mu(\bullet)$ the overall evaluation of a given fuzzy relation according to all the indicators taken into consideration, obtained by means of equation 3.6.

It is: $0 \leq \mu(\bullet) \leq 1$, with

$\mu(\bullet) = 0$ if no $\mu(\bullet)_i$ is greater than α;

$\mu(\bullet) = 1$ if $\mu(\bullet)_i \geq \alpha \; \forall \; i$, and $\mu(\bullet)_i > \alpha$ for at least one i.

This particular "concordance index" has the property of taking into account intensities of preference. However, the values do not completely compensate each other due to the value set for the parameter α, so it is partially compensatory in nature.

Now an aggregate fuzzy preference relation can be obtained: it is possible to use the term preference, since the closeness to 1 or 0 indicates an evaluation of the two alternative states, sustainability and unsustainability. In our example, by applying equation 3.6 with $\alpha = 0.3$ (the higher the value of α the less compensability is allowed in the model) the following fuzzy preference relation is obtained.

$$
\begin{cases}
\mu \,(\text{very close}) = 0.71 \\
\mu \,(\text{close}) = 0.78 \\
\mu \,(\text{intermediate}) = 0.8 \\
\mu \,(\text{distant}) = 0.85 \\
\mu \,(\text{very distant}) = 0.81
\end{cases}
$$

Overall Evaluation

The final output provided by the mathematical procedure proposed here, is the degree of truth (τ) of statement on the true overall condition of the country (e.g., good, moderate, or bad).

We have:

$$
\omega \,(\text{good}) = \frac{\mu \,(\text{very close}) + \mu \,(\text{close})}{\mu \,(\text{very close}) + \mu \,(\text{close}) + \mu \,(\text{intermediate}) + \mu \,(\text{distant}) + \mu \,(\text{very distant})}
\tag{3.7}
$$

$$
\omega \,(\text{moderate}) = \frac{\mu \,(\text{intermediate})}{\mu \,(\text{close}) + \mu \,(\text{intermediate}) + \mu \,(\text{distant})}
\tag{3.8}
$$

$$\omega \text{ (bad)} = \frac{\mu \text{ (distant)} + \mu \text{ (very distant)}}{\mu \text{ (very close)} + \mu \text{ (close)} + \mu \text{ (intermediate)} + \mu \text{ (distant)} + \mu \text{ (very distant)}}$$

$$(3.9)$$

A clear-cut evaluation is obtained if one and only one of the three possible situations should satisfy the linguistic quantifier *most,* corresponding to degree of truth of the evaluation, as defined by the following membership function.

$$\mu \text{ most } (\omega) = \begin{cases} 1 & \text{if } \omega \geq 0.8 \\ 3.33\omega - 1.66 & \text{if } 0.5 < \omega < 0.8 \\ 0 & \text{if } \omega \leq 0.5 \end{cases} \qquad (3.10)$$

On the other hand, if none of the three possible situations satisfies the linguistic quantifier *most* (e.g., all $\omega \leq 0.5$, then it is concluded that a situation of undecidability is present). What does a situation of undecidability mean? This is not an easy question to answer. From a purely technical point of view, this implies two situations:

(a) the values of the different fuzzy relations are more or less equally clustered on the two opposite situations, good and bad
(b) the values of the different indicators are more or less equally distributed into the three possible situations (i.e., the three statements are equally credible)

Situation (a) is a typical case of incomparability, as a strong conflict between different points of view exists (e.g., between economic and ecological indicators). A social conflict resolution process may be very difficult. In situation (b) the conflict between different points of view is weaker and the social conflict resolution process may be easier. The conflict resolution process is social in nature. In the area of environmental and resource management, and in policies aimed at ecologically sustainable development, many conflicting issues and interests emerge. In real world situations of public decision analysis two main cases can be distinguished.

1. broad similarity of goals, where secondary differences among parties are revealed through various trade-offs that are perceived to be in their best interest.
2. direct conflict of goals (i.e., a case where public policy involves an explicit division of resources among different sectors of the society or where

attitudes have led to irreconcilable strong differences, for example environmentalists versus industrialists).

In our opinion, the situation described in (a) fits more the case of direct conflicts of goals, while the one described in (b) is more a case of broad goals.

One possibility to arrive at a final evaluation is to attach weights to the different indicators; this implies subjective value judgements. However, these are always difficult to express. Moreover, when different interest groups exist, to find a set of weights that satisfies all the actors may be an impossible task (especially in the case of direct conflict of goals). In this case, a sensitivity analysis aimed at verifying (by means of different vectors of weights) the robustness and stability of the results obtained can be very useful.

In our example, by computing the values of ω (good), ω (moderate) and ω (bad), we have the following.

ω (good) = 0.37
ω (moderate) = 0.32
ω (bad) = 0.42

None of the values satisfies the linguistic quantifier *most* because all $\omega \leq$ 0.5, thus an undecidability case is created. To arrive at a conclusion saying that this situation can be considered good or bad, implies strong value judgements on the weighting of the economic and ecological indicators. For example, one could attach the following weights (already normalized to equal 1).

NES = 0.15
Ne - Nm = 0.15
Biodiversity = 0.10
NRS = 0.10
DGNP = 0.30
Unemployment rate = 0.20

If we use such weights to obtain revised values of the various ω's, we get ω (good) = 0.6 (considering the economic indicators as evaluators for good and the ecological indicators as evaluators for bad), thus it is possible to conclude that the overall situation of the country in question is good with a degree of truth = 0.33. However, this result implies quite a strong assumption, namely that the importance[2] of GNP is three times more than that of biodiversity! In our opinion, this is one of the most important characteristics of this procedure:

one can always play with numbers, but the assumptions leading to certain results are always very clear and transparent.

In an environmental decision-making process it is difficult to arrive at a straightforward and unambiguous solution. This implies that such a decision-making process will always be characterized by the search for acceptable compromise solutions, an activity which is compatible with the satisfying principle inherent to procedural rationality. Multi-criteria methods provide a flexible way of dealing with quantitative, qualitative, and multidimensional effects of decisions. However, this does not mean that multi-criteria analysis is a panacea which can be used in all circumstances without difficulties – it has its own problems (Munda, Nijkamp, and Rietveld 1994). Nevertheless, we have developed a specific multi-criteria procedure by using fuzzy set theory and have shown it can be used as a type of sensitivity analysis for policy prioritization depending on the levels decided for veto and satisfaction standards, and on relative weightings given for the different subgoals of sustainability.

CONCLUSION

Environmental approaches based on the Bayesian theory and on substantive rationality may address choice situations characterized by small scale, weak uncertainty, and reversible threats. Decision making in regards to the structural interactions between the economic system and the environment requires the adoption of more flexible models capable of dealing with strong uncertainty, irreversibility, and complexity. Multi-criteria decision aids could be relevant because they can be used as tools for framing decisions in a procedural rationality perspective, and assisting in negotiation taking various conflictual subgoals into account.

The main properties of the multi-criteria procedure we have proposed here can be synthesized as follows.

- The standards to be met are modeled as aspiration levels, thus a goal programming framework based on procedural rationality and satisfying behavior is used.
- Intensity of preference is taken into account, this implies that a certain degree of compensation (trade-off) between indicators is allowed; given the characteristics of the method our approach can be classified among partial compensatory methods.
- No weighting of the different indicators is used (in the first instance).
- Communication with the decision maker is required to elicit different relevant parameters, thus a constructive decision aid framework is used. This implies the risk of subjectivism.

- According to multi-criteria evaluation philosophy, the results obtained depend not only on the mathematical properties of the procedure used, but also on the way such a procedure is integrated in a decision process. In our case, this implies a social conflict resolution process characterized by deep uncertainties and complexity; thus we are in a typical post-normal science situation (Funtowicz and Ravetz 1991).

In reality, we have to take into consideration the dynamic aspect of the decision-making process. (For a detailed discussion about such a sequential and iterative decision-making process which suggests possible trajectories for implementing a sustainable development, see Faucheux and Froger 1997). For example, there may be possibilities of technological progress and of changes in production method and consumption patterns that would relieve pressures on natural resources and the environment, so that a country has new possibilities to reach a sustainable trajectory even if initially the indicators give unsatisfactory results. This kind of dynamic consideration should be incorporated in any decision-making analysis.

FOOTNOTES

1. We acknowledge the two referees for their insightful comments on earlier version of this chapter. Needless to say, they are not to blame for any remaining flaws. We thank also Martin O'Connor for his reading to improve the English.
2. Here the weights have the meaning of importance coefficients since they are used without the connected values of the indicators. For more information on this issue see Munda (1995).

REFERENCES

Asheim, G. B. and K. A. Brekke. 1993. Sustainability when resource management has stochastic consequences, paper presented for the Fourth Annual Conference of the European Association of Environmental and Resource Economists, INSEAD, Fontainebleau, France, June 30–July 3.

Ayres, R. U. and K. Martinas. 1995. Waste potential entropy: The ultimate ecotoxic? *Economie Appliquée* XLVIII (2):95–121.

Binmore, K. G. 1986. Remodeled rational players, manuscript. London School of Economics.

Daly, H. 1994. Operationalizing sustainable development by investing in natural capital. In *Investing in Natural Capital: The Ecological Economics Approach to Sustainability,* eds. A. M. Jansson, M. Hammer, C. Folke, and R. Costanza. Washington DC: Island Press.

de Finetti, B. 1937. La Prévision: ses lois logiques, ses sources subjectives. *Annales de l'institut Henri Poincaré* 7:1–68.

de Finetti, B. 1980. Foresight: Its logical laws, its subjective sources. In *Studies in Subjective Probability,* eds. H. E. Kyberg and H. E. Smokler. New York: R. E. Krieger.

Delorme, R. 1995. From first order to second order complexity in economic theorizing. Paper presented for the workshop on Self-organization and Transformations of Economic Systems, Paris, March 9–10.

Faucheux, S. and G. Froger. 1997. Decision-making under environmental uncertainty. *Ecological Economics* (forthcoming).

Faucheux, S. and M. O'Connor. eds. 1996. *Valuation for Sustainable Development: Methods and Policy Indicators.* Edward Elgar.

Faucheux, S. and G. Pillet. 1994. Energy metrics: On various valuation properties of energy. In *Valuing the Environment: Methodological and Measurement Issues,* ed. R. Pethig. Kluwer.

Froger, G. and E. Zyla. 1997. Towards a decision-making framework to address sustainable development issues. Forthcoming in *Sustainable Development: Concepts, Rationalities and Strategies,* eds. S. Faucheux, M. O'Connor and J. van der Straaten. Kluwer.

Funtowicz, S. O. and J. R. Ravetz. 1991. A new scientific methodology for global environmental issues. In *Ecological Economics: The Science and Management of Sustainability,* ed. R. Costanza. New York: Columbia University Press.

Funtowicz, S. O. and J. R. Ravetz. 1994. Uncertainty and Regulation. In *Scientific–Technical Backgrounds for Biotechnology Regulations,* eds. F. Campagnari et al. Netherlands.

Keynes, J. M. 1971[1921]. A Treatise on Probability, reprint as vol. 8 of *The Collected Writing of J. M. Keynes.* London: Macmillan.

Knight, F. H. 1921. *Risk, Uncertainty and Profit.* Boston, MA: Houghton and Mifflin.

Krutilla, J. V. 1967. Conservation reconsidere. *American Economic Review* 47:777–786.

Loomes, G. and R. Sugden. 1982. Regret theory: An alternative theory of rational choice under uncertainty. *Economic Journal* 92:805–824.

Lucas, R. E. 1986. Adaptive behavior and economic theory. *The Journal of Business* 59(4), reprint In *Rational Choice: The Contrast between Economics and Psychology,* eds. R. M. Hogart and M. W. Reder. 1987. Chicago, Il: Chicago University Press.

Machina, M. J. 1987. Choice under uncertainty: Problem solved and unsolved. *Journal of Economic Perspectives* 1:121–154.

Mäler, K. G. 1989a. Risk and Environment: An Attempt to a Theory. Stockholm School of Economics Research Paper 6390.

Mäler, K. G. 1989b. Environmental Resources, Risk and Bayesian Decision Rules. Stockholm School of Economics Research Paper 6391.

Munda, G. 1995. *Multicriteria Evaluation in a Fuzzy Environment. Theory and Applications in Ecological Economics.* Berlin: Physica-Verlag.

Munda, G., P. Nijkamp, and P. Rietveld. 1994. Qualitative multicriteria evaluation for environmental management. *Ecological Economics* 10:97–112.

Norgaard, R. 1994. *Development Betrayed: The End of Progress and a Coevolutionary Revisioning of the Future.* London: Routledge.

O'Connor, M. 1990. Time and Environment, Ph.D. thesis, University of Auckland.

O'Connor, M. 1994a. Complexity and coevolution: Methodology for a positive treatment of indeterminacy. *Futures* 26.

O'Connor, M. 1994b. Entropy, liberty and catastrophe: The physics and metaphysics of waste disposal. In *Economics and Thermodynamics: New Perspectives on Economic Analysis,* eds. P. Burley and J. Foster. Kluwer: Boston/Dordrecht/London.

O'Connor, M., S. Faucheux, G. Froger, S. Funtowicz, and G. Munda. 1995. Emergent complexity and procedural rationality: Post normal science for sustainability. In *Getting Down to Earth: Practical Applications of Ecological Economics,* eds. R. Costanza, O. Segura, and J. Martinez-Alier. Washington DC: Island Press

Passet, R. 1979. *L'Economique et le vivant.* Paris: Petit Bibliothèque Payot.

Peet, J. 1992. *Energy and the Ecological Economics of Sustainability.* Washington DC: Island Press.

Roy, B. 1985. *Méthodologie multicritere d'aide à la decision.* Paris: Economica.

Savage, L. J. 1954. *The Foundations of Statistics.* New York: John Wiley and Sons.

Shackle, G. L. S. 1955. *Uncertainty in Economics.* Cambridge: Cambridge University Press.

Shackle, G. L. S. 1969. *Decision, Order and Time in Human Affairs.* Cambridge: Cambridge University Press.

Simon, H. A. 1964. *Rationality. In A Dictionary of the Social Sciences,* eds. J. Gould and W. L. Kolb. Glencoe, III: The Free Press.

Simon, H. A. 1972. Theories of bounded rationality. In *Decision and Organization,* eds. C. B. Radner and R. Radner. Amsterdam: North-Holland Publishing Company.

Simon, H. A. 1976. From substantive to procedural rationality. In *Methods and Appraisal in Economics,* ed. J. S. Latsis. Cambridge: Cambridge University Press.

Stengers, I. 1986. Découvrir la complexité? In Cahiers du CREA, Centre de Recherche sur l' Epistémologie et l'Autonomie. Paris: Ecole Polytechnique.

Stengers, I., ed. 1987. *D'une science à l'autre: Des concepts nomades.* Paris: Seuil.

van den Bergh, J. and P. Nijkamp. 1991. Operationalizing sustainable development: Dynamic ecological economic models. *Ecological Economics* 4:11–33.

Vercelli, A. 1991. *Methodological Foundations of Macroeconomics: Keynes & Lucas.* Cambridge: Cambridge University Press.

Vercelli, A. 1995. From soft uncertainty to hard environmental uncertainty. *Economie Appliquée* XLVIII 2:251–271.

Victor, P. 1991. Indicators of sustainable development: Some lessons from capital theory. *Ecological Economics* 4:191–213.

Victor, P. 1997. How strong is weak sustainability? In *Sustainable Development: Concepts, Rationalities and Strategies,* eds. S. Faucheux, M. O'Connor and J. van der Straaten. Kluwer (forthcoming) .

Von Neumann, J., and O. Morgenstern. 1947. *Theory of Games and Economic Behaviour.* Princeton: Princeton University Press.

Wills, P. 1994. Correcting evolution: Biotechnology's unfortunate agenda. *Revue Internationale de Systémique* 8:455–469.

Zadeh, L. A. 1965. Fuzzy sets. *Information and Control* 8:338–353.

4 EMERGENT COMPLEXITY AND ECOLOGICAL ECONOMICS

Silvio Funtowicz
EC—Joint Research Centre
ISEInformatics, Ispra (Va) Italy

Martin O'Connor
Centre d'Economie et d'Ethique pour l'Environnement et le Développement (C3ED), Université de Versailles, Guyancourt, France

Jerry Ravetz
RMC Ltd, London, United Kingdom

INTRODUCTION

As the fledgling discipline of ecological economics strives to define itself in contrast to traditional tendencies in the field, new conceptions of science are employed. By these means, ecological economics is provided with a new conceptual framework, as an alternative to the antiquated conceptions of physical science which have been dominant hitherto in economics. We suggest one such conception of science appropriate for the new ecological economics. For epistemology there is the theory of systems, in particular emergent complex systems, in which thermodynamics and ecology are synthesized. For a guide to practice, there is the theory of post-normal science as the appropriate form of problem solving for the complex issues of environmental policy. In their terms, we can reassess the role of natural science as applied to decision making in economics and ecology.

Traditional economics has been largely bounded by a particular, now outdated, view of scientific knowledge, its progress and its application. As it developed in the nineteenth century, on the general model of Hobbes' atomistic conception of the natural and social worlds, mainstream economics was an attempt to reduce economic systems to mere complication or even simplicity. Ever since, economic analysis and its mathematical representations have

75

tended to portray the human economy as a machine whose functioning was largely amenable to scientific prediction and to mechanical control. Both of the ideal types, the planned economy on the one hand, and the decentralized market system on the other, are examples of this sort of conception. In both of these, the role of natural science was simple: it furnished the knowledge base for improvements in productive efficiency and for innovations in process technology and product types; it also provided a model for rational decision making. Thus scientific progress and economic progress (improved productivity and output growth) were to go hand in hand. Such a belief is still dominant among, for example, the advocates of global free trade (see Costanza et al. 1995).

This simple conception of the economic system is no longer appropriate when we come to deal with large-scale problems of economies within their ecological contexts. These are not amenable to control along the lines of classical paradigms of mechanics, engineering design, or even of cybernetic regulation. These systems of social-ecological action comprise physical and social interdependencies over wide ranges of space and time scales, as well as a variety of production and consumption processes and policy actions, and ultimately resources stocks that are increasingly recognized as finite or dwindling. Not surprisingly they are characterized by high levels of indeterminacy and conflict among the various stakeholders in policy issues.

A variety of attempts to reform scientific practice in relation to ecological problems have been taken. Fisheries scientists are reviewing the errors that yielded their contribution to the collapse of many major fisheries (MacKenzie 1995). Thus far these efforts have remained mostly at the level of what we call ordinary complexity, that is, operating at the lower dimensions of the total phase-space for knowledge of the whole ecosystem. These new scientific approaches, emphasizing interconnectedness of systems and their dynamic instabilities, can provide powerful heuristic tools for exploring small-scale and local processes. However, for the understanding and management of the interaction of qualitatively different subsystems, including those possessing consciousness, purposes and ethical judgments, it is necessary to extend scientific method further, to what we call emergent complexity.

In this chapter we discuss the theory of emergent complexity as it relates to ecological economics. We start by briefly explaining the new roles required of physical and ecological science to respond to urgent environmental problems. Next we explain and discuss the basis for characterization of the different types of complexity, ordinary and emergent. Finally we explain how sustainability and post-normal science link back the science of emergent complexity to key problem domains in ecological economics.

ECOLOGICAL ECONOMICS AND THE EMERGENCE
OF POST-NORMAL SCIENCE

In earlier work, post-normal science has been developed as the problem solving strategy that is appropriate to major contemporary environmental management issues (e.g., Funtowicz and Ravetz 1991, 1993; O'Connor et al. 1996). The post-normal science perspective is typically applied when facts are uncertain, values are in dispute, stakes are high, and decisions are urgent. We can visualize this situation as one where either "systems uncertainties" or "decision stakes" are large. When they are both small, traditional "applied science" is adequate. But when either is medium in intensity, then mere research expertise is insufficient. We may think of the tasks of the surgeon or architect involving personal judgment and responsibility to clients, and this is "professional consultancy" (see Figure 4.1). But in this new class of environmental problems, where either uncertainties or stakes are high, we require a new approach.

In particular, given the impossibility of effective quality assurance being conducted by some exclusive group of experts, we must reconsider the question of who can be a legitimate participant in the evaluation process. We recommend an "extended peer community," including all stakeholders in an issue who are prepared for a dialogue, regardless of their formal certification (Dryzek 1994). Such an extension is necessary, not merely for the acquiescence of communities in decisions taken on their behalf, but equally for the effective quality assurance of the scientific inputs into the decision process.

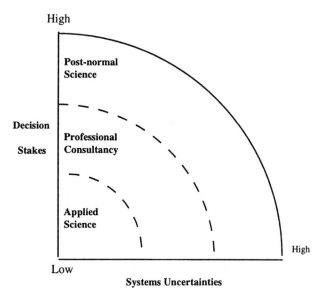

Figure 4.1. Professional consultancy

Such an extension and reorientation is necessary if natural science is to perform adequately the new roles required of it in environmental policy and decision making. These are to help guide and inform collective choices (community and political decisions at various levels) regarding the distribution of economic opportunity and of access to the services and benefits provided by the biophysical environment. The choices include an ethical component; this is seen in questions of present fairness, as in north–south redistribution, and also in equity issues relating to future generations and to the opportunities afforded to them and to the dangers and burdens we have imposed. In brief, the scientific perspective and practice that comprehends emergent complexity, i.e., post-normal science, is inseparable from explicit considerations of ethics and policy.

ECOLOGICAL DISTRIBUTION AND EXTERNALITY AS DOMAINS FOR POST-NORMAL SCIENCE

We can see what this reframing of science means with reference to the problems of environmental externalities (or unintended effects of economic production and consumption activity) and of social inequalities in ecological distribution and access to natural capital.

Our societies produce two sets of products, intended and unintended. The first of these categories is linked, in occidental ideology, to progress. The second is an aspect of what we might call *le revers du progrès* (Hanak et al. 1978; Dupuy and Robert 1976) as seen in litter, trash, chemical pollution, and urban and rural habitat degradation. Man makes history, but it is not wholly the history that he wants. Nor is industrial production confined to the products that he wants. Habitat degradation, due in large part to the production of waste (unavoidable though often accidental) as a by-product of commodity manufacture, transportation, and consumption activities is serious and widespread in all industrialized and industrializing societies. This distressing side of modern life, while unsought and unplanned, is nonetheless inherent in the modernization pathway chosen by these societies. It constitutes an inherent contradiction in the notion of resolving distributional conflicts in society through delivery of ever-increasing commodity wealth by unlimited industrial expansion.

In today's world, the goals of economic output growth and improved productivity are increasingly tempered by preoccupation with the unwanted by-production. The science of thermodynamics tells us that purposeful production will always be accompanied by unwanted wastes and disruptive environmental effects (O'Connor 1994a, 1994b). This becomes a global social problem. For example, as development theorist Gourlay writes (1992):

The more we consider the industrialized world of today, and the Third World of tomorrow, the more we realize that we live in a world dominated by waste, a World of Waste, most of it undesirable, and that unless we do something about it, humanity may disappear under its own detritus, and the world we know with it.

Science and economics have themselves emerged and coevolved within the larger social transformations of industrial revolution and modernization leading through to the present (Norgaard 1994). In peasant agricultural societies where there is little buffering against natural forces, humanity coexists closely with its by-products, which reenter local natural cycles along with detritus of other living systems. Economics for these societies was human ecology – management of nature's economy. Where natural resources come to be exploited more intensively, and populations gather more densely, degradation of the natural environment and of the human habitat inevitably becomes a problem. Examples in European history are extensive deforestation and water quality degradation since Roman times, and the filth and stench of the major cities over centuries. Where wastes could not be recycled profitably, they were simply endured. For example, when nineteenth century cities in Western Europe grew, and it became uneconomic for farmers to cart away rubbish and excrement from the dwellings of the poor, it simply accumulated as "midden" awaiting an occasional heroic exercise of removal.

The "modern" approach to unintended environmental effects began something over a century ago. One of the preoccupations of nineteenth century political economy was to describe and explain the process of capital accumulation. Another preoccupation, no less important, was to articulate political economy as the art of governance applied to commercial and production affairs, and to public administration. Nineteenth century industrial society already had its own theory and practice of externality regulation. For example, coinciding with the rise of large-scale industrial production, legislation prohibited factories from committing the most egregious forms of pollution. The domain of public health as a responsibility of municipal administrations and their corps of engineers and surveyors exemplified the new technological approach to managing environmental externality. Armies of "dustmen" removed wastes collected at residences or deposited on the streets by horses, and the system of sewer and flush toilet put in place a discreet transport of highly diluted human wastes to an elsewhere (preferably out of sight and out of line of smell).

This industrial theory and practice of economic development allied material progress to moral progress. The same dynamism of technological advance that produced industrial pollution on a large scale was also, rather paradoxically, heralded as ushering in an era of affluence, safety, and cleanliness. New techniques of production would be *cleaner* (less polluting) and wastes could be reused. Hence it became possible to imagine that the forthcoming era of mass-consumption was a pure good. Not only did the market deliver the enjoyable goods and services, but by the combined efforts of technological ingenuity and a benevolent social authority (the state, along with municipal powers, etc.) the "bads" and dirt could be suppressed and tucked away out of sight. Cleanliness was indeed close to "Go[o]dliness."

However, almost as soon as it became a reality in mass-consumption societies after World War II, this simple formula for material/moral progress began to fray at the seams. Wastes would not stay tucked away out of sight. Smog, poisoned waterways, traffic congestion, and roadside trash epitomized the "effluent society" and became the object of protestations by middle-class communities and hippie movements alike, culminating in events like the "Earth Day" celebrations in the United States and the Waldsterben panic in Germany. Rachel Carson's now classic book, *Silent Spring* (first published in 1962), detailed the irreversible poisoning of ecosystems and likely loss of species from extensive pesticide use, a quiet bomb that fractured optimism about technological solutions for agricultural productivity and disease control. The hazardous by-products of manufacturing ingenuity, such as CFCs, dioxins, genetic engineering, and nuclear fission residues, look likely to linger far more durably in our habitats than the manufactured goods themselves. The enlightenment notion of science as the basis of technological mastery of nature is put in question. By unlocking the secrets of nature, we bring upon ourselves (and those following us) unfathomed and mortal risks. The novelty and incessant innovation that is the mark of the technological society is matched by the novelty of uncontrolled and largely irreversible ecological change due to pollution and habitat disruption. Equally dramatic is uncontrolled social change. Transnationalization of investment, the routine transportation of commodities and manufacturing inputs between continents, and increased consumer affluence and mobility all contribute to social fragmentation, placing stress on traditional community structures and solidarity as well as on ecosystems. These are among the unintended effects of the progress of modern civilization (O'Connor and Ravetz 1996).

In fact, the past emphasis on economic growth as a desirable collective goal, and more particularly on output growth as a means of softening economic distribution contests (either through public policies of redistribution or the "trickle down effect" in mass consumer society), has itself been a powerful factor encouraging neglect of the environmental costs associated with economic expansion. We now see flagrant points of contradiction. The past marginalization of environmental issues relevant to economic growth and income distribution concerns has, cumulatively, led to the current sudden aggravation of issues of ecological distribution. While economic growth and population growth place increasing demands on the environment (on existing sources of natural capital and sinks for waste and pollution), it is not possible to enlarge the ecological pie upon which sustainable economic activity depends. Our ecological science and changed consciousness now leads us to emphasize the finiteness of our ecological capital, the fragility of our biosphere as a collective habitat and life support system, and the trade-offs between present and future associated with natural resource use (especially depletion of potentially renewable resources such as forests and fisheries) with land degradation and with the generation and disposal of wastes.

The emergence of the environmental movement and, in its wake, the recent development of concerted environmental policy at national and international levels, signals a very fundamental transition in public attitudes and policies – from a stance of benign neglect to one of concerted attention to these unintended environmental effects. However, any remedial action imposes costs on industry, government, and individuals. Indeed, while some of the problems are global in extent, affecting us all together (e.g., climate changes from greenhouse gases), their solutions are local, even individual (such as changes in technology and lifestyles necessary for problem reduction).

The practice of post-normal science that we describe here is a response to the changed role required of scientific inputs to policy decision making and to the social process requirements for effective conflict resolution.

Associated with the belief in the secular advance of science, technology, and civilization has been a strong emphasis in development thinking on economic growth. The enlargement of the economic pie has been promoted as the best way of alleviating distributional contests between social groups. Science and technology have been a principal means in the service of this strategy as technical knowledge was put to the service of production (aided by judicious investment strategy). The main focus of technological innovation and applied science during the industrial age was, thus, the domain of commodity production.

This was a plausible strategy only so long as environmental limits to economic output growth were not seen as limiting. However, the rise to prominence of environmental issues in the public policy domain, and with this the emergence of the discipline of ecological economics, signals the necessity to resolve not only economic distribution issues (income and marketable property), but also those of ecological distribution.

We define ecological distribution as the social, spatial, and intertemporal patterns of access to the benefits obtainable from natural resources and from the environment as a life-support system (Martinez-Alier and O'Connor 1996; Sachs 1993). The determinants of ecological distribution are in some respects natural (e.g., climate, topography, land quality, minerals, and rainfall patterns), and in other respects social and technological. We can speak of ecological goods and bads. For example, ecological goods and services include renewable and nonrenewable resources, the capacities for assimilation of pollution of the environment, species diversity, and amenity values of all sorts. Ecological bads include the risks and burdens falling on people as a result of pollution or exploitation, such as disturbed or degraded ecosystems, interruptions to ecological life-support cycles, and toxic substances in the environment. It has become commonplace to refer to ecological goods and services as deriving from existing stocks of natural capital. The prudent management of and investment in the maintenance, regeneration, and enhancement of natural capital is, correspondingly, receiving more attention. This immediately implies a critical role for physical, biological, and ecological sciences to furnish the knowledge base for this management. But the problems of managing ecosystem change and of resolving conflicts over ecological distribution are fundamentally different from those of augmenting economic productivity.

First, the supply and production (or "by-production") in the ecological domain of ecological goods and bads is not a controlled technological process. On the one hand, the biophysical milieu evolves under the influence of forces that in many respects are independent of human action. On the other hand, this same milieu is subject to uncontrolled (and increasingly severe) perturbation as a side effect of human economic activity.

Second, the distribution problem changes from one of sharing benefits of economic production (i.e., cutting the cake) to include the ethically and socially even more difficult problem of sharing bads – risk distribution and imposed suffering such as health damage and loss of food production capacity.

Third, the identities of the relevant agents and interested parties are not so accurately definable as in the case of commodity production and exchange. In some cases the interested parties are extremely diffuse (e.g., people suffering from health problems induced by or aggravated by urban pollution or carcinogenic substances) or hypothetical in character (e.g., future generations that may be affected by climate change, accumulation of toxic wastes, etc.). With regard to the costs and benefits themselves, there are fundamental difficulties with measurement and even with description. Ecological goods and bads cannot readily be divided into discrete units, measurable in terms of weight and volume. Even when the materials associated with environmental change (such as pollution discharges) are measurable in physical terms like volume, weight, or concentration, or when the ecological goods can be quantified in some respects (such as area of forest), these descriptions remain seriously incomplete. By contrast with intentional economic commodity production and use which is clearly localized in space and time, the unplanned side effects on ecological distribution (e.g., consequences of pollution and toxic waste disposal) will, in many cases, fully emerge only over long periods of time and across widely dispersed spatial domains. Moreover, the significance in economic welfare terms of a degraded ecosystem, or of changes in biodiversity, or of climate changes relating to greenhouse gas emissions, cannot be described exhaustively or evaluated quantitatively.

The nature of the scientific information required for understanding environmental externalities and for resolving ecological distribution issues with their associated uncertainties and long time horizons, is quite different from the fundamental and applied science for improving industrial productivity. Conflict resolution requires social processes of dialogue rather than scientific demonstration. Moreover, the purposeful social resolution of distributional contests and risk burdens associated with environmental issues depends on there being a sufficiently widespread acceptance of the very existence of these problems (e.g., impairment of life-support functions, or scarce physical resources, or acceptance of a duty towards future generations). At present there is evidence of widely contradictory perceptions and priorities, a situation we describe as fragmentation and conflict among plural attempted hegemonies. The common pattern in industrialized countries over the past few decades has been ad hoc bargaining in environmental policy-making with pressing industrial risk, environmental disruption, and ecological distribution issues resolved either implicitly (and in many cases simply by neglect) or through institutional channels not specifically intended for this purpose. Given this situation, scientific practice itself has become fragmented. Scientists in the environmental domains, and their work, have often been co-opted for policy legitimization purposes, without a clear understanding of the way that science, ethics, and policy are now inextricably meshed. Our discussion of emergent complexity and post-normal science is aimed at helping the reorientation of scientific practice to meet these new challenges.

ORDINARY AND EMERGENT COMPLEXITY

In post-normal science there is a plurality of legitimate perspectives, and this is essential. For, as we have seen in the case of environmental issues, distributional issues cannot now be sidetracked either by production increases or by scientific studies. In this new sort of problem solving context, the citizen stands alongside the expert and the official. This irreducible plurality of perspectives reminds us of the various well-known definitions of complexity. In this way, post-normal science provides a translation of complex systems theory into the science policy sphere. Motivated by the need to ground post-normal science in systems theory, we have introduced the concept of "emergent complexity."

Until now, science has advanced a great deal through analysis and reduction. The appropriate form of the societal system of research has mirrored this reductionist structure. Puzzle solving within compartmentalized disciplinary paradigms was the appropriate method for both scientific progress and personal advancement. The inadequacy of this traditional conception of science for our present tasks needs no argument here. The combination of fragmented research activity and hegemonic scientific method is now replaced by an awareness of contradiction and plurality, both in nature and in science. The metaphysical commitment of this program has been revealed by its comparative lack of success when applied to systems including the higher dimensions. For the behavioral sciences have never matured in the Kuhnian sense of providing stable paradigms for progress through puzzle-solving research. The downwards projection removed from the scientists' perspective (and therefore from the research work) precisely those higher-dimension properties that actually define emergent complex systems.

The metaphysical bias of reductionist science arose from the historic struggle between science and theology which continued well into the present century. Then holism (and previously design and vitalism) were foci of debate for they were associated with a particular strategy for the defense of spiritual realities. This involved the denial of the possibility of a (reductionist) scientific explanation of what we now call emergent properties, such as the phenomena characteristic of life. Against this have been ranged the reductionist philosophers of biology propounding counter-doctrines like "the selfish gene." In some ways the systems approach bridges the gap between holism and reductionism. Indeed, some elements of its origins are in the "holistic" tradition as shown by von Bertanlaffy, while others are in the "hard" sciences such as cybernetics. Although these ideological battles of the past are now over, knowing about them helps us identify their relics still persisting in particular theories and approaches.

Because the ecological–economic systems under study include awareness and conscious purposes as essential elements, the research system must also include awareness and self-awareness if it is to be effective. The puzzle-solving researcher, operating in an unquestionable paradigm laid down by the perceived views, has a limited role. When emergent complexity is recognized, but the societal system of research is not reformed, correspondingly we find calls for a vaguely understood interdisciplinary approach. In practice this usually means that each scientist does his or her own thing in the hope that somehow, somewhere it will all be integrated and made meaningful. Up to now the only means of real integration of effort has been on mission-oriented research conducted within institutionalized settings, but in that case the scientists' role is transformed, either upwards to manager or downwards to technician.

In recent years the theory of systems has been developed and enriched by a number of approaches in which dynamical properties have been grafted onto what was originally a rather static concept; among these is complexity which is now seen as manifesting in many scientific contexts. These new systems ideas, developed in conjunction with new concepts of structure, growth, qualitative change, and chaos have provided powerful tools of analysis, guiding practice in many fields. As the concepts have expanded in their application from the abstract fields of their origin to the study of phenomena in the biological and social worlds, the problems of their relation to external realities have needed to be addressed.

From systems theory we draw the distinction, which we shall expand below, between systems which are simple or merely complicated on the one hand, and those which are complex; the former are studied by classical physics, and the latter by biology and the human sciences. Complex systems are defined as those which cannot be captured by a single perspective (Casti 1986; Atlan 1991; O'Connor 1994b). For them, the reductionist program of physicalist natural science is definitely inappropriate. In order to study the systems where ecological economics is applied, it is necessary to further refine complexity into ordinary and emergent. Ordinary complexity is characteristic of biological systems. There is an absence of full self-consciousness and purposes. The most common organizational pattern in ordinary complexity is complementary of competition and cooperation, with a diversity of elements and subsystems. By contrast, emergent complexity (characteristic of systems, social, technical, or mixed, which includes humans) frequently oscillates between hegemony and fragmentation. Among both biological and social systems, diversity is now seen as desirable. This is particularly relevant to ecological economics, for diversity is the key to sustainability. In ordinary complexity, diversity occurs naturally while in emergent complexity it requires a special awareness and commitment for its achievement and maintenance (Funtowicz and Ravetz 1994a).

Emergent complexity can be distinguished from other aspects of physical phenomena studied in more classical scientific approaches in the following terms . The simplest state or manifestation of physical reality is that which can be captured by the tools of classical mathematical physics; this has functioned as the standard for generations of natural and social scientists. More recently, complication has been discovered, characterized by the nonlinearity of its processes and the loss of theoretically complete prediction. Beyond that lies ordinary complexity, defined by the incompleteness of any particular perspective – in living systems it usually involves structure and self-organization (implying some teleology). Whereas complication has no teleology (although there can be unidirection as in Fourier's theory of the flow of heat), ordinary complexity has a simple teleology. The boundaries between the various classes are not distinct; thus the dissipative systems studied by Prigogine are at the lower end of complexity. We can contrast ordinary and emergent complex systems in terms of their patterns of stability and change. Keeping biological species in mind as examples, we can list some relevant properties of ordinary complex systems. Much of their behavior can be explained in terms of mechanisms enriched with a functional teleology with simple systems goals such as growth and survival. The normal state for such systems is one of diversity of elements coexisting in (what we see as) a complementary state of competition and cooperation, perdition, parasitism or symbiosis. The ordinary complex systems tend to maintain a dynamic stability against perturbations until they are overwhelmed. This may be the result of direct assaults, such as by fire or aggressive invaders. For some purposes it is useful to enlarge the boundaries of the system to include such occasional extreme events. The new ideas of chaos and its edges enable simulations and analyses of processes of extraordinarily subtle articulation, variability, and apparent design.

Emergent complex systems, by contrast, cannot be fully explained mechanically and functionally; in them, at least some of the elements of the system possess individuality, along with some degree of intentionality, consciousness, foresight, purpose, symbolic representations, and morality. In ordinary complex systems, although numerical properties of subsystems (population size and density) can vary strongly, genuine novelty among the elements (a true origin of species as opposed to the formation of varieties) is very rare and still not easy to explain in mechanistic systems terms. On the other hand, continuous novelty and reflexivity may be considered among the characteristic properties of emergent complexity.

Some important aspects of emergent complex systems can be studied and successfully managed as if they were ordinarily complex. Indeed, since we are natural as well as social beings, the emergent aspects of our social and technical systems comprise only a small portion – the greater portion is ordinarily complex. On the other hand, it may be argued that in some respects there are no longer any cases of pure ordinarily complex systems. Any natural system that is of interest to us has properties that affect our welfare, but our perception of these natural features is mediated by culture. In a self-referring way, the ways that we describe systems and relations (e.g., the use of concepts like competition, to say nothing of selfishness) structure our research design and, beyond that, the whole institutional fabric of our research activities.

Emergent complexity is able to offer explanation of the phenomena of large-scale and long-lived hegemonies within the human species. By hegemony we understand a systems-state where the goals of one element or subsystem are totally dominant to the point where all others are either annihilated or survive on the margins. This state alternates (structurally and temporally) with fragmentation, which is a conflict among plural attempted hegemonies. The mixture of these polar opposite forms of relationships will depend strongly on the context, but the dangers of collapse of hegemonic human societies into fragmentation are greater than we had previously imagined. A similar phenomenon has been observed in the case of natural systems. For example, the Krumholz spruce can produce stands of very old trees with a high density of small trees and no understory – a sort of hegemonic biotic desert. In spite of under-performance this system can persist for a long time, resisting collapse, until an external force or a broader-scale phenomenon finally destroys it. Such analogies and borderline cases need not be used to reduce higher dimensions to lower; in cases like this they can illuminate phenomena from alternative perspectives.

THE DIMENSIONS OF EMERGENT COMPLEXITY

In order to better understand emergent complexity, we may borrow a mathematical metaphor from chaos theory (and before that from dynamical systems theory), that of a multidimensional phase space. The dimensions include those of the relevant mechanistic attributes (space, time, and measurable properties), the ordinary-complex attributes of structure and function, and in addition those of the technical, economic, societal, personal, and moral realms. These highest dimensions relate to knowledge and consciousness, and of course do not have the same type of metric relations as the lower dimensions. As Aristotle said, we cannot expect the same precision of reasoning in ethics as in geometry (Aristotle). We may use the term topology to indicate this difference: the lower dimensions have a *harder* topology, permitting measurement and quantitative gauges along with ordinal scales, while the higher dimensions have a *softer* topology in which the more qualitative properties are described.

In mathematics or physics, configurations of more dimensions are sometimes studied through their projections on subspaces of lower dimensions; thus in a four-dimensional problem, it can be useful to look at the various three-dimensional mappings of the object. The analogue in our interpretation of systems theory is the use of mathematical relationships to describe biological or social realities. However, it is also known in mathematics that the partial views of fewer dimensions do not encompass the whole; thus, even three-dimensional manifolds have properties that cannot be conceived in one or two dimensions. Or the higher-dimensional properties may appear paradoxical or counter-intuitive, as in the case of the well-known Möbius strip. These examples remind us that dimensions as deployed here are qualitatively different from the levels of integration that are familiar in biology. For those are generally stratified by inclusiveness; for example, the organism includes the cell, etc., whereas emergent properties apply to the more aggregated wholes. The dimensions in our systems phase-space overlap with those biological levels, but they extend over more aspects of systems, and there is no need for a higher dimension (as in the realms of symbolism and consciousness) to include the lower as a part of itself. The awareness that is fostered by this metaphor makes it easier to avoid some common errors in discussion of systems, such as those of being either anthropomorphic about lower dimensions or mechanistic about higher dimensions.

Flatland, the classic Victorian science fiction novel and social parody, provides a useful analogy (Abbot 1935). In this book, the inhabitants of spaces with more dimensions had a richer awareness of themselves, and also could see beyond and through the consciousness of the simpler creatures inhabiting fewer dimensions. At this stage it is not unfair to reveal the denouement of the story, namely that the Sphere of three-dimensional space was just as limited in his consciousness as were the flatlanders for he felt existentially threatened by the attempted generalization of reality to dimensions beyond his own familiar three.

By the use of the metaphor of phase-space, we hope to enable people of our own time to become aware and then transcend their own defensive limitations of imagination. An illustrative example of the relations among the dimensions of systems phase-space is that of the pendulum. The simple pendulum is indeed a classic case of successful mechanistic science. Its legendary origins are of a reductionist move: instead of responding to the aesthetic and religious aspects of the suspended censers in church, the young Galileo observed that their frequency of oscillation seemed to stay constant even as their swings diminished in amplitude. Now every student of mechanics learns the simple equation of pendulum motion whose solution yields a sinusoidal function. Few are told that this equation involves a move from complication to simplicity for the real dynamical equation of the simple pendulum is incapable of a formal solution. The student actually solves the equation for a pendulum-bob moving along a cycloid rather than a circle. All this was worked out within a short time of Galileo's publication of his results, mainly by Huygens. Why does (or did) all this matter? The pendulum seemed at that time to be the key to a technical problem with great policy consequences: the determination of longitudes. This was important for safe navigation, and also for statecraft, to determine the boundaries in overseas territories. So the errors in Galileo's theory of the circular pendulum, and their correction, were problems of considerable practical weight whose dimensions ranged from the mathematical and mechanical, all the way to the highly political, and they were fully appreciated as such by all those involved.

These examples remind us that no single perspective from within a subsystem of fewer dimensions can fully encompass the reality of the whole system. In the terms of our heuristic phase-space, a mathematical model of an ecosystem, although legitimate in its own terms, cannot be sufficient for a complete analysis of its properties – which include the human dimensions of ecological change and the transformations of human perceptions along the way. At the other end, institutional and cultural representations of the same system, also legitimate, are on their own insufficient for specifying what should be done on the ground in any particular case. The various dimensions are not totally disjoint; thus the institutional perspective can be a basis for the study of the social relations of the scientific processes. To take any particular perception, or projection onto a subspace, as the true, real, or total picture, amounts to reductionism, whether physical or sociological.

SUSTAINABILITY AND POST-NORMAL SCIENCE

Emergent complexity provides, we suggest, a coherent and rich theoretical framework through which ecological economics can transcend the restrictions imposed by the traditional disciplinary constraints of economics. We will illustrate this perspective with an application to the selection of priorities and standards in ecological and economic sustainability policies. (For a more comprehensive discussion, see Faucheux and O'Connor (1996).)

The setting of standards relates to a wide range of policy concerns, including matters of ecosystem conservation, maintenance of quality of the environment (including toxic waste management), and provisions for renewable resource use. Economic analyses of the basis for management of natural resources and the environment (now widely termed "natural capital") may be classified in terms of the "simple" or "complex" orders of explanation on which they depend.

At one extreme is what we might call monetary reductionism, which tries to represent all decision-making situations as problems of "optimal resource allocation" or "wealth maximization." This approach, underpinned by axiomatic assumptions about substitutability between production inputs and between sources of individual utility, derives in fact from a mechanistic analogy in the nineteenth century, and corresponds to what we have called a "simple" form of scientific analysis. The role of science would be, in this view, simply to provide estimates for the relevant model parameters, such as elasticity of substitution.

At another extreme are certain environmentalist approaches that reduce the complexity of decision making to the (moral) obligation of conservation. This is an understandable reflex when faced with alarming evidence of irreversible ecological changes, build-up of toxins, and so on. However, the determination of appropriate rules for ecological conservation and for sustainability is not a simple matter of scientific research and its application. There are irreducible social and political dimensions of judgment and choice as well.

Along the higher dimensions of emergent complexity are analytical approaches that emphasize problems of uncertainty and irreversibility, of social conflict, and of institutional change as irreducible dimensions of ecological management. Within this richer perspective, we reject the pursuit of optimizing solutions for natural capital management as illusory. Rather, social, economic, and ecological objectives must be established as explicit norms through processes of political negotiation involving compromise over matters of underlying dispute.

On the one hand, scientific analyses are not sufficient to determine sustainability requirements without ambiguity. This is partly because most environmental problems are characterized by a fluid and incomplete state of scientific knowledge, accompanied by the inherent unpredictability of complex systems. All environmental measurements are subject to uncertainties of various degrees of intensity and of qualitatively different types. Expressing environmental indicators to several significant digits amounts to a misleading hyperprecision (Funtowicz and Ravetz 1990). There are also problems with commensurability, which show up in difficulties with making meaningful aggregation of different sorts of physical quantities and properties expressed in a variety of units. If emissions of SO_2 diminish while those of NO_x rise, how can one decide whether the state of the environment has improved, gotten worse, or stayed the same? The highest policy levels are increasingly recognizing that no single "numeraire" can capture the diversity of perspectives and valuations that are present in any issue concerning the environment (European Communities 1993). Further, stakeholders may have commitments about their environment that are literally "beyond price," and in those cases all quantifications are profoundly misleading (European Communities 1993; Funtowicz and Ravetz 1994b).

On the other hand, because of uncertainties, complexity of ecosystem functions, and the long time scales involved, these norms cannot be set through use of conventional economic valuation methods, and in any case their achievement cannot be assured through market mechanisms of resource allocation alone. Thus, even if the scientific bases for decision making were clear-cut, there is no guarantee that norms proposed on a basis of specified biophysical goals would be backed by a social consensus. And it is now officially recognized that without a strong social commitment, there is no way in which respect of principles for environmental and economic sustainability can be assured (European Communities 1993; O'Connor and Ravetz 1996). This is one reason why, we argue, the environmental standards ought to be agreed to through a public participation process involving a wide range of stakeholders. The decision process would thus conform to a sort of procedural rationality, taking place through an iterative process of trade-offs and compromises with the aim of ending up with a solution that is satisfactory in terms of economic, social, and ecological imperatives. It might be said that the selection of the levels of environmental functions desired or to be sustained amounts to a choice of process that is essentially in the policy domain rather than the scientific. However, in practice the same is the case for the specification of a demand function for environmental quality and for the specification of a time-discount rate (relating to individual time preference and obligations to future generations) (European Communities 1993).

Broadly speaking, adopting sustainability as a policy norm means affirming a solidarity between present and future. This refers especially to the wealth-in-common of the biophysical milieu as a shared habitat. However, this generic formulation is not, on its own, sufficient for effective policy. In addition, there has to be a clear and explicit recognition of the necessity of making choices as to the particular interests (economic, societal, and ecological) that are going to be sustained. Sustainable environmental management involves making choices as to the particular ecosystems, species habitats, heritage values, and community structures that are to be preserved and provided for. Social groups differentiated by place, time, cultural heritage, collective identity, life experience, and hence preferences, will have widely different priorities. Sustainability policy therefore has to address and resolve two layers of distributional problems: what is, will be, or should be the distribution of welfare, that is, of wealth, of political and economic rights, of economic opportunity, and of access to environmental benefits and amenities within, first, the current generation, and, second, into the future? For example, the following questions need to be addressed.

- What effort is to be put into species conservation, and how should this be distributed between different species and different regions of a country or of the world?
- How urgently should standards relating to production, storage, and discharge of durable toxins like heavy metals, pesticide residues, and nuclear wastes be formulated, and according to what notions of prudence?
- What dangers to human health and ecological stability are deemed acceptable in the development of experimental bases and commercial application of biotechnologies involving genetically modified organisms?
- To what extent are native forests, wetlands, or other indigenous flora ecosystems to be modified or intruded upon for purposes of commercial gain (e.g., logging or farm development) or lifestyle preference (e.g., semi-rural housing, coastal developments for housing, tourism or recreational purposes)?

- Where should the boundaries of national parks or other reserve areas be drawn, and how rigidly should such boundaries preempt mining and other "exploitative" activities?
- How will the costs of major land, forest, and water quality conservation measures, such as pest control, soil erosion control programs, anti-desertification and anti-salinization programs, irrigation projects, and noxious plant eradication, be apportioned between private land-users and public agencies (and, within these latter, what division of responsibilities between local territorial, central government, and international bodies)?
- What taxation, "user-pays," or other revenue bases will be used to finance public expenditures on environmental management activities, and how will the fiscal burdens and the time burdens of management, policy-making, and decision-making processes be distributed within national units and between nations?

In a sense, all these sorts of issues are decided on a basis of balancing costs and benefits. But this is not an optimization process in the neoclassical wealth-maximizing sense. There is no avoiding the policy questions of costs for whom, benefits for whom, dangers borne by whom, and when and where? In other words, whose perceptions and principles are going to prevail, whose interests are to count more, and whose less? Here scientific practice, including the prioritizing of research and dissemination of results, is necessarily entwined with wider policy processes. How do we choose amongst the various particular economic and ecological outcomes that might be feasible within the framework of long-term sustainable activity? Effective sustainability policy depends on putting in place sociopolitical processes for deciding on the mix of economic, societal, and environmental purposes to be pursued. This is what the setting of ecological norms means in practice.

Scientific research for sustainability must be planned in close relation to the institutional framework for the environmental policy formation and decision process. On the one side, it is necessary to extend the category of the relevant facts for the analysis and management of environmental problems. On the other side, it is mandatory to extend the number and type of actors, both individual and collective, legitimated to intervene in the definition of the problems as well as the selection and implementation of the connected policies. This extension does not just fulfill the requirements of democratic decision-making, it also improves the quality of decisions. In other words, the very way of conducting a decision process dramatically influences its results. In addition to extended facts we must also recognize extended peer communities.

Natural resources use, ecosystem management, and conservation policies are, at root, matters of collective social choice that cannot be resolved at the level of individualistic approaches to valuation, choice, and resource ownership. The social acceptability of particular choices or proposals will depend very much on how the processes of scientific research and of decision-making are conducted, and on how people perceive the fairness of both the process and the outcomes of deciding the distribution of burdens, sacrifices, losses, and opportunities. Moreover, recent history has shown how large projects planned from the top-down, on the basis of apparently firm principles of science or of the market, have been vulnerable to large-scale failure; examples are the series of large dam projects in the Third World that have been canceled during construction. The knowledge and commitment of local peoples are at last becoming recognized as essential ingredients to genuine development (Norgaard 1994). To ignore the emergent aspects of such complex systems is to invite not merely ecological disaster in the long run, but also rejection and collapse of projects in the near future.

CONCLUSION

There is a complex feedback relationship between scientific theories and scientific understanding of ecosystem change on the one hand, and the evolution of social institutions and the cultural imaginary (habits of thought and norms) concerning the environment on the other. One implication of this complexity is that the role of scientific inputs in policy design becomes less simple to define than in the industrial age. Not only are the objectives of applying scientific knowledge matters of social controversy, but also there are major scientific uncertainties concerning risks and possible benefits where important decisions are having to be made. The demise of simple beliefs in material and moral progress, means that there is no longer the same confidence about solutions through technical expertise alone.

Dealing with environmental problems therefore requires opening the analytical and decision-making processes to broader categories of facts and actors than those traditionally legitimated. On the one hand, the old distinction between hard facts and soft values is being replaced by a soft facts/hard values framework. On the other hand, the distinction between experts and nonexperts is losing significance. In a sense, when facing an environmental problem, all stakeholders are experts – in different ways, from different points of view, and with regard to different aspects of the problem.

An epistemological perspective for the conception presented here of economics and ecological science is provided by the theory of emergent complex systems. Some aspects of economic activity do resemble the behavior of atoms, and they can be studied at the lower dimensions of the total system; these will include the highly aggregated measures of simple actions of many actors, as the movement of prices along a demand curve in markets like those imagined by neoclassical economists since Alfred Marshall. Those activities which involve structure and interactions among elements, the problems of economic organization and regulation properly speaking, are mapped in the middle dimensions, corresponding to ordinary complexity. And those involving policy, where purposes, awareness, uncertainties, and ethics are involved, belong to the higher, emergent dimensions.

Many environmental problems are so complex and diffuse that they are difficult even to grasp, let alone to manage effectively. Very often there are different definitions of the problem, different ways of selecting and conceiving its relevant aspects, as well as different goal definitions – depending on cultural/axiological factors and not only on conflict of interests. As a consequence, the traditional division of labor based on presumed knowledge and competence differentials between experts and lay people no longer applies.

The study of emergent complex systems, as in ecological economics, necessarily transcends traditional scholarly disciplines. It is impossible to have an effective process investigating such problems while remaining within the confines of a particular paradigm, which restricts the focus of research to a subset within the whole system, whether at the lower or at the higher dimensions. In this way, the principle of dialogue, expressed in post-normal science in relation to the policy stakeholders in an issue, applies here as well for the disciplinary stakeholders, be they natural or social scientists, or in the policy process itself. The theory of emergent complex systems, locating each disciplinary approach within its appropriate dimensions, enables all of them to gain perspective, and thereby enable a genuine integration of knowledge. With its means of effective management of uncertainty and value-commitments, post-normal science provides a viable mode of practice for ecological economics, whereby its major problems can be fruitfully investigated and resolved.

REFERENCES

Aristotle. *Nicomachean Ethics.* Translation by W. D. Ross. Oxford: Clarendon Press.

Abbott, E. A. 1935. *Flatland. A Romance of Many Dimensions.* Boston: Little, Brown & Co.

Atlan, H. 1991. *Tout non peut-être.* Paris: Editions du Seuil.

Carson, R. 1965. *Silent Spring.* Penguin.

Casti, J. L. 1986. On system complexity: Identification, measurement and management. In *Complexity, Language and Life: Mathematical Approaches,* eds. J. L. Casti and A. Karlquist. Berlin: Springer-Verlag.

Costanza, R., J. Audley, R. Borden, P. Ekins, C. Folke, S. O. Funtowicz, and J. Harris. 1995. Sustainable trade: A new paradigm for world welfare. *Environment* 37(5):16–20/39–44.

Dryzek, J. S. 1994. Ecology and discursive democracy: Beyond liberal capitalism and the administrative state. In *Is Capitalism Sustainable?,* ed. M. O'Connor. New York: Guilford.

Dupuy, J.-P. and J. Robert. 1976. *La Trahison de l'Opulence.* Paris: Presses Universitaires de France.

European Communities. 1993. Resolution of the Council ... on a community programme of policy and action in relation to the environment and sustainable development. *Official Journal* No. C 138 (17 May).

Faucheux, S. and M. O'Connor. eds. 1996. *Valuation for Sustainable Development: Methods and Policy Indicators.* Aldershot: Edward Elgar.

Funtowicz, S. O. and J. Ravetz. 1990. *Uncertainty and Quality in Science for Policy.* Dordrecht: Kluwer.

Funtowicz, S. O. and J. Ravetz. 1991. A new scientific methodology for global environmental issues. In *Ecological Economics: The Science and Management of Sustainability,* ed. R. Costanza. New York: Columbia University Press, pp. 137–152.

Funtowicz, S. O. and J. Ravetz. 1993. Science for the post-normal age. *Futures* 25(7):735–755.

Funtowicz, S. O. and J. Ravetz. 1994a. Emergent complex systems. *Futures* 26(6):568–582.

Funtowicz, S. O. and J. Ravetz. 1994b. The worth of a songbird: Ecological economics as a post-normal science. *Ecological Economics* 10:197–207.

Gourlay, K. A. 1992. *World of Waste: Dilemmas of Industrial Development.* London: Zed Books.

Hanak, J., S. Latouche, G. Leclercq, H. Philipson, J. P. Rouze, C. Sches, and R. Siorak. 1978. Le Revers de la Production: Eléments Pour une Approche Nouvelle des Mythes et des Réalités de la Pollution, document de travail. Centre d'Etude et de Recherche en Epistémologie de Lille (CEREL), Université de Lille, 59650 Villeneuve d'Ascq.

MacKenzie, D. 1995. The cod that disappeared. *New Scientist* 16 Sep, 24–29.

Martinez-Alier, J. and M. O'Connor. 1996. Ecological and economic distribution conflicts. In *Getting Down to Earth: Practical Applications of Ecological Economics,* eds. R. Costanza, O. Segura, and J. Martinez-Alier. Washington DC: Island Press.

Norgaard, R. 1994. *Development Betrayed: The End of Progress and a Coevolutionary Revisioning of the Future.* London: Routledge.

O'Connor, M. 1994a. Entropy, liberty and catastrophe: The physics and metaphysics of waste disposal. In *Economics and Thermodynamics: New Perspectives on Economic Analysis,* eds. P. Burley and J. Foster. Boston/Dordrecht/London: Kluwer.

O'Connor, M. 1994b. Thermodynamique, complexité, et codépendance écologique: La science de la joie et du deuil. *Revue Internationale du Systémique* 8(4-5):397–424.

O'Connor, M. and J. Ravetz. 1996. Social science and environmental policy science: Managing modernity's unintended effects. *International Journal of Environment and Pollution,* special issue on Decision Making and the Environment.

O'Connor, M., S. Faucheux, G. Froger, S. Funtowicz, and G. Munda. 1996. Emergent complexity and procedural rationality: Post-normal science for Sustainability. In *Getting Down to Earth: Practical Applications of Ecological Economics,* eds. R. Costanza, O. Segura, and J. Martinez-Alier. Washington DC: Island Press.

Sachs, W. ed. 1993. *Global Ecology: A New Arena of International Conflict.* London: Zed Books.

5 MULTI-CRITERIA EVALUATION AS A MULTIDIMENSIONAL APPROACH TO WELFARE MEASUREMENT

Giuseppe Munda

Departament d'Economia i d'Història Econòmica
Universitat Autònoma Bellaterra
08193 Bellaterra
Barcelona, Spain

INTRODUCTION

Cost–benefit analysis (CBA) is based on the neoclassical maximization premise of behavior, stating that rational decisions coincide with utility maximization. Consistency is considered an important characteristic of rationality; as a consequence, the preference structure is assumed to hold only the preference and the indifference relations and both relations are considered of a complete transitive type. No incomparability relation is allowed. Thus, it becomes possible to found the validity of a procedure either on a notion of approximation (i.e., discovering preexisting truths) or on a mathematical property of convergence (i.e., does the decision automatically lead, in a finite number of steps, to the optimum a*?).

The optimizing approach is based on the assumption that different objectives can be expressed in a common denominator by means of trade-offs (complete commensurability), so that the loss in one objective can be evaluated against the gain in another. The idea of compensatory changes underlies both the classical economic utility theory and the traditional cost–benefit analysis. From a theoretical point of view, the optimizing principle is elegant since it provides an unambiguous tool to evaluate alternative strategies on the basis of their contributions to community welfare. From an operational point of view, the value of the optimizing approach is rather limited, because the specification of a community welfare function requires complete information about all possible combinations of actions, about the relative trade-offs between all actions and about all constraints prevailing in the decision making process. Such information is generally not available in the context of environmental decision

96

making, and in any case the validity of the proposed trade-offs is likely to be contested by affected groups.

During the last two decades, more support has emerged for the view that welfare is a multidimensional concept, thus the conventional complete commensurability principle can be questioned. As a consequence one of the key problems a systemic approach must tackle is complexity. In economic theory three main conflicting values can be identified: allocation, distribution, and scale (Daly 1991). In an operational framework, this means that an exhaustive analysis has to take into consideration efficiency criteria, ethical criteria, and ecological criteria; thus a multidimensional approach is needed. The present chapter first addresses the issue of commensurability, then the main characteristics of multi-criteria evaluation are discussed. Finally, an empirical application showing a multidimensional evaluation of welfare in the nine provinces of Sicily is illustrated.

A KEY ISSUE IN ECOLOGICAL ECONOMICS: THE PRINCIPLE OF COMPLETE COMMENSURABILITY

Conventional cost–benefit analysis can be used only under the condition of strong commensurability (i.e., it is always possible to find a set of conversion factors able to transform all dimensions underlying a given action into a single composite measure). Such conversion factors are normally based on the market mechanism (Hanley and Spash 1993; Mishan 1971a; Pearce and Nash 1981). In order to be consistent with the objective of maximizing social welfare, it is necessary that the prices attached to the physical benefits and costs reflect society's valuations of the final goods and resources involved. Two questions immediately arise.

1. If markets do exist, to what extent will observed market prices reflect social valuations?
2. If markets do not exist (as it happens for most environmental goods and services), how are surrogate prices to be derived which, in turn, reflect social valuations?

In classical welfare economics, prices resulting from a competitive equilibrium can be considered to be a measure of social opportunity costs. Deviations from the neoclassical model originate from the so-called "market failures." As a result, prices may be bad indicators of the real scarcities and social evaluations in the economy. Some set of prices, called shadow or accounting prices, which reflects the true social opportunity cost of using resources in a given project, needs to be computed. In general, we would expect the marginal cost of a final good to indicate society's valuation of that good, since the marginal cost reflects consumers' willingness to use resources in that situation. As a first approximation, shadow prices are assumed to reflect marginal costs. However, the use of marginal cost pricing in the public sector with prices elsewhere diverging from marginal costs involves the "second best problem." The essential argument is that setting prices equal to marginal cost in one sector only may actually move the economy away from a Pareto optimum (Lipsey and Lancaster 1956).

Clearly, if market prices are to be corrected so that they reflect marginal costs, there is a practical problem of estimating marginal costs and a conceptual problem of justifying the procedure in the face of the second best theorem. Furthermore, marginal private cost will still not fulfill the role of a proper shadow price if private and social cost diverge. An important cause of divergence is the presence of an important category of market failures contributing to environmental degradation, namely externalities (Ayres and Kneese 1990; Mishan 1971b).

One should note that since externalities are characterized by the absence of markets, there will also be an absence of observable prices with which the cost–benefit analysis can work. Many external effect problems therefore reduce the issue of valuing intangibles.

In many applications of CBA to environmental issues, it is necessary to place monetary values on nonmarket goods such as clean air, water, and wilderness areas. Several methodologies have been developed to cope with such estimation requirements, the principal ones being contingent valuation, the travel cost method, hedonic pricing, and the shadow project approach. Among these only contingent valuation is universally applicable. An extensive discussion on the main properties of these valuation methods can be found in (Hoevenagel 1994; Kask, Shogren, and Morton, Chapter 13, this volume).

The aim of contingent valuation is to elicit valuations (or bids) that are close to those that would be revealed if an actual market existed. Respondents say that they would be willing to pay or willing to accept if a market existed for the good in question. In order to determine the value of environmental goods and services, economists try to identify how much people would be willing to pay (willingness-to-pay (WTP)) for these goods in artificial markets. Alternatively, the respondents could be asked to express their willingness-to-accept (WTA) compensation.

The respondents must be familiar with the good in question and with the hypothetical means of payment (payment vehicle). The quality of results in this method depends on how well-informed people are, moreover, the problem with these techniques is that respondents may answer *strategically*. For example, if they think their response may increase the probability of implementing a project they desire, they may state a value higher than their true value (free rider problem). In order to avoid free rider behavior people should really pay the amount of money they indicate (one should note that this is also needed by the consistency requirements of subjective probability theory; de Finetti 1974; Keynes 1921). Unfortunately in this case, WTP depends upon the ability to pay, thus projects that benefit higher income groups would generally be considered to be the best.

Distributional issues can also be one of the possible explanations of the difference found empirically between WTA and WTP measures in contingent valuation studies; since WTP bids are constrained by income, whereas WTA bids are not (one's WTP to save his life is bounded by his income and ability to borrow; one's WTA is probably infinite) (Hanley 1992). The divergence between WTA and WTP measures of value is a serious problem. This phenomenon can lead to projects passing the Kaldor-Hicks test[1] when payment measures are elicited for welfare losses, but failing it when compensation measures are obtained.

The income distribution problems connected with contingency valuation are also emphasized by Keeney and Raiffa (1976), who show formally that among the necessary validating assumptions of WTP there is also the condition that "the marginal rate of substitution between money and any other attribute does not functionally depend on the monetary level" (Keeney and Raiffa 1976).

For environmental problems the Kaldor-Hicks principle can be formalized simply as follows. Economic theory states that the utility derived from consumption can be captured in a so-called utility function (e.g., $U=U(M, E)$, where M represents monetary income and E is environmental quality). Given such a utility function, indifference curves are defined as the locus of points representing combinations of money and environmental quality that yield the same level of utility. What are the consequences of such a model?

From an environmental point of view, this model implies that it is always possible to find an amount of money in terms of WTP for environmental quality improvements or of WTA for environmental quality deterioration that keeps utility constant. It has to be noted that such models do not aim to achieve a better environmental quality, but only to incorporate the environmental impacts in the traditional price and market system. It has to be noted that since the objective is to keep utility constant, complete substitution between environmental quality and economic growth is always allowed, and thus a weak sustainability philosophy is implied (Pearce and Atkinson 1992, 1993).

From an intragenerational point of view, the compensation model presents strong distributive impacts; the monetary value of a negative externality depends on social institutions and distributional conflicts (WTP measures consider preferences of the higher income groups more important than the lower ones). If the people damaged are poor or of future generation, the cost of internalization will be lower ("the poor sell cheap") (Martinez-Alier 1994a, 1994b).

Martinez-Alier and O'Connor (1995) have introduced the concept of ecological distribution, referring to the social, spatial, and temporal asymmetries or inequalities in the use by humans of environmental resources and services. Thus, the territorial asymmetries between SO_2 emissions and the burdens of acid rain is an example of spatial ecological distribution; the intergenerational inequalities between the enjoyment of nuclear energy and the burdens of radioactive waste is an example of temporal ecological distribution. In the USA, "environmental racism" means locating polluting industries or toxic waste disposal sites in areas where poor people live. This is an example of social ecological distribution.

From an intergenerational equity point of view, since future generations are not on the market, their preferences do not count; however, society as a whole may have values that deviate from aggregated individual values. Society has a much longer life expectancy than individuals, thus the value society attaches to natural resources and the environment is likely to deviate from individual values, since the simple summation of individual preferences may imply the extinction of species and ecosystems. This implies that environmental policy cannot be merely based upon the aggregation of individual values and the estimation of WTP at any particular point of time (Klaassen and Opschoor 1991). It is interesting to note that surprisingly, Walras already noted that the market cannot be used as a basis for rational collective decision making and that "human destinies are not absolutely independent, but to some extent dependent on one another. There is a social morality which is distinct from individual morality" (Bürgenmeier 1994).

Finally, one should note that incommensurability (i.e., to take into account all the different dimensions of a decision problem without any monetary reductionism) does not imply incomparability. O'Neill (1993) distinguishes between the concepts of strong commensurability (common measure of the different consequences of an action based on a cardinal scale of measurement), weak commensurability (common measure based on an ordinal scale of measurement), strong comparability (there exists a single comparative term by which all different actions can be ranked) and weak comparability (one has to accept the existence of conflicts between all different consequences of an action).

Weak comparability can be considered to be the philosophical base of multi-criteria evaluation. The next section presents the main principles of multi-criteria evaluation.

TACKLING MULTIDIMENSIONALITY: MULTI-CRITERIA EVALUATION METHODS

The limits inherent in conventional decision theory methodologies and the necessity of analyzing conflicts between policy objectives have led to many calls for more appropriate analytical tools for strategic evaluation. This is the classic aim of multi-criteria evaluation. Furthermore, multi-criteria evaluation offers some way to cope with fundamental uncertainty; for example, by means of fuzzy set theory. As such multi-criteria decision aid does not itself provide a unique criterion for choice; rather it helps to frame the problem of arriving at a political compromise. The aim of this section is to present the principal methodological foundations of multiple criteria decision aid.

During the last two decades, more support has emerged for the view that welfare is a multidimensional concept that includes, inter alia, average income, economic growth, environmental quality, distribution equity, supply of public facilities, accessibility, and so on. This implies that a systematic evaluation of public plans or projects has to be based on the distinction and measurement of a broad set of criteria: private economic (investment costs, rate of return, etc.); socioeconomic (employment, income distribution, access to facilities, etc.); environmental (pollution, deterioration of natural areas, noise, etc.); energy (use of energy, technological innovation, risk, etc.); physical planning (congestion, population density, accessibility, etc.) and so forth (Nijkamp, Rietveld, and Voogd 1990).

In designing models for environmental and resource policy-making, the following three main types of policy objectives may be distinguished (van den Bergh 1996; Braat and van Lierop 1987; Dietz and van der Straaten 1992; Hafkamp 1984).

1. Nature conservation objectives (e.g., minimum exploitation of natural systems, optimum yield);
2. Socioeconomic objectives (e.g., maximum production of goods and services); and
3. Mixed objectives (e.g., maximum sustainable use of resources and environmental services at minimum private and social cost).

Such formulations remain vague, until constraints and performance criteria are defined. But, it is clear that in policy-relevant economic–environmental evaluation models, socioeconomic and nature conservation objectives are to be considered simultaneously. Consequently, multi-criteria methods are in principle an appropriate modeling tool for environmental decision-making issues:

a compromise solution taking into account different conflicting values can in principle be identified.

Multiple use refers to the simultaneous use of natural resources for different social and economic objectives. Such situations almost always lead to conflicts of interest and damage to the environment. The consequences range from suboptimal use due to unregulated access, to degradation of resource systems due to limited knowledge of the ecological processes involved. Thus, in the area of environmental and resource management, many conflicting issues and interests emerge. There is also a high degree of diverging public interests and conflicts among groups on society. For example, various hierarchical conflicts may emerge between regional government institutions and the central government which again implies a multiple objective decision situation.

As a tool for conflict management, multi-criteria evaluation has demonstrated its usefulness in many environmental management problems. From an operational point of view, the major strength of multi-criteria methods is their ability to address problems marked by various conflicting evaluations. Since real-world problems are generally not direct win–lose situations, a certain degree of compromise is needed. Multi-criteria evaluation techniques cannot solve all conflicts, but they can help to provide more insight into the nature of conflicts and into ways to arrive at political compromises in case of divergent preferences in a multigroup or committee system, so increasing the transparency of the choice process.

An important point is the way in which a problem is structured. The results of any decision model depend on the available information. Since this information may assume different forms, it is useful that decision models can take this differentiation into account. Another problem related to the available information concerns the uncertainty associated with this information. Ideally, in the Laplacian perspective on science and decision making, the information should be precise, certain, exhaustive, and unequivocal. But in reality, it is often necessary to use information that is known not to have those characteristics.

A variety of epistemological and methodological perspectives are possible. If it is impossible to establish exactly the future state of the problem faced, a stochastic uncertainty may be postulated; this type of uncertainty is well known – it has been thoroughly studied in probability theory and statistics. According to a well-established tradition originated by the classical contributions of Knight (1921) and Keynes (1921) a distinction is made between two kinds of uncertainty: a weak variety called "risk" and a strong one called "uncertainty." In particular, risk refers to probability distributions based on reliable classification of possible events and uncertainty refers to events whose probability distribution is not fully definable for lack of reliable classification criteria. Existing decision theories, based on substantive rationality, are limited for dealing with environmental decision situations characterized by a high degree of uncertainty about nature, incidence and/or timing of possible environmental costs, especially situations where the effects may be catastrophic for future generations (Froger and Munda 1994; Vercelli 1991).

Another framing of uncertainty called fuzzy uncertainty focuses on the ambiguity of information in the sense that the uncertainty does not concern the occurrence of an event but the event itself, which cannot be described unambiguously (Zadeh 1965). This sort of situation is readily identifiable in complex systems. Spatial-environmental systems in particular are emergent complex systems characterized by subjectivity, incompleteness, and imprecision (e.g., ecological processes are quite uncertain and little is known about their sensitivity to stress factors such as various types of pollution). Fuzzy set theory is a mathematical theory useful for modeling situations of this sort (i.e., it aims to portray in terms of fuzzy uncertainty some of the indeterminacies of the socioecological system under study).

Fuzzy sets as formulated by Zadeh are based on the simple idea of introducing a degree of membership of an element with respect to some sets. The physical meaning is that a gradual instead of an abrupt transition from membership to nonmembership is taken into account. An important feature of multicriteria evaluation methods is the possibility of also taking into account fuzzy information (Munda 1995).

A great number of multi-criteria methods have been developed and applied for different policy purposes in different contexts. In general, a multi-criteria model presents the following aspects (Munda, Nijkamp, and Rietveld 1994; Munda 1995).

1. There is no solution optimizing all the criteria at the same time and therefore the decision maker has to find compromise solutions.

2. The relations of preference and indifference are not enough in this approach, because when an action is better than another one for some criteria, it is usually worse for others, so that many pairs of actions remain incomparable with respect to a dominance relation.

The main advantage of these models is that they make it possible to consider a large number of data, relations, and objectives that are generally present in a specific real-world decision problem, so that the decision problem at hand can be studied in a multidimensional fashion. On the other side, an action *a* may be better than an action *b* according to one criterion and worse according to another. Thus when different conflicting evaluation criteria are taken into consideration, a multi-criteria problem is mathematically ill-defined. The consequence is that a complete axiomatization of multi-criteria decision theory is quite difficult (Arrow and Raynaud 1986). Since the problem is mathematically ill-structured, two cases are possible.

1. Leave the decision maker entire liberty for the decision (decisionism), or
2. Introduce consciously or not restrictive hypotheses, so that the problem can be solved by a classical method (rationalism).

Decisionism in practice maintains that decisions are blind actions, inspired by the subconscious and by the instincts, so that the act of reasoning over a decision is meaningless. On the contrary, rationalism assumes that in any decision problem an optimal precise solution always exists and that it is possible to find it by reasoning over the problem. Thus, using Socrates' words, "ignorance is the only cause of foolish or evil acts."

The methods used in multi-criteria analysis lie between these two extremes: they are based on (necessarily restrictive) mathematical assumptions as well as on information gathered from the decision maker. Thus the concept of "decision process" has an essential importance. According to Simon (1972, 1978, 1983), a distinction must be made between the general notion of rationality as an adaptation of available means to ends, and the various theories and models based on a rationality which is either substantive or procedural. This terminology can be used to distinguish between the rationality of a decision considered independently of the manner in which it is made (in the case of substantive rationality, the rationality of evaluation refers exclusively to the results of the choice) and the rationality of a decision in terms of the manner in which it is made (in the case of procedural rationality, the rationality of evaluation refers to the decision-making process itself) (Froger and Munda 1994).

According to Roy (1985), in general it is impossible to say that a decision is a good one or a bad one by referring only to a mathematical model: organizational, pedagogical, and cultural aspects of the whole decision process that leads to a given decision also contribute to its quality and success. As a consequence, it becomes impossible to find the validity of a procedure either on a notion of approximation or on a mathematical property of convergence. The final solution is more like a "creation" than a discovery. In multiple criteria decision aid (MCDA), the principal aim is not to discover a solution, but to construct or create something that is viewed as liable to help an actor taking part in a decision process either to shape, and/or to argue, and/or to transform his preferences, or to make a decision in conformity with his goals (constructive or creative approach).

Finally, we can conclude that the validity of a given procedure depends on two main factors.

1. Mathematical properties that make it conform to given requirements.
2. The way it is used and integrated in a decision process.

The constructive approach is much less ambitious in its objectives than rationalism, but is the best approach if we really wish that the application of mathematics to socioeconomic problems is meaningful.

From the above discussion, we can note that procedural rationality and multi-criteria decision aid are quite similar in spirit. They start with the basic assumption that the real world is complex, thus both are searching for satisfying compromise solutions, and finally, the decision process at hand is more important than the final solution found (Froger and Munda 1994).

In the next section, an application of a qualitative multi-criteria method, the so-called Novel Approach to Imprecise Assessment and Decision Environments (NAIADE)[2] method will be illustrated.

EXAMPLE OF A MULTIDIMENSIONAL EVALUATION OF WELFARE

A possible reduction of complexity, a precondition for management actions, consists in the aggregation of nonequivalent representations which arise in the interaction between the various observer subjects and the different systemic levels. The reduction of the number of nonequivalent representations introduces the problem of the descriptors: indicators and indices.

It is generally useful to distinguish between direct and indirect indicators. Direct indicators refer to objects, qualities, and attributes that have a direct connotation of value. Indirect indicators instead assign a magnitude of value to objects which in themselves do not possess it. As an example, the concentration of a pollutant in the atmosphere has an impact value on human health only as the result of the evaluation of a relationship between this concentration and a damage to people: these relationships are often based on long and uncertain event chains. Often the complexity of many real situations does not allow investigation of the long relational chains, possibly random, which assign the cause of an impact to the presence of an object of an attribute. In these cases the indicators constructed, as well as obviously being indirect, are called estimated. Their construction rests on analogies and similarities of behavior (i.e., on inferential models). The use of these indicators, although subject to discussion, is obviously very wide and often fundamental in describing the system being studied (Paruccini and Munda 1995).

As discussed before, the concept of welfare can be considered a multidimensional variable. A straightforward procedure to decompose this concept can be the "hierarchical decomposition" used in fuzzy set theory in order to represent linguistic variables with no meaning on interval or ratio scales (Zimmermann 1987). In this case, the qualitative information does not depend on a lack of information, but on the nature of the information that is essentially fuzzy (intrinsic fuzziness). For example, if linguistic propositions (like "pretty girl, beautiful flower, or quality of life") clearly have no quantitative base variable, how can we represent them?

Humans seem to have a set of hidden and fuzzy standards in their minds as justification for this type of concept, but they are more than a human being can rationally handle simultaneously. An approach to this problem may be to decompose the concept to be represented into a series of quantitative variables. This approach presents two main problems.

1. The explicit definition of the quantitative variables
2. The aggregation procedure to be used

As an illustrative example of the above considerations, here the nine provinces of Sicily will be evaluated according to the hierarchical decomposition

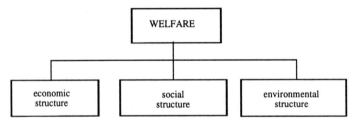

Figure 5.1. Hierarchical decomposition scheme of the concept of welfare

scheme illustrated in Figure 5.1. This scheme is also consistent with the main principles of procedural rationality. The implementation of procedural rationality may in fact imply the replacement of a global nonmeasurable objectives with intermediate objectives or intermediate subgoals whose achievement can be observed and measured. The dissociation process stops precisely at the point where each intermediate subgoal becomes homogeneously measurable. The decision maker does not choose the optimal solution, but arbitrates between the different intermediate subgoals and chooses the solution that he or she feels to be the most satisfactory after taking into account economic, ecological, social, and other imperatives (Froger and Munda 1994).

In the proposed scheme, the following indicators homogeneously measurable are taken into consideration.

I.   For the economic structure: activity index
    A.   Activity index (Ac. Ind)
    B.   ratio between real working population and the whole population (Cor. Act. Ind)

      C.   variation of the gross provincial product between 1980 and 1986 (Var. GPP)

      D.   value added per capita (VA. Cap)

      E.   gross provincial product per employee (GPP. Empl.)

      F.   consumption per inhabitant (Cons. Inhab.)

II. For the social structure:

      A.   percentage of graduate people (Grad. Peop.)

      B.   holders of a diploma (Hold. Diplo.)

      C.   illiterate people (Illit. Peop.)

      D.   diseases correlated to the territory (Disea. Terr.)

      E.   suicides (Suic.)

      F.   notified crimes (Not. Crim.)

      G.   notified minors (Not. Mino.)

III. For the environmental structure:

      A.   theoretical loads of nitrogen (N) and phosphorus (P)

      B.   theoretical evaluation of air pollution differences among the provinces (Air. Pol.)

      C.   percentage of irrigated surface (Irr. Surf.)

      D.   water available for zootechnical use (Wat. Zoot.)

      E.   percentage of woodland (Wood).

Munda (1989) provides a discussion on how these indicators are constructed.

In order to aggregate these indicators, a new multi-criteria method based on some aspects of the partial comparability axiom NAIADE is used (Munda 1995).

The concept of partial comparability is the base of the so-called "outranking methods" (Roy 1985). These are based on the understanding that generally, in multi-criteria problems the dominance relation is poor because it is based on a consensus of point of view. Thus, an action a outranks an action b only if a is at least as good as b on all the criteria considered. The concept behind the outranking methods is that the enrichment of the dominance relation can be done only if realistic information is available; so there is a formal structure between the dominance relation that is too weak and the utility functions complete pre-order. By using outranking methods some incomparable actions become comparable because realistic information exists, but other actions remain, nevertheless, incomparable. For an extensive discussion of the epistemological and methodological foundations of these methods, see Arrow and Raynaud (1986), Munda (1993), and Roy (1985).

NAIADE is a discrete multi-criteria method whose impact (or evaluation) matrix may include either crisp, stochastic, or fuzzy measurements of the performance of an alternative (a_n) with respect to a judgment criterion (g_m), thus it is very flexible for real-world applications. The NAIADE method presents different theoretical properties that are not shared by traditional multi-criteria methods in a fuzzy environment.

In a fuzzy context, any attempt to reach a high degree of precision on the results tends to be somewhat artificial; therefore a pairwise linguistic evaluation of alternatives is used. This is done by means of fuzzy relations and linguistic quantifiers. In the aggregation process, particular attention is paid to the problem of diversity of the single evaluations, while the entropy concept is used as a measure of the associated fuzziness. Such linguistic evaluations can be used in different ways according to the decision environment at hand.

In short, the main properties of the NAIADE method can be synthesized as follows.

Table 5.1. Economic Indicators of the Nine Provinces of Sicily

	Economic Structure					
	Ac. Ind.	Cor. Act. Ind.	Var. GPP	VA Cap.	GPP Empl.	Cons. Inhab.
Agrigento (AG)	63.60	45.80	138.30	7879.40	31265	5823.00
Caltanissetta (CL)	60.80	44.50	124.30	9373.60	34883	6106.40
Catania (CT)	67.60	50.20	142.00	10384.40	36124	7335.80
Enna (EN)	62.90	45.30	119.40	7932.40	30191	5517.70
Messina (ME)	72.20	52.70	134.00	10249.70	36410	8019.60
Palermo (PA)	66.00	48.50	135.60	9877.30	34417	8603.20
Ragusa (RG)	67.40	53.40	148.20	10047.20	33928	7128.20
Siracusa (SR)	65.90	48.60	114.50	11878.40	37933	6977.50
Trapani (TP)	65.00	50.40	134.20	9754.90	34461	7094.00

Table 5.2. Social Indicators of the Nine Provinces of Sicily

	Social Structure						
	Grad. Peop.	Hold. Diplo.	Illit. Peop.	Disea. Terr.	Suic.	Not. Crim.	Not. Mino.
AG	2.10	8.20	7.80	1.40	0.63	1.58	0.90
CL	1.90	8.30	8.20	1.30	0.61	1.85	5.72
CT	3.10	11.00	6.40	1.50	0.56	4.20	2.13
EN	1.80	8.50	9.30	1.40	0.85	0.81	4.21
ME	3.20	11.10	5.20	1.60	0.53	2.91	0.07
PA	3.50	9.90	5.40	1.50	0.32	4.17	2.15
RG	2.20	9.40	7.20	1.80	0.48	2.39	0.73
SR	2.40	11.10	5.90	1.40	0.38	2.65	2.14
TP	2.30	9.40	5.70	1.70	0.54	4.57	0.31

Table 5.3. Environmental Indicators of the Nine Provinces of Sicily

			Environmental Structure			
	N	P	Air Pol.	Irr. Surf.	Wat. Zoot.	Wood.
AG	7.70	0.99	good	5.14	5.40	5.12
CL	8.10	1.04	more or less bad	5.62	4.66	8.08
CT	4.30	0.81	more or less bad	17.09	5.91	8.84
EN	16.80	1.56	good	4.52	8.56	8.78
ME	5.23	0.88	more or less good	4.38	9.34	19.92
PA	4.97	0.87	very bad	4.32	10.10	7.63
RG	13.59	2	good	11.30	11.62	2.72
SR	5.94	0.89	bad	18.72	7.93	2.18
TP	5.75	0.88	good	5.79	4.86	5.56

- Communication with the decision maker is required to elicit different relevant parameters, thus a constructive decision aid framework is implied.
- The method is based on some aspects of the partial comparability axiom, in particular, a pairwise comparison between alternatives is carried out and incomparability relations are allowed.
- Intensity of preference is taken into account. This implies that a certain degree of compensation between criteria is allowed, and given the characteristics of the method it may be classified among partial compensatory methods.
- A partial (or total) order of feasible alternatives is supplied. It has to be noted that the final ranking is a function of all the alternatives considered, this implies that if a dominated or a dominating action is introduced, the ranking may change; moreover if the best action is eliminated, the ranking of the other alternatives may also change. In other words, Arrow's axiom of "the independence of irrelevant alternatives" does not hold.[3]

Taking into consideration these indicators, the NAIADE method will be applied. First we will consider each single point of view alone, and then all the indicators belonging to the three points of view will be used simultaneously.

I. Economic indicators

Applying NAIADE the following partial pre-order is obtained (high→ low).

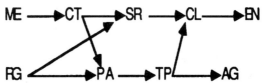

An incomparability relation exists between Messina (ME) and Ragusa (RG), between Ragusa and Catania (CT), between Agrigento (AG) and Caltanissetta (CL), and between Agrigento and Enna (EN). On the contrary, we can be sure that Messina is in a better position than Catania and that Ragusa is in a better position than Siracusa (SR) and Palermo (PA). In the last position are Caltanissetta, Agrigento and Enna.

II. Social indicators

Applying NAIADE the following partial pre-order is obtained:

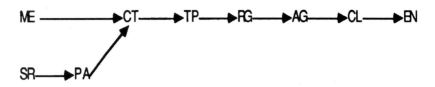

An incomparability relation exists between Messina and Siracusa and between Messina and Palermo. The other provinces form a very stable ranking.

III. Environmental indicators

Applying NAIADE the following partial pre-order is obtained:

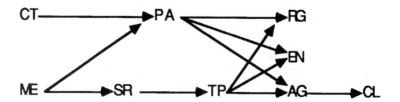

An incomparability relation exists between Catania and Messina, between Palermo and Siracusa, between Palermo and Trapani, among Ragusa, Enna and Agrigento, and among Ragusa, Enna and Caltanissetta. In any case, we can note that Messina is still in the first position.

IV. Global evaluation

Taking into consideration all the 19 indicators and applying NAIADE the following partial pre-order is obtained.

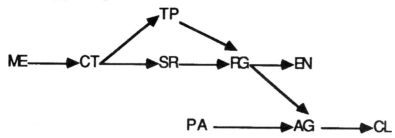

It is interesting to note the behavior of Palermo. Such a province is incomparable with other six provinces; on the contrary, we can be sure that it is better than Agrigento and Caltanissetta. The first position of Messina and the last positions of the tern Agrigento, Caltanissetta and Enna are very stable. It has to be noted that this ranking may be interpreted as an ordinal membership of the provinces to the fuzzy concept of welfare.

The results obtained depend on the indicators considered and on the method used. The indicators taken into consideration are constructed using data from the official statistics and from theoretical elaborations, therefore the results are theoretical in nature. Furthermore, in the NAIADE method, the intensity of preference is considered (i.e., how much an action is better than another one); if another method were used (e.g., ELECTRE 2; Roy 1985) that does not take into account the intensity of preference the results would be different. For example, with reference to the environmental indicators, one can see that Messina is better than Ragusa in the ranking; but such a result is completely dependent on the intensity of preference. In fact, there are exactly three criteria in favor of each of the two alternatives, and therefore, since all the criteria have the same importance, using ELECTRE 2 the two alternatives are indifferent.

Because of the deep uncertainties present in evaluation methods, it is a case of post-normal science. In such cases, the traditional subject speciality expertise is inadequate for peer review of quality. Quality assurance therefore requires extended peer communities, which include all those with a stake in the issue who are prepared to dialogue (Funtowicz and Ravetz 1991). The criteria of quality in this new context will, as in traditional science, presuppose ethical principles. But in this case, the principles will be explicit and will become part of the dialogue.

According to Funtowicz and Ravetz (1994) the traditional analytical approach, implicitly or explicitly reducing all goods to commodities, can be recognized as one perspective among several, legitimate as a point of view and as a reflection of real power structures, but not the whole story. To choose any particular operational definition for value involves making a decision about what is important and real; other definitions will reflect the commitments of other stockholders. How much is a songbird worth? To answer this question represents a new problem of valuation, one where measurements cannot pretend to be independent of methodology and ethics. As Funtowicz and Ravetz (1994) stated, "The issue is not whether it is only the marketplace that can determine value, for economists have long debated other means of valuation; our concern is with the assumption that in any dialogue, all valuations or 'numeraires' should be reducible to a single one-dimension standard."

CONCLUSIONS

Traditional economic theory is based on optimizing principles aiming at finding a precise *best* solution. CBA is based on strong commensurability and strong comparability; in order to find an optimum, a complete pre-order structure is needed. Most important is the quality of the final decision, not the quality of the decision process. Complete compensability and commensurability imply the inseparability between efficiency, equity, and environmental issues, and as a consequence no "objective, value-free" optimization of a monocriterion type can be done. A weak sustainability philosophy is always implied, since substitution between man-made capital and natural capital is a direct consequence of the compensation model. From an intragenerational point of view, the compensation model presents strong distributive impacts; the monetary value of a negative externality depends on social institutions and distributional conflicts. From an intergenerational equity point of view, since future generations are not on the market, their preferences do not count; thus the value society attaches to natural resources and the environment is likely to deviate from individual values, since the simple summation of individual preferences may imply the extinction of species and ecosystems.

Incommensurability, or taking into account all the different dimensions of a decision problem without any monetary reductionism, does not imply incomparability, weak comparability can be considered to be the philosophical base of multi-criteria evaluation.

Ecological economics explicitly recognizes that economy–environment interactions are also characterized by significant institutional, political, cultural, and social factors through which action is carried out. The use of a multidimensional approach seems desirable. This implies that in the framework of ecological economics, the strong commensurability and strong comparability premises of neoclassical economics have to be changed. Since multi-criteria evaluation techniques are based on a constructive rationality and allow one to take into account conflictual, multidimensional, incommensurable, and uncertain effects of decisions, they look to be a promising assessment framework for ecological economics. A systematic analysis of this possibility will be the aim of future research. Some tentative results can already be found in Faucheux, Froger, and Munda 1994, O'Connor et al. 1995, Munda, Nijkamp, and Rietveld 1995 and Munda 1995).

ACKNOWLEDGMENTS

I would like to thank Jeroen van den Bergh, Silvio Funtowicz, and Jan van der Straaten for their very helpful comments on previous drafts of this chapter.

Discussions with Sylvie Faucheux, Geraldine Froger and Martin O'Connor have been very fruitful for the understanding of the relationships between multi-criteria evaluation and procedural rationality.

FOOTNOTES

1. By this, the social cost of a given output is defined as the sum of money which is just adequate when paid as compensation to restore to their previous level of utility all who lose as a result of production of the output in question. In other words, the Kaldor-Hicks principle declares a social state y socially preferable to an existing social state x if those who gain from the move to y can compensate those who lose and still have some gains left over. Such a situation is consistent with a Pareto improvement since we have x indifferent to y for the losers (once they are compensated) and y preferred to x for the gainers (if they can overcompensate).
2. Naiade is the Italian name for the Greek nymphs of rivers.
3. Arrow's axiom of "the independence of irrelevant alternatives" states that the choice made in a given set of alternatives a depends only on the ordering made with respect to the alternatives in that set. Alternatives outside a (irrelevant since the choice must be made within a) should not effect the choice inside a. Unfortunately, empirical experience does not generally support this axiom; thus to exclude some actions already inside a may have even less justification (see Arrow 1951).

REFERENCES

Arrow, K. J. 1951. *Social Choice and Individual Values.* New York: Wiley.
Arrow, K. J. and Raynaud H. 1986. *Social Choice and Multicriterion Decision Making.* Boston: M.I.T. Press.
Ayres, R. U. and A. V. Kneese. 1990. Externalities: Economics and thermodynamics. In *Economy and Ecology: Towards Sustainable Development,* eds. F. Archibugi and P. Nijkamp. Dordrecht: Kluwer.
Braat, L. C. and W. F. J. van Lierop. eds. 1987. *Economic–Ecological Modeling.* Amsterdam: North-Holland.
Bürgenmeier, B. 1994. The misperception of Walras. *The American Economic Review* 84:342–352.
Daly, H. E. 1991. Elements of environmental macroeconomics. In *Ecological Economics: The Science and Management of Sustainability,* ed. R. Costanza. New York: Columbia University Press.

de Finetti, B. 1974. *Theory of Probability.* New York: Wiley.

Dietz, F. J. and J. van der Straaten. 1992. Rethinking environmental economics: Missing links between economic theory and environmental policy. *Journal of Economic Issues* 26:27–51.

Faucheux, S., G. Froger and G. Munda. 1994. Des outils d'aide à la decision pour la multidimensionalité systémique: une application au développement durable. *Revue Internationale de Systémique* 8:495–517.

Froger, G. and G. Munda. 1994. Methodology for decision support: Procedural rationality and multicriteria decision aid. Paris: Cahiers du C3E N. 94 –20, Université de Paris I.

Funtowicz, S. O. and J. R. Ravetz. 1991. A new scientific methodology for global environmental issues. In *Ecological Economics,* ed. R. Costanza. New York: Columbia.

Funtowicz, S. O. and J. R. Ravetz. 1994. The worth of a songbird: Ecological economics as a post-normal science. *Ecological Economics* 10:197–207.

Hafkamp, W. 1984. *Economic–Environmental Modeling in a National-Regional System.* Amsterdam: North-Holland.

Hanley, N. 1992. Are there environmental limits to cost–benefit analysis? *Environmental and Resource Economics* 2:33–59.

Hanley, N. and C. Spash. 1993. *Cost–Benefit Analysis and the Environment.* Aldershot: Edward Elgar.

Hoevenagel, R. 1994. The Contingent Valuation Method: Scope and Validity, Ph.D Thesis. Amsterdam: Free University.

Keeney, R. and H. Raiffa. 1976. *Decision with Multiple Objectives: Preferences and Value Trade-Offs.* New York: Wiley.

Keynes, J. M. 1921. *A Treatise on Probability.* New York: St. Martin's Press.

Klaassen, G. A. J. and J. B. Opschoor. 1991. Economics of sustainability or the sustainability of economics: Different paradigms. *Ecological Economics* 4:93–115.

Knight, F. H. 1921. *Risk, Uncertainty and Profit.* Boston: Houghton and Mifflin.

Lipsey, R. G. and K. Lancaster. 1956. The general theory of second-best. *Review of Economic Studies* 7.

Martinez-Alier, J. 1994a. Distributional issues in ecological economics. Paper presented at the Third International Meeting of Ecological Economics, San Jose, Costa Rica.

Martinez-Alier, J. 1994b. Distributional conflicts and international environmental policy on carbon dioxide emissions and agricultural biodiversity. In *Toward Sustainable Development,* eds. J. C. J. M. van den Bergh and J. van der Straaten. Washington, DC: Island Press.

Martinez-Alier, J. and M. O'Connor. 1995. Ecological and economic distribution conflicts. In *Getting Down to Earth: Practical Applications of Ecological Economics,* eds. R. Costanza, O. Segura, and J. Martinez-Alier. Washington, DC: Island Press.

Mishan, E. J. 1971a. *Cost–Benefit Analysis.* London: Allen and Unwin.

Mishan, E. J. 1971b. The postwar literature on externalities: An interpretative essay. *Journal of Economic Literature* 9:1–28.

Munda, G. 1989. Multiple criteria decision aid: Principi teorici ed applicazioni nel campo delle scienze regionali. In proceedings of the 10th meeting of the Italian Regional Sciences Association, Rome 2:1225–1244.

Munda, G. 1993. Multiple criteria decision aid: Some epistemological considerations. *Journal of Multi-Criteria Decision Analysis* 2:41–55.

Munda, G. 1995. *Multicriteria Evaluation in a Fuzzy Environment. Theory and Applications in Ecological Economics.* Berlin: Physica-Verlag.

Munda, G., P. Nijkamp, and P. Rietveld. 1994. Qualitative multicriteria evaluation for environmental management. *Ecological Economics* 10:97–112.

Munda, G., P. Nijkamp, and P. Rietveld. 1995. Monetary and non-monetary evaluation methods in sustainable development planning. *Economie Appliquée* 48:145–162.

Nijkamp, P., P. Rietveld, and H. Voogd. 1990. *Multicriteria Evaluation in Physical Planning.* Amsterdam: North-Holland.

O'Connor, M., S. Faucheux, G. Froger, S. O. Funtowicz, and G. Munda. 1995. Emergent complexity and procedural rationality: Post-normal science for sustainability. In *Getting Down to Earth: Practical Applications of Ecological Economics,* eds. R. Costanza, O. Segura and J. Martinez-Alier. Washington, DC: Island Press.

O'Neill, J. 1993. *Ecology, Policy and Politics.* London: Routledge.

Paruccini, M. and G. Munda. 1995. Scientific tools to support the environmental management. In *Chemistry and Environment: Legislation, Methodologies and Applications,* eds. S. Facchetti and D. Pitea. Dordrecht: Kluwer.

Pearce, D. W. and G. D. Atkinson. 1992. Are national economies sustainable? Measuring sustainable development. CSERGE Working Paper GEC 92–11.

Pearce, D. W. and G. D. Atkinson. 1993. Capital theory and the measurement of sustainable development: An indicator of "weak" sustainability. *Ecological Economics* 8:103–108.

Pearce, D. W. and C. A. Nash. 1981. *The Social Appraisal of Projects.* London: MacMillan.

Roy, B. 1985. *Méthodologie Multicritere d'Aide à la Decision.* Paris: Economica.

Simon, H. A. 1972. *Theories of Bounded Rationality. Decision and Organization,* eds. C. B. Radner and R. Radner. Amsterdam: North Holland.

Simon, H. A. 1978. On how to decide what to do. *The Bell Journal of Economics* 9:494–507.

Simon, H. A. 1983. *Reason in Human Affairs.* Stanford: Stanford University Press.

van den Bergh, J. 1996. *Ecological Economics and Sustainable Development: Theory, Methods and Applications.* Aldershot: Edward Elgar.

Vercelli, A. 1991. *Methodological Foundations of Macroeconomics: Keynes and Lucas.* Cambridge: Cambridge University Press.

Zadeh, L. A. 1965. Fuzzy sets. *Information and Control* 8:338–353.

Zimmermann, H. J. 1987. *Fuzzy Sets, Decision Making, and Expert Systems.* Dordrecht: Kluwer.

PART II

MACRO-SCALE

6 EFFECTIVE DEMAND AND WEAK SUSTAINABILITY: A MACROECONOMIC MODEL

Carlos Eduardo Frickmann Young
Department of Economics
University College London
London, United Kingdom

INTRODUCTION

The environmental economic literature concerning economic growth usually follows the standard neoclassical approach, which does not consider the effective demand problem (see Hartwick 1977, 1978; Solow 1986; Pezzey 1992). All emphasis is put on the long-term problem (i.e., the sustainability of a certain level of economic activity). Some empirical case studies present qualitative comments about the relationship between unemployment and natural resource depletion or degradation (Cruz and Repetto 1992; Jonish 1992). However, unemployment is never considered in the formal models presented (Young 1993).

On the other hand, standard Keynesian macroeconomics focuses on the unemployment problem, but does not pay attention to the sustainability issue. The intertemporal linkages between current production and long-term effects of man-made capital accumulation are analyzed in the multiplier-acceleration interaction models. The most famous of these models, the Harrod–Domar equation, shows the investment required to assure growth with a desired level of employment (Harrod 1939; Domar 1946). Nevertheless, problems concerning changes in the stocks of nonproduced assets, such as resource exhaustion or pollution, are not formally addressed.

The objective of this chapter is to link both modeling traditions in the context of a developing country undergoing a structural adjustment program. The determination of the aggregate level of product (the simplest way of dealing with the effective demand problem) is the short-term problem to be considered. The maintenance of a nondecreasing total stock of assets (the weakest definition of sustainability) addresses the long-term problem. The point to be emphasized is the dual nature of resource depletion: it presents opposite effects to effective demand and sustainability. In the short-term, natural asset depletion will have positive impacts on employment because it represents addition to effective demand. However, natural resource depletion reduces the total asset stock, compromising future economic activity.

The solution to this apparent contradiction rests on combining higher investment levels with lower resource depletion because investment in man-made capital has the advantage of increasing effective demand and the asset stock simultaneously. However, private investment is not fully controlled by policymakers, and this ideal solution is not easily achievable for developing countries. This problem is stressed during structural adjustment programs when the economy is under pressure to achieve short-term objectives. The examples of the Philippines and Indonesia show that the economy may fail to achieve the sustainability objective independently of restoring (or not) short-term economic growth. These results illustrate some of the criticisms about environmental consequences of adjustment programs.

THE SHORT-TERM PROBLEM: FULL EMPLOYMENT

The original problem addressed by Harrod (1939) and Domar (1946) was the instability created by the dual character of investment. In the short-run, investment represents an additional source of demand, contributing positively to the level of employment through the multiplier principle. But when the investment project is finally converted into productive capital, there is an addition of potential capacity, but no increase in effective demand, constituting a threat to full employment (the accelerator principle). Though a very simple model, it shows how difficult it is for the economic system to keep on a growth path with sustained full employment.

It should be noted that the Harrod–Domar model does not emphasize input substitution because the concern is not on the possibilities on the production frontier (full employment), but how to reach this frontier. This is a fundamental difference to the neoclassical growth model tradition which assumes that "full employment is perpetually maintained" (Solow 1970). The neoclassical problem is to determine what is the optimal input allocation or output composition (consumption or investment) given that the economy always operates on the production frontier. This difference usually leads to the inappropriate conclusion that the Harrod–Domar economy is rigid in the sense that input substitution is not possible. In reality, the main problem addressed concerns the possibility of future unemployment generated by current decisions of increasing the capital stock.[1]

Since the determination of the level of employment in a dynamic context is the objective of the model, the discussion is centered on the demand for labor. However, production factors other than capital and labor are crucial to the potential output of the economy, with explicit reference to natural resources and technological progress (Domar 1946). There is the possibility that not only labor, but other production factors are utilized at less than their maximum capacity.

In the case of natural resources, changes in their consumption level will affect both demand and supply equations. From the demand perspective, natural resource depletion is analogous to investment: both represent an increase in effective demand. Therefore standard Keynesian analysis would encourage natural resource depletion to promote economic growth and employment. However, from the supply perspective, there is a fundamental difference to investment: current consumption results in reduced productive capacity (and employment) in the future.

This dual character of natural resources has not received attention from the subsequent Keynesian literature. The objective of the model presented below is to discuss this unique characteristic of natural resources in the context of economic growth, and at the same time establish a connection to the modern debate concerning sustainability.

MODELING EFFECTIVE DEMAND

The model is based on the standard macroeconomic equation (1), where Y_t is the aggregate demand, C_t is final consumption, I_t is investment, X_t is exports, and M is imports. We assume that the country is specialized in exporting exhaustible natural resources, being a price taker in the international market.[2]

$$Y_t = C_t + I_t + X_t - M_t \qquad (6.1)$$

The final consumption and the level of imports are considered functions of the aggregate demand.

$$C_t = c\,Y_t \qquad (6.2)$$

$$M_t = m\,Y_t \qquad (6.3)$$

Therefore, the level of demand is determined by the exogenous expenditures in investment and resource depletion, through the multiplier (a).

$$Y_t = \frac{1}{1 - c + m}\,(I_t + X_t) = a\,(I_t + X_t) \qquad (6.4)$$

The investment ratio (r_t) relates the level of investment to the total stock of produced assets (Km_t).

$$I_t = r_t Km_t \qquad (6.5)$$

The depletion ratio (q_t) relates the level of exports of natural resources to the stock of natural assets (Kn_t), both expressed in monetary values.

$$X_t = q_t Kn_t \qquad (6.6)$$

Equation (6.4) can be rewritten in order to express the aggregate demand as a function of the investment and depletion ratios. Accumulation of produced assets and liquidation of natural assets are substitute forms of increasing short-term economic activity.

$$Y_t = a\,(r_t\,Km_t + q_t\,Kn_t) \qquad (6.7)$$

For a constant level of aggregate demand $(Y_t = Y^*_t)$ the depletion and accumulation ratios present a negative relationship in equation (6.7).[3] This is shown in equation (6.8), which provides the combination of accumulation and depletion necessary to achieve full employment.

$$q_t \;=\; \frac{Y^*_t}{a\,Kn_t} - r_t\,\frac{Km_t}{Kn_t} \qquad (6.8)$$

The policy implication is clear: reducing depletion will have negative impacts on the economic activity and employment. Therefore, investment in man-made capital should replace falling levels of depletion, if full employment is a policy concern.

Figure 6.1 provides a graphical interpretation of the discussion above. The usual situation refers to points on the left of the full employment boundary. The policy problem is to increase economic activity. There are two ways to do so, more investment (upward shift) or more depletion (rightward shift). Points on the right of the full employment boundary represent over-employment situations, usually characterized by inflation. In this case, restrictive policies to contain excessive demand is the most suitable policy recommendation.

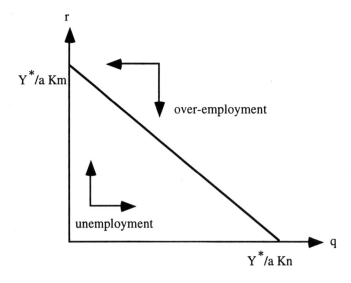

Figure 6.1. The short-term problem: effective demand

Similar results can be obtained using a Harrod–Domar dynamic model. The incremental man-made capital-output ratio is expressed by (Rm_t).

$$Rm_t = \frac{I_t}{\Delta Y_t} \tag{6.9}$$

Reorganizing equation (6.4), the share of investment on total output can be expressed as follows.

$$\frac{I_t}{Y_t} = 1 - c + m - \frac{X_t}{Y_t} \tag{6.10}$$

Combining (6.9) and (6.10), the output growth rate (y_t) is determined by the propensity to consume (c), the propensity to import (m), the share of exports in total output (X_t/Y_t), and the incremental man-made capital-output ratio (Rm_t).

$$y_t = \frac{\Delta Y_t}{Y_t} = \frac{1 - c + m - \frac{X_t}{Y_t}}{Rm_t} \tag{6.11}$$

The objective of the Harrod–Domar equation is to determine the "warranted" rate of growth of income or output which assures full employment (y^*). Equation (6.12) shows that the warranted rate is a function of natural resource depletion and the incremental man-made capital-output ratio:

$$y^* = \frac{1 - c + m - \frac{q_t Kn_t}{Y_t}}{Rm_t} \tag{6.12}$$

Equation (6.12) states that the higher the depletion ratio (q_t), the easier it will be to achieve the warranted rate, a result equivalent to the one obtained with the static model. More generally, this is the basic conclusion of standard macroeconomics: higher levels of natural resource depletion make full employment an easier target in the short run.

However, no consideration has yet been made about future consequences of resource depletion. If the economy is based on the extraction of natural resources, current depletion may affect future economic activity. In that sense, it is crucial to introduce a sustainability condition dealing with long-term consequences of current economic growth. This is the objective of the next section.

THE LONG-TERM PROBLEM: SUSTAINABILITY

Sustainability, like other principles such as democracy and justice, is easy to pronounce but hard to define. In the environmental economics literature, the debate concerning the definition of sustainability is polarized in two concepts: *weak* and *strong* sustainability.

The weak sustainability test is an intuitive rule based on the assumption of unconstrained substitutability between produced and nonproduced assets. An economy is considered unsustainable if the total savings are lower than the combined depreciation of produced and nonproduced assets, the former usually restricted to man-made capital and the latter to natural resources (Pearce and Atkinson 1993, 1995). The idea behind this is that investment compensates future generations for the asset losses caused by current production and consumption (formally represented by the "Hartwick rule"; see Hartwick 1977).

This approach is heavily criticized in terms of the assumptions adopted (external criticism) and methodological inconsistency (internal criticism). The external criticism focuses on the incapacity of substitution of vital services provided by some categories of natural resources. The weak sustainability approach fails to recognize this different characteristic of natural resources because they are nonproduced assets, they cannot be replaced by human action. In that sense, the consumption of natural capital may be irreversible, and the simple aggregation with man-made capital is meaningless (Victor, Hanna, and Kubursi 1994).

The internal criticism refers to the inconsistency in the valuation of capital, an argument similar to the aggregation problem in the "Cambridge versus Cambridge" debate on capital theory (Victor 1991). The objective of the weak sustainability approach is to obtain one aggregate, combining man-made and natural capital. This requires a common numeraire, a function attributed to the existing price system. To be valued, natural resources need to be referred to existing prices (man-made capital is estimated by actual market prices). However, the existing price system should not be the numeraire because it does not address many environmental issues (which is exactly the original problem motivating natural resource valuation). A proper price system would have to consider how every good would be affected if all environmental functions are monetized, but environmental functions can only be monetized if the price system is known. This circular problem makes the use of market prices in reaching a conclusion whether economies are developing sustainably "a rather questionable procedure" (Victor, Hanna, and Kubursi 1994).

In opposition to the weak sustainability approach, strong indicators are suggested. Strong indicators would identify and measure critical natural capital such that any positive depreciation would be a sign of nonsustainability (and not the total aggregate). Critical natural capital would be delineated by interdisciplinary scientific work, incorporating issues such as the definition of minimum safety standards and maximum carrying capacity.

However, there is still a huge gap between the principles behind strong sustainability and the elaboration of indicators which can be consistently used with the existing macroeconomic framework. This gap comprises data difficulties and the incompatibility between ecological procedures and traditional macro-economic concepts. Therefore, despite the problems presented above, most empirical studies at the national level adopt the weak sustainability approach, including all the environmental accounting exercises (Repetto et al. 1989; Cruz and Repetto 1992; Bartelmus, Lutz, and Schweinfest 1993; van Tongeren et al. 1993; Young and Seroa da Motta 1994).

For the same reasons, this chapter will adopt the weak sustainability approach. The weak sustainability approach provides a necessary but not sufficient condition; if the economy fails this test, it will probably fail other more rigorous tests.[4]

MODELING (WEAK) SUSTAINABILITY

In formal terms, the (weak) sustainability condition can expressed as:

$$\Delta Km_t + \Delta Kn_t \geq 0 \tag{6.13}$$

The changes in the stock of produced assets are determined by the difference between gross investment and depreciation. The average depreciation is expressed as a rate (d) of the stock of produced assets.

$$\Delta Km_t = (r_t - d)\, Km_t \tag{6.14}$$

The changes in the stock of natural assets are determined by the difference between the natural growth of the resources and actual depletion, both expressed in monetary values. The average natural growth of the resources is expressed as a rate (g) of the stock of natural assets.

$$\Delta Kn_t = (g - q_t)\, Kn_t \tag{6.15}$$

Therefore, the sustainability principle requires that net investment should not be smaller than net depletion.

$$(r_t - d)\, Km_t \geq (q_t - g)\, Kn_t \tag{6.16}$$

It is clear that the accumulation of produced assets and the liquidation of natural assets present opposite results for the objective of sustainability. Assuming a given level of investment, there is a maximum amount of resource depletion that the economy can afford without compromising its sustainability.

$$qt \leq (r_t - d)\, \frac{Km_t}{Kn_t} + g \tag{6.17}$$

In other words, the sustainability condition imposes a limit on how far depletion can go without putting at risk the future productive capacity of the economy. This is an important policy result because natural resource exhaustion is usually seen as a costless way to finance economic development. Establishing such a limit is even more important in developing economies which are often resource dependent. Furthermore, policy makers have more control on the rate at which their natural resources are depleted than on the aggregate level of investment.

This limit is represented by the line illustrated in Figure 6.2. The economy is operating at a sustainable level if the combination of accumulation and depletion rates appear on or above the line; any combination below the line means that the economic activity is being sustained through a net loss of wealth.

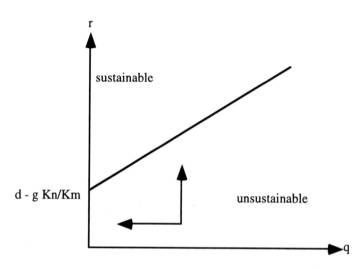

Figure 6.2. The long-term problem: (weak) sustainability

COMBINING SHORT-TERM AND LONG-TERM OBJECTIVES

The achievement of simultaneous success in the short and long-term objectives should be a prior concern of policy-makers. In formal terms, it is equivalent to determining values for (q_t) and (r_t), obeying simultaneously the full employment requirement (equations 6.8 or 6.12) and the sustainability principle (equation 6.17).

Equation (6.18) presents both requisites in terms of growth rates,[5] resulting in a more restrictive expression for the warranted rate. The impact of introducing the sustainability condition is to raise the warranted rate of growth whenever net depletion exceeds net investment.

$$y^* = \frac{1-c+m}{Rm_t} \cdot \frac{1}{1+\dfrac{q_t\,Kn_t}{r_t\,Km_t}} \quad st \quad q_t \leq (r_t-d)\,\frac{Km_t}{Kn_t} \; +g \tag{6.18}$$

In other words, the introduction of a sustainable condition may imply higher levels of investment even if full employment has already been achieved (this would be the conventional neoclassical situation of diminishing consumption to increase investment).

However, investment is relatively rigid in response to policy instruments, especially in developing countries. In that situation, the control of resource depletion becomes the only available instrument to achieve two different objectives: full employment and sustainability. However, it is possible that both objectives imply contradictory policy recommendations. This is shown in Figure 6.3, which combines the results from the previous sections.

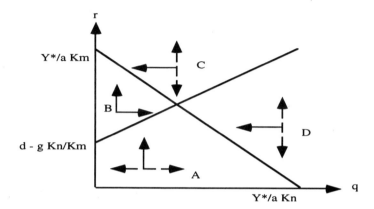

Figure 6.3. Combining short-term and long-term conditions

Areas (C) and (D) (including the full employment boundary) represent the situations usually covered by the conventional environmental economics literature. The typical neoclassical situation occurs at the points precisely on the full employment boundary. There is no consideration of the effective demand problem because every factor of production is considered to be fully employed. On the contrary, excessive nominal demand should be contained in order to avoid inflation. In both areas, the impact of reducing resource depletion is unambiguously positive because sustainability is increased without facing the risk of short-term unemployment.[6]

The symmetric situation is described in area (B), the typical Keynesian situation. There is no sustainability problem, and unemployment is the only problem to be solved. Hence, an increase of the activity level should be pursued, and depletion can be stimulated together with investment.

The situation in area (A) is far more complicated, and is closer to the reality of developing countries in economic and environmental crisis. The best policy recommendation is to increase the investment level because this promotes economic activity and increases the accumulation of capital. However, as discussed above, economic policy has limited power in the determination of investment level. Private and foreign investment are determined exogenously to governmental decisions, and the expansion of public investment has important funding constraints. In developing countries, the control of resource depletion is a much easier instrument to deal with, and in many circumstances the only instrument available. However, the two policy objectives present contradictory guidelines to depletion management. On the one hand, the depletion should be stimulated in order to increase the employment level. On the other hand, depletion should be decreased in order to achieve sustainability.

This dilemma illustrates the controversy about adjustment programs in developing countries (for a review see Young and Bishop 1995). Defenders argue that adjustment reforms are essential to private business, favoring investment. In this case, the contradiction is solved through the rise in the investment level. Path (a) in Figure 6.4 illustrates this optimistic point of view – the economy moves in the direction of the full employment and sustainability boundaries simultaneously.

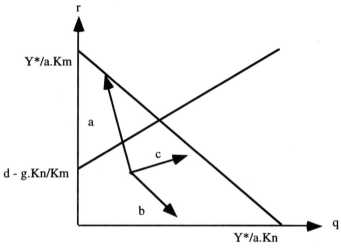

Figure 6.4. Structural adjustment policies: alternative perspectives

Nevertheless, many critics argue that adjustment results in the opposite impact on investment. The contraction of public investment, the increase of interest rates due to tough monetary policies, and the fall of real wages would depress rather than stimulate private investment. Consequently, increasing unemployment and poverty would result in more depletion. This pessimistic situation is illustrated in path (b): the falling investment is partially compensated by raising depletion, and the economy becomes even farther from a sustainable position.

An intermediate position is also possible. Empirical studies show that investment has increased in successful adjustment experiences, but depletion has increased too. In other words, economic growth may be achieved at the cost of losing natural resources. Path (c) illustrates this situation: the economy moves upward and rightward, coming closer to the full employment boundary. The impact on sustainability depends on the net balance between the increase of produced assets and the decrease of natural assets.

APPLYING THE MODEL TO DEVELOPING COUNTRIES: INDONESIA AND THE PHILIPPINES

Indonesia

Indonesia is considered to have had one of the most successful adjustment experiences. Adjustment took place after 1981, under conditions much less adverse than in most other indebted countries. The revenues from petroleum exports and a relatively well-controlled public deficit prevented the adoption of tough measures. Economic growth has been sustained at high averages, and social indicators presented an improvement in the period (Thorbecke 1991).

However, the country still faces many problems, and the acceleration of natural resource depletion is one of the most important. Despite the industrial boom, the economy is still dependent on natural resources. Repetto et al. (1989) estimate that 88% of 1988 exports were based on natural resources. Deforestation is a major environmental problem caused by timber harvest and human migration for agricultural purposes. Soil erosion is increasing and pollution affects millions of people in urban centers.

Table 6.1 and Figure 6.5 present the estimates for the accumulation and depletion ratios. During the adjustment years the growth trend was maintained. The investment ratio (r) and the share of gross domestic investment (GDI) to GDP increased. The same happened to the depletion ratio (q) and to the share of resource depletion to GDP; both variables presented significant increases.

These results indicate that accumulation of produced assets has not resulted in the reduction of natural resource depletion. Indeed, the data suggests that investment and depletion are interlinked. The revenues obtained from timber and oil extraction might have financed the boom of industrial investment, and investment was required to afford the expansion of resource extraction. Therefore, the Indonesian example seems to be closer to the intermediate situation described by path (c) in Figure 6.4.

Table 6.1. Indonesia 1971 to 1984

Year	GDP growth (%)	GDI/GDP (%)	r (%)	DEPL/GDP (%)	q (%)
1971	5.5	15.8	7.9	10.6	0.6
1972	9.4	18.8	9.7	13.7	0.8
1973	11.3	17.9	9.6	17.6	0.9
1974	8.0	16.8	9.2	24.6	1.2
1975	4.6	20.3	10.8	19.3	1.5
1976	6.9	20.7	10.9	20.8	1.4
1977	8.9	20.1	10.7	20.8	1.6
1978	7.7	20.5	10.9	18.2	1.6
1979	6.3	20.9	10.9	22.9	1.1
1980	9.9	20.9	11.0	28.0	1.3
1981	7.9	22.4	11.7	25.7	1.7
1982	2.2	22.6	11.1	19.0	1.3
1983	4.2	29.4	13.5	24.0	2.3
1984	5.3	26.3	11.6	18.6	1.7

Note: Estimates based on Repetto et al. (1989).

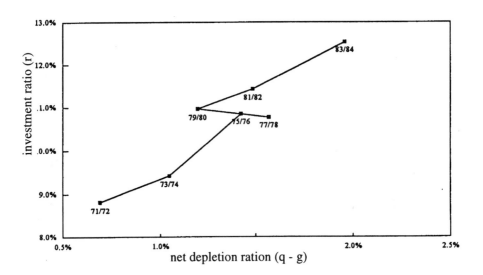

Figure 6.5. Indonesia 1971 to 1984: investment and net depletion ratios

The Philippines

By contrast, the Philippines has experienced a painful adjustment process. The adjustment programs started in 1981 and were followed by a deep recession. Real wages and employment fell drastically with important consequences for poverty incidence. Migration and resource depletion and degradation are pointed to as consequences of such a process (Cruz and Repetto 1992).

Table 6.2 presents estimates of economic growth, investment, and resource depletion in the Philippines. Depletion is restricted to net changes in the timber stock due to the lack of data for other resources. The growth trend from the 1970s was stopped and investment started to fall. On the other hand, depletion has accelerated after the adjustment programs.[7]

Table 6.2. The Philippines 1971 to 1987: investment and net depletion ratios

Year	GDP growth (%)	GDI/GDP (%)	r (%)	DEPL/GDP (%)	q - g (%)
1971	5.2	21.2	10.2	4.2	2.2
1972	5.2	20.9	9.9	3.8	2.0
1973	6.6	20.6	9.9	5.1	1.9
1974	6.6	20.8	11.4	6.3	2.2
1975	6.6	24.4	12.5	6.4	3.0
1976	8.0	27.7	12.1	6.0	1.9
1977	6.1	27.4	11.3	7.1	2.2
1978	5.5	26.5	11.5	6.8	2.3
1979	6.3	27.9	11.9	9.4	1.8
1980	5.2	29.9	11.0	13.0	2.3
1981	3.9	28.8	10.3	11.3	2.9
1982	2.9	28.3	9.3	8.7	2.5
1983	0.9	26.7	8.3	10.0	3.4
1984	-0.6	25.0	5.4	14.1	2.0
1985	-4.3	17.9	3.6	18.4	2.8
1986	1.5	12.8	3.8	18.0	2.7
1987	5.1	13.7	4.4	20.5	2.7

Note: Estimates based on Cruz and Repetto (1992).

Figure 6.6 shows the evolution of the net depletion ratio (q - g) and the investment ratio (r). These results suggest that resource depletion was stimulated in order to compensate the decline of economic activity. Consequently, the Philippines experience seems to be closer to the pessimistic case described by path (b) in Figure 6.4.

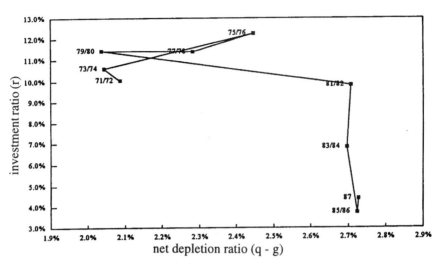

Figure 6.6. The Philippines 1971 to 1987: investment and net depletion ratios

Sparse information and qualitative references concerning other resources show that natural asset losses extended beyond timber loss. Cruz and Repetto (1992) point out a strong relationship between increasing rural poverty, migration to mountain areas, and soil erosion. Another flow described concerns fishery overharvest caused by migration to coastal areas. These elements suggest that resource overuse has been more dramatic, challenging the argument that environmental conservation benefits from economic stagnation.

POLLUTION AND OTHER LIMITATIONS

So far the problem of sustainability has been restricted to the depletion of marketable natural resources. However environmental degradation is another dimension increasingly relevant in both developed and developing countries.

The consideration of pollution and other degradation impacts is important because economic activities are subject to multiplier effects. For example, the expansion of an industry requires inputs from other industries, each one with different environmental standards. The whole chain of effects derived from the original investment should be considered, requiring an input–output approach which has not been included in this analysis.

A possible way to overcome this limitation is to consider environmental quality as another form of natural capital (Kq). Damages caused by environmental degradation can be valued in monetary terms and regarded as capital losses (van Tongeren et al. 1993). The new condition for "weak" sustainability becomes:

$$\Delta Km_t + \Delta Kn_t + \Delta Kq_t \geq 0 \qquad (6.19)$$

Therefore only *clean* investment in man-made capital has unambiguous positive impacts on effective demand and the environment. *Dirty* investment (i.e., investment which causes direct or indirect expansion of environmentally harmful industries) will increase the stock of man-made capital, but at the cost of reducing natural capital. The net impact on total stock would be obtained by extracting the total extension of degradation costs from the value of the investment. The final result would be more restrictive conditions to simultaneously achieve short-term full employment and long-term sustainability.

CONCLUSIONS

The linkages between unemployment and overuse of natural resources have been regarded with increasing attention in empirical research. Unfortunately, this trend has not been shared by the theoretical literature. The model presented in this chapter is a preliminary attempt to link both issues, integrating the concept of effective demand into environmental economics.

Despite important limitations, the model can be helpful in discussing concrete policy issues. One is the increasing pressure on developing countries to lower their chosen path of natural resource exploitation. Assuming that unemployment should be avoided because of its social and even environmental consequences, the best solution is to increase investment in man-made capital in such countries. Thus, the international community should be able to help developing countries finding alternative options to economic development, if it is concerned about the way resources have been depleted in the Third World.

Nevertheless, the net capital flows in many developing countries have been negative. Short-term pressures created by economic crises result in long-term environmental sacrifices. The examples of Indonesia and the Philippines illustrate this situation. In both cases resource depletion was accelerated after adjustment programs, even though the conventional economic variables presented distinct performances (economic recovery in Indonesia and stagnation in the Philippines). Even though these results should be used with caution, given the preliminary character of methodology and data, they do suggest that adjustment programs have been careless of natural resource concerns in these countries.

ACKNOWLEDGMENTS

This chapter is part of my ongoing Ph.D. thesis, Adjustment Policies and the Environment: A Case Study for Brazil, under the supervision of D. W. Pearce, University College London. I am also grateful to J. C. J. M. van den Bergh, J. van der Straaten, G. Atkinson, and K. Hamilton for their valuable comments.

FOOTNOTES

1. Domar (1946) was particularly aware of changes in the capital intensity of the economy caused by the addition of new plants.
2. This assumption highlights the role of depletion as a source of effective demand. However, it is not crucial to the model since a variable concerning exports nonrelated to depletion can be attached with no significant changes in the results.
3. The notation (*) denotes full employment.
4. It is theoretically possible that an economy fails the weak sustainability test without failing the strong sustainability criteria. This may be the case of an economy under declining economic activity which temporarily survives by the consumption of man-made capital previously accumulated, but does not deplete/degrade its natural resource allowance. However, the most likely situation of a society becoming economically poorer is that the pressure for depleting natural resources will increase, with the economy failing both weak and strong sustainability tests.
5. The equation on the right side of expression (18) is obtained by applying equations (5), (6) and (9) to equation (12).
6. The difference in the two areas concerns policy recommendations about investment. Increases in nominal investment would result in more inflation (reduction of real consumption through forced savings), but getting closer to a position of sustainability. In area (C), it is not a positive recommendation because the economy is already sustainable, but in area (D) it may be interesting. Nevertheless, this conclusion is unlikely to occur in reality because inflation tends to depress real investment. Reduction of the depletion rate is a much easier, safer, and more efficient way to reduce nominal aggregate demand in both situations.
7. This result contradicts the conclusion of Cruz and Repetto (1992) who assume that depletion has decreased as a share of GDP. The reason is due to the methodology used to estimate resource depletion. Cruz and Repetto (1992) considered the revaluation of remaining stocks as an income increase, basing their depletion estimates on the differences between the monetary values of initial and closing forest stocks. This stock difference has increased less than actual depletion because timber net prices have increased faster than the area deforested. This revaluation effect led Cruz and Repetto (1992) to conclude that the ratio of timber asset loss to the GDP has decreased during adjustment. However, the same data show that commercial harvest has steadily increased during the whole period analyzed.

REFERENCES

Bartelmus, P., E. Lutz, and S. Schweinfest. 1993. Integrated environmental and economic accounting: A case study for Papua New Guinea. In *Toward Improved Accounting for the Environment,* ed. E. Lutz. Washington, DC: World Bank.

Cruz, W., and R. Repetto. 1992. *The Environmental Effects of Stabilization and Adjustment Programs: The Philippines Case.* Washington, DC: World Resources Institute.

Domar, E. 1946. Capital expansion, rate of growth and unemployment. *Econometrica* 14:137–147.

Harrod, R. F. 1939. An essay in dynamic theory. *Economic Journal* 49:13–33.

Hartwick, J. M. 1977. Intergenerational equity and the investing of rents from exhaustible resources. *American Economic Review* 5:972–974.

Hartwick, J. M. 1978. Substitution among exhaustible resources and intergenerational equity. *Review of Economic Studies* 45(2):347–354.

Jonish, J. 1992. *Sustainable Development and Employment: Forestry in Malaysia.* Working Paper n.234. Geneva: ILO.

Pearce, D. W., and G. Atkinson. 1993. Capital theory and the measurement of sustainable development: An indicator of "weak" sustainability. *Ecological Economics* 8(2):85–103.

Pearce, D. W., and G. Atkinson. 1995. Measuring sustainable development. In *Handbook of Environmental Economics,* ed. D. W. Bromley. Oxford: Blackwell.

Pezzey, J. 1992. Sustainable Development Concepts: An Economic Analysis. World Bank Environment Paper n.2. Washington, DC: World Bank.

Repetto, R., W. Magrath, M. Wells, C. Beer, and F. Rossini. 1989. *Wasting Assets: Natural Resources in the National Income Accounts.* Washington, DC: World Resources Institute.

Solow, R. 1970. A contribution to the theory of economic growth. In *Growth Economics: Selected Readings,* ed. A. Sen. Harmondsworth: Penguin.

Solow, R. 1986. On the intergenerational allocation of natural resources. *Scandinavian Journal of Economics* 88(1):141–149.

Thorbecke, E. 1991. Adjustment, growth and income distribution. *World Development* 19(11):1595–1614.

van Tongeren, J., S. Schweinfest, E. Lutz, M. G. Luna, and G. Martin. 1993. Integrated environmental and economic accounting: A case study for Mexico. In *Toward Improved Accounting for the Environment,* ed. E. Lutz. Washington, DC: World Bank.

Victor. P. A. 1991. Indicators of sustainable development: Some lessons from capital theory. *Ecological Economics* 4:191–213.

Victor, P. A., E. Hanna, and A. Kubursi. 1994. How strong is weak sustainability? Paper presented at the International Symposium Models of Sustainable Development: Exclusive or Complementary Approaches of Sustainability?" Universite Pantheon-Sorbonne, Paris 16–18 March 1994.

Young, C. E. F. 1993. Sustainability, economic growth and employment. In *Three Essays on Sustainable Development,* eds. A. Gomez-Lobo, K. Hamilton, and C. E. F. Young. GEC Working Paper 93–08. London: CSERGE.

Young, C. E. F., and R. Seroa da Motta. 1994. Measuring Sustainable Income from Mineral Extraction in Brazil. Environmental Economics Programme Discussion Paper 94–01. London: IIED.

Young, C. E. F., and J. Bishop. 1995. Adjustment Policies and the Environment: A Critical Review of the Literature. CREED Working Paper 1. London: IIED.

7 THEORIES OF INTERNATIONAL TRADE AND THE ENVIRONMENT: COMPARISON AND CRITIQUE

Cees van Beers
Department of Economics
Faculty of Law
Leiden University
Leiden, Netherlands

Jeroen van den Bergh
Department of Spatial Economics
Free University
Amsterdam, Netherlands

INTRODUCTION

The environmental economics literature up to 1985 gives the impression that environmental problems are generally considered as occurring on restricted spatial scales. Indeed, economic research has long been concentrated on the local dimension of environmental pollution and natural resource use. In the 1960s local air and water pollution received much attention. During the next decade, environmental economics focused primarily on the policy analysis of closed economies (see Baumol and Oates 1988). However, since the beginning of the 1970s many researchers have been investigating the links between international trade and the natural environment. Early contributions are Baumol (1971), GATT (1971), Siebert (1973, 1974), Markusen (1975), Walter (1975, 1976). These papers show a variety of approaches ranging from Heckscher-Ohlin to general equilibrium analysis based on trade theories. Additionally, in the study of environmental problems, open systems were employed with a perspective on transboundary pollution issues, such as acid rain (see Walter 1976). In this case, the foreign trade dimension was usually not incorporated. In the 1980s, a widespread concern for global issues and long-term environmental phenomena emerged, leading to research on sustainable development and global environmental issues such as climate change (WCED 1987). The attention given to the interdependence of trade and environment has also increased significantly (Anderson and Blackhurst 1992; Low 1992; Folke, Ekins, and Costanza 1994; van Ierland 1994). Both conventional trade theory with partial analysis and modern trade theories of imperfect competition analysis have been applied to deal with issues of international trade and environment. New related topics in this context are those of policy coordination, including strategic policy (Carraro 1994) and environmental policy impact on location of firms, which causes shifts in trade patterns (Markusen, Morey, and Olewiler 1993; Motta and Thisse 1994). As in the case of transfrontier pollution, no trade dimension is necessary, although several authors focus on some combination of these ingredients.

All these approaches have focused on a number of specific issues.

a. Environmental factors as determinants of international trade.
b. The impact of international trade on environmental quality and natural resources.
c. The impact of environmental policy on competitive strength and trade flows.
d. Substitution or complementation between foreign trade policy and environmental policy measures.

For each of these issues, a number of approaches based on different theories and methods can be chosen, not necessarily leading to the same conclusion. As indicated above, environmental economists have mainly been concerned with environmental externalities and environmental policy issues in closed economies, while trade economists have focused on other imperfections, such as imperfect market structures and economies of scale. Some mix of externality and trade theories is required for answering relevant fundamental and policy questions. Additional theories can come from growth theory and spatial economics theory (including regional and continuous space models). Figure 7.1 shows how they all can be linked to the concepts and methods or models.

In the following sections different approaches are considered in detail. A distinction is made between theories of foreign trade according to whether they are based on the notion of a general or a partial equilibrium. Trade theories of a general equilibrium nature (Ricardo, Heckscher-Ohlin) are implicitly based on a set of underlying micro-relations. The emphasis in such theories is on the determinants of foreign trade and their impact on the domestic income distribution and production structure. These theories are discussed in the next section. Then we present a comparative static analysis in a partial equilibrium setting based on the assumption of perfect competition. Partial equilibrium theories consider the factors that determine foreign trade from the perspective of isolated markets. They provide a clear view on how certain environmental

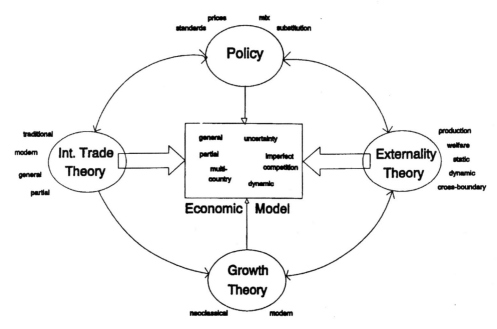

Figure 7.1. An overview of model approaches and inputs for environment-trade analysis

policy interventions or environmental factors influence foreign trade directly. Next we extend the discussion to imperfect competition, and discuss the implications of modern trade theory for the relationship between trade and environment. The main disadvantage of partial equilibrium models is that they offer no insights about the interactions between markets or distributional effects, for instance, in terms of income groups or sectors. Then we focus on general equilibrium models which do explicitly include such effects, based on the perspective of multiple interactive markets. The difference with the Ricardian and Heckscher-Ohlin models is that here the attention is focused on modeling economy-wide effects based on microeconomic relationships. Foreign trade in these models is therefore explicitly linked to the behavior of individual agents in the economy, and likewise to environmental externalities in production and utility functions. Next a short comparison table of the formal methods is presented, followed by a discussion of the neglected issues, including remaining methods related to multiregional issues, growth, and uncertainty. We then present critical notes on the use of models related to substantive discussions about institutions and sustainability, as well as to the lack of empirical testing. A short account is given of points of critique on the formal, mainstream approaches. Finally we present our conclusions.

GENERAL TRADE THEORIES AND ENVIRONMENTAL EXTERNALITIES

International trade theories can be distinguished in two types: those emphasizing the importance of demand factors, and those focusing on supply factors. An example of the former one is the analysis presented by Linder (1961). Two well-known supply-oriented theories are formalized in the Ricardian and the Heckscher-Ohlin models. The interface between foreign trade and environmental quality seems to be predominantly regarded as a matter of supply factors, as reflected by the current focus of general and environmental economic research. Therefore, the demand-oriented theories are not discussed here. The trade theory of Ricardo implicitly uses differences in labor productivity as the cause of comparative advantages. This theory does not deal with other determinants of comparative advantage. The main contribution of Ricardo has been the revelation of the notion of comparative cost advantage versus absolute cost advantage. Consideration of the interaction between foreign trade and environmental quality can focus on environmental quality and policy as factor endowments that determine the structure of foreign trade. This justifies a closer look at the Heckscher-Ohlin (HO) model.

The factor endowment theory of Heckscher and Ohlin focuses primarily on the relative availability of capital and labor as the main causes of differences in comparative advantage and therefore of the emergence of foreign trade. The domestic effects of the trade flows are revealed by the equalization of production factor prices among countries like wages and capital rents.[1] The theory assumes the existence of perfectly competitive markets which implies an efficient allocation of economic resources. The main result of the HO model is stated as:

> A country has a comparative advantage in producing and exporting a commodity in the production of which, compared with other countries, relatively much of the relatively abundant production factor at home is used.

The HO result is based on the following six assumptions:

1. There are two countries producing *n* commodities with endowments of *m* production factors that is different between the two countries.
2. There are no technological differences between countries (i.e., for a given commodity the production function is the same in all countries). Furthermore commodities are produced under constant returns to scale.
3. The supply of the production factors in the country is completely inelastic (i.e., independent of the rewards of the production factors).

4. Mobility of production factors is perfect among domestic industries but impossible internationally.
5. There are no externalities in production (i.e., the output of the production process of the commodities is only determined by the quantity of the production factors).
6. The preferences of the consumers are the same and hemostatic in all countries.

The central question now is how environmental elements can be included in this theory. There are two options, namely to include environmental elements in the model with standard assumptions as mentioned above, or to relax the standard assumptions that are related to a treatment of the environment as a supply factor in international trade. For the first option, the reader is referred to Walter (1976), Siebert (1987), and van Beers and van den Bergh (1996). Here the focus is on relaxing the standard assumptions of the HO model.

Changing Assumptions of the Standard Model

The possibility of incorporating environmental elements in the factor endowment model can be realized by changing the assumptions of the model. The assumptions (2), (4), and (5) are the most essential here, whereas assumptions (1), (3), and (6) are necessary to retain the supply orientation. Relaxing of the latter three assumptions will require a more disaggregate approach, as in the general equilibrium models we discuss later.

The second assumption can be relaxed by assuming the existence of technological differences. Trade models have been developed to explain trade patterns out of technology differences (e.g., Posner's technology gap model, 1961). Technology differences have their own influence on the pattern of trade even when factor endowments are not different. Falvey (1994) distinguishes two types of technology differences.

1. Product augmenting (i.e., a country can produce more output with the same factor inputs in a particular sector than another country).
2. Factor augmenting (i.e., a factor of production is more productive than the same factor in the other nation independent of the sector in which the factor is employed).

The second type of technology difference between countries offers a particular opportunity for introducing environmental aspects into the model, based on the inclusion of environmental goods or services as a production factor in the HO model. Suppose a country is relatively less well endowed with capital in comparison to another country. In the traditional HO model the country would have a comparative advantage in exports of labor-intensive commodities. However, if technology differences allow, for example, a higher productivity of capital, it is possible that the country obtains a comparative advantage in the exports of relatively capital-intensive goods. Then the quantities of labor and capital will be measured in effective units (i.e., their productivity is taken into account). The central question is whether it is possible to combine this kind of technology difference with the environment as a production factor. Now, the environment as a factor can be more productive in one country as compared with another, since it is possible that technological differences are such that in one country the use of a "unit of environment" generates more output than another. There will be a shift in the environmentally more productive country towards pollution-intensive products.

This result is very straightforward, but a static model leaves unnoticed the fact that technological progress is a dynamic process. In the HO model it is possible to analyze differences between technologies at a certain moment. If technological changes of the environment as a production factor are expressed in effective units, it is possible to analyze changes in this model as a change of the effective units.

According to assumption (4), for each industry all factors of production have internationally a supply elasticity of zero (i.e., they are fixed and internationally immobile). However, factors like capital and labor are mobile in the real world. It is important to note that environmental services just like natural resources are immobile. In a "Heckscher-Ohlin world" with one immobile factor, intercountry equalization of the factor price of the immobile factor will result when either one of the other production factors is mobile, or when exchange of commodities occur (Deardorff 1984). However, this result is only valid when the mobility of the other production factors is independent of the endowment of the immobile factor. It is conceivable that the mobility of labor depends on the presence of environmental services. Indeed, labor will not only migrate to areas with higher wage rates but also to areas where better environmental conditions prevail. This means that when the home country exports the pollution-intensive commodity, wages may need to rise substantially to compensate the resulting lower level of environmental quality. The factor labor becomes more expensive and the wage level can be interpreted as a proxy for the price of environmental quality. The question is therefore what wage should be paid to attract labor into less environmentally desirable areas. Extending the HO model to incorporate the relationship between the mobile factor(s) and the immobile factor is not an easy task. It is necessary then to work out the underlying micro-relations more explicitly possibly by means of general equilibrium models.

About assumption (5) we can be brief. As environmental damage is an externality caused by the production of pollution-intensive commodities it is not incorporated in the standard HO model. An extension by Siebert (1987) focuses on the incorporation of environmental quality as a separate factor of production. A larger availability of environmental assimilative services relative to other production factors leads to export of pollution-intensive goods.

Environmental externalities can also be modeled via a production factor variable, not as an independent one. This would proceed through a negative influence on the conventional production factors labor and capital. The productivity of labor and capital is dependent on the environmental production factor. Extension of the HO model with an environmental externality therefore implies the incorporation of the dependence of the productivity of capital and labor on environmental quality, which is used up by these production factors. Modeling these elements will give rise to all kinds of counteracting forces which require a more explicit treatment of the microeconomic relations underlying the HO model structure. Also for this purpose, a general equilibrium treatment of the open economy seems to be more adequate.

PARTIAL EQUILIBRIUM MODELS OF INTERNATIONAL TRADE AND ENVIRONMENT

The absence of externalities in trade theories presented in the previous section is a drawback for analyzing the relationship between trade and environment. Two alternative approaches are available to deal with the environment in terms of externalities, namely the general equilibrium type of economic models and partial equilibrium models. In both cases the method of comparative static analysis is used.

An important division of partial equilibrium trade models is based on the assumption regarding the market structure of the commodity considered, namely perfect or imperfect competition. The first category is part of standard welfare economics while the second one is often referred to as modern trade theory. The models of both categories are of a partial equilibrium nature as they analyze only situations of a single isolated market without taking into account the interactions with other markets. This certainly restricts the relevance of the results although the main advantage is that very clear conclusions can be derived about essential relationships between international trade and environmental externalities. Thus it seems useful to consider the consequences of environmental policies on trade, and of trade policies on the environment in a static partial equilibrium context.

Anderson (1992) performs a partial comparative static analysis to investigate how social welfare and the environment of a country are influenced by opening up to or liberalizing its trade and by the implementation of appropriate environmental policies when opening up to or liberalizing trade.

Two types of externality may be distinguished, namely a production externality (i.e., in the country of production), and a consumption externality (i.e., in the country of consumption). In addition, a distinction is made between small and large country cases (i.e., whether world prices are exogenous or can be influenced).

We consider only the cases of production externalities in small and large countries since the analysis presented can easily be extended to many consumption externalities. This is graphically illustrated in Figures 7.1 and 7.2, where a shift in supply from private cost pricing (MPC) to social cost pricing (MSC) is considered, with no shift in demand (D).[2] In Anderson (1992) and van Beers and van den Bergh (1996) the small country case is analyzed, which has become quite standard in arguing for or against certain trade policy measures in the face of environmental externalities. Instead of completely discussing the graphical analysis here, the combinations of policy, externalities, and openness are considered and compared in the following.

Assuming the absence of environmental policy, opening up trade in a good whose production is pollutive will increase social welfare and improve the environment if the good is imported. If the good is exported, however, environmental quality decreases so that a negative welfare effect results, in addition to the positive effect caused by a larger producer surplus. Therefore the direction of change in social welfare, which is equal to the sum of private welfare and the social or external benefits resulting from less pollution, is ambiguous.

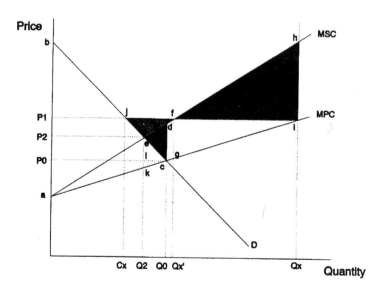

Figure 7.2. An environmental externality and an exported commodity in a small open country

Increasing imports of a good whose production is pollutive will replace domestic production and therefore reduce environmental damage. In the case of exports the increase in producer surplus is due to an international relative price that is higher than the domestic relative price. This works out positively on social welfare but the increased domestic production reduces environmental quality and therefore decreases social welfare. The strongest of these two offsetting forces will determine whether social welfare will increase or decrease. If a socially optimal environmental policy (such as a production tax) is implemented, increase of imports will be the result. Domestic production becomes more expensive and will decrease. Moreover, pollution will decrease too and environmental quality and social welfare will increase. If the good is exported introduction of a production tax reduces producer surplus and improves environmental quality. The effect on social welfare is ambiguous again.

This conclusion can be found via Figure 7.2, where the situation is shown for a commodity that is imported. The demand curve (D) and the marginal cost curves are marginal private costs of production (MPC) and marginal social costs of production (MSC), where the latter is obtained by adding private production costs and external costs. The prices are relative to all other prices in the economy. In the situation of autarky and no environmental policies, Q_0 is produced and consumed at a relative price of P_0. If there is no externality net social welfare is abc (sum of producer and consumer surplus). In the case of pollution, net social welfare is lower, namely abc - acd, where acd is the external cost. Suppose that the relative price at which foreign countries (the world market) offer the good is $P_1 < P_0$. Then imports are $Q_m C_m$. In that case net social welfare is abfg - ahg. The gain in social welfare (with respect to the autarky situation with no environmental policies) consists of ghcd (less pollution) and cfg (more consumer surplus).

In Table 7.1 four situations are shown which can be investigated in this partial analysis. Three comparisons between two situations are relevant. In the case of a shift from A to C one is concerned with the welfare effect of opening up an autarkic economy with externalities. A change from B to D is similar but in the presence of environmental policy. Finally, a shift from C to D means a focus on the welfare effect of environmental policy in an open economy. For each effect one can ask two questions.

- How to determine the price range for which no sign switch in the effect occurs.
- How to establish whether an effect is unambiguous in terms of its sign.

The latter is summarized in Table 7.2. By combining the prices in Figure 7.2 with the signs in Tables 7.1 the first question can be answered for specific cases.

Table 7.1. Relevant Situations in Comparative Static Analysis of Trade and Environment

	Environmental externalities and no policy	Environmental externalities and policy
Autarky	A	B
Open economy	C	D

Table 7.2 summarizes the welfare effects for different situations in terms of areas in Figure 7.2. The table shows that the shifts go along with the following total welfare effects: for A to B the area edc; for A to C the area jfe+edc-fhi; for B to D the area jfe; for C to D the area fhi; and for A to D the area jfe+edc. These results can easily be checked with Figure 7.2.

Table 7.2. Net Welfare Decomposition for the Four Situations of Table 7.1: The Export Case

1. net welfare = 4–5	2. producer surplus	3. consumer surplus	4. total surplus 2+3	5. external cost
A. abe - edc	ap_0c	bp_0c	abc	adc
B. abe	$ap_0c - klc + p_0p_1el$ $=ap_1ek$	p_1be	abc-kec= abek	adc-edck=aek
C. abjf - fhi	ap_1i	p_1bj	abji	ahi
D. abjf	$ap_1i-fig = ap_1fg$	p_1bj	abji - fig = abjfg	ahi - fhig = afg

Note: Combinations of letters a to k denote areas in Figure 7.2.

Large Country Case

When the social welfare of a large country changes, then two additional effects result. First, as a large country is able to influence world market prices, both its export supply and import demand curve will not be horizontal as it would be for a small country. Second, when a large country starts to import a pollutive commodity instead of producing it domestically, it will increase production abroad because of trade creation, and this may affect pollution generation abroad. Some analyses also include international pollutive spill-overs which cause negative welfare effects. It is doubtful whether these spill-overs are a relevant factor. The same effects are valid when a large country exports a pollutive commodity and introduces a production tax at home.

The resulting analyses of large country cases can be summarized as follows. When a large country enters international trade by opening up the import of a pollutive commodity, rather than producing it domestically, then the gain in social welfare will be unambiguous but smaller than can be achieved in a small country. The main reason is that the import price will be higher, which decreases consumer surplus as compared with the small country case. This is the terms-of-trade effect (Anderson 1992).

When a large country enters international trade by opening up the export of a pollutive commodity the gain in social welfare will be ambiguous as it depends on two opposite welfare effects.

1. A negative welfare impact resulting from a larger supply at the world market, depressing the export price and causing a loss of producer surplus and an increased domestic production which stimulates domestic pollution.
2. Less transfrontier pollution resulting from less foreign production may increase domestic welfare.

Finally, Krutilla (1991) presents one of the rare studies dealing with large country cases. Krutilla considers the case of a large open country in which environmental policy can influence the economy's terms of trade.[3] In such a case a comparison between regulatory impacts and comparative advantage is insufficient. Also offsetting terms-of-trade effects have to be included in a comparison. Optimal taxes will differ from the standard Pigouvian ones as a result of the terms-of-trade effect. This works in opposite directions for consumption and production taxes. The optimal consumption (production) tax is lower (higher) than the standard Pigouvian tax in the case of a net exporting (importing) country, in order to have the optimal trade-off between the second-order effects related to trade losses (gains) and the environmental benefits (costs) of lower consumption (higher production). An interesting idea mentioned by Krutilla is that the optimal environmental policy depends on the tariff parameter, such that one can vary this so as to find a zero environmental tax (i.e., trade policy is used as environmental policy). The resulting optimal tariff, a mix of the standard Pigouvian tax and standard optimal tariff, is, like other first-best optimal combinations, not generally attainable. The reason is that both instruments are generally chosen so as to maximize separate objectives, rather than maximizing social welfare of an open economy.

MODERN TRADE THEORY AND ENVIRONMENTAL EXTERNALITIES

The analyses discussed so far have been based on the assumption of perfectly operating domestic markets. However, the assumption of perfect competition seems restrictive for many product markets where the use of market power is present. A second category of partial equilibrium analysis known as modern trade theory, is based on imperfect competitive markets. Since the beginning of the 1980s increasing attention has been given to imperfect competition in explaining international trade. There are many assumptions possible, often with slightly different implications. The most influential model of imperfect competition has been developed by Dixit and Stiglitz (1977). Helpman and Krugman (1985) and others have extended this work in different directions Smith (1994).

The major consequences of the introduction of environmental policy in open country models with imperfect competition are indicated here. In the case of the perfect competition models we can distinguish between a commodity that can be imported or exported (see Figure 7.3). We assume that the commodity is domestically produced by a firm with monopoly power. It is further assumed that there is perfect competition at the world market, so that the firm is a price taker internationally.[4] If the world market price is below the autarky price (P_{pf}) level (resulting under perfect competition in the domestic market), the commodity will be imported. In that case, in the absence of trade barriers against the commodity, the monopolist will lose its market power. Then the case of the monopolist will be analogous to that of perfect competition discussed in the previous section (but now at world level).

The more interesting case is therefore to assume that the price at the world market (P_w) is higher than the autarky price but lower than the domestic mo-

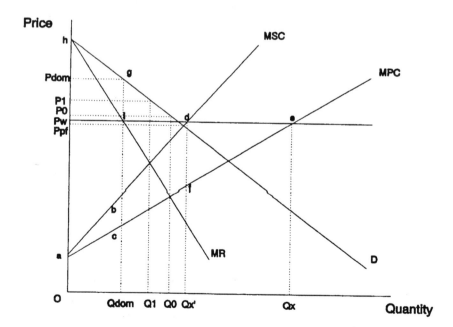

Figure 7.3. Imperfect competition in the domestic market of a commodity which is exported and generates environmental externalities

nopolistic price (P_0). The monopolist will then decide to export, which would not be the case if these prices would represent situations where the firm would face perfect competition. For all quantities less than Q_{dom}, marginal revenue in the domestic market is higher than at the world market ($MR > P_w$). For quantities higher than Q_{dom} the situation is reversed ($MR < P_w$). Therefore, up to Q_{dom} the domestic market is served, while it is profitable for the monopolist to export then Q_x- Q_{dom} (i.e., until marginal profits are zero ($MPC = P_w$)). The firm maintains monopoly power in the domestic market in spite of a lower world market price, because it is still the only supplier.[5] Note that P_{dom} is higher than the autarky monopoly price (P_0).

The external effects for the export case in the absence of environmental policy can be split into abc (externalities via pollution caused by production for the domestic market) and bdec (externalities via pollution caused by producing for the world market).

Introducing an environmental tax in the autarkic situation would increase the domestic price from P_0 to P_1. The monopolist will reduce its domestic supply in that case from Q_0 to Q_1. In case of an open economy the introduction of an environmental tax results in an unchanged domestic price P_{dom}, given that the intersection of MSC and P_w is not to the left of point I.[6] The monopolist will first cut production for the export market, since marginal revenue in the domestic market is higher than in the export market. Exports will decrease to (Q_x - Q_{dom}). Consequently, pollution will be reduced with def. Domestic consumer surplus (hg P_{dom}) remains unchanged. Only producer surplus will decrease by the area ade.

The example presented here has been kept tractable by assuming that the imperfect competition is of the monopoly type. Other kinds of imperfections, such as oligopolistic ones, can also be analyzed, which would give rise to game theoretical models (Dixit 1984; Eaton and Grossman 1986). For both firms and governments elements of strategic behavior can be analyzed. Examples of such analyses in the context of environmental policy and externalities are Ulph (1991), Verdier (1993), Kennedy (1994a, 1994b), Conrad (1993, 1994), and Feenstra et al. (1995). Ulph concludes in a model of strategic international trade that there is a preference for pollution standards rather than pollution taxes as environmental policy instruments. Kennedy and Conrad show that imperfect competition in global markets is a reason for strategic behavior of governments in deciding about domestic environmental regulation. This can lead to distortion of pollution taxes. Objectives in strategies may be focused on gaining competitive advantage or shifting pollution, and an equilibrium results from the trade-off between these. When transboundary pollution is included in a multicountry setting this may change the outcome. For instance, with perfect transboundary pollution there is no shifting pollution effect.

GENERAL EQUILIBRIUM ANALYSIS, TRADE, AND ENVIRONMENTAL POLICY

General equilibrium (GE) models that reflect the economy-wide perspective are discussed in this section. These type of models allow for including descriptions of international trade, environmental externalities, environmental production factors, and combinations of policies. First, a short introduction is given on the methodology. Subsequently, the combination of trade and environmental issues is discussed.

Theoretical and Applied General Equilibrium Models

The standard GE framework is based on the interaction between various behavioral models given that market clearing conditions are satisfied. Consumers are supposed to choose a consumption bundle in order to maximize welfare given income and prices. Producers are supposed to choose a mix of cost-minimizing input and profit-maximizing output, given input and output prices. In a competitive equilibrium without externalities, markets will be cleared for all factors and commodities while every actor can achieve his objectives. If convexity conditions are satisfied, uniqueness of the equilibrium is guaranteed. Stability of an equilibrium means that no actor has an incentive to divert from the equilibrium (Arrow and Hahn 1971).

The potential advantages of the GE approach to trade and environment can be summarized by a number of effects of trade and environmental policies that can be analyzed with it: resource allocation; distributional consequences in terms of households, income groups or sectors; welfare, income and employment effects; prices of commodities, wages, and capital rents; effects on the trade balance and the terms of trade; substitution effects between goods or between production factors; impact on public finance; and impact of policy instruments. Of course, not all of these potential advantages are realized in all applied studies, as this would give rise to complex general purpose models. For the issues involved here the specific questions addressed will determine which elements will be useful. Examples are desegregation of income groups for dealing with ecological tax revision proposals, or disaggregation of energy products and a distinction between more and less energy-intensive goods in the context of carbon tax studies.

GE models are specifically useful for comparing trade and environmental policies with regard to their respective economic and distributive effects as long as they realize the same environmental objective. Of course, there must be a caveat somewhere, and it is the increasing complexity that results from the fact that everything indirectly depends on everything else. In a theoretical analysis it is possible to add additional assumptions simplifying the analysis. The only alternative is to numerically solve (applied) general equilibrium models. Many of the applied models do not take the individual actors as the decision units, as the Arrow–Debreu theory does, but instead adopt a multisectoral approach, originated by Johansen (1960).[7] The applied general equilibrium models are usually disaggregating sectors. From such a perspective they can be considered as an extension upon the traditional economy-wide framework for multisector analysis (i.e., the input–output model). This framework has been used in trade analysis (e.g., Moses 1955; Leontief and Strout 1963) as well as in environmental analysis (Leontief 1970). However, combinations are rare (see Leontief, Carter, and Petri 1977).

The equilibrium models are usually associated with neoclassical assumptions of smooth, monotonous, convex functions and competitive market assumptions that allow for a single equilibrium. One may, however, use model structures and functional specifications for which proof of existence and uniqueness are unavailable. Solutions are then still possible (see Dervis, De Melo, and Robinson 1982), but the interpretations are uncertain. Another application is extending the GE approach to include rigid prices or quantity constraints for markets that do not clear and imperfect market characteristics. The latter type of models are still exceptional, for reasons of analytical and numerical complication (see Harris 1984; Norman 1990; Burniaux and Waelbroeck 1992).

Environment and Trade in GE Models

Trade GE models are distinguished by an orientation to a single-country or multicountry system. As stated by Shoven and Whalley (1984) these models originate from different sources and have a more diffuse focus than the other important field of GE modeling (i.e., taxation analysis). Some models are general purpose models of open countries, while others are exclusively oriented to trade policy issues. Many of the empirical models apply to developing countries and are oriented toward specific trade policy questions (see Srinivasan and Whalley 1986). The multicountry GE models differ from the standard theoretical trade model of Heckscher-Ohlin in that trade is not only determined by intercountry differences in relative factor endowments, but also by differences in production and demand parameters. These multicountry models may be very suitable for dealing with global issues such as the determination of effects of GATT agreements.

Many single-country GE models, although not explicitly focusing on trade issues, are concerned with small open economies. *Small* means that the economy is a price-taker on international markets. *Open* means that trade is relatively important (i.e., it requires to be dealt with in the GE formulation). The price-taking aspect may present inconsistency in a GE approach where prices are typically determined endogenously.[8] The perfect substitutability assumption usually employed in trade theory exaggerates the power of trade policy over the domestic price system and economic structure. Such an approximation is not a workable one in a GE context. An escape from both extreme specialization (with endogenous prices) and exogenous prices (i.e., smallness) is to assume that domestic and foreign products are imperfect substitutes. Generally, for every open economy, one has to deal with substitution between inputs of the same kind supplied by different origins, both in utility and production functions. Usually this is solved by some assumption of imperfect substitution via the Armington assumption (e.g., Dervis, De Melo, and Robinson 1982).

General equilibrium analysis in the field of environmental economics has focused on the effects of environmental policy and abatement (investment) on distribution, factor rewards, and public finance (see Comolli 1977; Yohe 1979; Steininger 1994a). Other examples of GE applications to environmental issues are Bovenberg and de Mooij (1994) focusing on the "double dividend hypothesis," where the interaction between public sector budget, taxation, environmental policy, and employment is studied. A shift in the tax base from labor to environmental production factors would, according to the hypothesis, have two beneficial effects: more environmental quality and more employment. Although possible, this seems to hinge on a restrictive set of assumptions regarding production and utility parameters. Several studies deal with energy, starting with Hudson and Jorgenson (1975). A number of recent studies look at the effects of environmental policies: country-specific (Hazilla and Kopp 1990; Nestor and Pasurka 1992; Conrad and Schroder 1991); acid rain oriented (Boyd and Krutilla 1992); carbon dioxide emissions (Burniaux et al. 1991; Piggott, Whalley, and Wigle 1992); and long-run growth (Jorgenson and Wilcoxen 1990). Bergman (1991) discusses the economy-wide effects of tradeable permits on energy use in the context of an applied CGE model. Often, interactions between production inputs receive a lot of attention via nested production relationships, usually represented by flexible CES functions. It should be noted that most applied models of environmental policy impact analysis are concerned with open economies and are therefore of some relevance in the present context. However, it should also be clear that trade is not always dealt with explicitly or consistently in such models.

Theoretical GE models that address the relationship between trade and environmental policy are few in number. Some different approaches can be found in Pethig (1976), Asako (1979), McGuire (1982), Merrifield (1988), and Steininger (1994a). Several attempts have been made to model the effects of environmental policies on foreign trade flows. Such models include environmental quality as a productive factor or a welfare determinant. Pethig (1976) and Asako (1979) deal with international trade of a polluting commodity in a general equilibrium framework. They both conclude that expansion of trade may be bad for the exporting country if the export good is the more polluting commodity, since additional pollution damages may offset the usual gains from trade. Another important conclusion is that with binding environmental policy constraints, the country with the least restrictive policy will export the pollution-intensive commodity.[9] Finally, an interesting result is that harmonization (i.e., striving for the same environmental quality) should not be interpreted as implying equally restrictive environmental controls.

In general, one can deal with two types of externalities in the GE context (see model specifications in van Beers and van den Bergh 1994). First, there are externalities that only affect welfare. This is the type most commonly focused on. The other approach focuses production effects of environmental damage. Siebert et al. (1980) have dealt with this issue very extensively. They analyze pollution as joint outputs of production activities, small-country and two-country models, two-sector and two-factor models with or without abatement, recycling and capital mobility in open economies.

While another approach can be considered to include both types of effects simultaneously, the externality can also be modeled in different ways. Sometimes, emissions are explicitly modeled as part of production (i.e., leading away from the standard production function). Usually, emissions are regarded as an input with standard properties (substitution). However, one can expect different outcomes when a more complex approach is adopted, namely dealing explicitly with complementations between production levels and emissions (multiproduct relationships). The same holds, however, for complementarity versus substitution of regular commodities and environmental quality in utility functions. In terms of having externalities between countries, one may develop models of trading countries that cause each other negative externalities by way of cross-boundary pollution. This, however, presents particular cases which are not at the heart of the environment-trade problem.

It should be noted that empirical studies on the relationship between environment and trade have mainly focused on energy and carbon dioxide emissions, largely because these allow for finding significant economy-wide effects as the required policy interventions are quite severe. Piggott, Whalley, and Wigle (1992) study this by focusing on production or consumption substitution across countries; terms of trade effects involving energy products; and terms of trade effects involving energy-intensive and other products. Since environmental quality at the global level (typical of carbon dioxide emissions) has the character of a public-good, unilateral actions may generate benefits that also accrue to other countries. An example of effect-chains is that cutting production (consumption) in a country leads to higher producer (lower consumer) world prices and increased production (consumption) in other countries, thus generating adverse spill-over effects to the country.

A COMPARISON OF FORMAL APPROACHES

Each specific approach deals with particular issues and can address different questions. Table 7.3 summarizes some essential differences between the main approaches. Three categories of environmental issues are distinguished: environmental externalities, environmental production factors, and environmental sustainability (or long-run environmental quality). Of course, it is possible to link the three issues in a dynamic model, which is not separately considered here.

Table 7.3. A Rough Comparison Between Three Methods for Environment-Trade Analysis

Model Type	Ext.	Envr. Prod. Factor	Sust.	No. of Goods	Market Structure	Policy
general trade	no	yes	no	>1 (2)	perfect	environmental policy = trade policy
partial equilibrium	yes	no	no	1	perfect or imperfect	environmental policy = trade policy
general equilibrium	yes	yes	partly	$\geq 1 (>>)$	mainly perfect	whole set of specific policies; distinction environmental / trade policies

Key: Ext = Externality, Envr. Prod. = Environmental Production, and Sust. = Sustainability.

The table shows that the main distinction between the trade, partial and general equilibrium models relates to the inclusion of externalities and environmental production factors. Whereas the first two approaches can only deal with one of these, the GE approach allows for considering both simultaneously. The most important difference between the partial analysis and the economy-wide analysis (GE models) is that the first comes with firm conclusions based on a simple model, while the second is focusing on the significance of various effects operating within a complex system. A disadvantage of GE models is that everything is related to everything else, which makes these models very difficult to operationalize and validate. The advantage is that the effect of various demand and production parameters on the allocation of factors and goods and the (factor or sectoral) distribution of welfare effects can be analyzed. In a way the partial and general equilibrium approaches can be regarded as complementary, although it is also interesting to see where they are overlapping and consistent. The consistency has been noted also for open economy general equilibrium models and general trade theories à la Heckscher-Ohlin, which focus on trade-offs between different activities, given availability of primary resources.

Other criteria that may be relevant are the dimensions and market structure. The dimensions of models are determined by the number of production factors, households, and production sectors. In a general equilibrium model typically all dimensions can be chosen freely, whereas this is more difficult, albeit possible, in general trade models and partial equilibrium models. Models incorporating imperfect competition throw light on the relationship between market structure, foreign trade and environmental policy. These analyses may play an important role in future research. The effects of environmental policy on foreign trade patterns are dependent on the kind of competition present in domestic and foreign markets, which can be combined in a general equilibrium setting.

NEGLECTED ISSUES: SPACE, DYNAMICS, AND UNCERTAINTY

Although some of the above approaches may address the important dimensions of space, dynamics, and uncertainty, in general these have not received very much attention. In the following discussion we explain the entry to these important issues.

Multicountry and Multiregion Models

A theme that requires attention from a policy, environmental, and trade-economic point of view is the regional disaggregation in GE models. Multicountry models may be useful for a number of reasons. They can deal with international trade more explicitly, thereby linking imports and exports (i.e., providing for a more complete perspective). Also they may be extended to allow for relocation process analyses. Furthermore, they can address environmental interdependence on an international scale, such as global and cross-boundary environmental processes. In addition, policies on different, hierarchical levels may be dealt with simultaneously; for example, the EU and the national level. Finally, policy coordination and strategic behavior of policy authorities may be studied with them, possibly giving rise to game-theoretic models. However, in the present context such models are interesting when they provide for a link between strategic trade and environmental policy on the one hand, and international trade flows on the other hand (Ulph 1991).

A special type of approach to equilibrium analysis of the interface between trade and environmental policies that is less well known to trade economists is the Spatial Price Equilibrium (SPE) model (see Takayama and Judge 1971; Takayama and Labys 1986). These models take as a departure various locations linked in an (international) transport network. In each location supply and demand functions are given. The static problem is to solve a constrained (quasi-) social welfare program, in which the sum of consumer and producer surpluses less transport costs is maximized, subject to market clearing conditions for each location. In an extended version of this model, one can combine production and transport with externality generation in both type of sectors and associate two types of environmental policies: one aimed at production and consumption at locations and the other aimed at mobile sources related to transport or trade. Given either type of policy one may then derive second-best rules policies. An example of such an approach can be found in Verhoef and van den Bergh (1995, 1996). The main advantage of SPE models is that derivation of solutions is less difficult than in the case of GE models, while extending the equilibrium notion to multiple dislocated markets.

Environmental and Spatial Sustainability

The formal approaches (previously discussed) consider environmental externalities or environmental production factors, but do not deal with the issue of environmental sustainability. Formal approaches that do consider sustainability and trade are rare. The potential conflict between growth and environmental sustainability is considered in a multiregional growth context in van den Bergh and Nijkamp (1995), and Verhoef and van den Bergh (1995 and 1996). In van den Bergh and Nijkamp, economic and environmental processes of two regions and their trade and environmental interactions are dynamically specified. Using numerical simulation, the resulting model is used to trace, among other things, sustainable growth in an open economy, the effect of dissimilarity between regional environmental processes, and the role of technological progress and diffusion. Essential for the outcomes is the endogenous pattern of interregional trade in the model. Sustainability has here a spatial dimension, and the global environmental quality is regarded in terms of an aggregation of the regional environmental qualities. Especially interesting in the above examples is the trade-off between efficiency and sustainability in a multisector production–consumption system, since it can be analytically linked to a trade-off between the absolute volume or size of each sector, its relative size in the economic structure, and the level of "environmental technology" adopted in each sector. In an operational sense this may be done by using indicators for efficiency and sustainability.

Dynamics and Growth

Growth means that one is concerned with long-run policy issues, which may differ from the environmental and trade policy issues. In this case the static "flow analysis" is replaced by a dynamic "stock analysis." This means, for instance, that capital accumulation, labor force growth, technical progress, and expansion of knowledge are included. In addition, it means that the dynamics of accumulation and degradation of resources and pollution also can be addressed. This implies furthermore that one extends the flow-based analysis of environmental issues of the previous sections. In other words, pollution may be regarded in terms of a stock that is accumulated from emissions and negatively affects welfare or production. Finally, it is worth stressing that the supply–demand integration of the last section is abandoned for a supply-orientation. This is a common approach in growth theories.

Two approaches in formal growth analysis are relevant for linking formally growth to trade and environmental variables. First is a neoclassical-oriented approach that extends the well-known Solow growth model to include environmental variables, such as stocks and flows of resources or pollution, which has received a lot of attention. A good review is offered by Kamien and Schwartz (1982) and Toman, Pezzey, and Krautkraemer (1994). Most of these models, however, fail in linking pollution with resource extraction, with only a few exceptions (Tahvonen and Kuuluvainen 1991, 1993). A more recent approach is an extension of modern growth theory to open economies, which is concerned with positive externalities of capital (infrastructure, human capital, education, knowledge, and designs), When confronting these positives with negative externalities arising from environmental use – in a broad sense – by economic activities, the outcome in terms of the necessity of further economic growth evaluated in terms of social welfare is uncertain. Therefore, formal analysis may render insights into whether and under what circumstances one should foster and control growth. This will ultimately come down to a trade-off between positive and negative external effects of growth (Gradus and Smulders 1993; Smulders 1994). Specific elaborations towards international trade of neoclassical growth theory are rare and differ from the traditional approaches. Recent (partial) extensions of new growth theories to trade are provided in Grossman and Helpman (1990, 1991).

Finally, as an example of dynamics of trade, growth and pollution one may consider an early analysis by Asako (1979). When he takes pollution accumulation into account he obtains the conclusion that: "when a country has a comparative advantage (or disadvantage) in the pollution-intensive commodity so that it exports (or imports) that commodity, international trade activities should be curtailed (or promoted) over time as pollution accumulates. This enables the country to transfer indirectly pollution to foreign countries." So it seems relevant to take into account the possibility of pollution stocks decreasing or increasing over time, in order to determine optimal trade from the exporting or importing country perspective.

Uncertainty in an Open Economy and Environmental Policy

Though it seems extremely relevant, uncertainty has received relatively little attention in environmental economics. In the context of environmental policy in closed economies various results have been obtained (e.g., Baumol and Oates

1988). Uncertainty can be caused by a lack of information, problems of control and enforcement, and stochastic processes. For an open economy there are three main sources of uncertainty: shifts in production costs, shifts in external costs, and random world prices of traded goods. Choi and Johnson (1992) analyze the problem of ranking second-best policies in this case by combining a general equilibrium model of an open economy with expected utility analysis. An optimal tax schedule dominates the optimal quantity standard when the world price is random, and they are equivalent when the marginal externality cost is random. Ranking is ambiguous if the marginal production cost is random. Further studies linking international trade and environmental quality and policy with explicit and formal treatment of uncertainty are rare.

CRITIQUE ON THE MAINSTREAM APPROACHES

A broader critique of the formal mainstream approaches that deals with the environment-trade conflict states that the crucial assumptions are not satisfied in most real world situations. Examples are the assumptions of perfectly competitive markets, the absence of transport costs, the complete mobility of factors within countries and immobility between countries (see Folke, Ekins, and Costanza 1994). According to Daly and Goodland (1994), the fact that capital is internationally mobile takes away much ground for the free trade proponents. Daly and Cobb (1989) and Røpke (1994) are of the opinion that political, sociological, historical, and distributional aspects require more attention in addition to the economic ones. They argue that economic decentralization is necessary for influencing the conditions of local communities and for closing materials and product cycles. This would require increasing self-sufficiency and therefore a reduction of trade. A danger often mentioned by opponents of this view is that protectionist policies regarding specific markets where some of the assumptions do not hold can quickly lead to reactions in other markets and by other countries, and give rise to a process of mutual and increasing protectionism that is difficult to reverse. Negotiations within the GATT/WTO over the last decades have shown how slowly the process of removing protectionist measures proceeds.

More specifically, in terms of model use there is the issue of criteria for policy analysis. Economic models of trade and environment focus usually on efficiency, either in terms of optimal social welfare (in a partial or general context) or Pareto improvement. Other criteria such as feasibility and equitability are not considered in these models. The reaction to such a critique is of course that the models are not normative (i.e., their outcomes should be inputs in a larger set of analyses and considerations to support the choice of policies and institutions). Of course, economic models can still be used to perform equity impact analyses and sensitivity analyses with regard to the assumed initial distributional characteristics of the system under study. Further-more, policy analysis can be approached from a cost-effectiveness perspec-tive, combined with one or multiple criteria other than efficiency. Still, the various approaches outlined in the preceding sections can be helpful in so far as they allow the depiction of ideal or optimal cases; realistic or second-best cases given market and institutional barriers; or effects of policies on a number of economic and environmental indicators, ranging from unemployment to energy use and acid deposition. Models are certainly not only used in academia for this purpose, but also to support the preparation of policies on various lev-els of policy-making.

Another fundamental point of critique is that in reality there are many kinds of institutional, cultural, and social impediments to changes that policies aim to set in motion. In other words, models can be too optimistic about the as-sumed flexibility of economies to respond to policies. On the other hand, how-ever, it is possible to claim that over longer periods of time economies have shown to be more responsive than has been assumed in many scenario and modeling projections related to technology, sectoral shifts, and labor markets. However, it is certainly true that there are a number of barriers to environmen-tal policy in an international context that models cannot easily address; barri-ers related, for instance, to the difficulty of transforming or establishing inter-national agreements. There is literature available on coalition formation, in which some of these issues are addressed from an economic, game-theoretic point of view (e.g., Barret 1995).

It may be useful to repeat that free trade will be socially optimal when imperfections and externalities are taken away by measures like direct (source oriented) and efficient (price oriented) measures. Hampering free trade should be the last option considered, after introduction of these other measures has failed. Røpke (1994) argues that optimal policy seems to be impossible as long as transport externalities are not optimized. Alternatively, when policy mea-sures are successfully applied, the international system of specialization and trade may develop to an environmentally sustainable system in the long-run. Still, at least one critic argues that "countries need to be allowed to introduce at-the-border measures to counterbalance differences in environmental control costs such that they can choose independent levels of environmental strin-gency" (Steininger 1994b). This indicates that trade measures should be based on differences in the use of matter, energy, and emissions, established via product life cycle analyses. However, even when one can agree with such a perspective it seems that this should be linked to a distinction between subnational and supranational externalities. In the first case there may be a conflict between ethical or environmental perspective and national sovereignty. One may also argue that although a world with small self-sufficient communities has some advantage, the internationalization process, which has been going on for at least several centuries, cannot be reversed. It is like asking to omit a part of our history. Furthermore, in order to provide for international political stability, communication between countries is a prerequisite, and cannot take place without trade.

At a more fundamental level the goal of environmental sustainability has led some authors to criticize the mainstream approaches. Clearly, the approaches previously discussed do not explicitly deal with sustainability. Sustainability essentially means that a dynamic approach is necessary. To make things complex in the context of trade and environment, trade should be linked to growth, and growth to environmental sustainability. Since the linkage between growth and trade has, not been dealt with very extensively until recently, this area is still very much open. The sketched linking can only be taken well into account in a dynamic setting, or one should see it in terms of a fixed limit determined by scientists (e.g., biologists) that is to be allocated over space (spatial sustainability) or over sectors. The latter case may be dealt with in a multisectoral general equilibrium setting, similar to the analysis of tradeable permits (Bergman 1991). Generally, global sustainability can mean that regions specialize in those production activities in which they have an environmentally comparative advantage. In such a framework, sustainability and trade should not be conflicting. However, current models are not complex enough to deal with this issue.

Lack of Empirical Research

Finally, a general critique of trade theory and environmental economic theory has been that they have not been well tested. In other words, the question is raised as to whether empirical studies support theoretical findings. This holds for the effect of environmental factors on trade and development, as well as for the impact of strictness of environmental policy on the international competitive position of a country and its trade flows. Generally, the trade theories and the partial equilibrium models previously discussed have not seen much application in the context of environmental factors, externalities, and policies. They have been mostly used for obtaining partial theoretical insights. Some general equilibrium models have been applied. Thus it seems that theoretical research has received much more attention than empirical studies. Two explanations can be offered for this. First, not all theoretical models allow for immediate testing or application because of their abstract nature. Second, it is very difficult to link monetary and physical dimensions, and to define and measure unambiguous indicators (e.g., environmental effects, specific environmental measures, or strictness of environmental policy). This is partly a fundamental problem, and partly a matter of lacking data. It is, for instance, only recently that the World Bank Atlas started to publish national figures on the environment. In order to ameliorate such problems, one may use simple indicators such as ratios and trade variables to estimate the effects of, for instance, environmental policy on trade; this can be done by comparison of values of such indicators before and after implementation of policy in a specific country, or by country-wise comparison. An alternative is to adopt econometric or statistical (correlation) analysis based on single-country (time-series) or country-wise (cross-section) analysis as, for instance, in Tobey (1990) and van Beers and van den Bergh (1997). Finally, one may note that statistical evidence on certain relationships between trade, environmental quality, and policy may not be found when explanatory variation in the data is weak. This can be caused by unobserved technological processes, imperfectly operating markets, rigid prices, exogenous shocks, or just because policies have not been that strict. This problem is also found in studies dealing with the effect of environmental factors and regulation on location decisions (e.g., Low and Yeats 1992).

CONCLUSIONS

The diverse and multifaceted relationship between international trade and environmental externalities calls for a pluralistic approach. This has been the basis of this chapter. A number of formal models are available to deal with environmental issues from the perspective of environmental externalities, environmental factors of and conditions for production and consumption, impacts of environmental policy on foreign trade, and economic indicators. In addition, there are many important aspects of environmental policy that models cannot address, particularly related to institutional complexities. The foregoing overview hopefully clarifies that although most methods offers a limited and partial insight, they can still stimulate thought about what kinds of effects may be expected and how these can be evaluated.

We recognize that there are a number of neglected topics. An important one is the link between long-run sustainability and international trade, and related to that, the choice of locations by firms. Most analyses of trade and environment adopt a static framework. However, the dynamics of locations and trade should be guided so that overall sustainability coincides with local sustainability and welfare. Traditional growth analysis does not seem to offer much new food for thought on trade and environmental issues. To address long-run environmental quality there is some need for linking trade and growth in models for environmental policy analysis, preferably to regional disaggregated models. Spatial and multiregional model types may serve a useful purpose here. Little work has been done yet, although there seem to be several areas where further investigation may be fruitful. It is clear that international coordination of environmental policy is a necessity for maintaining as much as possible the elements of free trade. Such issues, although not given much attention here, are attracting more attention from economists. In this context, formal modeling, often based on game theory, can also be useful in dealing with relevant questions. Interaction between policy coordination, transboundary pollution, and international trade is certain to remain a focus of research in the future.

As previously stated, the use of formal models for studying the interface of environment and trade can only be pursued on the basis of abstractions and simplifications. Therefore, care has to be taken in translating conclusions obtained from model exercises to implications for policy. Instead, results from separate model-based and other studies should be combined, since each will shed unique and necessarily partial light on the issue. Finally, perhaps the most important focus of future work should be the empirical testing of theories and hypotheses.

ACKNOWLEDGMENTS

We are grateful to Jan van der Straaten for suggestions to improve and extend the contents of this chapter.

FOOTNOTES

1. Domestic effects are expressed more extensively in the Stolpher-Samuelson theorem (influence on factor prices) and the Rybczynski theorem (influence on quantities exported) (see Falvey 1994).
2. In addition to these assumptions, the regular assumptions necessary for a comparative-static analysis are also adopted (i.e., no changes in tastes and technology change, and no international factor mobility).
3. According to Krutilla (1991) the assumption of a large country is similar to imperfect competition in international markets since prices can be influenced. It should be clear that this is imperfect competition at the world market level and that no specific assumptions are made for competition in the domestic markets. This is explicitly done in the field of "modern trade theory," discussed in the section on general equilibrium analysis, trade, and environmental policy.
4. See Dixit and Stiglitz (1977) for the case of imperfect competition internationally.
5. Here it is assumed of course that the lower world market price does not give the domestic consumers the opportunity to import the commodity because of trade barriers that make the firm able to maintain its monopoly power.
6. In the case where the optimal environmental taxes (and externalities) are extremely high so that the intersection of MSC and P_w is to the left of i, exports will disappear, the domestic supply is decreased, and the domestic price P_{dom} increases. Left of i, the marginal revenue is higher at the domestic than at the world market, and the monopolist will only supply the domestic market. In other words, only for extremely high externalities will the domestic market be affected by the introduction of environmental policy measures.
7. Bergman (1990) gives a typology and overview of CGE model applications: static models based on social accounting matrices; dynamic models based on econometric estimation using time series data; and planning model formulations.
8. This inconsistency follows from the theoretical result established by Samuelson (1953) that with constant returns to scale in production and with domestic and foreign identical goods

being perfect substitutes, the domestic economy will produce only as many different kinds of tradable goods as it has primary inputs.
9. Restrictiveness of environmental policy is a relative notion, and is difficult to test (Tobey (1990). Pethig (1976) defines "more restrictive" in terms of relative emission standards or (not necessarily equivalent) relative emission prices in autarky. Van Beers and van den Bergh (1997) use narrow and broad aggregate indicators of environmental policy stringency.

REFERENCES

Anderson, K. 1992. The standard welfare economics of policies affecting trade and the environment. In *The Greening of World Trade Issues,* eds. K. Anderson and R. Blackhurst. New York: Harvester Wheatsheaf.

Anderson, K. and R. Blackhurst. eds. 1992. *The Greening of World Trade Issues.* New York: Harvester Wheatsheaf.

Arrow, K. J. and F. H. Hahn. 1971. *General competitive analysis.* San Francisco: Holden-Day.

Asako, K. 1979. Environmental pollution in an open economy. *The Economic Record* 55:359–367.

Barret, S. 1995. Toward a theory of international environmental cooperation. Nota di lavoro 60.95. Milan: Fondazione Eni Enrico Mattei.

Baumol, W. J. 1971. *Environmental Protection, International Spillovers and Trade.* Stockholm: Almqvist and Wiksell.

Baumol, W. J. and W. E. Oates. 1988. *The Theory of Environmental Policy,* 2nd ed. Cambridge: Cambridge University Press.

Bergman, L. 1990. *The development of computable general equilibrium modeling. In General Equilibrium Modeling and Economic Policy Analysis,* eds. L. Bergman, D. W. Jorgenson, and E. Zalai. Oxford: Basil Blackwell.

Bergman, L. 1991. General equilibrium effects of environmental policy: A CGE-modeling approach. *Environmental and Resource Economics* 1:43–61.

Bovenberg, A. L. and R. A. de Mooij. 1994. Environmental policy in a small open economy with distortionary labor taxes: A general equilibrium analysis. In *International Environmental Economics: Theories, Models and Applications to Global Warming,* International Trade and Acidification, ed. E. C. van Ierland. Amsterdam: Elsevier Science Publishers.

Boyd, R. and K. Krutilla. 1992. Controlling acid deposition: A general equilibrium assessment. *Environmental and Resource Economics* 2:307–322.

Burniaux, J. M., J. P. Martin, G. Nicoletti, and J. Oliveira-Martins. 1991. GREEN – A Multi-Region Dynamic General Equilibrium Model for Quantifying the Costs of Curbing CO_2 Emissions: A Technical Manual. Working Paper 89. OECD, Department of Economics and Statistics, Paris.

Burniaux, J. M. and J. Waelbroeck 1992. CGE and imperfect competition model for EC. *Journal of Policy Modeling* 14:65–92.

Carraro, C. 1994. *Trade, Innovation, Environment.* Dordrecht: Kluwer Academic Publishers.

Choi, E. K. and S. R. Johnson. 1992. Regulation of externalities in an open economy. *Ecological Economics* 5:251–265.

Comolli, P. 1977. Pollution control in a simplified general equilibrium model with production externalities. *Journal of Environmental Economics and Management* 4:289–304.

Conrad, K. 1993. Trade policy under taxes and subsidies for pollution intensive industries. *Journal of Environmental Economics and Management* 25:121–135.

Conrad, K. 1994. Emission taxes and international market share rivalry. In *International Environmental Economics: Theories, Models and Applications to Global Warming,* International Trade and Acidification, ed. E. C. van Ierland. Amsterdam: Elsevier Science Publishers.

Conrad, K. and M. Schroder. 1991. The control of CO_2-emissions and its economic impact. *Environmental and Resource Economics* 1:289–312.

Daly, H. E. and W. Cobb. 1989. *For the Common Good: Redirecting the Economy Toward Community, the Environment and a Sustainable Future*. Boston: Beacon Press.

Daly, H. and R. Goodland. 1994. An ecological–economic assessment of deregulation of international commerce under GATT. *Ecological Economics* 9:73–92.

Deardorff, A. V. 1984. Testing trade theories and predicting trade flows. In *Handbook of International Economics*, eds. R. W. Jones and P. B. Kenen. Amsterdam: Elsevier Science Publishers.

Dervis, K. J., De Melo, and S. Robinson. 1982. *General Equilibrium Models for Development Policy*. Cambridge: Cambridge University Press.

Dixit, A. 1984. International trade policy for oligopolistic industries. *Economic Journal Supplement* 1–15.

Dixit, A. K. and J. E. Stiglitz. 1977. Monopolistic competition and optimum product diversity. *American Economic Review* 67(3):297–308.

Eaton, J. and G. M. Grossman. 1986. Optimal trade and industrial policy under oligopoly. *The Quarterly Journal of Economics* vol. CI:383–406.

Falvey, R. E. 1994. The theory of international trade. In *Surveys in International Trade*, eds. D. Greenaway and L. A. Winters. Oxford: Blackwell Publishers.

Feenstra, T., P. Kort, P. Verheyen, and A. de Zeeuw. 1995. Standards versus taxes in a dynamic duopoly model of trade. Nota di lavoro 62.95. Milan: Fondazione Eni Enrico Mattei.

Folke, C., P. Ekins, and R. Costanza. 1994. Trade and Environment. *Ecological Economics* vol. 9, special issue.

GATT. 1971. Industrial Pollution Control and International Trade. GATT studies in International Trade No. 1, General Agreement on Tariffs and Trade, Geneva.

Gradus, R. and S. Smulders. 1993. The trade-off between environmental care and long-term growth: Pollution in three prototype growth models. *Journal of Economics* 58:25–52

Grossman, G. M. and E. Helpman. 1990. Comparative advantages and long-run growth. *American Economic Review* 80:796–815.

Grossman, G. M. and E. Helpman. 1991. *Innovation and Growth in the Global Economy*. Cambridge, MA: MIT Press.

Harris, R. G. 1984. Applied general equilibrium analysis of small open economies and imperfect competition. *American Economic Review* 74:1016–1032.

Hazilla, M. and R. J. Kopp. 1990. Social cost of environmental quality regulations: A general equilibrium analysis. *Journal of Political Economy* 98:853–873.

Helpman, E. and P. R. Krugman. 1985. *Market Structure and Foreign Trade: Increasing Returns, Imperfect Competition, and the International Economy*. Cambridge, MA: MIT

Hudson, E. A. and D. W. Jorgenson. 1975. U.S. energy and economic growth 1975–2000. *Bell Journal of Economics and Management Science* 5:461–514.

Johansen, L. 1960. *A multisectoral study of economic growth*. Amsterdam: North-Holland.

Jorgenson, D. W. and J. Wilcoxen. 1990. Intertemporal general equilibrium modeling of US environmental policy. *Journal of Policy Modeling* 12:715–744.

Kamien, M. I. and N. L. Schwartz. 1982. The role of common property resources in optimal planning models with exhaustible resources. In *Explorations in Natural Resource Economics*, eds. V. K. Smith and J. V. Krutilla. Baltimore: Johns Hopkins University Press.

Kennedy, P. 1994a. Equilibrium pollution taxes in open economies with imperfect competition. *Journal of Environmental Economics and Management* 27:49–63.

Kennedy, P. 1994b. Environmental policy and trade liberalization under imperfect competition. In *International Environmental Economics: Theories, Models and Applications to Global Warming, International Trade and Acidification*, ed. E. C. van Ierland. Amsterdam: Elsevier Science Publishers.

Krutilla, K. 1991. Environmental regulation in an open economy. *Journal of Environmental Economics and Management* 20:127–142.

Leontief, W. W. 1970. Environmental repercussions and the economic structure: An input–output approach. *Review of Economic Studies* 52:262–271.

Leontief, W., A. P. Carter, and P. A. Petri. 1977. *The Future of the World Economy.* New York: Oxford University Press.

Leontief, W. and A. Strout. 1963. Multiregional input–output analysis. In *Structural Interdependence and Economic Development,* ed. T. Barna. New York: St. Martin's Press.

Linder, S. B. 1961. *An Essay on Trade and Transformation.* Upsala: Almquist and Wiksell.

Low, P. 1992. International Trade and Environment. World Bank Discussion Papers, 159. Washington, DC: World Bank.

Low, P. and A. Yeats. 1992. Do "dirty" industries migrate? In P. Low, International Trade and Environment. World Bank Discussion Papers, 159. Washington, DC: World Bank.

Markusen, J. R. 1975. International externalities and optimal tax structures. *Journal International Economics* 5:15–29.

Markusen, J. R., E. R. Morey, and N. D. Olewiler. 1993. Environmental policy when market structure and plant locations are endogenous. *Journal of Environmental Economics and Management* 24:69–86.

McGuire, M. C. 1982. Regulation, factor rewards, and international trade. *Journal of Public Economics* 17:335–354

Merrifield, J. D. 1988. The impact of selected abatement strategies on transnational pollution, the terms of trade and factor rewards: A general equilibrium approach. *Journal of Environmental Economics and Management* 15:259–284.

Moses, L. N. 1955. The stability of interregional trading patterns and input–output analysis. *American Economic Review* 45:803–832.

Motta, M. and J.-F. Thisse. 1994. Does environmental dumping lead to delocation? *European Economic Review* 18:563–576.

Nestor, D. V. and C. A. Pasurka. 1992. *General Equilibrium Model of German Environmental Regulation.* Washington, DC: US Environmental Protection Agency, Economic Analysis and Research Branch.

Norman, V. D. 1990. Assessing trade and welfare effects of trade liberalization: A comparison of alternative approaches to CGE modelling with imperfect competition. *European Economic Review* 34:725–751.

Pethig, R. 1976. Pollution, welfare and environmental policy in the theory of comparative advantage. *Journal of Environmental Economics and Management* 2:160–169.

Piggott, J., J. Whalley, and R. Wigle. 1992. International Linkages and Carbon Reduction Initiatives. In *The Greening of World Trade Issues,* eds. K. Anderson and R. Blackhurst. New York: Harvester Wheatsheaf.

Posner, M. V. 1961. International trade and technical change. *Oxford Economic Papers* 323–341.

Røpke, I. 1994. Trade, development and sustainability–A critical assessment of the "freetrade dogma." *Ecological Economics* 9:13–22.

Samuelson, P. A. 1953. Prices of factors and goods in general equilibrium. *Review of Economic Studies* 21:1–20.

Shoven, J. B., and J. Whalley. 1984. Applied general-equilibrium models of taxation and international trade: An introduction and survey. *Journal of Economic Literature* 22:1007–51.

Siebert, H. 1973. Comparative advantage and environmental policy: A note. *Zeitschrift fur Nationalokonomie* 34:397–402.

Siebert, H. 1974. Environmental protection and international specialization. *Weltwirtschaftliches Archiv* 110:494–508.

Siebert, H. 1987. *Economics of the Environment: Theory and Policy.* Berlin: Springer-Verlag.

Siebert, H., J. Eichberger, R. Gronych, and R. Pethig 1980. Trade and environment: A theoretical enquiry studies. In *Environmental Science 6.* Amsterdam: Elsevier Science Publishers.

Smith, A. 1994. Imperfect competition and international trade. In *Surveys in International Trade,* eds. D. Greenaway and L. A. Winters. Oxford: Blackwell Publisher.

Smulders, S. 1994. Growth, Market Structure and the Environment: Essays on the Theory of Endogenous Economic Growth. Ph.D. thesis. Tilburg: Tilburg University.

Srinivasan, T. N. and J. Whalley. 1986. *General Equilibrium Trade Policy Modeling.* Cambridge, MA: MIT Press.

Steininger, K. 1994a. *Trade and Environment: A Computable General Equilibrium for Vienna, Austria.* Austria: Physica-Verlag.

Steininger, K. 1994b. Reconciling trade and environment: Towards a comparative advantage for long-term policy goals. *Ecological Economics* 9:23–42.

Tahvonen, O. and J. Kuuluvainen. 1991. Optimal growth with renewable resources and pollution. *European Economic Review* 35:650–661.

Tahvonen, O. and J. Kuuluvainen. 1993. Economic growth, pollution and renewable resources. *Journal of Environmental Economics and Management* 24:101–118.

Takayama, T. and G. Judge. 1971. *Spatial and Temporal Price and Allocation Models.* Amsterdam: North-Holland.

Takayama, T. and W. C. Labys. 1986. Spatial equilibrium analysis. In *Handbook of Regional and Urban Economics,* ed. P. Nijkamp. Amsterdam: North-Holland.

Tobey, J. A. 1990. The effects of domestic environmental policies on patterns of world trade: An empirical test. *Kyklos* 43:191–209.

Toman, M. A., J. Pezzey, and J. Krautkraemer. 1994. Neoclassical economic growth theory and "sustainability." In *Handbook of Environmental Economics,* ed. D. Bromley. Oxford: Blackwell.

Ulph, A. 1991. The choice of environmental policy instruments and strategic international trade. In *Conflicts and Cooperation in Managing Environmental Resources,* ed. R. Pethig. Berlin, Springer-Verlag, pp. 111–128.

van Beers, C. and C. J. M. van den Bergh. 1994. Environmental and foreign trade policies in a small open economy. In *Quantitative Economics for Environmental Policy,* eds. R. de Mooij and H. Vollebergh. Rotterdam: OCFEB, Erasmus University.

van Beers, C. and J. C. J. M. van den Bergh. 1996. An overview of methodological approaches in the analysis of trade and environment. *Journal of World Trade* 30:143–167.

van Beers, C., and J. C. J. M. van den Bergh. 1997. An empirical multi-country analysis of the impact of environmental regulations on foreign trade flows. *Kyklos* 50:29–46.

van den Bergh, J. C. J. M. and P. Nijkamp. 1995. Growth, Trade and Sustainability in the Spatial Economy. *Studies in Regional Science* 25:67–87.

van Ierland, E. C. ed. 1994. *International Environmental Economics: Theories, Models and Applications to Global Warming, International Trade and Acidification.* Amsterdam: Elsevier Science Publishers.

Verdier, T. 1993. Strategic Trade and the Regulation of Pollution by Performance or Design Standards. Nota di Lavoro della Fondazione Eni Enrico Mattei, University of Venice, No. 58.

Verhoef, E. T. and C .J. M. van den Bergh. 1995. Transport, spatio-economic equilibrium and global sustainability: Markets, technology and policy. TRACE Discussion Paper TI 95-80, Amsterdam-Rotterdam: Tinbergen Institute.

Verhoef, E. T. and C. J. M. van den Bergh. 1996. A spatial price equilibrium model for environmental policy analysis of mobile and immobile sources of pollution. In *Recent Advances in Spatial Equilibrium Modelling,* eds. J. C. J. M. van den Bergh, P. Nijkamp, and P. Rietveld. Berlin: Springer-Verlag.

Walter, I. 1975. *The International Economics of Pollution.* London: Macmillan.

Walter, I. 1976. *Studies in International Environmental Economics.* New York: Wiley.

WCED. 1987. *Our Common Future. World Commission on Environment and Development.* Oxford/New York: Oxford University Press.

Yohe, G. W. 1979. The backward incidence of pollution control – Some comparative statics in general equilibrium. *Journal of Environmental Economics and Management* 6:187–198.

8 TRADE, EQUITY, AND REGIONAL ENVIRONMENTAL SUSTAINABILITY

John Gowdy

Department of Economics
School of Humanities and Social Sciences
Rensselaer Polytechnic Institute
Troy, New York

INTRODUCTION

The recent NAFTA debates in the United States and Mexico focused attention on arguments by environmentalists, specifically that regionally based economies are more likely to promote environmental sustainability than those based on trade with distant markets (Daly 1993). There is considerable evidence for this position, particularly with regard to sustainable agriculture. Norgaard (1988) describes the loss of agricultural diversity in traditional agricultural societies which results from a switch from what he calls "coevolutionary agriculture" to monocrop production for export. Martinez-Alier (1994, 1995) cites evidence for the loss of genetic diversity in local agricultural systems as a result of specialization and trade. There are numerous examples of GATT, NAFTA, and European Community policies that undermine efforts to protect local environmental resources (Arden-Clarke 1992; Hines 1990; Phillips 1993). Common sense tells us that economies dependent on local resources must have greater incentives to preserve them than economies which can trade for these resources (or for substitutes) with distant markets.

On the other hand, there is considerable evidence that scores of region-based[1] economies with little or no trade have overexploited their resource base and collapsed. For example, the first agriculture-based civilizations in southwest Asia caused widespread environmental disruption relatively soon after their formation. Eventually soil exhaustion, increased salinity through irrigation, deforestation, and overpopulation resulted in the disintegration of these civilizations when they could no longer cope with inevitable environmental shocks, such as prolonged drought. Numerous examples from history and prehistory suggest that although a regionally-based economy may have a greater incentive to conserve its natural resources, there is no guarantee that it will. In these early societies there must have been powerful factors involved in decisions about resource use that overrode conservation and led to eventual resource exhaustion and societal collapse. Most likely, a central element was the control of economic surpluses by elites, a characteristic of human cultures since the widespread adoption of agriculture. In case after case as early agricultural societies began to experience environmental limits to growth and declines in living standards, there was increasing religious fanaticism and intensification of the very behavior that had driven them to the brink of disaster (Ponting 1991; Bahn and Flenley 1992; Malone et al. 1993). This is an important point to consider when formulating environmental protection policies that threaten economic and political elites.

When developing policy recommendations concerning trade it is difficult to sort out which negative aspects of trade can be corrected within the existing system and which cannot. Many of the criticisms of free trade by Daly (1993) and others are criticisms of the current industrial system and its apparent dependence on economic growth and income inequality. In an analysis of the effects of trade on the environment we should be careful to separate the negative effects due to increased economic growth and those which are due to trade itself.

There are positive aspects of trade, particularly for income levels in underdeveloped countries, which are not discussed in detail here. It should be noted, however, that in terms of environmental impacts, rising income levels have some positive and some negative effects. The standard argument that rising incomes first have a negative then a positive effect on environmental quality (the inverted U-shaped curve) does not hold for all negative environmental impacts of income growth (Arrow et al. 1995).

There are many examples to suggest that trade itself may undermine local efforts to promote environmental sustainability. This chapter looks at these questions by examining the role of trade in hunting and gathering and early agricultural societies. Two insights that arise from this brief survey are (1) local self-sufficiency alone is not enough to insure sustainability or equality, and (2) even in these early societies trade sometimes reinforced inequality and environmentally unsustainable practices. These observations have relevance for current trade policy.

SOCIETY AND ENVIRONMENT BEFORE THE INDUSTRIAL REVOLUTION: HUNTER–GATHERERS AND AGRICULTURALISTS

Before turning to the issue of trade I will briefly survey the relationship between the level of technology, social structure, and the environment before the industrial revolution. For 99% of human existence, or about two million years, we lived as hunter–gatherers more or less in harmony with the natural world

(Shepard 1973; Ponting 1991; Orr 1992; Gowdy 1994). Hunter–gatherers most likely modified their environment, being a large mobile species, but there is scant evidence that human presence was detrimental to overall biodiversity, habitat, or any other indicator of ecosystem health. One of the most remarkable changes in scientific opinion in recent years has been the change in the evaluation of the hunter–gatherer way of life. In the early 1960s, the predominant view echoed Hobbes' description of a life that was nasty, brutish, and short. By the early 1970s, hunter–gatherers were described as the original affluent society (Sahlins 1972), a view that has stood up remarkably well during the past two decades (Bird-David 1992).

Hunting and gathering societies were not only environmentally sustainable, they were also characterized by social equality. Based on field studies of the hunter-gatherer culture of Tanzania, the Hadza, James Woodburn (1982) describes some of the characteristics of hunter-gatherer societies that serve to promote social equality. These include:

1. Social groupings are flexible and are constantly changing in composition;
2. Individuals have almost complete freedom of choice as to whom they associate with in residence, and in trade and exchange;
3. Individuals are not dependent on specific others for access to basic requirements; and
4. All relationships stress sharing and mutuality without requiring long-term binding commitments.

In this type of social organization societies' individuals have no real authority over each other. Furthermore, all of these characteristics are consciously protected as part of what Woodburn calls an "aggressively egalitarian" social strategy. He writes:

> In these societies equalities of power, equalities of wealth and equalities of prestige or rank are not merely sought but are, with certain limited exceptions, genuinely realized. But, the evidence suggests, they are never unchallenged. People are well aware of the possibility that individuals or groups within their own egalitarian societies may try to acquire wealth, to assert more power or to claim more status than other people, and are vigilant in seeking to prevent or limit this. (1982)

Woodburn argues that social equality is also related to environmental sustainability. With the abandonment of the hunting and gathering way of life in most regions of the world, stratified societies appeared about ten thousand years ago and were characterized by rapid growth, followed by resource exhaustion and social disintegration. According to many commentators (Graham and Lundelius 1984; Harris 1978), agriculture was adopted as a response to climate change after the last glaciation and the subsequent extinction of big game animals on which Pleistocene hunters depended. Once agriculture was adopted as the predominant source of food, societies became locked into an agricultural mode of production as their populations increased beyond a level that could be supported by hunting and gathering. These societies soon became stratified and tightly controlled by religious and political elites.[2]

Compared to the minimal impact of hunter–gatherer economic systems on the environment, agricultural economic systems led relatively quickly to huge increases in population and large-scale environmental disruption. Ponting (1991) writes:

> Recent evidence from central Jordan suggests that as early as 6000 BC, within about a thousand years of the emergence of settled communities, villages were being abandoned as soil erosion caused by deforestation resulted in a badly damaged landscape, declining crop yields and eventually inability to grow food.

Weiss et al. (1993) document the pattern of rapid growth, environmental degradation, and abrupt collapse of the Akkadian empire in Mesopotamia in the third millennium BC, a pattern that was repeated throughout the world in early agriculture-based civilizations. The Mayan civilization, which expanded by an increasingly intensive system of cultivation until it collapsed around 600 AD, shows the typical process of overshoot and collapse. According to Ponting (1991):

> By using the natural resources readily available to them, by finding ways of exploiting these more fully and, in some cases, by creating artificial environments, the Maya were able to build a complex society capable of great cultural and intellectual achievements, but they ended up destroying what they had created. Perhaps the more complex the superstructure, the more difficult it was to retain an awareness of the connections or to alter course.

There are examples of environmental over-exploitation even in very simple, localized agricultural economies with little or no contact with other cultures. One of the most dramatic examples of shortsighted neglect of ecological limits is the case of Easter Island, best known for its large (2–10m) stone figures.

Easter Island is possibly the most isolated human habitation in the world, lying thousands of kilometers from its nearest inhabited neighbors. It was first settled around 700 AD (Bahn and Flenley 1992) probably by voyagers from Polynesia. The island is small, less than 100 square miles. When the first settlers landed the island was forested with palm trees. The soil was not particularly fertile, but was rich enough to support an agricultural base for a population that peaked at about 7,000 people.[3] The diet of these settlers depended on the chickens and Polynesian rats they brought with them, and on sweet potatoes. Due to the extreme isolation of Easter Island both flora and fauna were extremely limited. There were far fewer species of fish compared to other inhabited islands. The lack of a coral reef meant that shellfish were also limited in numbers (Bahn and Flenley 1992; Diamond 1995).

The isolation and ecological fragility of Easter Island should have been obvious to its inhabitants. In spite of this they stripped the island of almost all trees, overworked the soil, and in general created an environmental catastrophe for themselves. When Europeans arrived in 1722, the population had been reduced to a few hundred impoverished residents living in squalid caves. Apparently the island was controlled by religious cults based on the construction and worship of the huge figures for which the island is famous. All the island's trees were cut down to make skids to transport the stone statues from quarries to religious centers. In a frequently recurring pattern, as the resource base of the island became more and more precarious, religious fanaticism became more pronounced until even the most modest efforts of resource conservation were ignored.

Past civilizations have taught us that political pressures from elites bent on preserving their power at all costs will inevitably result in perpetuating unsustainable systems, that is, until environmental degradation leads to social disintegration. Easter Island's society collapsed even though there were no outside forces such as military threats or social disruption through trade. Easter Islanders used only indigenous resources. If such obvious self-inflicted environmental collapse could happen in isolated island societies where environmental damage is immediate and obvious, this indicates that there are no natural mechanisms present in post-hunter–gatherer societies to halt environmental degradation. There is apparently no negative feedback mechanism in complex societies strong enough to halt environmental destruction even when it threatens the economic resource base.

A number of recent studies point to the relationship between environmental degradation, social disruption, and the power structure of human societies (Gurr 1985; Homer-Dixon 1991). In this context it is revealing to contrast the egalitarian social structure of hunting and gathering societies to the authoritarian structure of agricultural and industrial economic systems. In hunting and gathering economies access to the means for making a living is free and open to all. Material technology is limited. The basic requirement to survive in these societies is the knowledge that is freely given to all members of the group. With agriculturally based economies and permanent surpluses came social divisions and the control of production and distribution by elites.

TRADE AMONG HUNTER–GATHERERS AND EARLY AGRICULTURALISTS

Trade, even in economically simple agricultural societies, can serve to reinforce social divisions and create dependencies on specific others. Even in very early agricultural societies we begin to see evidence of trade items used to reinforce the power and authority of social elites. There is a clear relationship between trade, the creation of economic surplus, equity, centralized decision-making, and environmental sustainability.[4]

As a justification for promoting trade as a means of protecting biodiversity, some writers (Stiles 1994) point to the fact that trade has existed among human societies for tens of thousands (perhaps hundreds of thousands) of years. Although true, this overlooks the facts that (1) there is a difference between trade as the bilateral exchange of exotic items and trade as a means of reinforcing and expanding the power of elites, and (2) although market trade as a means to expand economic surplus may have existed for millennia, it also has a long record of promoting environmental abuse. Although there are vast differences between modern Western market economies and early agricultural chiefdoms and states, there are also similarities in the role of trade in these two categories. In both systems trade is a means of augmenting personal wealth and reinforcing class differences, a characteristic of trade that is not present, or present in a very limited way, in hunter–gatherer societies.

Evidence for trade among prehistoric hunter–gatherers is, of course, limited to physical archeological evidence. We can only speculate about the role of trade in hunter–gatherer social relationships but, given the egalitarian nature of historic hunter–gatherer cultures, one would expect that trade items would have a utilitarian function. This seems to be confirmed by historical accounts of trading practices among recent hunter–gatherers. Among the Australian Aborigines of present-day Queensland and the Northern Territory a variety of items were traded. Axe heads mined from quarries near Mount Isa in northwest Queensland were traded as far as the Gulf of Carpentaria to the north and the Great Australian Bight to the south. Pituri, the nicotine-based drug which grows on the eastern margin of the Simpson Desert was traded in all directions over an area of some 500,000 square km. Ochers used for body decoration and painting were also widely traded. There is even evidence from

19th century accounts that ceremonies (different kinds of dances, for example) were traded in an elaborate system of year-to-year exchange from the coast of South Australia to the Alice Springs area in central Australia (Davidson 1993). In the Pacific islands there is evidence for the widespread trade of obsidian, used to make projectile points, at least 19,000 years ago (Loy 1993). Trade in these societies is characterized by the exchange of useful exotic goods not available locally.

In early agricultural systems trade begins to take on a dynamic role in reinforcing power relationships among individuals and classes. The most famous example of trade in the anthropological literature is Malinowski's (1961 [1922]) description of the kula ring of the Trobriand Islanders. The kula ring is a circular system of reciprocal exchange among some eighteen island communities off the coast of Papua, New Guinea. Kula exchange is governed by an elaborate system of rules that do not apply to simple barter exchange. Two kinds of valuables such as necklaces and armshells are periodically exchanged by two communities. Only certain kinds of objects can be exchanged for each other. A completed exchange is called a "marriage" (Hage, Harary, and James 1986). Kula ring valuables are not held permanently, but continually circulate around the ring. Brunton (1975) argues that chiefdoms among the Trobriand Islanders emerged as a result of kula trading. Although the details of Bruton's theory have been challenged (Irwin 1983), the theory that trade is important in establishing and reinforcing power relationships in the Trobriands is generally accepted.

Milicic (1993) used graph theory to examine the most favorable locations in terms of trade possibilities for the community of Hvar in the Eastern Adriatic during the Venetian period (1420–1797). He found a systematic relationship between trade, locational advantage, and social stratification. He writes:

> Under these conditions [locational advantage and an excellent harbor] internal social stratification, both urban and rural, developed and was sustained through the transfer of wealth and through marriage alliances. In addition to an elaborate social stratification in towns, concentrated around harbors, the rural areas on the island of Hvar also developed three main social strata differentiated by land ownership. With its relative lack of natural resources the island's production was primarily aimed for trade. In the case of Hvar the external trade network set up the conditions for internal stratification based on the differentiation in the degree of access to exchange and, consequently, wealth.

Graph-theoretic models of trade possibilities have been used to explain social stratification based on favorable trade location for the prehistoric city of Cahokia along the Mississippi river (Peregrine 1991) as well as in the Trobriand Islands discussed above (Hage and Harary 1991). The very first large (although with only a few hundred residents) human settlements in Jericho and Catal Huyuk (both about 8500 b.p.) were based on trade for, respectively, water and obsidian (Ponting 1991).

The expansion of trade had a negative impact on many previously egalitarian, unstratified societies. Accounts of Plains Indian tribes indicate a dramatic alteration of social norms as a result of their involvement in a trading network. Adams (1992 [1974]) writes:

There was a growing dependence on certain categories of trade goods, leading to the disappearance of their native cognates and hence to an even greater, and presently irrevocable, involvement in the commerce in furs... It appears that widespread polygyny, a tendency toward social stratification, and a shift toward economically acquisitive, venture-taking, individualistic patterns of leadership all can be traced to the influence of trade.

Evidence from Madagascar (Kottak 1972) suggests that trade alone can completely disrupt economies based on local ecosystems and "rapidly elevate a strategically situated chiefdom to the status of a predatory state" (Adams 1992 [1974]). Meillassoux (1971) argues that long-distance trade in Africa was an indigenous phenomenon whose disruptive effects on local cultures were not due to European influence.

These brief considerations of the social effects of trade in nonindustrial societies reinforce Daly's (1993) warnings about neglecting the community welfare dimension of trade. There is certainly a social welfare difference between trade as a means of acquiring useful objects not available locally and trade as a means of acquiring power and prestige. As social stratification becomes a characteristic of human society, trade not only increases the availability of communities as its proponents claim, it also becomes an avenue to increase the political and economic power of elites.

THE STANDARD VIEW OF FREE TRADE

Trade as a means to acquire political power seems to be a recent phenomenon going back ten thousand years or so at the most. Such trade could only develop within societies having elite groups whose power depended on the control of economic surplus, that is, with the social stratification that accompanied the transition to agricultural-based societies.[5] Production solely for market exchange is a recent phenomenon. It is only in the last two hundred years or so that societies have emerged in which resource use is driven by production for market exchange. The subordination of all production and distribution considerations to the generation of market values has taken hold worldwide only in this century. In modern market economies the economic justification for trade is centered around its role in rationalizing production and in promoting economic growth. A major function of neoclassical economic theory is to provide the ideological justification for markets as the sole authority for production and allocation decisions. Expanding the possibilities for exchange through trade is a natural extension of the neoclassical analysis of market behavior. The brief examples given above of the relationship between trade, social structure, and environmental degradation point to gaps in the neoclassical view. Although economic critiques of free trade dogma usually focus on problems with the theory of comparative advantage (Daly 1993; Daly and Cobb 1989), the neoclassical argument for trade can be more easily seen in the standard model of market exchange. Any voluntary exchange must obviously be mutually beneficial. This was in fact Adam Smith's argument for trade in *The Wealth of Nations* (Lea 1994). The neoclassical model describes the static market exchange of a fixed amount of existing goods among consumers or of productive inputs among producers. The model, as any good model does, focuses on a few essential features and ignores most others. The purpose of the model is to describe the pure exchange of a fixed amount of goods or inputs. It ignores space, time, society, and the biophysical world. Neoclassical trade theory essentially treats trade among countries as being the same as the static exchange of market goods or inputs among individuals or firms (Gowdy and O'Hara 1995).

The standard Edgeworth box diagram of exchange shows how two individuals go about maximizing their utility by trading two goods. Before the analysis can begin, the amounts of the goods to be traded must be given and the initial distribution of the goods between the two individuals must also be given. If the initial distribution of goods is non-Pareto optimal, it can be easily shown that both individuals can be made better off by trading. If one individual trades some of one good with another individual for some of the other good, both move to higher indifference curves, indicating that both achieved a higher level of utility after the trade. Unhindered trading will lead to a point in the Edgeworth box where the rate at which the consumers are willing to trade one good for the other is the same and no further trading can improve the welfare of one without decreasing that of the other. This Pareto optimal situation is the ultimate objective of neoclassical policy, including trade policy. Anything that interferes with the free exchange of goods, including trade barriers between countries, will thwart the achievement of maximum welfare (given the two initial assumptions above).

If one keeps in mind exactly what the neoclassical model says and does not say, it can be a very useful tool for the analysis of how markets work. The problem is that neoclassical economists can become mesmerized by the power of the model and forget the physical and social realities that surround simple, static market exchange. In the basic neoclassical model of trade all the assumptions of perfect competition are invoked plus some others which are at least as restrictive. A few problems with the basic neoclassical model of trade as illustrated by the Edgeworth box analysis follow:

1. It ignores the dynamics of real-production in real time. As economists from Ricardo to Daly have pointed out, the arguments about the benefits of trade break down when the mobility of factors of production (especially capital) is taken into account (Daly and Cobb 1989).
2. It retains the simplistic treatment of the future through discounting. As legions of economists and ecologists have pointed out (Georgescu-Roegen 1976; d'Arge, Schultze, and Brookshire 1982; Hueting 1991; Hanley and Spash 1993) the existence of a positive discount rate works against the notion of environmental sustainability.
3. It assumes that all market goods are on an equal footing. The downward sloping indifference curve, which is the foundation of modern economic analysis, implies a willingness to trade (Georgescu-Roegen 1968). In neoclassical utility theory lexicographic preferences do not exist; anything may be traded for anything else.
4. It ignores the effects of distribution on production and exchange. As Lea (1994) points out, trade may be beneficial for the parties actually doing the trading, but its total impact may still be negative.

All these shortcomings result from the exclusive reliance on market exchange as the determinate of economic value, and this total economic value as the determinate of human well-being. In the neoclassical view there is no physical or social context for exchange, only ill-defined human preferences (however they arise) to be traded-off and balanced among competing individual interests. In the same *Scientific American* issue as Daly's article on the perils of free trade, Bhagwati gives the neoclassical view of trade and the environment. He writes: "Employment in the Mexican tuna fishery may offset the saving of dolphins that would result were the industry to forgo purse-seine nets. Countries should not be faulted for placing human welfare ahead of concerns specific to other cultures" (Bhagwati 1993). The implication is that protection of the biosphere is only a human preference having no objective basis in reality; the proper level of environmental quality is a matter of human preference just like any other market good. Biodiversity (Edwards 1987) [6] or even a stable climate (Nordhaus 1992) [7] may be treated as any other market goods to be discounted and traded in the open market.

It should be pointed out that not all neoclassical economists accept without question the idea that free trade is always beneficial. There is a rich literature which examines the assumptions of the basic model and discusses the limitations (Krugman 1987). Nevertheless, the basic neoclassical theory of production and distribution leads directly to the notion that increased trade is always positive. Ekins, Folke, and Costanza (1994) and Røpke (1994) discuss the ideology of trade and provide fascinating examples of how clearly thought-out theoretical statements about trade (Samuelson 1962, 1969) are restated as simple-minded ideology (Bhagwati 1969, 1993).

The standard economic analysis of trade necessarily ignores the role of trade in maintaining and extending existing power relationships. This neglect is critical because, to the extent that trade is controlled by economic and political elites, it may (1) exacerbate existing social inequality including gender inequality, and (2) wreak environmental havoc because those who make the decisions about environmental exploitation for trade are those who gain the most and who suffer the least from environmental destruction.

TRADE, ECONOMIC SURPLUS, AND EQUITY: WHAT CAN BE LEARNED FROM THE PAST?

From the brief discussion of the role of trade in history and prehistory we can begin to develop criteria for evaluating the desirability of trade. Below are some basic questions about the interrelated social and environmental effects of trade.

1. What is the effect of trade on the distribution of wealth?

In the neoclassical theory of exchange, income distribution is taken as given. Pareto optimality is independent of the distribution of goods or productive inputs. Likewise, the core arguments for trade made by economists usually focus only on the prospect of increased total output. By this view, if the total effect of trade on economic growth is positive, that is enough justification. But, as discussed above, income inequality is likely to have negative effects on environmental sustainability.

The importance of the effect of trade on distribution is illustrated by the controversy surrounding rainforest harvesting. Promoting the sustainable economic use of rainforests seems unambiguously to be a good idea. If sustainable rainforest products such as Brazil nuts can earn enough income then not only can the rainforests be saved, but the indigenous people of the forest can reap some of the economic benefits. Some of the main groups supporting the idea of rainforest harvest are Cultural Survival International, The Body Shop,

and Ben and Jerry's ice cream (Davenport 1997). In spite of the good inten-
tions of these organizations the effect on native rainforest people of increased
trade appears to have been negative. Cultural Survival has been accused of
buying Brazil nuts not from indigenous people, but from well-established bro-
kers who continue to exploit indigenous people (Corry 1993; Davenport 1997).
Even more troubling is the evidence that income from rainforest harvesting is
promoting the creation of social elites within indigenous tribes. A number of
authors have charged that income from international trading of forest products
has created large social differences within formally egalitarian tribes (e.g.,
Davenport 1997). There is evidence that elites are emerging in forest tribes
who control the distribution of income from forest products and who use this
power to oppress the majority of their own people.

The analysis referred to above, based on graphical analysis of trade-route
possibilities, suggests that power centers will emerge in rainforests along
favorable trading routes. Corry (1993) writes:

> If the "harvest" spreads it will affect only a few, selected rainforest com-
> munities – those which are near viable methods of transport, which have
> something of interest to outsiders, which have the time and desire to
> harvest for cash instead of subsistence, which are able to cope with re-
> ceiving and allocating considerable amounts of money and which have
> been approached by a foreign company willing to buy from them. A
> handful may earn a substantial amount of money, even get rich. But they
> will have no influence over this: they will earn as much, or as little as the
> company wants to pay.

It is well known that an influx of wealth into previously egalitarian societies can have unanticipated and devastating impacts on local cultures (Yellen
1990). There is no reason to think that tribal people are any less susceptible to
the addiction of modern industrial goods than the rest of us. An influx of market goods will inevitably follow the influx of cash into the forests.

A related question, going to the heart of the argument for regional-based
economies, is the accountability of local versus multinational firms. Daly (1993)
writes:

> The broader the free trade area, the less answerable a large and footloose
> corporation will be to any local or even national community. Spatial
> separation of the places that suffer the costs and enjoy the benefits be-
> comes more feasible. The corporation will be able to buy labor in the
> low-wage markets and sell its products in the remaining high-wage, high

income markets. The larger the market, the longer a corporation will be able to avoid the logic of Henry Ford, who realized that he had to pay his workers enough for them to buy his cars. That is why transnational corporations like free trade and why workers and environmentalists do not.

It is not sufficient to argue that trade will increase total economic output and, even if some members of society are made worse off, they can be compensated for their loss through other redistribution policies. The question of the effect of trade on relative incomes should be dealt with directly in free trade legislation (Daly and Goodland 1994; Ekins, Folke, and Costanza 1994).

2. What is the effect of trade on environmental quality?

If decisions about how trade is to take place are made by an elite who will benefit most by its expansion, these decisions will naturally downplay the importance of environmental and distribution consequences. Under the various GATT treaties individual governments have less ability to override the market to achieve social and environmental goals (Daly and Goodland 1994). Goods produced by child labor or by ecologically destructive practices cannot be treated differentially under the existing GATT treaty and even less under the proposed extensions of the treaty (Daly 1993; Daly and Goodland 1994). Among the environmental rulings of the GATT Secretariat are the inadmissibility of raising tariffs to take account of pollution abatement costs and the refusal to adopt the polluter-pays principle (Daly and Goodland 1994).

International trade agreements should be written to explicitly take into account the link between trade and the environment. There are many excellent recommendations for reforming the GATT agreements, such as regulations to prevent ecodumping (Daly and Goodland 1994), enforcement of the polluter-pays principle in trade agreements (Young 1994), and a harmonization of environmental standards (DeBellevue et al. 1994). Again, it is not enough for free-trade advocates to argue that with more trade total output will rise and more income will be available to correct environmental damages. Trade agreements such as GATT and NAFTA contain very specific rules and regulations regarding the conduct of economic activity between sovereign nations. It is not inconsistent with the spirit of these treaties to advocate trade-related environmental agreements which would move us toward sustainable economic activity.

3. Is trade disruptive to the sustainability of local environments and indigenous communities?

As we move toward a single worldwide economy a matter of great concern is the loss of indigenous cultures and regional biodiversity. One of the most serious negative impacts of increased trade is its impact on local cultures. It is widely recognized that indigenous people possess an extensive knowledge of local environmental resources. Tribes in the Amazon, such as the Kayapo Indians of Brazil have sustainably managed forest resources for a millennia (Posey 1985). Gadgil, Berkes, and Folke (1993) argue that societies whose subsistence is based on sedentary fishing, horticulture, or subsistence agriculture, with considerable dependence on hunting, are most likely to exhibit patterns of sustainable resource use and of conservation of biodiversity. They write:

> Self-regulatory mechanisms tend to evolve in such societies when they are faced with resource limitations. Among these mechanisms is a recognition and accumulation of knowledge about the important role that species play in generating ecological services and natural resources.

This knowledge is not only vital to the sustainability of indigenous cultures, it may also be of considerable value in efforts by Northern governments to protect biodiversity. An unintended consequence of trade may be to break down indigenous beliefs and customs which have traditionally maintained ecosystem functions.

Brush (1986) discusses the importance of the thousands of varieties of ancestral crops which he calls "landraces."[8] Because of the penetration of markets into traditional agricultural systems there has been widespread "genetic erosion" of traditional crop varieties. This erosion not only makes indigenous people more dependent on imported agricultural goods, it also means the loss of valuable genetic information which could be of tremendous value to the North. For example, the corn blight that devastated the U.S. corn crop in the 1970s was defeated using a hybrid developed from a traditional variety of corn from Mexico. Brush argues that the effect of increased dependence of traditional peoples on global markets is to break down the traditional agricultural system. In the last twenty years thousands of ancestral crop varieties have been replaced by a few scientifically bred varieties (Brush 1986).

The influx of cash from trade into indigenous communities will create a demand for more industrial goods and a demand for more income from the forest to pay for them. The land ethic generally held by indigenous people will be lost. Davenport (1997) writes: "As indigenous societies become bound to the world economic system, the world is losing the lessons they can teach us about mutual survival."

Martinez-Alier (1993) argues that the current proposed revisions to GATT and the recently passed NAFTA agreement will accelerate the decline in traditional agriculture in Mexico. The neoclassical explanation of genetic erosion is the lack of property rights for genetic resources. NAFTA and GATT would extend property rights to "intellectual property," that is, to knowledge about and use of agricultural plant varieties. According to Martinez-Alier (1993): "The threat to this agricultural diversity comes, above all, from the extension of the market, and from the fact that decisions relating to production are taken to a greater and greater extent on the basis of priorities indicated by price." Under NAFTA, the introduction of cheaper corn and other agricultural products grown by the U.S. factory system will have the effect of pushing Mexico's traditional agricultural system toward a Northern style monoculture dependent on large inputs of fertilizer and energy. Genetic diversity will suffer as will the peasant farmers who will face competition from cheaper agricultural products from the U.S.

SUMMARY AND CONCLUSIONS

Many environmentalists advocate regionally-based economies and call for restrictions on international trade. There are many good environmental arguments for local production. However, evidence from the past shows that regionally-based economies have not always been environmentally sustainable. The problem of environmental sustainability involves more than physical production and consumption. It is intimately connected with power relationships and the distribution of economic surpluses (Boyce 1994; O'Hara 1994). The importance of social structure on trade and sustainability can be seen in a comparison of the role of trade in hunting and gathering as opposed to agricultural societies. Among hunter–gatherers, trade did not adversely affect environmental quality nor did it have a negative impact on the generally egalitarian social structure of these societies. With the widespread adoption of agriculture came social stratification and the concentration of decisions involving production and consumption in a few hands. Among early agriculturalists there are numerous examples of trade leading to increased social stratification. Social stratification, and the control of economic surpluses by political or religious elites, can be linked to the environmental degradation and eventual collapse of many ancient civilizations.

Examining the positive and negative roles of trade in preindustrial societies can be useful in developing criteria for evaluating the environmental and social desirability of trade in modern economies. Questions that arise from such an examination concern the effect of trade on distribution, the role of trade in promoting efficiency and economic growth, and the effect of trade on local environments and indigenous cultures. As the example of Easter Island shows, there is no guarantee that regionally-based economies with no trade at all will be environmentally sustainable. The collapse of numerous past civilizations, from the Sumerians to the Mayans, shows that (1) isolated societies with little trade with the outside world may be incapable of changing their patterns of behavior even when this behavior results in complete social collapse, and (2) this inability to change is most likely the result of the concentration of power in the hands of a few.

The following are recommendations for current trade policy.

1. Trade agreements should explicitly take into account the impact of trade on income inequality.
2. Trade agreements should be written to explicitly deal with potential negative effects on environmental quality.
3. The potential devastating effect of trade on indigenous cultures, including agricultural biodiversity in indigenous agriculture, is of particular importance.

Many of the criticisms environmentalists make of free trade are criticisms of economic growth and the sustainability of the world economic system itself. The incompatibility between economic growth and environmental sustainability is a matter of increasing concern (Arrow et al. 1995). Current trade agreements such as GATT and NAFTA fail to recognize this incompatibility and are, in fact, based on the belief that continued growth is the only solution to the problems of income inequality and environmental degradation. Progressive forces should put pressure on governments to directly address these questions in trade agreements, rather than to assume that market forces will eventually correct them. The issue of trade can be a mechanism for raising larger questions about the long-run viability of our socioeconomic system, and the lessons learned from constructing environmentally sound trade treaties could be a model for moving the entire economy toward environmental sustainability.

ACKNOWLEDGMENTS

This chapter is a revised version of a paper presented at the October 1994 meeting of the International Society for Ecological Economics in San José, Costa Rica. The author would like to thank Juan Martinez-Alier and Sabine O'Hara for helpful comments.

FOOTNOTES

1. Defining an economic "region" in the modern world economy is problematic. In hunting and gathering type economies, economic regions were coterminous with what we call today "bioregions." Cultures were systematically adapted to deserts, seashores, rainforests, and so on, and compared to contemporary regional economies there was little overlap between them in terms of imports, exports, or other external influences (see the discussion of regions and sustainability in Verhoef and van den Bergh 1997; van den Bergh and Nijkamp 1994).

2. There is no sharp distinction between hunting and gathering and agriculture. Wild plants were cultivated and tended for tens of thousands of years before the so-called "Neolithic revolution." Herds of wild animals were managed in varying degrees by humans for millennia before they were domesticated.
3. A maximum population of 7,000 people is the most widely quoted figure, but other estimates go as high as 20,000 (Diamond 1995).
4. A great deal of literature in ecological anthropology exists on the relationship between economic surplus and power. See, for example, the discussions of Sahlins (1958) and Rappaport (1979) about social stratification and ecology in Polynesia.
5. There are examples of (somewhat) hierarchical societies who do not practice agriculture. The Northwest Coast Indians, for example, had permanent economic surplus, permanent settlements, and chiefs because of the great abundance of salmon which provided a dependable food source that could be stored.
6. In defense of neoclassical environmental economics Edwards (1987) writes: "In this context, the cold truth is that there is nothing unique about an apple, a day of fishing, a scenic vista, a blue whale, or a bequest of clean ground water to future generations."
7. Nordhaus (1992) uses a CES utility function to represent human preferences. The degree of substitutability between any pair of goods in consumers choice set is mathematically constrained to be the same. There is nothing unique about any good.
8. Some authors consider the term "landrace" to be negative and propose the word "folkseed" because the varieties have coevolved with human agricultural practices (Martinez-Alier 1993).

REFERENCES

Adams, R. 1992 [1974]. Anthropological perspectives on ancient trade. *Current Anthropology* 33:141–160.
Arden-Clarke, C. 1992. *International Trade, GATT and the Environment.* World Wildlife Fund for Nature. Gland, Switzerland.
Arrow, K. et al. 1995. Economic growth, carrying capacity, and the environment. *Science* 268:520–521.
Bahn, P. and J. Flenley. 1992. *Easter Island, Earth Island.* New York: Thames and Hudson.
Bhagwati, J. 1969. *Trade, Tariffs and Growth.* London: Weidenfeld and Nicholson.
Bhagwati, J. 1993. The case for free trade. *Scientific American* 269:42–49.
Bird-David, N. 1992. Beyond the original affluent society. *Current Anthropology* 33:25–47.
Boyce, J. 1994. Inequality as a cause of environmental degradation. *Economics* 11:169–178.
Brunton, R. 1975. Why do the Trobriands have chiefs? *Man* 10:544–558.
Brush, S. 1986. Genetic diversity and conservation in traditional farming systems. *Journal of Ethnobiology* 6:151–167.
Corry, S. 1993. The rainforest harvest: Who reaps the benefit? *The Ecologist* 23:148–153.
Daly, H. 1993. The perils of free trade. *Scientific American* 269:50–57.
Daly, H. and J. Cobb. 1989. *For the Common Good.* Boston: Beacon Press.
Daly, H. and R. Goodland. 1994. An ecological–economic assessment of deregulation of international commerce under GATT. *Ecological Economics* 9:73–92.
D'Arge, R., W. Schultze, and D. Brookshire. 1982. Carbon dioxide and intergenerational choice. *American Economic Review* 72:251–256.
Davenport, D. 1997. Compensation for biodiversity preservation: Questions raised by the biodiversity convention. *Ecological Economics* (forthcoming).
Davidson, I. 1993. Archaeology in the Selwyn Ranges. In *People of the Stone Age,* ed. G. Burenhult. New York: Harper Collins.

DeBellevue, E., E. Hitzel, K. Cline, J. Benitiez, J. Ramos-Miranda, and O. Segura. 1994. The North American Free Trade Agreement: An ecological–economic synthesis for the United States and Mexico. *Ecological Economics* 9:53–71.

Diamond, J. 1995. Easter's end. *Discover* 16:62–69.

Edwards, S. 1987. In defense of environmental economics. *Environmental Ethics* 10:55–74.

Ekins, P., C. Folke, and R. Costanza. 1994. Trade, environment, and development: The issues in perspective. *Ecological Economics* 9:1–12.

Gadgil, M., F. Berkes, and C. Folke. 1993. Indigenous knowledge for biodiversity conservation. *Ambio* 22:151–156.

Georgescu-Roegen, N. 1968. Utility. In *The International Encyclopedia of the Social Sciences,* vol. 16. New York: MacMillan.

Georgescu-Roegen, N. 1976. *Energy and Economic Myths.* New York: Pergamon Press.

Gowdy, J. 1994. *Coevolutionary Economics: The Economy, Society and the Environment.* Boston: Kluwer Academic Press.

Gowdy, J. and S. O'Hara. 1995. *Economic Theory for Environmentalists.* Delray Beach, FL: St. Lucie Press.

Graham, R. and E. Lundelius, Jr. 1984. Coevolutionary disequilibrium. In *Quaternary Extinctions,* eds. P. Martin and R. Klein. Tucson: University of Arizona Press.

Gurr, T. 1985. On the political consequences of scarcity and economic decline. *International Studies Quarterly* 29: 51–75.

Hage, P. and F. Harary. 1991. *Exchange in Oceania.* New York: Oxford University Press.

Hage, P., F. Harary, and B. James. 1986. Wealth and hierarchy in the Kula ring. *American Anthropologist* 88:108–114.

Hanley, N. and C. Spash. 1993. *Cost–Benefit Analysis and the Environment.* Brookfield, Vermont: Edward Elgar.

Harris, M. 1978. *Cannibals and Kings.* New York: Random House.

Hines, C. 1990. *Green Protectionism: Halting the Four Horsemen of the Free Trade Apocalypse.* London: Earth Resources Institute.

Homer-Dixon, T. 1991. On the threshold: Environmental changes as causes of acute conflict. *International Security* 16:76–116

Hueting, R. 1991. The use of the discount rate in a cost–benefit analysis for different uses of a humid tropical forest. *Ecological Economics* 3:43-58

Irwin, G. J. 1983. Chieftainship, Kula, and trade in Massim prehistory. In *The Kula: New Perspectives in Massim Exchange,* eds. J. W. Leach and E. Leach. Cambridge: Cambridge University Press.

Kottak, C. 1972. A cultural adaptive approach to Malagasy political organization. In *Social Exchange and Interaction,* ed. E. N. Wilsen. Lansing: University of Michigan Anthropological Papers 46:107–28.

Krugman, P. 1987. Is free trade passe? *Journal of Economic Perspectives* 1:131–144.

Lea, L. 1994. GATT justice: Who gets the gains of trade? *Challenge* September/October, 11–17.

Loy, T. 1993. From stone to tools: Residue analysis. In *The First Humans,* ed. G. Burenhult. New York: Harper Collins.

Malinowski, B. 1961 [1922]. *Argonauts of the Western Pacific.* New York: E. P. Dutton.

Malone, C., A. Bonanno, T. Gouder, S. Stoddart, and D. Trump. 1993. The death cults of prehistoric Malta. *Scientific American* 269:110–117.

Martinez-Alier, J. 1993. On the valuation of wild and agricultural biological diversity. Working Paper, Universitat Autnoma de Barcelona.

Martinez-Alier, J. 1994. The merchandising of biodiversity. *Ethnoecologica* 2:69–86.

Martinez-Alier, J. 1995. The environment as a luxury good or too poor to be green. *Ecological Economics* 13:1–10.

Meillassoux, C. 1971. *The Development of Indigenous Trade and Markets in West Africa.* London: Oxford University Press.

Milicic, B. 1993. Exchange and social stratification in the Eastern Adriatic: A graph-theoretic model. *Ethnology* 375–395.

Norgaard, R. 1988. The rise of the global exchange economy and the loss of biological diversity. In *Biodiversity,* ed. E. O. Wilson. Washington, DC: National Academy Press.

Nordhaus, W. 1992. An optimal transition path for controlling greenhouse gases. *Science* 258:1315–1319.

O'Hara, S. 1994. Economic aggression – ecological destruction. Paper presented at the International Sociology Association Conference, Bielefeld, Netherlands, July.

Orr, David. 1992. *Ecological Literacy.* Albany: SUNY Press.

Peregrine, P. 1991. A graph theoretical approach to the evolution of Cahokia. *American Antiquity* 56: 67–75.

Phillips, D. 1993. *The Case Against Free Trade.* San Francisco: Earth Island Press.

Ponting, C. 1991. *A Green History of the World.* New York: Penguin Books.

Posey, D. 1985. Indigenous management of tropical forest ecosystems: The case of the Kayap Indians of the Brazilian Amazon. *Agroforestry Systems* 3:139–158.

Rappaport, R. 1979. *Ecology, Meaning, and Religion.* Berkeley: North Atlantic Books.

Røpke, I. 1994. Trade, development and sustainability: A critical assessment of the free trade dogma. *Ecological Economics* 9:13–22.

Sahlins, M. 1958. *Social Stratification in Polynesia. American Ethnological Society Monographs.* Seattle: University of Washington Press.

Sahlins, M. 1972. *Stone Age Economics.* Chicago: Aldine.

Samuelson, P. A. 1962. The gains from international trade once again. *Economic Journal* 72:820–829.

Samuelson, P. A. 1969. The gains from international trade once again. In *International Trade,* ed. J. Bhagwati. Harmondsworth: Penguin.

Shepard, P. 1973. *The Tender Carnivore and the Sacred Game.* New York: Charles Scribner's Sons.

Stiles, D. 1994. Tribals and trade: A strategy for cultural and ecological survival. *Ambio* 23:106–111.

van den Bergh, J. and P. Nijkamp. 1994. Sustainability, resources, and region. *The Annals of Regional Science* 28:1–5.

Verhoef, E. T. and C. J. M. van den Bergh. 1995. Transport, spatio-economic equilibrium and global sustainability: Markets, technology and policy. *Environment and Planning A.* (forthcoming).

Weiss, H., M.-A. Courty, W. Wetterstrom, F. Guichard, L. Senior, R. Meadow, and A. Currow. 1993. The genesis and collapse of third millennium North Mesopotamian civilization. *Science* 261:995–1004.

Woodburn, J. 1982. Egalitarian societies. *Man* 17:431–451.

Yellen, J. 1990. The transformation of the Kalahari! Kung. *Scientific American* April, 72–79.

Young, M. 1994. Ecologically-accelerated trade liberalization: A set of disciplines for environment and trade agreements. *Ecological Economics* 9:43–51.

9 SUSTAINABLE AGRICULTURE AND RURAL DEVELOPMENT IN CHINA: PAST EXPERIENCES AND FUTURE POTENTIAL

Futian Qu
College of Land Management
Nanjing Agricultural University
China

Arie Kuyvenhoven
Nico Heerink
Teunis van Rheenen
Department of Development Economics
Agricultural University of Wageningen
Wageningen, Netherlands

INTRODUCTION

As a new strategy sustainable development has become part of the agricultural policy framework in many countries. Due to its complexity and the diversity of prevailing situations in different countries, the implementation of sustainable development policies in less-developed countries (LDCs) faces crucial problems related to food shortages, farmers' poverty, and severe environmental degradation. Apart from the limited availability of resources to apply policy instruments that promote sustainable agriculture, the real difficulty in most LDCs is the lack of experience with integrating sustainable agriculture and rural development, and in particular with the choice of goals and appropriate strategic measures of sustainable agriculture policies.

China is the world's largest developing country. With only 0.08 ha of agricultural land per capita, however, its land is scarce. In 1990, cereals output per capita amounted to 322 kg. Over the past three decades China has adopted yield-increasing, high external-input production technologies to complement its traditional organic technologies and practices in order to match food output with increasing population pressure. According to FAO-estimates, fertilizer use per ha of arable land has increased from 42 kg in 1970 to 301 kg in 1993, a level approximately equal to that of the United Kingdom and higher than that of France, Germany, or Denmark (World Bank 1985, 1995). China's efforts to increase food production and to meet other socioeconomic objectives have certainly had a destructive impact on the environment through serious soil erosion, increasing desertification, and intensified environmental pollution. To address these problems, since the beginning of the 1980s, China has increasingly paid attention to practices of sustainable agriculture[1] to suit its own national conditions. The development of sustainable agriculture gradually evolved into a process characterized by goals that integrate socioeconomic benefits and ecological objectives, and comprehensive measures that combine rural transformation (in particular structural changes and poverty alleviation) with sustainable development. These characteristics, arising from the prevailing situation in China and differing from those of developed countries, have had significant effects on the rural environment and its development during the past decade.

Problems of food shortage, rural poverty and a degrading environmental base during the process of agricultural development and rural transformation are typical for many LDCs. In this chapter, the characteristics of sustainable agriculture in China are compared with those in developed countries with the purpose to draw some general conclusions with regard to the goals and strategic options of sustainable agriculture in LDCs. The characteristics of sustainable agriculture in China are also discussed and compared with those of sustainable agriculture practices in developed countries. From this comparison, a number of conclusions are drawn with respect to the development of sustainable agriculture in other LDCs. Next, the impact of sustainable agriculture practices on rural development in China is examined. The section starts with an analysis of economic and environmental achievements thus far, and subsequently discusses a number of unaddressed environmental problems that will have to be taken up in the near future. Finally, we present some strategic suggestions for dealing with remaining problems in China's sustainable agriculture.

CHARACTERISTICS OF SUSTAINABLE AGRICULTURE IN CHINA

The Development of Sustainable Agriculture in China

The practice of sustainable agriculture in China began by the end of the 1970s and has since undergone three successive phases. The first phase or preparatory period can be defined as the period from 1980 to 1983. It is characterized by academic preparation, particularly the definition and classification of basic concepts and major functions of sustainable agriculture, and by the organization of scientific and technical personnel in order to start pilot research projects.

The second phase, from 1983 to 1986, can be characterized as a period of intensive experimentation and demonstration. By 1986, 300 experimental sites had been set up. The third phase, from 1987 to the present, is the demonstration and extension period. This period is characterized by the strengthening of the demonstration farms or sites and massive extension. By 1990, about 29 sustainable agriculture pilot units had been set up at the county level, 138 at the township level and more than 1,200 at the village or farm levels (Table 9.1). The purpose of these pilot units is to carry out the experimentation and demonstration of sustainable agriculture programs. They are scattered over all provinces and municipalities in Mainland China, except for the Tibet Autonomous Region. As a result of massive demonstration and extension efforts, we expect to see increasing numbers of areas, at different levels, incorporated into sustainable agriculture in the near future.

Table 9.1. Recent Development of Sustainable Agriculture Pilot Units in China

	Pilot Level			Pilot area (million ha)		Population
Year	County	Town	Village	Arable land	Forest / grass land	(million)
1988	14	27	429	1.69	0.17	13.14
1990	29	138	1200	2.09	1.11	25.61

Source: The Ministry of Agriculture PRC; Sun (1993).

China's sustainable agriculture can be characterized as a comprehensive agrosystem. It is based on a multitiered and multipurpose intensive management system and draws on successful experiences with agricultural practices, especially those of China's traditional organic farming. This agrosystem is designed and managed in accordance with ecological and economic principles and systematic agrotechnical and biophysical methodology and by applying advanced science and technology. Three principles are stressed (Luo and Han 1990).

1. The protection and conservation of natural resources and environment are the foundation for sustainable agricultural productivity; at the same time, food security and sufficient income generation are prerequisites for reducing the pressure on the environment.

2. Important relationships exist between different components within the agro-ecosystem and between the agro-ecosystem and its physical and socioeconomic environment.

3. Agricultural resources should be saved and recycled within the production system in order to reduce the negative impact of external inputs and production wastes on the environment and to lower the production costs of agricultural products.

The Implementation of Ecological–Economic Principles

As an important alternative to industrial agriculture (which is based on mechanization, chemical input use, and new crop technologies), the concept of sustainable agriculture was first proposed in the United States in the early 1980s (Harwood 1990). According to Parr et al. (1990), a workable concept of sustainable agriculture is a low-input farming system that seeks to optimize the management and use of internal production inputs (i.e., on-farm resources) in ways that provide sustainable crop production yields and livestock production and result in acceptable income levels. This low-input farming system emphasizes such farm management practices as crop rotation, recycling of animal manure, and conservation tillage to control soil erosion and nutrient losses and to maintain or enhance soil productivity. In developed countries sustainable agriculture implies many synonymous concepts or systems, including biological, biodynamic, ecological, ecobiological, low-input, low resources, organic, and regenerative agriculture. Each urges low chemical resources and energy conserving and resource efficient farming methods and technologies. In fact, sustainable agriculture in North America is mainly a low-input farming system, while biodynamic agriculture is the dominant form of sustainable agriculture in Western Europe.

Many aspects of sustainable agriculture in China, especially the overall goals and measures to achieve these goals, are similar to those in developed countries (Cheng and Taylor 1992). Both types have a definite holistic system orientation. Both are concerned with the long-term environmental sustainability and economic viability of the agricultural production system. Both give major attention to crop rotation and other soil-building practices. Both emphasize man as an ally with nature, rather than man trying to conquer nature.

In some important respects, however, China's sustainable agriculture differs from that practiced in developed countries. These differences are to a large extent determined by the basic physical and socioeconomic conditions of the country (see Table 9.2). First of all, the objectives are given different priorities. In developed countries, the priority of sustainable agriculture is mostly given to the improvement of the ecological/environmental base, even to the extent of sacrificing output or other economic objectives. This may be possible in developed countries because of over-cultivation of the soil, vast surpluses of agricultural products, higher prices for ecological products, and available resources for subsidizing farmers. Thus, the economic objective of sustainable agriculture in developed countries may be an acceptable level of sustainable crop yields and livestock production that results in economically profitable returns. Even if crop yields from low-input farming systems are lower than existing ones, the bottom line is whether an acceptable net return can be obtained with the lower yield (Parr et al. 1990). Some reports indicate that the yield or total income of sustainability-oriented farms in America and Switzerland is lower by 5%–17% compared to existing agriculture (Sun 1993).

Table 9.2. Some Basic Indicators for China and Other Selected Countries (1989–1990)

Countries	Population density (hbts/km²)	Per capita GNP (US $)	Per capita GDP (Int'l $ ICP)	Agricultural land per capita (ha)	Per capita cereals output (kg)	Fertilizer use (kg/ha)
China	119	370	1,950	0.08	322	262
India	258	350	1,150	0.20	235	69
Indonesia	94	570	2,350	1.22	286	117
Japan	327	25,430	16,950	0.04	116	418
U.S.A.	27	21,790	21,360	0.07	1,137	99
Germany	223	23,320	16,290	0.10	328	317

Source: World Bank (1992).

In China, however, with the prevalence of rural poverty and food shortages, more emphasis is given to "win–win" solutions in which output and income increase while the resource base is maintained and improved. According to the World Bank, per capita cereals output in China was only 322 kg in 1990 (see Table 9.2). With continuing population growth, the growing demand for food has to be met by highly productive, sustainable agriculture (provided China does not want to rely on the world food market to feed its immense population). If not, environmental degradation will intensify, and social security will be threatened because of insufficient food supply.

An important goal of sustainable agriculture development in China is income generation. In 1990, per capita GNP in China was only US$370.[2] Net income per capita of farm households was about US$130. Rural poverty is not only indicative of agricultural backwardness, but is also closely related to environmental degradation. For example, during the period from 1981 to 1983, 225 counties in China (out of a total of more than 2,200 counties) were below the poverty level, had an annual average per capita income of less than 200 yuan (about US$100) and a per capita grain production of only 200 kg per year. All of these counties are located in the serious soil erosion regions in China (Wen, 1993). Sustainable agriculture in China should evidently contribute to income generation at the farm household level. Otherwise, its viability is likely to disappear because of lack of participation by farmers. The focus of sustainable agriculture in China on income generation guarantees to a large extent the integration of economic objectives at the farm household level with food security and ecological objectives at the national or regional level.

A second difference of sustainable agriculture between China and developed countries lies in the strategy and the *industrial organization* of sustainable agriculture. Because of its limited land resources, China's strategy for promoting sustainability in agriculture focuses on a broad structural adjustment of the agro-ecosystem and an optimization of regional resource allocation. It not only takes into consideration the horizontal relations between agricultural sectors (cropping, forestry, animal husbandry, and fishery), but also the vertical relations between primary activities and agro-processing in order to ensure a balanced development of the entire system in which each sector promotes higher efficiency in other sectors. Within each farm or village, crop production is combined with other activities (e.g., animal production, forestry, or agro-processing in order to minimize nutrient losses and to integrate biological and economic circles). Accordingly, an efficient industrial organization is an important characteristic of China's sustainable agriculture, in which economic integration through the creation of industrial links increases agricultural productivity and product value and improves the profitability of sustainable agriculture. In developed countries, however, the macro strategy of sustainable agriculture usually focuses on some specific environmental problems or activities and on the legislation of agricultural environmental protection rather than on a broad structural adjustment of the agro-ecosystem. As a result, industrial organization of sustainable agriculture is mainly confined to crop planting and animal breeding with a focus on soil and water conservation.

A third significant difference between sustainable agriculture in China and developed countries is the intensive input system. Unlike many developed countries, China emphasizes the necessity of high external input use in agriculture. Consequently, appropriate use of chemical fertilizers and pesticides is not excluded from the input systems (see also Table 9.2), and extensive use is made of modern agrotechnical and biophysical science in sustainable agriculture. A fundamental reason for the relatively low emphasis on reduced chemical fertilizer use in China is the much smaller difference between the nutritional need and economic demand for food and the capacity to produce food in China compared to most Western countries (Cheng and Taylor 1992). Compared with developed countries, large output increases can be obtained when external input is raised because agricultural input use is too low in most agricultural areas of China (as a result of credit unavailability or other factors). Estimates from

Chen and Zhang (1990) based on data from 1983 to 1987 indicate, for example, that the elasticity of wheat output with respect to chemical fertilizer input equals 9.60 on the average for the country. For labor, the elasticity equals 4.69 and for other inputs (machines, pesticides, and irrigation) the elasticity equals 7.79. These results imply a great potential of increasing wheat output through increased use of external input. Evidently, increases in the levels of input use, particularly of chemical inputs, may cause environmental damage like soil and water pollution. The societal costs of this damage will have to be weighted against the costs in terms of reduced food production of lower chemical input use in agriculture.

Thus, sustainable agriculture in China at present may be characterized as intensive, high external-input sustainable agriculture (HEISA). It is a logical result of the prevailing physical, economic, and demographic conditions in China.[3] The most important form of sustainable agriculture in developed countries, on the other hand, is called low external-input sustainable agriculture (LEISA). In Western Europe and North America most of the relevant literature discourages the use of agrochemicals and fossil fuels and advocates greater reliance on animal and green manure, leaf mulch and crop residues so as to lower the risk of farmer management, to reduce pollution and to improve soil quality (Hulse 1991).

Finally, sustainable development in China is characterized by effective initiation and intervention by the government. The government was the initial and primary moving force underlying the recent thrust toward sustainable agriculture in China, beginning during the late 1970s. Because of the prevalent socioeconomic system in China – characterized by food procurement, guaranteed prices for many crops, and absence of agricultural land markets – price policy is not a real option for stimulating sustainable agriculture development. Since 1985, sustainable agriculture has been incorporated into the agricultural and rural development planning of every province and region. In 1989, special departments of the Ministry of Agriculture (MA) and the State Environmental Protection Agency (SEPA) were identified to carry out experimentation and extension. With government support, specific (green label) markets were created for certain products based on sustainable agriculture. Sustainable agricultural practices in developed countries, on the other hand, are to a large extent spontaneous, scattered activities of pressure groups, researchers, and farmers. In the U.S., for example, significant initiatives in the private sector (e.g., by the Rodale Institute) preceded by decades the government promotion of sustainable agriculture that started in the mid-1980s (Cheng and Taylor 1992).

The foregoing comparison of sustainable agriculture between China and developed countries has been summarized in Table 9.3.

Table 9.3. A Comparison of Sustainable Agriculture (SA) Between China and
Developed Countries

Items	SA in Developed Countries	SA in China
Emphasis of goals	Protecting environment and maintaining resource base with acceptable yield of return	Integration of raising yield and income, and improving ecological and social impacts
Strategic options	Environmental protection through specific projects, legislation, and market intervention	Broad structural adjustment of agro-ecosystem and optimization of regional resource allocation
Industrial organization	Cropping and breeding focusing on soil conservation and water resource protection	Integrated development of cropping, forestry, processing and environmental engineering
Input use	Low external-input, self-maintaining system with much emphasis on reduced chemical use	Intensive use of modern techniques, labor, and chemical inputs
Development and organization	Spontaneous and scattered activities of individual groups; sluggish promotion by government	Government initiates supports, and directly intervenes

Contribution of China's Sustainable Agriculture Towards the Goals of the Den Bosch Declaration: Some Experiences

There has been a debate about the socioeconomic viability of low-input sustainable agriculture[4] even in developed countries. Ruttan (1991) has proposed that the strategy of sustainable development should be changed from the *preventist* to the *adaptionist*. The first urges the reduction of fossil fuel use, the intensity of agricultural production and biomass burning. The latter implies moving as rapidly as possible to design and put in place institutions needed to remove the constraints that intensification of agricultural production is currently imposing on sustainable increases in production. When Crosson (1991) discusses sustainable agriculture in North America, he defines it as a production system "which meets demand for food and fibre into the indefinite future at economic, environmental, and social costs which do not imperil the per capita welfare of present or future generations."

For most LDCs low output never becomes a feasible option for achieving sustainable agricultural development because of its adverse effects on farmers' incomes and food security. For that reason, the Den Bosch Declaration (FAO and LNV 1991) has developed the concept of sustainable agriculture and rural development (SARD). Because "underdevelopment, poverty, and the social inequalities of the rural world" are recognized as the "root of the problem" of unsustainable land use, the essential goals of SARD are defined as "food security"; "employment and income generation in rural areas, particularly to eradicate poverty"; and "natural resource conservation and environmental protection." The Declaration also highlights several "fundamental changes and adjustments" needed to achieve these goals: a greater role in the design and implementation of development projects for farmers and local farm-based organizations; the need for a plurality of institutions and new forms of cooperation among government, NGOs, and rural leaders in decision making; clearer rights to land and other natural resources; new investments in natural resource conservation; and changes in macroeconomic and agricultural policies (FAO and LNV 1991; Benbrook 1991).

From the analysis of its characteristics, it follows that China's sustainable agriculture is rather close to the FAO concept of SARD. Most importantly, the emphasis of essential goals in China's sustainable agriculture is similar to that of SARD. Furthermore, the attempts to broaden the agro-industrial organization have, in fact, combined sustainable agriculture and rural development. It can therefore be concluded that China's sustainable agriculture would fit well into the implementation of SARD.

Reviewing the previous analysis of China's sustainable agriculture, some useful conclusions can be drawn for the implementation of SARD in other LDCs. First of all, the determination of the goals regarding SARD should depend on a country's physical and socioeconomic situation as indicated by the ratio of population to land, the level and manner of agricultural production, the living standard of farmers, the phase of rural transformation and the available economic resources. For many LDCs, the most crucial problem is a chronic shortage of food and the prevalence of rural poverty. Import of food is usually no real alternative, because it makes great demands on scarce foreign exchange reserves. Meeting increasing food demand and improving farmers' income should therefore be incorporated into the goal system of sustainable development. With increasing population pressure, most LDCs cannot afford to rely on low-input agriculture (Hulse 1991). Thus LEISA is not feasible in areas with high population pressure; HEISA is a better alternative.

Secondly, sustainable agriculture should be incorporated into the entire rural transformation process. Rural industrialization and urbanization in LDCs will change both the location and the magnitude of ecological or environmental problems in the future. These changes should be taken into consideration in the choice of structure design and measures to achieve sustainable agriculture. The industrial organization of sustainable agriculture in China, especially the integration of processing and environmental engineering industry in China's sustainable agriculture, supplies useful experiences to realize this objective (Qu and Liu 1988).

Finally, active instigation and effective intervention by the government is another important aspect. Sustainable development deals with reducing the externalities of economic activities and cannot be realized without effective government intervention. Especially in LDCs, where poverty and environmental ignorance of farmers are pervasive, government initiation and intervention is necessary to achieve sustainable development in agriculture. On the other hand, government policies intended to promote nonenvironmental goals may themselves be an important cause of environmental damage. Promotion of sustainable agriculture development may therefore also necessitate reforms of nonenvironmental policies, such as price policies or industrialization policies (e.g., Gillis et al. 1993).

IMPACT OF SUSTAINABLE AGRICULTURE ON RURAL DEVELOPMENT IN CHINA

Economic and Environmental Achievements

Since the late 1970s, the number of pilot units of sustainable agriculture in China has reached nearly 1,400, and the number of sustainable agriculture households in the country is going up too. For example, in Sichuan Province alone there are at least 10,000 such households. Furthermore, most of the nation's provinces, municipalities, and autonomous regions are continuing to expand demonstration units. At the moment, 5% of rural laborers are involved in sustainable agriculture practices (Sun 1993). The pilot projects have been successful in most areas.[5]

The introduction of sustainable agriculture practices during the last decade has had significant effects on agricultural environment and rural development. The most important achievement, however, is that sustainable development has become a dominant strategy for agricultural modernization and rural transformation. The successful adjustment of the agricultural structure from the beginning of the 1980s, for instance, is largely a result of the strategic transition towards sustainable agriculture. During the adjustment, cultivation practices on environmentally sensitive soils such as marginal lands, steep lands, and wetlands has changed from cropping to forestry or grass. Mono-planting of grain in farming, which led to serious soil erosion and nutrient depletion, has been replaced by a diversified structure of cropping with a wider range of ecological suitability. Recently, 46 million ha of land with serious soil erosion (i.e., one third of the total land area in China) has been placed under conservation programs which, to a large extent, consist of the technical systems of sustainable agriculture. Preliminary results of pilot areas in the Loess Plateau indicate that structural changes from cropping to planting trees, shrubs, and grasses have reduced the soil erosion rates by 70%–80% (Wen 1993). With increasing output and economic benefits, the ecological instability of agricultural production in China is more and more controlled.

A second important effect is the fact that more labor can be used in sustainable agriculture. According to available survey information, labor absorption in pilot areas has increased by 10–20% (Zhang and Qu 1992). Although the creation of employment opportunities will to a large extent depend on off-farm development and urbanization, the potential of sustainable agriculture for absorbing more surplus labor will be of great significance for rural development. Another effect of sustainable development is the emergence of an "ecological market." The production of ecological products which contain little chemical residues has been included into the sustainable agriculture program. Its production is located in areas least polluted by industry. In addition, increasing numbers of green label products have emerged in markets. Some ecological products such as tea, vegetables, and fruits have been exported abroad. Thus, ecological products with a higher economic value are being accepted in the market as a new way to realize sustainability, especially in relatively developed areas.

Improved benefits and higher income generation turn out to be feasible in most pilot areas of sustainable agriculture. In China, the important options adopted in sustainable agriculture refer to a better use of external inputs and to more industrial diversity of the agro-ecosystem. Intensive input use has resulted in high agricultural output and improved food security which have, to some extent, alleviated the pressure of population growth on environmental resources. Adjustment of the industrial structure according to ecological–economic principles has not only maintained the natural resource base, but has also contributed to higher, more diversified and more stable incomes. According to McLaughlin (1993), in Dingxi County (Gansu Province) the elasticity of income with respect to soil conservation practices (terrace construction and use of biological methods) was 0.76 during the period from 1982 to 1986. An evaluation of integrated ecological–economic benefits of two typical pilot areas of sustainable agriculture (at the county level and the village level) made by Zhang and Qu (1992) indicates that, with ecological improvement, the economic benefits have also increased considerably (see Table 9.4).

Table 9.4. Integrated Evaluation of Sustainable Agriculture in Wenxi County and Chuanziying Village

Index of Benefits[*]	Wenxi County			Chuanziying Village		
	1983	1986	1989	1982	1986	1990
Ecological benefit	0.072	0.292	0.185	0.107	0.526	0.689
Economic benefit	0.275	0.409	0.706	0.000	0.467	0.881
Social benefit	0.018	0.482	0.538	0.000	0.492	0.976
Integrated benefit[**]	0.148	0.398	0.763	0.046	0.474	0.832

[*]The indices of ecological, economic, and social benefits are derived from a number of indicators of ecological, economic, and social benefits, respectively.

[**]The integrated index is a well-weighted average of ecological, economic, and social benefit indicators. See Zhang and Qu (1992) for more details.

With the implementation of sustainable agriculture programs, more advanced techniques are applied to agricultural production. The increasing demand for new technologies is likely to lead to a further technical transformation in agriculture. So far, new microtechniques such as genetic and ferment engineering are increasingly applied.

Remaining Problems in China's Sustainable Agriculture

Despite these recent achievements, a number of problems exist that will continue to affect agricultural sustainability in the near future. First of all, the still increasing population pressure is intensifying the friction between population and resources. Although the population increase has been checked since the beginning of the 1970s, population growth is still 1.4%. Population projections for 2000 and 2025 amount to 1.3 and 1.5 billion, respectively (Lu 1992). Soil overcultivation and marginal land development will remain major obstacles in realizing sustainability, especially in the south and northwest of China. According to estimates of the Chinese Academy of Sciences in 1989, the area in which food demand of the population exceeds the carrying capacity of land resources now occupies 38% of the total area of China. The area comprises 22% of the total arable land and 27% of the total population (Hu and Wang 1989).

The second problem concerns the acceleration of rural industrialization and its environmental pollution, in particular of water resources. As a major component of rural transformation, rural industry has increased by 28.5% annually from 1978 to 1993 and its value now equals 37% and 70% of national output and rural output, respectively. Pollution arising from rural industrialization has a serious impact on the agricultural resource base. In 1989, 1.83 billion tons of wastewater was spilled out, only 16.3% of which had been treated according to official criteria because of limited equipment and funds. The experiences of the U.S. and Japan indicate that effective treatment of environmental pollution may start when GNP per capita reaches middle-income levels (Ye and Peng 1992). Assuming that China's development will follow a similar pattern, this would imply that more intensive pollution arising from rural industry will be inevitable for a considerable period. Furthermore, the scattered distribution of rural industry with few linkages with agro-processing and the more rapid diffusion of pollution to arable land will lead to relatively more serious and direct environmental damage to soil and water resources.

The instable economic policy is another problem affecting sustainable development of agriculture. The dispersed and small-scale land units limit the creation of a rational economic sector structure and the public action necessary for resource conservation and ecological projects. China's fluctuating price policy affects the stability and sustainability of the agro-ecosystem. Investments are increasingly shifted from agriculture to the nonagricultural sectors because of significant differences in benefits between the two sectors arising from policies that depress relative prices in agriculture. The current system of land property rights frustrates farmers' incentives to conserve or protect land resources (Qu, Heerink, and Wang 1995). In addition, the policy of lagged urbanization that retains labor on overcultivated land increases population and employment pressures on the environment.

CONCLUSIONS AND RECOMMENDATIONS

Sustainable agriculture in China differs in a number of respects from sustainable agricultural practices in developed countries. These differences arise from China's different physical and socioeconomic conditions, such as the high population pressure, the long history of farming, the primary phase of agricultural development, and the household management of very small-scale land units. Important characteristics of sustainable agriculture in China are the high importance attached to the goals of food security and income generation, the diversified structure of agro-ecosystems, the integration of different agricultural sectors and agro-processing industry at the farm and village level, the intensive external input use, and the instigation and intervention by the government. Thus, sustainable agriculture in China is close to the concept of sustainable agriculture and rural development (SARD) proposed by the FAO, and may serve as a good example of its implementation.

During the last couple of decades, the upsurge of sustainable agriculture accomplished some important achievements with respect to the agricultural environment and rural development in China. Sustainable development has become the main strategy of agricultural and rural transformation. The agricultural structure has been transformed accordingly. An integrated system of techniques in sustainable agriculture results in innovation and application of new techniques. Ecological product markets, such as the market for green label products, emerge in more developed areas. The more intensive use of labor in sustainable agriculture alleviates to some extent employment pressures caused by increasing population in the rural areas. In most sustainable agriculture programs, output and farmers' incomes have increased while simultaneously improving and maintaining the natural resource base and environmental quality.

Several problems, however, stand in the way of a further realization of sustainable agricultural development. Among them are the increasing population size, the accelerating rural industrialization, and the unstable economic policies. In order to deal with these problems, appropriate adjustments of strategy and policy are needed. Creating an avenue in which rural surplus labor can be shifted to nonagricultural sectors and urban areas offers great potential for alleviating population and employment pressure on land resources. Rural industry should be concentrated more and the development of small- to medium-size cities or towns should be given priority. Meanwhile, innovation and application of new techniques of pollution prevention and treatment should be promoted. Providing the necessary economic incentives to farmers for practicing sustainability and stabilizing the structure and functions of the agro-ecosystem should be the objectives of economic policy reform. With market reform and price liberalization, prices that are important for maintaining the resource base and agro-ecosystem stability should be set at levels such that serious fluctuations of the agro-ecosystem can be avoided. On the other hand, ecological markets or green food markets should be promoted so that markets that maintain natural resources and the environment can be developed into effectively functioning markets. Sustainable development also requires investment and credit availability for vast numbers of small farmers. Thus, investment promotion and credit policies directed toward sustainable agriculture are needed. Finally, land property rights and land use policy should be further reformed so that effective and secure land rights can be established, which will stimulate farmers to maintain resources and achieve sustainable development.

ACKNOWLEDGMENTS

The authors wish to thank Philip G. Pardey, Ruerd Ruben, Jeroen van den Bergh, and Jan van der Straaten for their helpful comments on a previous drafts of this chapter.

FOOTNOTES

1. The alternative to the existing farming system since the end of the 1970s was originally called "ecological agriculture" in China. Because its concept and contents are different

from that of ecological agriculture in developed countries, more and more agricultural scientists and economists denote "ecological agriculture" in China as "sustainable agriculture" (Cheng and Taylor 1992; Lu 1992).

2. There is a widespread presumption that Chinese GNP data seriously underestimate production and consumption, substantially more than the common underestimation in LDCs. Estimates of GDP per capita, based on purchasing power parities (PPP) instead of exchange rates as conversion factors, give an indication of the extent of overestimation. These estimates are presented in Table 9.2. Per capita GDP in China is estimated to be around $1,950 in 1990, that is more than five times the conventional GNP p.c. estimate. For India and Indonesia, the PPP-estimates equal three to four times the conventional GNP p.c. estimates. The differences with per capita GDP estimates for developed countries, however, remain very large.

3. A similar conclusion has been drawn from a study on Africa by Van Keulen and Breman (1990). They argue that input use in Sahel countries can alleviate soil mining and stimulate the sustainability of agriculture. Thus a new concept, HEISA, is proposed as an alternative for LEISA.

4. For a discussion of suitable methods for economic appraisal of low-input sustainable agriculture, see Ruben and Heerink (1995).

5. Four villages in China won the top prize of the global environmental project award from the UNEP between 1987 and 1991 for their outstanding achievements in sustainable agriculture development.

REFERENCES

Benbrook, C. 1991. Grappling with the challenges of sustainability: The Den Bosch Declaration. *Canadian Journal of Agricultural Economics* 39:581–586.

Chen, S. and Y. Zhang. 1990. Degrading land and losing arable land in China. In China's Association of Science & Technology, Study on Land Degradation in China. Beijing: China Science and Technology Press. [In Chinese]

Cheng, X. and D. C. Taylor. 1992. Sustainable agriculture development in China. *World Development* 20:1127–1144.

Crosson, P. 1991. Sustainable agriculture in North America: Issues and challenges. *Canadian Journal of Agricultural Economics* 39:553–565.

FAO and the Ministry of Agriculture, Nature Management and Fisheries of the Netherlands (LNV), 1991. *The Den Bosch Declaration and Agenda for Action on Sustainable Agriculture and Rural Development.* Rome: FAO.

Gillis, M. et al. 1993. *Economics of Development,* 3rd edition. New York : W. W. Norton.

Harwood, R. R. 1990. A history of sustainable agriculture. In *Sustainable Agricultural Systems,* eds. C. A. Edwards et al. Ankeny: Soil and Water Conservation Society.

Hu, A. and Y. Wang. 1989. *Existence and Development.* Beijing: Science Press. [In Chinese]

Hulse, J. H. 1991. Global perspectives on sustainable development: Implications for agriculture. *Canadian Journal of Agricultural Economics* 39:541–551.

Lu, L. 1992. Development and perspectives of sustainable agriculture. *Agricultural Tech-economics* 2:1–4. [In Chinese]

Luo, S. and C. Han. 1990. Ecological agriculture in China. In *Sustainable Agricultural Systems,* eds. C. A. Edwards et al. Ankeny: Soil and Water Conservation Society.

McLaughlin, L. 1993. A case study in Dingxi County, Gansu Province, China. In *World Soil Erosion and Conservation,* ed. D. Pimentel. Cambridge: Cambridge University Press.

Parr, J. F. et al. 1990. Sustainable agriculture in the United States. In *Sustainable Agricultural Systems,* eds. C. A. Edwards et al. Ankeny: Soil and Water Conservation Society.

Qu, F., N. Heerink, and W. Wang. 1995. Land administration reform in China: Its impact on land allocation and economic development. *Land Use Policy* 12:193–203

Qu, F. and S. Liu. 1988. Rural industry and eco-economic construction in China. In *Proceedings of International Agro-eco-engineering Conference*, ed. H. Sun. Beijing.

Ruben, R. and N. Heerink. 1995. Economic evaluation of LEISA farming. *ILEIA Newsletter* 11(2):18–20.

Ruttan, V. W. 1991. Constraints on sustainable growth in agricultural production: into the 21st century. *Canadian Journal of Agricultural Economics* 39:567–580.

Sun, H. 1993. *Theory and Methodology of Ecological Agriculture Jinan*. Shandong Science and Technology Press. [In Chinese]

Van Keulen, H. and H. Breman. 1990. Agricultural development in the West African Sahelian region: A cure against land hunger agriculture. *Ecosystems and Environment* 32:177–197.

Wen, D. 1993. Soil erosion and conservation in China. In *World Soil Erosion and Conservation*, ed. D. Pimentel. Cambridge: Cambridge University Press.

World Bank. 1985. *World Development Report 1985*. Oxford: Oxford University Press.

World Bank. 1992. *World Development Report 1992*. Oxford: Oxford University Press.

World Bank. 1995. *World Development Report 1995*. Oxford: Oxford University Press.

Ye, X. and B. Peng. 1992. An analysis of the environmental economical characteristics of rural industrialization in China. *Eco-economics* 2:1–3. [In Chinese]

Zhang, R. and F. Qu. 1992. Theory and methodology of the evaluation of sustainable agriculture. *Jiangsu Rural Economics* Special Issue. [In Chinese]

10 STRUCTURAL CHANGE, GROWTH, AND DEMATERIALIZATION: AN EMPIRICAL ANALYSIS

Sander de Bruyn
Jeroen van den Bergh
Department of Spatial Economics
Free University, De Boelelaan 1105
1081 HV Amsterdam, The Netherlands

Hans Opschoor
Institute of Social Studies, The Hague, The Netherlands

INTRODUCTION

Sustainable development in an expanding economy requires that the detrimental effect of growth on the environment should continuously be compensated. Initially, remedial environmental technologies can be successful. When such opportunities have been exhausted, more fundamental technological and structural changes are required.

From this point of view, a preventive environmental policy may be aimed at stimulating structural change in the productive side of the economy, leading to changes in the consumption of materials and energy. Structural change implies a reduction in the resource input of production, so that materials throughput will be reduced and less emissions and waste may be generated (Simonis 1989). Such a strategy may play a decisive role in achieving sustainability because the application of end-of-pipe technology may not be sufficient to reduce emissions such as of carbon dioxide. Economic growth will eventually boost these emissions up to the point where irreversible environmental changes may occur. Environmental protection, especially in the long run, will therefore necessarily have to be conceived in terms of structural policy. This has been called the "ecological/economic imperative" (Jänicke, Monch, and Binder 1993).

Many studies note that in developed economies the consumption of several materials and energy has declined, both in relative (per unit of GDP) and in absolute terms. This phenomenon has been labeled as "dematerialization" (Schmidt-Bleek 1993), "ecological structural change" (Simonis 1989) or "de-linking" (Jänicke et al. 1989; Opschoor 1990). According to Simonis (1989) this "ecological structural change" is the result of a combination of process integrated investments that have led to a more efficient use of energy and materials, and a shift in the structure of final demand towards less polluting products.

This chapter explores the question whether the de-linking of materials and energy consumption from economic growth has actually occurred in developed economies. First, a review is given of contributions that have concluded that de-linking may have taken place in developed economies. Special attention will be given to the methodologies that have been implied in these studies and the implication of these methodologies for the interpretation of the observed developments. Next, new analyses will be given that suggest a development of re-linking (i.e., increases in materials and energy consumption in several developed economies since the mid-1980s). This suggestion is further investigated using time-series analysis on energy, steel, and cement consumption for Japan, the Netherlands, and the United States which identifies economic growth as an important determinant of material and energy consumption. More explanations on the observed developments are provided using a decomposition method that is being applied to energy consumption in the Netherlands. The analysis presented in this chapter will provide some insight into the driving forces behind apparent de-linking and re-linking tendencies in the data.

A REVIEW OF EMPIRICAL INVESTIGATIONS

There is a vast body of literature in resource economics on empirical studies of the consumption of materials and energy (Barnett and Morse 1973; Malenbaum 1978; Bossanyi 1979; Larson, Ross, and Williams1986; Tilton 1990). Many of these investigations indicate structural reductions in the demand for materials and energy since the first oil crisis. Often the concept of the intensity of use is applied, defined as the ratio between the physical inputs (materials) and monetary outputs (GDP). Malenbaum (1978) presents the hypothesis that the relationship between the intensity of use and income over time can be described as an inverted U. This has been called the "intensity of use hypothesis." More precisely, this states that the intensity of use increases in early stages of economic development, then reaches a turning point and finally declines. The last stage is often referred to as de-coupling or de-linking materials and energy consumption from economic growth.

Tilton (1986) elaborates these reasons for de-linking:

1. Technological change, such as materials' saving production techniques and the substitution of metals by lighter chemical products, and
2. Structural changes in the economy, such as the shift from an economy oriented towards heavy industry to an economy primarily relying on services.

The inverted-U curve and falling consumption of energy and materials relative to income in developed economies have been confirmed by empirical observations on metal use (Larson, Ross, and Williams 1986; Tilton 1990; Valdes 1990) and energy use (Bossanyi 1979; Chesshire 1986; Goldemberg 1992). Other empirical studies indicate that Third World countries (Radetzki 1990; Suslick and Harris 1990) and COMECON-economies (Jänicke et al. 1989; Dobozi 1990) did not experience such a de-linking. As described by the intensity-of-use hypothesis, this implies that they have not yet reached the turning points.

Simonis (1989), Jänicke et al. (1989), Jänicke, Monch, and Binder (1993), von Weizsacker and Schmidt-Bleek (1994) and others have interpreted these findings from an environmental perspective. They pointed out that by reducing the resource input of production less emissions and wastes will occur that have a negative impact on the natural environment. This can be related to Daly's (1991) emphasis on the reduction of throughput, defined as the entropic physical flow of matter-energy from natural sources, through the human economy and back to nature's sinks (Daly 1991).

Some empirical evidence for a reduction in throughput was found in Jänicke et al. (1989), who compared the changes in a weighted sum of four indicators: the per capita consumption[1] of steel; the per capita consumption of energy; the production of cement; and the tons freight-transport between 1970 and 1985 for 31 industrialized countries. These four indicators were regarded as an approximation of the volume of throughput of a country.[2] For 1970 and 1985, each indicator has been calculated as the percentual deviation from the sample mean in these two years. The resulting (dimensionless) indicators are then aggregated into an Index of Environmental Deterioration (IED), giving equal weighting to all indicators (see Appendix 1 on the calculation of the IED).

In a cross-section analysis, Jänicke et al. (1989) regress the IED on the level of income and then compare 1970 to 1985. The results of their analysis are given in Table 10.1 (t-statistics were not provided).

The table shows that per capita income in 1970 gave a much better explanation for the environmental index than in 1985: the slope is less steep in 1985 than in 1970 and the measure of strength has decreased substantially.[3] The explanation for the decreasing slope is that the volume of (approximated) throughput increased in the poorer countries (e.g., in Bulgaria, Greece, Portugal, and Turkey), whereas it decreased in several richer countries. The fact that the measure of strength has decreased can be explained by the divergent developments of middle-income socialist countries (Czechoslovakia, DDR, Hungary, and Poland), which showed a high growth in materials and energy consumption, while the growth in materials and energy consumption of middle-income countries of the OECD (Ireland, Italy, New Zealand, and Spain) declined. These

Table 10.1. Relationships Between IED and GDP for 31 Countries

Regression Equation: $IED_t = \alpha + \beta GDP_t + e_t$

Years	1970	1985
Slope β	0.17	0.046
Intercept α	−1.2362	−0.3951
Measure of strength R^2	0.57	0.09

Note: Per capita GDP is measured in 1,000 1980 US$. Table taken from Jänicke et al. (1989).

developments are depicted in Figure 10.1 where arrows indicate linearized changes between 1970 and 1985 for various countries.

The analysis by Jänicke et al. has been interpreted as evidence of de-linking materials and energy consumption from economic growth through structural change in developed economies (Simonis 1989; RIVM 1991; Von Weizsacker and Schmidt-Bleek 1994). Several economies (e.g., Belgium, Denmark, France, Sweden, United Kingdom, and West Germany) showed "absolute structural improvements" (Jänicke et al. 1989) (i.e., their approximated throughput declined in absolute levels despite the growth in GDP).

The cross-section analysis by Jänicke et al. (1989) is in fact equivalent to the intensity of use hypothesis, as can be seen by Figure 10.2. This figure gives hypothetical intensity of use curves for four countries (C1,...,C4) with a shift-

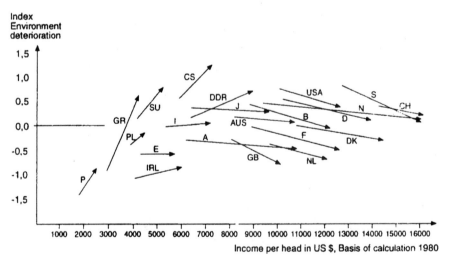

Source: von Weizsacker and Schmidt-Bleek (1994), after Jänicke et al. (1989).

Figure 10.1. De-linking economic growth from approximated throughput for some countries

ing inward for poorer countries resulting from the diffusion of technology as mentioned by Malenbaum (1978). Because of the diffusion of technological knowledge, poorer countries nowadays will have lower intensities than richer countries in the past for comparable income levels. The bold line in each curve illustrates the developments during the period of measurement (time 1,2,3) for each country. If these countries are included in a cross-section regression analysis for each period of time, the slope will decrease while the intercept will increase for later periods of time.

Concluding, the cross-section analysis of Jänicke et al. (1989) may confirm inverted-U shaped curves for the intensity of use of individual countries. Interpreted in this way, the Jänicke results can indeed be regarded as suggesting a process of de-linking materials consumption from economic growth for the more developed countries over the respective period.

Other investigations have disclosed similar tendencies for a number of pollutants. Inverted-U curves have been found in panel data analysis of the relationship between per capita income and air pollutants such as sulfur dioxide, nitrate, nitrite, and Suspended Particulate Matter (Shafik and Bandyopadhyay 1992; Selden and Song 1994).[4]

INTERPRETATION OF THE RESULTS OF PREVIOUS STUDIES

The results of Jänicke et al. (1989) and others have given an impetus for the suggestion that it would be possible to mitigate environmental problems in a

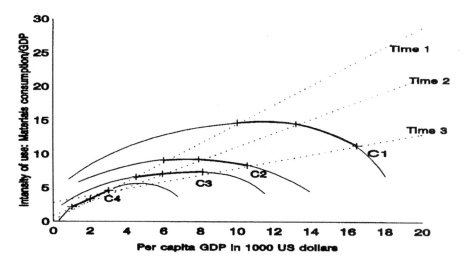

Note: The assumption here is that income rises over time.

Figure 10.2. An illustration of the outcomes of cross-section analysis in three periods, assuming inverted U-shaped intensity of use curves

growing economy through structural change. The perceived dematerialization is therefore an important issue in economic-environmental forecasting. The Dutch Environmental Planning Institute (RIVM) assumes that materials consumption per unit income in the Netherlands will decline by 20% in the year 2015 (RIVM 1991). But before interpreting the results from metal and energy demand studies in terms of dematerialization and structural change, we need to consider the following points.

First, only in closed economies does resource input in production equal emission and wastes in the long run.[5] International trade causes the inputs and outputs to diverge quite substantially. The perceived dematerialization in developed economies may therefore be entirely due to trade and relocation effects, and particularly to a relocation of energy and material-intensive industries to poor countries (Opschoor 1990). By importing the final products from these countries, production patterns are dematerialized, but consumption patterns are not. This phenomenon may be called import-substitution or exporting environmental pressure (Opschoor and Reijnders 1991). By importing products from dirty industries located abroad, developed countries deteriorate the environment in less developed countries. There is some evidence that this kind of import-substitution may be relevant. Al-Rawahi and Rieber (1991) show that the perceived decrease of the copper intensity of use in the U.S. economy could almost entirely be contributed to the increased import of embodied copper in (semi-)finished products. Total consumption of copper, both embodied and as raw material, grew almost at the same rate as income. For steel, however, Tilton (1990) reaches an opposite conclusion: the intensity of use in developed economies was lower when corrected for trade in steel embodied in finished products. The few case studies that are available, however, are too fragmentary to draw general conclusions about the effect of import-substitution on the intensity of use hypothesis. Moreover, the data on materials embodied in final products are being constructed from (monetary) trade statistics. This approach may not be very reliable (Tilton 1990). The materials and energy embodied in trade flows is a topic that deserves more attention in future research.

A second remark is that all dematerialization studies focus only on energy and a few types of metals. Wadell and Labys (1988) have proposed that dematerialization can generally better be described as "transmaterialization" since there is some evidence that lower quality bulk materials are being replaced by technologically superior lighter materials. Steel and cement are typically low quality materials, and plastics, platinum, titanium, and advanced ceramics are typical high quality materials. The demand for these is strongly increasing nowadays, whereby substitution is an important driving force. Therefore we need to incorporate more types of materials in dematerialization studies. Here we encounter a problem when aggregating several materials. Substitution of steel for plastics, for example in automobiles, will show up as dematerialization of the total product. Moll (1993) finds strong dematerialization tendencies for the United States if several materials are aggregated on weight. However, if the aggregation is performed on volume (m^3), no such de-linking can be found (Moll 1993). The question of which aggregation scheme is favorable from the environmental point of view is also a topic that deserves more attention.

A third remark is that none of the studies distinguishes between primary and secondary metals consumption. This distinction is not important if the purpose of the study is to predict or describe consumption. However, when we wish to equate materials and energy consumption with environmental pressure, the distinction between recycled and virgin materials is essential.

The above remarks indicate that a reduction in the consumption of energy and materials cannot be simply translated into environmentally beneficial dematerialization. It is clear that before anything definite can be said about dematerialization and de-linking, more data and alternative methods should be investigated. However, the problem is that few environmental data are available over a long time span (Jänicke et al. 1989). In the following sections we will therefore mainly consider alternative methods for expressing changes in the throughput of an economy, and search for explanations on the observed and estimated patterns.

IN-DEPTH CROSS-SECTION ANALYSIS

In this section we examine the study by Jänicke et al. (1989) in more detail, try to improve the method, and repeat the analysis using more data. The cross-section analysis by Jänicke et al. (1989) only contains samples for two years. No insight is obtained in the development of the approximated throughput during years in between. Hence the analysis is too general to draw strong conclusions about the stability of the de-linking process. It may be possible that the approximated throughput declined from 1970 to 1980 as a result of the two oil crises, but increased again after 1980. This would indicate that de-linking is not a continuous and stable process that autonomously leads towards dematerialization in the future. Also an observation can be made on the representation of the research results. Figure 10.1 showed the IED for each country for both 1970 and 1985 as the deviation from the sample mean of the per capita consumption of the selected indicators in 1970 and 1985, respectively. The arrows indicate developments in terms of this indicator for the two years. Since the indicators for both years are only measured in relative terms, Jänicke et al. cannot compare the developments in absolute levels between 1970 and 1985.[6] In other words, declining vectors in the figure do not automatically imply declining absolute levels of approximated throughput. Figure 10.1 only shows that the consumption of materials and energy in the countries with a lower per capita GDP rose relatively faster than in countries with a higher per capita GDP. Interpreted in this way, Figure 10.1 indicates convergence of levels of approximated throughput between countries over time and not necessarily de-linking. This fact, although recognized by Jänicke et al. seems to be over-looked by other studies referring to the work of Jänicke et al. (e.g., Simonis, 1989; Opschoor 1990; RIVM 1991; von Weizsacker and Schmidt-Bleek 1994).

In order to provide a more complete insight into the process of structural change and de-linking, the analysis of Jänicke et al. is here repeated, taking the above remarks into account. Data have been collected for steel, energy, and cement consumption and transport for a sample of nineteen countries[7] including all the years between 1966 and 1990 (see Appendix 2). This data collection diverges from the one by Jänicke et al. since fewer countries but more years have been included. Secondly, the indicator of cement production is replaced by cement consumption to diminish the sensitivity of the IED import substitution.

The IED for each country has been calculated as the deviation from the sample mean per capita consumption of the selected indicators. Contrary to the analysis of Jänicke et al., only one sample mean has been calculated as the average consumption over all countries and over all the years. Calculated in this way, absolute increases in throughput will result in an increase of the IED.

In order to obtain an overall and yet comprehensive view of the relationship between IED and GDP, the period under study was divided into four subperiods of seven years: 1966–1972, 1972–1978, 1978–1984, and 1984–1990. In the first period, economic growth was high and not disturbed by external shocks. The second period was characterized by the aftermath of first oil crisis in 1973, which influenced several economic parameters. The third period was marked by the second oil crisis and the subsequent negative growth rates in the beginning of the 1980s for most economies. The last period is characterized by a recovery of economic growth in the Western economies and by a disintegration of economic structures in formerly socialist economies. The IED and GDP of each country have been calculated as their average values in each period of seven years. This way yearly and incidental shocks in the economies or data are leveled out.

Jänicke et al. conclude that in 1985 the relationship between the IED and GDP, as measured by the coefficient of determination (R^2), was weakened and that the slope was less steep compared to 1970. The regression of IED on income for four periods with an improved IED calculation gives a more subtle representation of the development of this relationship (see Table 10.2). This table shows that the relationship between the IED and GDP was not stable over time. The second and third period give both a lower slope, a higher inter-

cept, and a lower coefficient of determination (R^2) compared to the first period. This is similar to the conclusion of Jänicke et al. (see Table 10.1). However, this development of de-linking comes to an end in the fourth period. The
slope rises, the intercept declines, and the coefficient of determination increases
compared to the third period. Interpreted in the framework by Jänicke et al.
this would mean that the de-linking phase for developed economies has come
to an end in the last period under study.

Table 10.2. Descriptive Statistics of Cross Section Analysis for Four Periods

Regression Equation: $\text{IED}_t = \alpha_t + \beta_t \text{GDP}_t + \varepsilon_t$

Years	1966–1972	1972–1978	1978–1984	1984–1990
Slope β	0.0765	0.0552	0.0409	0.0435
(t- value)	(5.830)	(3.926)	(3.381)	(4.711)
Intercept α	-0.5892	-0.4188	-0.3938	-0.4624
(t- value)	(-6.725)	(-3.800)	(-3.734)	(-5.061)
R^2	0.666	0.476	0.402	0.566

Note: Income measured in 1,000 US$ per capita in 1985 prices.

Although, apparently, structural change has played a role in the second and
third period, it has ceased to do so for developed economies in the 1980s. It
seems that these economies are entering a period of re-linking rather than de-
linking. This is clarified more explicitly in Figure 10.3, which presents the

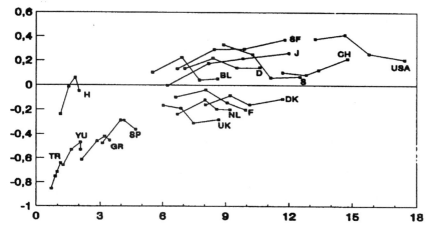

Note: Countries' symbols refer to international number plates, except for Spain (SP)
and Belgium-Luxembourg (BL).

*Figure 10.3. Developments of selected countries from 1966–1990 in levels of per
capita GDP and IED*

developments for several individual countries from period to period. Each dot indicates one period and the lines connect the dots for each country. As can be seen from this figure, three groups of countries can be distinguished. First, Turkey is an example of a group of countries that has not yet experienced any structural change. The IED has been rising faster than GDP in each period. Secondly, Greece, Hungary, Poland, Spain, and (former) Yugoslavia are countries that have experienced absolute improvements in the last period (1984–1990) compared to the third period (1978–1984).[8] After rapid increases in their levels of IED in the second and third period these countries now find themselves in a period of de-linking.

The group of richer countries shows more internal differentiation in the developments of the IED. However, most countries showed absolute improvements in the third period, between 1978–1984. This development of de-linking continued in the last period only for France and the United States. It is remarkable that all the other countries showed a rise in their levels of the approximated throughput in that period. For Finland and Japan this has been the case in each period, but the growth in their levels of IED has been declining.

Having noticed that the absolute improvements as measured and reported by Jänicke et al. (1989) are an exception (induced by the years of measurement) rather than a general rule, the question arises whether the developed countries are still de-linking in relative terms: the levels of approximated throughput may increase, but yet at a structurally slower rate than the increase in GDP. This would result in a continuously lower intensity of use. This is not the case for several countries as shown in Table 10.3.

This table shows for selected countries the developments of the intensities of use of steel, cement, energy, and transport during the 1980s. Overall, it appears that the process of structural change has been rather weak. In the Netherlands, United Kingdom, and Belgium–Luxembourg, the intensities of steel and cement have been increasing, especially after 1986. This implies that the consumption of these materials has grown at a higher rate than the economy. Only France and the United States experienced decreases over all periods. This apparent re-linking phase after a period of de-linking, forecasted by Pezzey (1989) and Opschoor (1990), and confirmed by some empirical investigations (c.f. Jänicke, Monch, and Binder 1992; Vial 1992), will be elaborated in the next section where we estimate several models for the consumption of energy, steel, and cement.

TIME SERIES ANALYSIS AND DE-LINKING

The analysis in the previous section suggests that in developed economies, for some materials, a period of de-linking may be followed by a period of re-

Table 10.3. Developments of the Intensity of Use in Selected Countries for Steel, Cement, Energy, and Transport (1966 = 100)

		Steel	Cement	Energy	Transport	IED
Belgium	1981	51.20	56.38	83.29	85.89	65.68
	1986	56.25	44.54	81.37	91.16	60.94
	1989	55.97	51.95	77.06	107.44	62.29
France	1981	62.34	63.25	98.28	81.31	68.92
	1986	50.88	48.30	99.50	68.26	58.21
	1989	50.98	47.58	95.32	69.87	57.85
Netherlands	1981	74.27	69.44	108.86	99.20	80.71
	1986	71.01	56.28	105.76	98.09	74.00
	1989	75.15	61.98	100.18	102.98	75.42
United Kingdom	1981	47.03	56.22	79.13	94.06	61.95
	1986	39.82	54.04	71.90	86.13	55.89
	1989	43.83	62.60	66.40	94.81	58.45
United States	1981	58.37	79.43	92.68	95.11	74.17
	1986	49.93	86.87	82.94	85.93	66.34
	1989	48.01	79.94	81.82	87.08	64.21

linking. This would not only invalidate the conclusions by Jänicke et al. (1989), but would also challenge the intensity of use hypothesis, which predicted continuously lower income elasticities of demand once economies have reached the turning points. The question is whether a de-linking as proposed by the intensity of use hypothesis is virtually nonexistent or whether high economic growth in the second half of the 1980s simply has resulted in an increase in demand that counteracted the materials and energy savings due to technological and structural changes.

To test the influence of economic growth on the demand for energy and materials, we construct three models that all use the following identity.

$$I_t = i_t \cdot Y_t \tag{10.1}$$

where I_t is the demand for materials and energy, i_t is the intensity of use, and Y_t the level of GDP in year (t). The question here is thus whether the variation in the demand for I_t is mainly driven by variation in the level of GDP (the growth effect) or by the variation in the level of the intensity of use (the intensity of use effect). To answer this question we transform (10.1) into logarithms and take the first difference in order to obtain the growth rates of all variables.

$$\Delta \ln l = \ln l_t - \ln l_{t-1} = (\ln (i_t) - \ln (i_{t-1})) + (i\, n\, Y_t - \ln Y_{t-1}) \qquad (10.2)$$

By adding an error term to (10.2), we construct three growth models that can be estimated.[9] These models differ in the way the change in the intensity of use is explained.

Model 1: The demand for materials and energy is solely explained by economic growth (i.e., the intensity-of-use effect is absent).

$$\Delta \ln l = \beta_1 (\Delta \ln Y) + u \qquad (10.3)$$

Model 2: The demand for energy and materials follows an inverted-U shaped curve (i.e., the intensity-of-use effect is explained by economic growth).

$$\Delta \ln l = \beta_1 (\Delta \ln Y) + \beta_2 \{(\ln Y_t)^2 - (\ln Y_{t-1})^2\} + u \qquad (10.4)$$

This model is the first difference of the translog models that have been used to estimate material demand according to the inverted-U shaped intensity of use curve (Suslick and Harris 1990).[10] It assumes that the intensity-of-use effect is dependent on economic growth. Under conditions of zero economic growth, the change in materials consumption will also be absent. This means that structural and technological changes responsible for the de-linking phase are a function of economic growth itself.

Model 3: The demand for materials and energy is a function of economic growth and the level of income.

$$\Delta \ln l = \beta_1 (\Delta \ln Y) + \beta_2 (\ln Y_t) + u \qquad (10.5)$$

According to this model, the intensity-of-use effect is explained by the level of income, and will result in more material and energy savings in rich economies than in poor economies.

In all models, it is expected that β_1 has a positive sign (representing the growth effect). Furthermore, in models 2 and 3, β_2 is expected to have a negative sign (representing the intensity-of-use effect).

These models have been estimated for the per capita consumption of steel, cement, and energy for each of the nineteen countries mentioned in the previous section. Income has been calculated as per capita GDP in US$1,000 constant (1985). The price changes of steel, cement, and energy for the U.S. market have been added as an additional explanatory variable (using parameter β_3). [11]

Table 10.4 gives the results for Japan, the Netherlands, and the United States. The first model offers a poor explanation in general. It is unlikely that the growth in the demand for materials can be explained by prices and growth in income only. The second model's explanation of the growth in materials and energy consumption is not much better than the first model. The parameter β_2 is nowhere significant at the 5% level, indicating that the intensity of use effect is either absent or poorly specified in this model. Furthermore the signs of steel and cement consumption in the Netherlands and steel consumption in the United States are the opposite of our expectations. The third model gives the best fit: all parameters have the expected signs and most of them are significant. The first parameter β_1 estimates the growth effect of the economy on materials consumption. For the countries selected in this table, this growth effect is significant at the 5% level for all materials and energy.

According to the estimators, an economic growth of 1% results in an increase in the steel consumption of 2.4% in Japan, 3.4% in the Netherlands, and even 4.8% in the United States. This growth effect is, however, counteracted by the intensity of use effect (parameter β_2). The intensity of use effect is appropriately specified as being dependent on the levels of income, being significant on the 5% level for all cases except for steel consumption in Japan and energy consumption in the Netherlands and the United States, which fall inside 10% significance level. There are also differences concerning the substances taken into account. According to model 3, the intensity of use effect in all countries is greater in the case of steel than in the case of cement or energy. This may reflect material substitution of steel for plastics as well as technological improvements in the molding and cutting of steel (McSweeney and Hirosako 1991). Furthermore, each of the models gives a better explanation for energy than for steel and cement. This can be explained by looking at the measurement of the data. Energy consumption data reflect *actual* consumption while the data on steel and cement consumption reflect *apparent consumption* including changes in stocks. Hence, an increase in stocks will be incorrectly counted as an increase in consumption and vice versa. Such developments may be reflected via a larger residual term.

The outcome of the time-series estimations indicates that the increase observed in the consumption of materials and energy during the 1980s (see Table 10.3) is simply the result of an increase in economic growth. Since the estimators for the growth effect range between 0.97 and 4.8, a higher economic growth leads to a more than proportional increase in the consumption of energy, steel, and cement given the reductions due to the intensity of use effect. Chow-tests

Table 10.4. *Results from Estimation of Alternative Models for Materials and Energy Consumption*

Country	Material	Model 1: $\Delta\ln(I) = \beta_1\Delta\ln Y) + \beta_3\Delta\ln(P)$			Model 2: $\Delta\ln(I) = \beta_1\Delta\ln Y) + \beta_2\{[\ln(Y_t)^2 - \ln(Y_{t-1})^2]\} + \beta_3\Delta\ln(P)$				Model 3: $\Delta\ln(I) = \beta_1\Delta\ln(Y) + \beta_2(\ln Y_t) + \beta_3\ln(P)$			
		β_1	β_3	R^2/DW	β_1	β_2	β_3	R^2/DW	β_1	β_3	β_4	R^2/DW
Japan	Steel	1.457 (3.28)	-0.055 (-0.12)	24.7% 2.224	3.370 (1.25)	-0.503 (-0.72)	-0.103 (-0.22)	26.4% 2.337	2.354 (3.36)	-0.029 (-1.62)	-0.016 (-0.04)	32.7% 2.318
	Energy	0.939 (7.40)	-0.330 (-1.47)	62.4% 1.979	2.249 (3.18)	-0.343 (-1.88)	-0.300 (-1.41)	67.6% 2.323	1.379 (6.41)	-0.013 (-2.42)	-0.056 (-0.24)	70.3% 2.442
	Cement	0.916 (3.94)	-0.142 (-0.42)	33.6% 1.167	2.722 (2.05)	-0.482 (-1.38)	-0.274 (-0.79)	41.6% 1.262	1.578 (4.74)	-0.021 (-2.56)	-0.101 (-0.33)	51.1% 1.425
Nether-lands	Steel	1.807 (2.48)	-0.479 (-1.21)	24.5% 2.303	-4.792 (-0.49)	1.643 (0.67)	-0.468 (-1.16)	26.0% 2.294	3.396 (3.43)	-0.030 (-2.19)	-0.517 (-1.41)	37.9% 2.547
	Energy	1.464 (5.49)	-0.692 (-2.84)	60.7% 1.691	5.422 (1.54)	-0.984 (-1.13)	-0.668 (-2.75)	62.9% 1.913	2.032 (5.26)	-0.010 (-1.94)	-0.553 (-2.30)	66.4% 1.942
	Cement	0.779 (1.95)	-0.164 (-0.55)	16.3% 2.284	-1.067 (-0.20)	0.460 (0.34)	-0.152 (-0.47)	16.7% 2.282	1.624 (3.02)	-0.016 (-2.16)	-0.254 (-0.90)	31.0% 2.806
United States	Steel	2.610 (3.35)	0.026 (0.06)	32.2% 1.945	-12.159 (-0.59)	2.748 (0.72)	0.017 (0.04)	33.7% 1.897	4.786 (7.16)	-0.035 (-5.29)	0.129 (0.47)	70.2% 2.734
	Energy	0.773 (5.19)	-0.353 (-2.75)	64.6% 1.111	5.488 (1.47)	-0.879 (-1.27)	-0.368 (-2.89)	67.0% 1.360	0.970 (5.00)	-0.003 (-1.53)	-0.284 (-2.14)	68.0% 1.230
	Cement	1.901 (3.68)	-0.201 (-0.55)	41.2% 1.261	0.522 (0.04)	0.257 (0.10)	-0.196 (-0.52)	41.2% 1.265	2.920 (5.40)	-0.017 (-3.19)	-0.255 (-0.82)	59.8% 1.541

Notes:

1. Figures in parenthesis are t-statistics.
2. Income levels have been calculated in US$1,000 constant (1985) per capita.

214

were conducted to test for structural breaks in the data after 1985 and were all rejected so that we can assume that the estimated relationship is stable over time. This leads us to the conclusion that the intensity of use hypothesis is too static and deterministic for predicting the patterns of material and energy consumption, a fact that restates the criticism of others on this hypothesis (Auty 1985; Tilton 1986; Roberts 1990). The predictive power from translog models describing an inverted-U curve turned out to be rather poor, especially after 1980 (Valdes 1990; Vial 1992). The increase in consumption during the second half of the 1980s cannot be explained by dropping prices of metals and energy. In all the models, prices (parameter β_3) are insignificant at the 5% level, except the prices for energy in the Netherlands and the United States. This is in line with a number of other studies which found that in general prices of materials are not an important variable for determining materials consumption (Auty 1985; Holmes 1990a, 1990b; Tilton 1990; Mannaerts 1993). The demand for materials is typically a derived demand (i.e., dependent on the demand for final consumption goods). Material costs are only a small proportion of the total costs of producing these goods (Malenbaum 1978).

THE RATE OF SUSTAINABLE GROWTH

The existence of two counteractive effects, economic growth and intensity of use, implies that under conditions of low economic growth the consumption of materials and energy may decline. This provides a link with the literature on steady state economics and sustainable development. Daly (1991) proposes the installation of depletion quotas for exhaustible resources: "to be set near the existing extraction rates. The first task would be to stabilize, to get off the growth path. Later we could try to reduce quotas to a more sustainable level, if present flows proved too high." So in a first step towards a steady state, economic growth would only be acceptable if it does not result in a higher level of materials and energy consumption. We, rather informally, label this rate of acceptable growth here as *sustainable* growth, without claiming that economic growth that does not result in an increase in the consumption of materials and energy is sustainable in terms of all environmental aspects.[12]

From model 3 of the previous section, we can calculate which rate of economic growth does not result in a growth of materials consumption, but solely stems from improvements in the efficiency of transforming materials into valuable products and income. This rate of sustainable growth can be calculated by setting the right-hand side of equation (10.5) smaller than or equal to zero. This gives the following condition.

$$\text{ß}_1 \,(\Delta \ln Y) + \text{ß}_2 \,(\ln Y_t) \leq 0 \qquad\qquad (10.6)$$

This equation can be expressed as:

$$\ln\left(\frac{Y_t}{Y_{t-1}}\right) \leq -\frac{\text{ß}_2}{\text{ß}_1} \cdot \ln Y_t \qquad\qquad (10.7)$$

By solving the right-hand side of this equation for the parameters estimated from model 3 given a certain level of income, the maximum rate of sustainable growth is obtained. It indicates which rate of growth will not result in a higher consumption of the selected materials. Table 10.5 gives the application of condition (10.7) to the United States, Japan, and the Netherlands for energy, steel, and cement, where the prices have been assumed to remain constant over the whole period. The average level of GDP and the average growth between 1966–1990 have been chosen as explaining variables. In Table 10.5 the calculated rate of sustainable growth is compared with the actual rate of economic growth over the time period considered. In order to determine the accuracy of the calculations, Table 10.5 also gives a comparison of the actual annual growth rates of materials and energy consumption with the predicted growth rates according to the model. The predicted growth rates have been calculated using model 3 with the average level of GDP and the average economic growth rates between 1966–1990 with constant prices. In the last two columns of this model the actual and predicted growth rates of steel, cement, and energy have been given. This shows that the prediction of the model is rather good, except for energy consumption in the Netherlands and cement consumption in the United

Table 10.5. Annual Sustainable Growth Rates (1966–1990)

		GDP growth		Growth Consumption	
		Sustainable	Actual	Predicted*	Actual
Japan	Steel	2.68%	4.56%	4.19%	3.67%
	Energy	2.05%	4.56%	3.32%	3.39%
	Cement	2.92%	4.56%	2.43%	2.48%
Netherlands	Steel	1.83%	2.21%	1.19%	2.21%
	Energy	1.05%	2.21%	2.30%	0.94%
	Cement	2.08%	2.21%	0.16%	0.18%
United States	Steel	1.98%	1.56%	-2.11%	-1.71%
	Energy	0.80%	1.56%	0.72%	0.66%
	Cement	1.58%	1.56%	-0.10%	0.47%

*Calculated using average income level and average annual rate of growth between 1966–1990 and the parameters from OLS regression of model 3.

States. In column 3 the rate of sustainable growth, as has been calculated from equation (10.7), is presented.

In most cases, the rate of sustainable growth is below the actual annual growth rates over the period 1966–1990, indicating that the consumption of energy, steel, and cement has risen over the period considered. It is also interesting to notice that the rate of sustainable growth in all countries is lower for energy than for cement and steel, which indicates that economic growth will sooner result in a rise in energy consumption than in a rise in steel or cement consumption. Finally, it appears that the rate of sustainable growth in Japan for all materials is about 1% higher than in the Netherlands and the U.S. This indicates that the process of structural change may have played a more pronounced role in the Japanese economy than in the Dutch and U.S. economies.

The calculated rate of sustainable growth can also be placed in the light of sustainable development, as put forward in the Brundtland report (WCED, 1987). The Brundtland Commission estimated that an economic growth of 3% in developed economies would not be in conflict with the sustainable development. From our estimations we can see that an economic growth of 3% would in all cases lead to increasing consumption of steel, energy, and cement. This indicates that with present rates of technological and structural changes, an economic growth of 3% should not be termed sustainable.

DETERMINANTS OF THE DECLINE IN THE INTENSITY OF USE

The previous sections have shown that structural changes in material and energy consumption are determined by the intensity of use effect. It appeared that the intensity of use hypothesis underestimates the progressive influence of economic growth on material and energy demand. Yet, the intensity of use has declined in many developed countries. This phenomenon is poorly understood (Auty 1985). In order to predict future material demand, Tilton (1986) and Radetzki and Tilton (1990) have stressed the need for identifying the factors underlying the decline in the intensity of use. They emphasize two factors: changes in the structure of the economy and changes in technology. This distinction is also of importance for sustainable development. It has been stated that shifts in the structure of the economy are needed in order to transform our economies toward a sustainable economy (WCED 1987; Jänicke et al. 1989). Technological improvements, on the other hand, may come to an end once the opportunities for win-win situations have been exhausted. It will be clear that the prices of materials and energy should be an important determinant of technological changes.

In order to distinguish between both factors we propose a decomposition method of the intensity of use that employs sectoral data. We can then decompose the intensity of use into intrasectoral and intersectoral changes. Intrasectoral changes are changes of the intensity of use within a sector. The intensity of use within a sector may decrease as the result of increased process-efficiency (less inputs) or increased knowledge intensity of the products (more value added). These can be labeled as technological changes. Intersectoral changes refer to shifts in the composition of income: (i.e., changes in the economic structure). These can be labeled as structural changes.

The distinction between intrasectoral and intersectoral changes in the intensity of use can formally be specified and empirically applied. It requires that data are available on the input of material I, $I_{j,t}$, and value added $Y_{j,t}$ for a range of $\{j=1...n\}$ sectors in the economy of a country. The intensity of use of material i by the total economy in year t (i_t) is then defined as:

$$i_t = \frac{I_{i,t}}{Y_t} \tag{10.8}$$

The sum of the value added of every sector gives (Y_t), the GDP of an economy.

$$Y_t = \sum_{j=1}^{n} Y_{j,t} \tag{10.9}$$

The sum of $I_{i,j,t}$, the consumption of material i by sector j gives the total demand for this material.

$$I_{i,t} = \sum_{j=1}^{n} I_{i,j,t} \tag{10.10}$$

Equation (10.8) can now be rewritten as the sum of the intensity of use of the individual sectors by weighting them with their market shares in outputs, skipping the material index i of the intensity of use variable I.

$$i_t = \sum_{j=1}^{n} \left(\frac{Y_{j,t}}{Y_t} \cdot \frac{I_{j,t}}{Y_{j,t}} \right) \tag{10.11}$$

The first ratio on the right hand side of (10.11) gives the market share of sector j, defined as the value added of a sector divided by the total value added of the economy. The second ratio gives the intensity of use of sector j. Taking the differences from equation (11) may result in the following expression for the change in the intensity of use of the whole economy, specified in changes in the intensity of use of the individual sectors.[13]

$$\frac{I_{t+1}}{Y_{t+1}} - \frac{I_t}{Y_t} = \sum_{j=1}^{n} \left(\frac{Y_{j,t}}{Y_t} \cdot \left(\frac{I_{j,t+1}}{Y_{j,t+1}} - \frac{I_{j,t}}{Y_{j,t}} \right) \right) +$$

$$\sum_{j=1}^{n} \left(\left(\frac{Y_{j,t+1}}{Y_{t+1}} - \frac{Y_{j,t}}{Y_t} \right) \cdot \frac{I_{j,t+1}}{Y_{j,t+1}} \right) \tag{10.12}$$

The first term on the left-hand side of equation (10.12) gives the intrasectoral changes as the sum of the changes in the intensities of use of the sectors individually, multiplied by their market shares. The second term on the left-hand side gives the intersectoral changes as the sum of each sector's change in market shares multiplied by the intensity of use. Simple rewriting will confirm that the sum of intrasectoral and intersectoral changes equals the total change in the intensity of use. It will be clear that the precise distinction of intersectoral and intrasectoral changes will depend on the number of sectors that will be used in the analysis. If data can be found that are sufficiently detailed, one could treat the lowest level of aggregation as the fabrication process itself. Intrasectoral changes would then truly represent actual improvements in physical efficiency.

This decomposition model will be used to determine which factors (structural or technological changes) have been most influential in the development of the energy intensity of the Dutch economy. Three years of reference have been chosen: 1970, 1980, and 1990. Data for these years have been collected on commercial energy consumption and value added of ten industrial and six nonindustrial sectors (Appendix 2). The industrial classification consists of the following manufacturing sectors: foodstuffs, textiles, paper, chemicals, fertilizers, refineries, building materials, base metals, metal products, and other industry. The nonindustrial classification consists of: agriculture, mining, power generation and distribution, other public utilities, construction and the service-sector, which includes commercial and governmental services. Energy consumption is measured as commercial energy input used for fuel combustion. This means that energy use by households and energy embodied in the final products (for example, naphtha as the output of refineries) has not been taken into account. A second consequence is that the consumption of electricity taken from public power plants is not counted as energy input for the industrial sectors. The energy input used for electricity generation is contributable to the power generation sector only. In general, the share of electricity in the total energy requirement is rather low in Dutch industry.

Table 10.6 shows that the energy intensities differ substantially between sectors. Especially the fertilizer industry and power generation have high intensities. Both typically have labor extensive and energy intensive production so that they add relatively little value compared to their energy inputs. Construction has the lowest energy intensity because of the labor intensive character of production.

Over the time period considered, energy intensities have changed considerably, as can be seen by the index numbers for 1980 and 1990. These indices show that the energy intensity of the whole Dutch economy has declined between 1970–1990. Considering sectoral developments, the decrease in the energy intensities of the public utilities and the mining sector is remarkable. The reason is the large-scale extraction of natural gas and the closing down of several coal mines. As the extraction of natural gas requires less energy than the

Table 10.6. Developments of Energy Intensities and Market Shares in the Netherlands for Selected Sectors (1970–1990)

Sector	Energy Intensity			Market Share		
	1970	1980	1990	1970	1980	1990
	Value	Index numbers (1970–100)				
Agriculture/Fisheries[1]	5.01	217	128	5.7%	3.6%	4.3%
Mining	9.60	6	20	1.6%	5.9%	3.2%
Total Industry	9.52	102	76	26.8%	18.5%	20.1%
Foodstuffs	5.41	118	83	4.7%	3.3%	3.7%
Textiles	4.95	119	53	1.1%	0.5%	0.4%
Paper	15.78	84	65	0.8%	0.6%	0.6%
Fertilizers	107.44	45	83	0.3%	0.2%	0.1%
Other chemicals	13.63	226	116	3.3%	1.7%	2.8%
Building materials	15.64	101	67	1.1%	0.8%	0.7%
Base metals	14.32	119	99	1.3%	0.8%	0.7%
Metal products	1.19	147	68	8.6%	5.7%	6.3%
Oil industry[2]	43.29	87	59	1.8%	1.2%	1.5%
Other industry	2.03	64	33	3.7%	3.7%	3.2%
Electricity[3]	99.63	98	80	1.6%	1.5%	1.5%
Other utilities	11.34	2	19	0.6%	0.7%	0.3%
Construction	0.84	67	29	8.0%	7.3%	5.5%
Service-sector	1.56	51	44	55.6%	62.6%	65.2%
Total economy[4]	5.60	78	61	100.0%	100.0%	100.0%

Notes:
1. Only commercial energy meant for fuel combustion is taken into account.
2. Energy data only for agriculture.
3. Oil industry consists of refineries and coke fabrication.
4. Electricity includes production and distribution of electricity.
5. Total economy excludes the consumption of fuel types by households.
6. Energy counted as TJ input, Value added in millions Dutch constant (1980) guilders.

extraction of coal, this has led to a much lower energy intensity for the mining sector. For the public utilities, the distribution of natural gas instead of the gasification of coal has resulted in much less energy use. On the other hand, energy intensities in the agriculture sector and the chemical industry more than doubled in 1980 compared to 1970. Cheap deliveries to horticulture of natural gas for heating purposes has increased the energy intensity in the agricultural sector.

In 1980 industry as a whole had a slightly higher energy intensity than in 1970. However, in 1990 energy intensity also declined in total industry. The share of industry in total GDP (the last three columns of Table 10.6) declined in 1980, but increased afterwards to 20% in 1990. The market share for the mining sector almost quadrupled due to the large scale extraction of natural gas. The contributions of base metals and building materials industry to the GDP have declined over all the years.

Using equation (10.12) for these data, it is possible to calculate which factors have contributed to the decreases in the energy intensity in the Netherlands. The results are depicted in Table 10.7. The time period under study is divided into two periods: 1970–1980 and 1980–1990. It is remarkable that explanations for the observed decline in the intensity of use differ completely for both periods in the context of the present method. In the first period, the energy intensity of the whole economy declined by more than 24%. It appears that this is solely explained by intersectoral changes. The structure of the Dutch economy has become less energy intensive. Despite the increase in prices in this period, technological changes (measured as intrasectoral changes) have played a marginal role during this decade. It appears that energy saving considerations within sectors were not an important aspect of production (this is largely due to the increase in energy consumption in the chemical sector). The explanation for the declining intensity of use in the second period is completely different: the individual sectors have succeeded in an energy saving per unit output of more than 22% due to technological changes. The structure of

Table 10.7. Decomposition of Energy Intensities in the Netherlands: Intrasectoral Changes and Intersectoral Changes (Expressed as Percentage Change)

	1970–1980	1980–1990
Total economy	-24.14%	-19.80%
o.w. intrasectoral	-0.53%	-22.46%
o.w. intersectoral	-23.61%	2.67%
Total industry	1.97%	-25.57%
o.w. intrasectoral	12.83%	-28.56%
o.w. intersectoral	-10.87%	2.99%

the economy, however, has become more energy intensive. Changes in the structure of the Dutch economy have resulted in an increase in the energy intensity of more than 2.5%.

If decomposition is performed for the Dutch industry only (i.e., excluding the service sector, transport, and communication sector) the above-described developments are more pronounced. As has already been noted, the energy intensity in Dutch industry increased slightly in 1980 compared to 1970. The reason is that, despite the shifts towards a less energy intensive production structure, the individual sectors showed a rise in their energy intensities, leading to an intrasectoral effect of almost 13%. It appears that Dutch industry was unsuccessful in applying energy saving technology until 1980.

In the second period this picture is reversed. The total energy intensity declined by more than 25%. The explanation for this decrease is intrasectoral change, indicating an increase in efficiency at the sectoral level. The intersectoral effect now is positive, indicating that in the 1980s the structure of production has become more energy intensive. This case study shows that the method of decomposition can provide additional insights into issues of dematerialization and de-linking. As a main conclusion of the application of this method to the Dutch economy, one can notice that the effect of the first oil shock (1973) resulted in a change in the structure of the Dutch economy, while the second oil shock (1979–1981) resulted in technological changes in production towards energy saving. These latter technological changes may have been accelerated by policy programs since the Dutch government launched a number of projects to promote energy efficiency in the 1980s.

CONCLUSIONS

There are serious drawbacks in equating an observed decline in materials and energy demand with dematerialization and ecological structural change. Studies that do so find important evidence for dematerialization and structural change, especially after 1970. The cross-section analysis performed in this chapter confirms that pattern, but adds the insight that the consumption of several materials and energy has increased in most developed economies since the mid-1980s. A time-series analysis was presented which provides insight into this apparent pattern of re-linking. It appears that materials and energy consumption is not necessarily de-linked from economic growth in general. An increase in economic growth may result in a more than proportional increase in the consumption of materials and energy. Furthermore, the growth rates of the Dutch, Japanese, and U.S. economies between 1966 and 1990 have been well above the rate of sustainable growth (i.e., the rate of growth below which the increase in income does not lead to a higher consumption of materials).

A statistical decomposition method can provide more insight into the factors underlying the changes in the intensity of use. Application of the method to commercial energy consumption in the Netherlands makes clear why energy saving was higher in the 1970s than in the 1980s despite the launching of energy saving programs in the 1980s. The process of structural change turned out to be rather absent in the 1980s. Contrary to the 1970s, the structure of the Dutch economy has become more energy intensive: sectors with a high energy intensity have expanded their production more than the sectors with a low energy intensity. This all casts serious doubts on the stability of the processes of dematerialization and structural change.

ACKNOWLEDGMENTS

The authors would like to thank Jan van der Straaten and Roebijn Heintz for comments on earlier drafts. All remaining errors are ours.

FOOTNOTES

1. Throughout this chapter consumption and income refer to per capita consumption and income.
2. It may be noted that in 1990 in the United States cement consumption accounted for 18% and steel consumption for 22% of all industrial minerals and metals consumed in the U.S. economy (construction materials like crushed stone, sand, and gravel excluded) (Berry 1994). The weight of freight transport in tons can be seen as a general indicator of the volume aspect of production.
3. It should be noted, however, that with such a low R^2 the decreasing slope is difficult to interpret and may fall within the statistical confidence intervals.
4. For a critical review of these studies on methodological grounds, see Stern et al. (1995) and De Bruyn, van den Bergh, and Opschoor (1995).
5. A considerable amount of resource input is being "stored" in the products that have been produced which become wastes after they have been discarded.
6. The sum of the deviations from the sample mean is zero by definition. Therefore, the arrows of individual countries indicate the developments from the relative position in 1970 to the relative position in 1985.
7. The sample consists of Belgium–Luxembourg, Denmark, Finland, France, Greece, Hungary, Italy, Japan, Luxembourg, the Netherlands, Norway, Poland, Spain, Sweden, Switzerland, Turkey, United Kingdom, the United States, Western Germany, and (former) Yugoslavia.
8. Poland has not been given in this figure for reasons of clearness.
9. The error term in the models is calculated as the first difference of the logarithmic expression for the usual error term. It should be added that first difference models have been chosen for ease of interpretation and that it does not necessarily mean that the lag structure is properly specified in this way.
10. The inverted-U form of the intensity of use curve has been given by Suslick and Harris (1990):

$$I_t / Y_t = a_1 Y_t^{(a2 + 82 \ln Yt)} + \varepsilon_t$$

From this the demand function for I_t can be derived as:

$$I_t = a_1 \cdot Y_t^{(\beta1 + \beta2 \ln Yt)} + \varepsilon_t$$

where $ß_1 + α_2$. This model implies an income elasticity of demand that varies with the income level, which is characteristic for the inverted-U shaped intensity of use curve. Estimation of model 2 will thus, in general, give a higher value for $ß_1$ than of the other models.

11. This may give a bias for the other countries involved in the estimations, because their rate of price increase may differ from the U.S. market. Unfortunately we have not been able until now to collect all the price indices for each country individually.

12. Some authors have pointed out that to realize sustainable development on a global scale, the developed countries should even reduce their consumption of materials and energy in order to create "environmental space" for growth in the consumption of materials and energy in developing countries (Weterings and Opschoor 1992).

13. This decomposition is not unique; there are other decomposition methods possible that give a different division between intersectoral and intrasectoral changes.

REFERENCES

Al-Rawahi, K. and M. Rieber. 1991. Embodied copper: Trade, intensity of use and consumption forecasts. *Resources Policy* 17:2–12.

Auty, R. 1985. Materials intensity of GDP: Research issues on the measurement and explanation of change. *Resources Policy* 11:275–283.

Barnet, H. J. and Ch. Morse. 1963. *Scarcity and Growth: The Economics of Natural Resource Availability.* London: Johns Hopkins Press.

Berry, D. 1994. Information needs for sustainable resource policy. In *Sustainable Resource Management and Resource Use: Policy Questions and Research Needs,* eds. F. J. Duinhouwer, G. J. van der Meer, and H. Verbruggen. Raad voor Milieu en Natuur Onderzoek (RMNO), RMNO, nr. 97:175–90.

Bossanyi, E. 1979. UK primary energy consumption and the changing structure of final demand. *Energy Policy* 7:253–258.

Chesshire, J. 1986. An energy-efficient future: A strategy for the UK. *Energy Policy* 14:395–412.

Daly, H. E. 1991. *Steady State Economics.* San Francisco: Freeman.

De Bruyn, S. M., J. C. J. M. van den Bergh, and J. B. Opschoor. 1995. Empirical Investigations in Environmental–Economic Relationships: Reconsidering the Empirical Basis of the Environmental Kuznets Curves and the De-linking of Pollution from Economic Growth. Tinbergen Discussion Paper, TI 95–140. Amsterdam: Tinbergen Institute.

Dobozi, I. 1990. The centrally planned economies: Extravagant consumers. In *World Metal Demand: Trends and prospects, Resources for the Future,* ed. J. E. Tilton. Washington DC.

Goldemberg, J. 1992. Energy, technology, development. *Ambio* 21:14–17.

Holmes, M. J. 1990a. Material substitution in battery electrodes: The UK 1983–1987. *Resources Policy* 16:22–34.

Holmes, M. J. 1990b. Material substitution in the UK window industry, 1983–1987. *Resources Policy* 16:128–142.

Jänicke, M., H. Monch, and M. Binder. 1992. *Environmental Improvement by Industrial Structural Change?* (in German). Berlin: Edition Sigma.

Jänicke, M., H. Monch, and M. Binder. 1993. Ecological aspects of structural change. *Intereconomics Review of International Trade and Development* 28:159–169.

Jänicke, M., H. Monch, T. Ranneberg, and U. E. Simonis. 1989. Economic structure and environmental impacts: East-west comparisons. *The Environmentalist* 9:171–182.

Larson, E. D., M. H Ross, and R. H. Williams. 1986. Beyond the era of materials. *Scientific American* 254: 34–41.

Malenbaum, W. 1978. *World Demand for Raw Materials in 1985 and 2000.* New York: McGraw-Hill.

Mannaerts, H. J. B. M. 1993. *The use of non-energetic resources in the long run* (in Dutch). Onderzoeksmemorandum 109. Den Haag: Centraal Planbureau.

McSweeney, Ch. and M. Hirosako. 1991. Understanding crude steel consumption: The perils of ignoring the role of technological change. *Resources Policy* 17:258–270.

Moll, H. C. 1993. *Energy Counts and Materials Matter in Models for Sustainable Development: Dynamic Lifecycle Modelling as a Tool for Design and Evaluation of Long-term Environmental Strategies.* Groningen: Styx.

Opschoor, J. B. 1990. Ecologically sustainable economic development: A theoretical idea and a refractory practice (in Dutch). In *Het Nederlands Milieu in de Europese Ruimte: Preadviezen van de Koninklijke Vereniging voor Staathuishoudkunde,* pp. 77–126, eds. P. Nijkamp and H. Verbruggen. Stenfert Kroese, Leiden.

Opschoor, J. B. and L. Reijnders. 1991. Towards sustainable development indicators. In *Search of Indicators for Sustainable Development,* eds. H. Verbruggen and O. Kuik. Dordrecht: Kluwer Academic Press.

Pezzey, J. 1989. Economic Analysis of Sustainable Growth and Sustainable Development. Environment Department Working Paper No 15. Washington DC: The World Bank.

Radetzki, M. 1990. Developing countries: The new growth markets. In *World Metal Demand: Trends and prospects,* ed. J. E. Tilton. Washington DC: Resources for the Future, pp. 77–112.

Radetzki, M. and J. E. Tilton. 1990. Conceptual and methodological issues. In *World Metal Demand: Trends and prospects,* ed. J. E. Tilton. Washington DC: Resources for the Future, pp. 13–34.

Rijksinstituut voor Volksgezondheid en Milieuhygiene (RIVM). 1991. *National Environmental Outlook 2* (in Dutch), Alphen aan de Rijn: Samson-Willink.

Roberts, M. C. 1990. Predicting metal consumption: The case of US steel. *Resources Policy* 16:56–73.

Schmidt-Bleek, F. 1993. MIPS Re-Visited. *Fresensius Environmental Bulletin* 2:2–7.

Selden, T. M. and D. S. Song. 1994. Environmental quality and development: Is there a Kuznets curve for air pollution emissions? *Journal of Environmental Economics and Management* 27:147–162.

Shafik, N. and S. Bandyopadhyay. 1992. Economic Growth and Environmental Quality: Time-Series and Cross-Country Evidence, World Bank Working Papers WPS 904, Washington DC.

Simonis, U. E. 1989. Industrial Restructuring for Sustainable Development: Three Points of Departure. Science Centre Berlin FS II 89-401, Berlin.

Stern, D. I., M. S. Common, and E. B. Barbier. 1996. Economic growth and environmental degradation: A critique of the Environmental Kuznets Curve. *World Development* 24:1151–1160.

Suslick, S. B., and D. P. Harris. 1990. Long-range metal consumption forecasts using innovative methods: The case of aluminium in Brazil to the year 2000. *Resources Policy* 16:184–199.

Tilton, J. E. 1986. Beyond intensity of use. *Materials and Society* 10:245–250.

Tilton, J. E. 1990. The OECD countries: Demand trend setters. In *World Metal Demand: Trends and prospects,* ed. J. E. Tilton. Washington DC: Resources for the Future, pp. 35–76.

Valdes, R. M. 1990. Modelling Australian steel consumption. *Resources Policy* 16:172–183.

Vial, J. 1992. Copper consumption in the USA: Main determinants and structural changes. *Resources Policy* 18:107–121.

von Weizsacker, E.U., and F. Schmidt-Bleek. 1994. Signs of hope for the 21st century? (In Dutch) Committee for Long-Term Environmental Policy. *The Environment: Towards a Sustainable Future.* Dordrecht: Kluwer Academic Publishers.

Wadell, L. M. and W. C. Labys. 1988. Transmaterialization: Technology and materials demand cycles. *Materials and Society* 12:59–85.

Weterings, R. A. P. M. and J. B. Opschoor. 1992. The Ecocapacity as a Challenge to Technological Development. Advisory Council for Research on Nature and Environment, Rijswijk.

World Commission on Environment and Development (WCED). 1987. *Our Common Future.*
   Oxford: Oxford University Press.

APPENDIX 1

A METHODOLOGY FOR THE CALCULATION OF THE INDEX OF ENVIRONMENTAL DETERIORATION (IED)

The calculation of the Index of Environmental Deterioration (IED) in this chapter involves a two-step procedure. First, sample means have been calculated for all countries and all years. For each indicator this was done using the following formula:

$$\bar{X}_i = \frac{\sum\limits_{t=1966}^{1990} \sum\limits_{c=1}^{20} C_{i,c,t}}{\sum\limits_{t=1966}^{1990} \sum\limits_{c=1}^{20} POP_{c,t}} \tag{10.13}$$

where i = indicator (1..4), c = country (1..20), t = year (1966..1990), Xi = per capita consumption of indicator (i), POP = population, Ci = measured yearly consumption of indicator i.

The environmental index (IED) for each country (c) and for each year (t) is calculated by adding the relative deviations from the mean per capita consumption of each indicator ($X_{i,c,t}$), dividing it by four which results in an equal weighting of each indicator. In formula this becomes:

$$IED_{c,t} = \sum\limits_{i=1}^{4} \frac{1}{4} \cdot \left(\frac{x_{i,c,t} - \bar{x}_i}{\bar{x}_i} \right) \tag{10.14}$$

The formula used by Jänicke et al. (1989) differs from this since the sample mean was year-specific (i.e., the summation signs over the years 1966–1990 in equation (10.14) were not taken into account). Both for 1970 and 1985 they calculated the IED as the deviations from the mean for, respectively, 1970 and 1985.

APPENDIX 2

DATA SOURCES AND DATA QUALITY

Our data were taken from a number of international sources as listed below.

Cement Consumption

Economic Commission for Europe of the United Nations: Annual Report on Housing and Building. United States: CRB: Commodity Yearbook. For Italy, Japan, Spain, and Turkey cement production has been taken as a proxy for consumption. Production data from Statistical Office of the United Nations: Statistical Yearbook.

Energy Consumption

Measured as Total Primary Energy Supply (TPES). International Energy Agency (IEA): Energy Balances of OECD Countries, Energy Balances of Non-OECD countries, World Energy Statistics and Balances; For Hungary, Poland, and Yugoslavia before 1971 growth rates extracted from: United Nations: "World Energy Supplies" (Total Final Consumption).

Steel Consumption

Until 1987: United Nations: Statistical Yearbook. After 1987: Eurostat: Eisen undStahl for EC members, Economic Commission for Europe of the United Nations: Annual Steel Statistics for Europe for non-EC members. Series have been standardized on each other using three-year averages.

Freight Transport

Economic Commission for Europe of the United Nations: Annual Bulletin of Transport Statistics for Europe. International Road Federation: World Road Statistics. European Conference of Ministers of Transport (ECMT): Transport Statistics. Especially for road transport series show differences. Series have been standardized. Rail transport has been used for all countries, road transport for all countries except the United States, Spain, Italy, and Greece. For these countries the quantity of freight transport was measured by train only. This is the same routine as Jänicke et al. took in their investigations in 1989.

Population

Worldbank: Worldtables.

Gross Domestic Product

Worldbank: Worldtables, 1992. For Yugoslavia, Poland, and Hungary before 1971 growth rates have been extracted from: Summers, R. A. Heston: A new set of international comparisons of real product and price levels estimates for 130 countries, 1950–1985 In: Income and Wealth 1988.

Structure of Dutch Economy

Value added data have been extracted from the Dutch Statistical Office (CBS) (1985): Nationale rekeningen 1969–1981 met herziene reeksen voor de jaren 1969–1976. From 1977 and on: CBS (1978–1991): Samenvattend overzicht industriestatistieken" For the fertilizer industry data taken from: Statistical Yearbook of the Netherlands (1972–1993). For power generation by public utilities, data taken from: Statistiek van de elektriciteitsvoorziening in Nederland

(1970–1991). Value added has been calculated as gross value added using market prices.

Energy Input in Dutch Economy

Delivered from CBS databases.

PART III

ECOSYSTEM SCALE

11 ECONOMIC CULTURES AND ECOLOGY IN A SMALL CARIBBEAN ISLAND[1]

Sam Cole
Department of Geography and Planning
Center for Regional Studies
State University of New York at Buffalo
Buffalo, New York

INTRODUCTION

Challenges for Ecological Economics

In what she sees as a turning point for ecological economics, Duchin (1994) argues that the discipline's second stage will focus on building concrete, situation-specific strategies for sustainable development and an analytic framework for evaluating the environmental, social, and economic trade-offs among them. She assesses the ambition of ecological economics to provide guidance for achieving sustainable development so as to bring environment-related considerations into a formal quantitative framework. Unfortunately, she concludes, there has been a substantial disjuncture between verbal description about the role of quantitative analysis and its application: ecological economists now must endeavor to bridge this gap and incorporate qualitative information into an integrated, formal evaluation framework, providing an empirical analysis (rather than simply an application of abstract facts). This goal unites with the recommendations of UNEP and their aim to adopt the SNA (System of National Accounts) Framework for Integrated Environmental and Ecological Accounting (United Nations 1994; Bartelmus, Stahmer, and Tongere 1991). Academics such as Duchin and policy agencies such as the UN DSMS (Development Support and Management) advocate the use of social accounting type models, extensions of Leontief's original input–output tables, in order to reveal issues of economic equity in development (Stone 1973). The UN suggests that the Cultural Accounting Matrix (CAM) approach provides a valuable starting point for modeling the developing island economies, especially if it can be tailored directly to the needs of the planning process.

231

There are at least three aspects of the need to establish a better integration between the qualitative and quantitative dimensions of ecological economics. The first is to place our analysis within a broad historical, present, and future context. For example, Duchin notes that to evaluate alternative development strategies we need a theory that can situate activities and social actors within the natural world in a concrete and useful way. The UN recommends that modelers base their work on analysis and understanding of the social, economic, and political processes influencing development (United Nations 1994). The second aspect is to bring new ecology-related social variables into formal and empirical models. For example, Duchin (1995) argues the necessity to construct a new classification scheme rather than those based on income or urban versus rural location. She suggests also the need to integrate anthropological studies into a generalized social accounting structure. Related to this is the need to provide useful data on the environmental variables that link to different lifestyles and cultures. Third is a concern with the interface between ecological economic modeling and complex public policy, in order to put models into the social frame of policy-making. Here the UN (Morrison 1994) notes the paradox that mathematical models often serve only to mystify, frustrating public participation, and advocates that models used for planning should be based on clear principles and be as simple as possible.

Lessons from Small Islands

This chapter describes one attempt to address these issues within the context of a specific community—the small Caribbean island nation of Aruba.[2] Historical, ethnographic, and empirical analyses are employed to gain an understanding of the island's present situation, and possible future paths of development, and to shed light on some of the concerns noted above. While many ecological concerns are global, the impacts often depend on local scale ecologies and societies – in this sense small islands provide a laboratory and techniques that can address their situation may have wider applicability.

Most small islands have been impacted by the successive waves of global economic change usually associated with a major new commodity or industry. For most islands in the Caribbean, this was sugar cane production and refining. In Aruba it was cattle ranching, gold mining, and oil refining, and most recently, international tourism. Often the economies and environments of islands were simply reconfigured to meet the needs of the metropolitan economies, with the local populace displaced or marginalized. With each new industry comes new populations and environmental perils, often with devastating cultural and ecological consequences. The smallness of indigenous island populations relative to the number of immigrants and visitors means that they are particularly vulnerable to external cultural forces. With present-day restructuring of the global economy, these processes are set to accelerate. Compared to many small islands, Aruba is relatively prosperous. Their high income has made native Arubans proud of their island, and also allowed them to maintain the reality and the myth of their rural past as a source of identity. This not-uncommon dichotomy between a desire for modernity based on access to commodities, and a sense of identity harking back to traditional lifestyles is the focus of the calculations at the end of this chapter.

In broad terms, the chapter accepts Duchin's assessment of the new agenda for ecological and equity economics, and the recommendations of the UN DSMS for small islands. In particular, a modified social accounting framework is used to describe the relationship between populations with distinctive economic cultures, and their social, economic, and physical environment.[3] The categories adopted arise from a fairly long acquaintance with the island – as a consultant preparing a development plan for the island's independence, and later as a researcher concerned with finding analytic means to describe the complex social history and present cultural mosaic of the island. Any differences from Duchin's recommendations arise in the nature of the compromises that might be required for the kind of analysis they advocate. This is especially applicable to the balance between qualitative and quantitative components, including the tension between the high level of spatial and other detail that are needed for empirical analysis and the practical constraints of providing useful long-run analysis for the policy arena.[4]

In their guidelines for planning sustainable development in island nations, the UN (United Nations 1994) notes that in addition to their singular environmental situation island economies are faced with special difficulties arising from rapid cultural and economic change, and that both sustainability of growth and development are of vital concern.[5] They also note that while the concept of economic growth is quantitative, the concept of development – more closely related to cultural needs – is qualitative and less amenable to measurement. Indeed, concepts such as Duchin's "the natural world" have fluid meanings that vary across social groups and across time (e.g., Strathern 1995), and notions such as "community" are inherently ambiguous (e.g., Cohen 1985).[6] Thus, although one contribution of this chapter may be that it provides a set of accounts with actors subdivided according to their economic cultures, the goal has been rather to develop these accounts within an historical explanation of how the prevailing cultural division of labor has arisen, and what constraints this history imposes physically, economically, and politically on the possibilities for future change.

There is another tremendous tension here. On the one hand, a crucial consideration for small islands (and other small communities) is how best to utilize their limited planning resources, for example, by accepting that a single framework must serve several purposes (United Nations 1994). On the other hand, it is seldom that a particular historic explanation or a single model could ever be acceptable to all groups within a small community. Planners usually face a situation where there are numerous interest groups among which there is a need to establish cooperation and consensus (Morrison 1994). In terms of making models more useful to this process of negotiation, it might turn out that models which help distinct groups to evaluate and present their position more cogently are likely to be the most useful.

A second concern is the several time scales over which analysis should be conducted. The UN notes that sustainability is defined over the medium to long term and involves a secular trend largely independent of shorter-term oscillations which are characteristic of the business cycle (United Nations 1994). This apparent negation of the importance of short-run phenomena can be highly misleading since island economies tend to move from crisis to crisis. Indeed, as the same document also points out, island countries depend on a limited range of export products which makes them highly vulnerable to externally determined conditions. The way in which the short-run crises (as well as those from natural disasters) are dealt with has a tremendous impact on the possibilities for sustainable development. In particular, this determines social attitudes to the long run as reflected in high discount rates, the maintenance of local and transnational kinship networks, defensive strategies to change, and so on. Munasinghe (1993), for example, observes that a loss of ecological resilience depends on the capacity of human societies to adapt and continue functioning in the face of stress and shocks. These linkages are apparent in the example given in this chapter. The modeling framework is used for short-run emergency management of conditions of insecurity that frustrate longer-run aspirations for sustainable development. The link is inescapable. For observers such as Jones (1982), disasters are part and parcel of development and provide opportunities for a more protected future (Aysan, Coburn, and Spence 1989).

The Scope of the Chapter

This chapter provides a brief historical review of economic, demographic, cultural, and environmental changes in Aruba from colonial times to the present. Over the centuries the population built up layer-by-layer to form a complex hierarchical society, comprising different lifestyles, cultures, and goals. This sets the present condition of the island in a wider context, showing how a diversity of economic cultures compete to determine the ecological future of the island. It also provides the context for an empirical analysis of ongoing and future temporal and systemic changes on the island. Then I discuss the use of an extended input–output approach to quantify specific links between the island's economic cultures and key components of the island's environmental support system – energy and water, and selected policy – and relevant environmental indicators such as land use and emissions (as both endogenous and satellite accounts). This matrix, called an Ecological Cultural Accounting Matrix (or EcoCAM), has been developed at varying levels of aggregation, including individual processes and firms, groups of like-activities and lifestyles, and public activities. The aim is to use the matrix to explore the implications of continued economic growth and changing lifestyles, the tension between the traditional and the modern, and competing visions of the island's future, the vulnerability of these alternatives, the relationship between the physical and economic carrying capacity, and hence the possibilities for sustainable development on the island. In each case, some empirical and institutional limitations arising from efforts to use the model within a policy context are indicated, exploring compromises in achieving Duchin's challenge to ecological economics.

HISTORICAL ANALYSIS[7]

This section provides a historical overview of Aruba showing how the island's economy, demography, and environment have evolved in response to a succession of external forces.

From Past to Present

The island is twenty miles long by six miles wide, and is located close to the Maracaibo basin in Venezuela. With low and variable rainfall, an arid, rocky, windswept, and unvegetated terrain subject to occasional hurricanes, even minor earth tremors, Aruba is now home to about 78,000 people. Although today best known for her fine tourism, Aruba was once the site of the largest oil refinery in the world, and before that was the world's largest producer of aloe and a major exporter of phosphates and gold. All of these activities have had a dramatic impact on the people and nature of the island. In several respects Aruba is a case study in ecological devastation. But, beyond this, the island has unique natural environments and cultures, and the resilience to selectively restore, preserve, and adapt its remaining heritage.

Like all other islands of the Caribbean, Aruba passed through a succession of distinctive global epochs mainly driven by sweeping political, technological, and economic changes. Through each historical era, external actors sought specific environmental resources, such as natural harbors, mineral and agricultural products. Today, the primarily resources sought are sun, sand, and sea, the raw materials of modern tourism. In each global age the importance of all these resources has varied tremendously in a manner dictated by the attitudes, products, and technologies of the prevailing global powers.

In pre-Colombian times, Aruba was on the fringes of the great civilizations of South America. During the European Age of conquest and colonization, Aruba faced the civilizing forces of Spain, Britain, Holland, and France. Throughout much of the present (American) century, however, the island's economy has been a subsidiary of a major multinational oil enterprise (Exxon). Thus, in the postwar era the island has faced the dual forces of neocolonialism and global corporatism, and evolved its own institutions and cultures for dealing with this (e.g., Cole 1985). In 1986, Aruba attained *status aparte* from the Netherlands Antilles, but retained strong links with Holland, in principle guaranteeing the islands strategic and financial security. The principle demographic, economic, and environmental characteristics of the island that arose over these years are indicated in Table 11.1.

Long subject to spates of rapid growth and decline, Aruba's economy has expanded very rapidly in the last few years. This has been a remarkable recovery following the closing of the oil refinery in the mid-1980s. This recovery, with a threefold increase in the level of tourism and a great influx of new immigrants, is placing an increasing burden on the island's physical resources, as well as forcing new and rapid changes in the composition and geography of the island's economy, demography, and ecology. In the long run, it is not clear in what sense the present path might be considered ecologically recoverable or

Table 11.1. Main Characteristics of Historical Epochs in Aruba

EPOCH	POPULATION	ECONOMY	ENVIRONMENT and IMPACTS
PRE-COLUMBIAN (~1400BC) (intermittent settlement)	Arawak -Caiquetio	Fishing Manioc Hunting	Small Settlements Cave Dwelling
COLONIAL ERA (~ 1500) Spanish (1500-1634) Dutch (1634 on)	Spanish Dutch Sephardics African Red Indians	Ranching Goat Herding Gold and Phosphates Aloe Plantations Subsistence Farming Fishing Laundering Hat Weaving Sailoring Migrant Labor	Smallholdings Bario Settlements Small Townships De-Vegetation Land Clearance Land Enclosure Tree-Felling Soil Erosion
AMERICAN ERA (~1930) Dutch	North Americans West Indians Surinamse Venezuelans Middle Easterns Chinese Portugese More Dutch 48 Nationalities	Transhipment Oil Refining Commerce Construction Maintainance Light Industry Tourism Government	Squatter Settlement Urbanization Land Abandonment Salination Oil Seepage Road Building Rubbish Dumping
NATIONAL ERA (~1975) Status Aparte (1986)	More Dutch More Americans Haiti Dominica Hong Kong Philippines Colombia Costa Rica China	Service Off-Shore Banking Container Harbor Condominiums Cruise Tourism	Urban Sprawl Suburbanization Rural Encroachment Tourist Strip Tropicalisation Bird Sanctuary Natural Park Golf Course

sustainable. With these changes Aruba is becoming increasingly vulnerable to internal changes (such as provision of fuel and water) and external changes (such as fluctuations in international markets or climate).

The Aruban Economy

Even in the last century, when the population numbered less than 5,000, many Arubans were impoverished by periodic droughts. The domestic economy consisted of commerce, subsistence agriculture, and fishing (Hartog 1958). At times as many as half of the island's men were obliged to work overseas while the women barely sustained a living through agriculture, hat weaving, and laundering for visiting ships. In the late 1920s, the island was delivered from its nineteenth-century poverty by the setting up the Lago oil refinery, later to become one of the largest refineries in the world. This driving force in the island's transition from subsistence to modernity brought with it a variety of social problems (Wever 1970). Within one decade the population increased several-fold. After the war, the refinery began to rationalize its technology and lay off workers, and in the 1960s the island turned to tourism as an alternative source of income, having failed in its efforts to introduce import-substitution manufacturing. With its warm climate, political stability, and gentle people, by the mid-1970s Aruba was already a favored resort (Spinrad 1981). The impact of these changes on the island is illustrated by Figure 11.1 (which shows levels of total employment in Aruba, and key sectors during the present century).

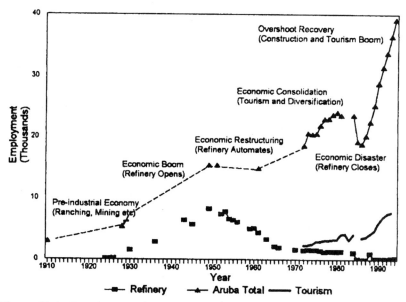

Figure 11.1. Trends in employment in Aruba from 1900 to 1990

When the Lago refinery closed in 1985, Aruba successfully confronted a potentially disastrous economic upheaval just as the island was gaining greater political autonomy, i.e., semi-independence called *status aparte* (Cole 1986). The only solution was to attempt a very rapid expansion of tourism by 1990. Despite the odds this goal was more than exceeded, and soon led to a situation of economic overshoot. In less than a decade, employment in Aruba first fell by over 30% in 1985, and then rose to more than 30% above its original level by 1990, reaching nearly 38 thousand by 1994 (AIB 1995). This was one of the fastest national growth rates in the world. Many new hotels were constructed and many foreign workers came to the island. By the early 1990s, tourism had become the new life and livelihood of the island, reportedly supplemented by "hot" money from the international drug trade and international offshore finance.[8] To top this, in 1990 the oil transshipment terminal reopened (now owned by Wickland), and soon after the refinery was purchased by Coastal. Both are expanding their operations rapidly although under far less generous conditions than those that prevailed under Exxon.

Because the island's population in the 1930s was so small, most native islanders and immigrants gained materially from the wealth generated by Lago. The mammoth refinery is generally considered to have been a great benefactor to the island despite the unwanted side effects discussed later in this chapter. Even in the late 1970s and early 1980s, for example, the taxes paid by the refinery roughly settled the public sector wage bill. Coupled with considerable Dutch development assistance, this provided the Arubans with an unusually prosperous situation in the Caribbean. This both supported a nationally high standard of living, and enabled the rural population to maintain a welfare-subsidized traditional lifestyle in their cunucu homes (Cole 1986).

Demography and the Cultural Division of Labor

The population of Aruba has risen and fallen with the fluctuating fortunes of her economy in drought, boom, and recession. Successive migrant communities are partially squeezed out with each recession only to be replaced by another when the economy rebounds—a constantly replenished "reserve army." By the beginning of the present century this included many people with mixed blood descended from the native Arawaks, as well as African slaves and mulattos brought from Curaçao to the aloe plantations and as house servants for Dutch settlers who, with Sephardics and renegade Venezuelans, became the patriarchs of the island's kinship, regional, economic, and political system. Although the island was for most of this time a subcolony of Curaçao (within the Netherlands Antilles), it evolved a Spanish Indian culture. The arrival of the oil refinery exacerbated further the segmentation of the Aruban society; for example, the American work force lived in a well-appointed colony, separate and protected from the hastily constructed shacks of the West Indian migrant workers.

The structure laid down by this layering process is still evident in most activities, and institutions – social variables such as ethnicity and national origins, religion, education, region and community, language, social class, and attitudes to environment are well correlated with economic variables such as occupation, activity sector, ownership, consumption, access to public and natural resources. Such features have been observed by structural anthropologists following Furnival (Clarke 1984). Some of the more apparent segmentation is summarized in Table 11.2, under the headings of politics, economy, and society. (Relationships with the natural environment will be considered later.) One of the most important distinctions drawn is that between real Arubans and outsiders – the former all speak the local language Papiamento and are divided between an urbanized commercial elite and a rural, more traditional group, the latter subdivided between relatively wealthy expatriates and temporary migrants and settlers mainly from the Caribbean Basin.[9] In both cases there is a distinctive income and ethnic hierarchy found in many Caribbean islands (see Hoetink 1967; Clarke 1984). For reasons of both income and national and social origins, these various populations display quite different consumption

Table 11.2. Characteristics of Cultural, Economic, and Social Divisions in Aruba

	EXPATRIATE	METROPOLITAN ARUBAN	RURAL ARUBAN		MIGRANT ARUBAN	
POLITICAL STRUCTURE						
STATUS	Transient	Outsiders Settled	Insiders	Insiders	Outsiders Settled	Transient
ORIGIN	Dutch American European	Europe Mid-East Asian	Dutch European Venezuelan	Iberain Indian African	English Caribbean	Haiti Caribbean Basin Asia
ARRIVAL	1925-on	1930-on	1700-1900	~1400-1850	1930-1950	1970-
AFFILIATION	None	AVP	AVP	MEP	(PPA)	None
ECONOMIC STRUCTURE						
OCCUPATION	Professional Management	Management Administration Education	Entrepreneur Commerce	Clerical Laboring	Technical Skilled	Laboring Domestic Casual
ACTIVITY	Tourism Refining Finance	Commerce Tourism Business	Commerce Manufactirong Construction	Informal Small Business	Maintenance Hotels	Hotels Service Informal
LIFESTYLE	Middle to Upper Income Luxury Homes Apartments Beach Houses	Wealthy Luxury Homes Villas	Middle Income Suburban Ranchos	Low to Middle Income Small Town Barrios Public Housing	Urban Poor Lower Middle Dense Village Public Housing Multiple Units	Ghetto Poor Small Apartments Squatter Shacks
SOCIAL STRUCTURE						
RELIGION	Mixed	Protestant (various)	Catholic	Catholic	Protestant (various)	Catholic
LANGUAGE	English Dutch	Dutch English	Papiamento Dutch	Papiamento	English	French Spanish Chinese
SETTLEMENT	Oranjestad Malmok Enclaves	Oranjestad Suburbs	Oranjestad Seveneta	Santa Cruz Noord Cunucu	San Nicolas Dakota	San Nicolas Oranjestad

patterns and lifestyles. The groups are also organized socially in different ways. Rural Arubans especially have close-knit kinship networks (often centered on a particular barrio of family), elite Arubans and expatriates have special "clubs" and homes overseas, while immigrants tend to maintain Caribbean-wide (even worldwide) links, with some circulatory migration. This networking is reflected directly in their work, trading. For example, for traditional Arubans, historically, the construction of dwellings has provided a symbolic and material component of their economic culture. A social process and a mode of industrial organization (using local materials, knowledge, and networks) have evolved through which extended families work together to build homes and incur reciprocal obligations (Cole 1993). These various institutions also insure them through crisis and uncertainty.

The essential point here is that the island's population exhibits a marked cultural division of labor with both horizontal and vertical divisions on the supply and the demand side. Each group has a distinctive economic culture.[10] Economic cultures may be labeled in various ways. For example, in literature on development economics' stylized descriptors such as "traditional," "dependent," "migrant," or "metropolitan" are often used to characterize the organizational and economic traits of a population including knowledge and resource base, technology, needs and skills, and patterns of consumption. The demographic groupings in Aruba can be considered to fall into similar categories, but each with their own distinctive flavor.

Duchin (1995) observes, "if we want to give both qualitative and quantitative meaning to livelihood, households need to be classified so that the households within each culture have roughly similar patterns of both production and consumption activities." Table 11.2 lays the ground for one such categorization. It correlates attributes such occupation, education, income, gender, and ethnicity, as well as the various community and public sector biases to the physical, economic, and technological context, and recognizes the importance of social and other networks.[11] This includes distinctive subcategories within each of these divisions and a variety of reinforcing links within, and barriers to transactions between them.[12] In the empirical accounts presented below households, the work force, and all economic activities are subdivided into groups based on the clusters of attributes shown in Table 11.2. There are clear compromises with any such classification – a division that best addresses ecological issues will be less suitable for social or regional issues, and so on. This loss of significance becomes especially acute in small islands when one attempts to use a single framework for several purposes.

Moreover, while statistical analysis can reveal many of these biases and relationships in some detail, it is doubtful whether quantification can capture more than a small part of the full implications of the social and political attributes listed in the table. For this reason, in seeking a balance between the quantitative and the qualitative dimensions of analysis, the aim in later empirical analysis has been to capture only the essential broad characteristics of the island's cultural division of labor within the social accounting model. Further, it allows a qualitative analysis to assess the meaning of the various transactions and any forecasts made using the model, even if this means that the interpretation remains ambiguous.[13]

Regional Settlement and Environment

Over the centuries, with each wave of development, the economic locus has shifted back and forth along the full length of the island. Early settlements by various groups of Indians are found at the back of the island. The Spanish settled in Saveneta (to the west of San Nicolas) which offered a sheltered harbor behind the reefs. When the Dutch took the island they adopted the harbor at Oranjestad because it permitted larger vessels. This situation began to reverse again when phosphate mining began in the 1870s, but Oranjestad and Santa Cruz remained the main population centers until the Lago refinery was established. By the 1940s, San Nicholas was again the growth pole of the island's economy.

With the closing of the refinery in 1985, and the rise of tourism, most new commercial development is in Oranjestad or Noord adjacent to the tourist strip. In addition, with rising incomes, more Arubans are moving to the suburbs which are beginning to cover the entire Western end of the island (see Figure 11.2a). Residential changes are slowed only by the cultural and administrative traditions. For example, at the end of slavery in the mid-nineteenth century people born free on the island were allocated a plot of land (in order to encourage slaves to leave the island), and this distribution has left a complicated regional and local-level patchwork of land and dwelling ownership in Aruba. As new populations arrive on the island their residential location is circumscribed by this and other socioeconomic considerations. Figure 11.2b shows the location of non-Papiamento speaking residents.

The island's varied past, and the abandonment of industrial sites such as ranches, mines, aloe plantations, oil refineries, and the transshipment terminal, has left her with a legacy of present and future environmental problems across most of the island. In addition, international tourism, overpopulation, and conspicuous consumption are among the new problems facing Aruba. Even by the 1920s when the oil refinery first arrived in Aruba, the island's ecology already had been undermined by tree felling to smelt gold and land clearing for aloe plantations. Subsistence cultivation, damage caused by goats, poor drainage, and occasional torrential rains have led to soil erosion and frustrated recent efforts toward revegetation. The stones used in the cunucu walls were taken as foun-

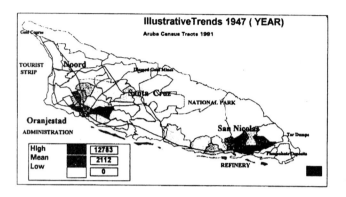

Figure 11.2a. The population density in 1991

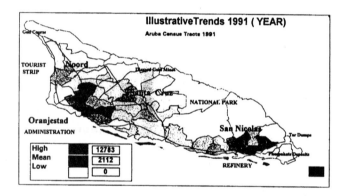

Figure 11.2b. The distribution of non-Papiamento speaking residents

dations for the refinery whose operations subsequently depleted the ground water. Throughout World War II massive amounts of oil tar and bulk were literally dumped on the beaches or shallow pits, and not removed until the 1980s, after a long legal wrangle. Solid wastes are dumped or burned on coastal sites, tides carry any seepage away from the island, and trade winds carry airborne toxins to neighboring countries in Central America. Aruba, in turn, is the landfall for casual waste from Atlantic shipping and nearby Curaçao. The present Coastal and Wickland transshipment facilities carry the risk of spills which may spoil beaches or pollute the drinking water. In Aruba, most potable water is distilled from sea water; only the old style traditional homes have cisterns for capturing rain water. Agricultural water is recycled sewage, or rain water captured in small ponds or "tankis."[14] Water is a perennial problem in Aruba, and for this reason is given prominence in the social accounts.

Government Institutions

In small societies, such as Aruba, government plays a pivotal role in the economy, enabling redistribution of assets to reflect historical kinship patterns, as well as ideological dispositions (Benedict 1978; Henry 1989). Until the end of the Second World War, electoral representation in Aruba was restricted and based on a property qualification. The island's polity essentially consisted of patriarchal extended family cliques with strong regional associations, some in a client relationship with the refinery (Verton 1973; Cvejanovich 1985). Even though the island has a dynamic political system with regular elections and changes in the ruling parties, patronage is evident and has resulted in a bloated public sector, which also cushions the population against economic fluctuations (NCEER 1993). In a covert fashion, the island government largely manages to resist Holland's compulsion to manipulate its affairs (Sedoc-Dahlberg 1989). The current ruling party, the Arubaanse Volks Partij (AVP), represents the interests of the old urban elite (essentially a small business party), but relies heavily on the financial support of the leaders of the prosperous tourism and commerce sectors. Although bent on modernizing the Aruban work force, this party is obliged to give way to demands from the commercial sector to relax immigration. The current opposition, Movimento Electoral di Pueblo (MEP), has its own business supporters, but with strong backing from the traditional cunucu dwellers, is equally trapped between the need to educate this population and retain its vote through its appeal to nativeness and tradition. This dilemma confounds the need to encourage traditional Arubans to reconsider their relationship with the environment through means such as restraining their predatory goats and raising skill levels so that productivity matches lifestyle.

Implicit in these positions are two contrasting versions of the island's economic and demographic future: a prosperous Aruba for its citizens (but with no policy to implement it), and a modern open economy (that offers no real safeguards to protect the interests of traditional Arubans against opportunistic foreign and local entrepreneurs) with a steadily increasing, mainly alien population. In this, most new citizens are virtually disenfranchised (since the demise of the Partido Patriotica Arubano (PPA)). The upshot of this dichotomy is stop-go and a systemic dysfunctionality of key departments concerned with economic development and the environment as ministers, policies, and personnel are changed. With this new phase of growth, land is becoming increasingly scarce and the need for new and effective zoning regulations has become far more pressing. Thus, even though the most recent wave of economic development is placing such an unaccountable burden on the island's physical resources, an institutional complicity between government and developers places few checks on the dramatic shifts in the composition and geography of the island's economy, demography, and ecology.[15]

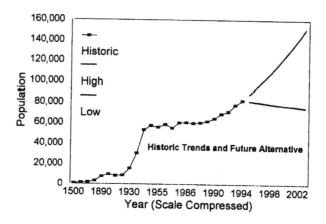

Figure 11.3 Demographic trends and alternatives in Aruba

Prevailing political and cultural forces imply quite different levels of impact on environment. Current arguments range between advocating an increase in population to around 120,000, to maintaining (or even decreasing) present levels. As Figure 11.3 shows, population trends are moving rapidly to the higher level. Despite this, there is rather little discussion about the outlook for the future. This is hardly surprising on an island with a discount rate upwards of 30%, and where most economic events are determined from outside, and most of the population is in the process of taking advantage of them while the good times last. Most islanders recognize the government's limitations and develop their own strategies for dealing with uncertainty. During the last crisis, for example, depending on their circumstances, the different communities took advantage of bank accounts in Miami, refuge in Holland, secure jobs in government, extended families in Aruba, circulatory migration around the Caribbean, and a worldly variety of informal sector activities. Even the goats are an insurance. Only the threats to tourism from a littered environment or downswings in the North American economy are treated as somewhat more sonorous.

EMPIRICAL ANALYSIS: CULTURAL–ECOLOGICAL ACCOUNTING

The empirical work summarized in this section attempts to make the economic structure described in Table 11.2 more concrete. This is done by constructing an ecological–cultural accounting matrix (EcoCAM), based on a cultural accounting matrix method (Cole 1993, 1994). This is then extended to include specific ecological variables pertinent to present environmental concerns in Aruba. Each item in the table has a direct relationship with elements of the earlier discussion and illustrates empirical issues. In principle, therefore, the historical analysis, the model, and its results mutually inform each other.

Cultural Accounting

Cultural accounting matrices (CAM) are an obvious extension of the input–output tables first introduced by Leontief, and the later social accounting matrices (see Pyatt and Roe 1977; Adelman,Taylor, and Vogel 1988). Input–output tables, in general, offer a way to represent the flow of goods, income and people between businesses, households, and public service within an economy, or between neighboring localities and regions. As such they afford a useful starting point for the economic evaluation of economy–ecology relationships. They provide a picture of how the different parts of a community are linked together as a productive technological and social network, and at least some links to the physical world, especially inputs of raw materials such as land, energy, and water, and outputs of pollutants (gaseous and solid waste and emission).

The cultural accounts are designed to serve several purposes – to better the understanding of distribution mechanisms in small multicultural societies (Cole 1994), provide the basis for short-run project evaluation and cost–benefit analysis of certain emergency preparedness measures in key livelihood and lifeline sectors (e.g., Cole 1995), and to be used as an input into discussions of sustainable development scenarios for Aruba (e.g., Aruba Today 1995). While a single table can contribute to all these goals, it must be used in different ways.

The items to be included in the Aruba accounts, and the way in which the information is organized within the matrix, are shown in Table 11.3. One pervading concern in constructing social accounts is to find an appropriate level of aggregation for each activity (e.g., Pyatt and Roe 1977; United Nations 1994). Here, one attractive facility of input–output type tables is that they allow a mixed representation so that individual processes within a production unit or networks of activities can be juxtaposed with a macro-level model, or a national model may be subdivided by geographic region.

The Aruba CAM has four components, each subdivided in different ways. In the first, the "lifeline" activities of energy and water production are treated as separate processes in individual enterprises. In the second, the principal livelihood sector, tourism, is broken down by style of tourism (stayover versus cruise visitors), class of hotel, and ancillary activities (such as taxi tours, restaurants, and specialty retailing). All other private sector activities are combined into the conventional Standard Industrial Classification (SIC). The community (household) sector is subdivided according to different population groups, as discussed above, each associated with characteristic occupations and lifestyles. Other public sector activities, such as education, are combined into a single sector.[16] For some applications, the data are subdivided further (into large and small enterprises or by region of the island).

The Aruba cultural accounts for the year 1990 are shown in Table 11.4. Each entry represents a transaction – the amount paid in millions of Aruban florins (AFl) by one actor (i.e., business, sector, or class of household) to another over the course of the year. For example, the AFl 67 million of fuel oil purchased by WEB from the oil refinery appears in the top-left of the matrix. The columns show the expenditures by each actor, and the rows show their purchases. Total income and expenditures for each actor are approximately equal.[17] With their intrinsic network structure, an extended input–output table such as the CAM allows the direct and indirect consequences of changes for actors in a community to be represented and calculated. It is important to note that one value of the table as a device for studying the distributional consequences of structural economic change arises because the cultural division of labor has greater permanence than the sectorial divisions – the migrant groups, for example, roll over into the same lowly positions even as the economy restructures.

As well as being a statistical reconciliation of many data, the table also implies an underlying round-by-round process of income accumulation (e.g., Miller and Blair 1985). This last point may be understood by reading along the migrant household income row (the largest contribution to their income comes from unskilled labor: AFl 22 million) then by reading along the low-skilled labor income row to see that the largest contribution to low-skilled workers comes from the construction sector (AFl 40 million). Thus we should expect that the employment and livelihood of immigrants is especially sensitive to fluctuations in the construction industry. Carrying this process further, we see

Table 11.3. Items Included in the Cultural-Environmental Accounts

Category	Production	Labor	Households	Government	Investment	Extra-regional	
Production	Transactions by types of production activity		Household consumption by population subgroups	Public expenditures by activity		External sales of goods and services	T o t a l
Labor	Wage income by skill or education			Government wages		Wage income from outside	
Households	Entrepreneurial income by household	Wage transfers to population subgroups	Informal transfers by households	Public transfers to households	Investment income by subgroup	Household income from outside	
Firms and Capital	Capital payments by type of ownership		Savings by households	Financial transactions by government	Financial transactions by subgroups	Outside investment and balance of payments	I n c o m e
Government	Indirect taxes	Wage taxes	Direct taxes		Corporate taxes	Economic assistance	
Extra-regional	Imports	Other extra-regional payments					
	Total Expenditures by Each Activity						

Note: Items in upper left box may be sub-divided by region.

Table 11.4. *The Aruba Cultural Accounts with Tourism and Lifeline Sectors.*

SECTOR or ACTIVITY	1 Wick	2 Coas	3 WEB‑E	4 WEB‑W	5 ELMA	6 Tran	7 High	8 LowR	9 Tour	10 Bars	11 Casi	12 Taxi	13 Indu	14 Cons	15 Othe	16 Othe	17 Labo	18 Labo	19 Labo	20 Depr	21 Loca	22 Trad	23 Metr	24 Migr	25 Exps	26 Firm	27 Gove	28 Hous	29 Firm	30 Gove	31 Stay	32 Crui	33 Impo	34 Over
1 Wickland Terminal																																	2023	
2 Coastal Refinery			57																														2001	
3 WEB‑Electric	2	3		40	51		5	9					1			3						4	16	1	3		1							
4 WEB‑Water	2	4			2		5	2					2			4						6	23	2	4		2							
5 ELMAR	2	2																																
6 Transport‑Telecom																																		
7 HighRise Hotels																						0	1	0	0		1		14		159			
8 LowRise Hotels																						0	1	0	0						119			
9 Tourist Shops																						18	35	0	6						41			
10 Bars/Cafes																						1	3	0	3						23			
11 Casino																						1	1	0	0						74			
12 Taxi/Tours																															20			
13 Industry/Agriculture													17	30	1	24						57	138	14	24		6		66	22	8		26	
14 Construction													6		0	14						1	6	0	1		1	46	211	9				
15 Other Commerce													30	15	20	14						102	257	26	45		66			2			218	
16 Other Service													26	23	23	57						46	149	12	26	9	40			3	107	14	179	
17 Labor (low education)							65	50	69	14	20	6	34			16																		
18 Labor (middle education)							13	9																										
19 Labor (high education)							15	10																										
20 Depreciation							33	5			4																							
21 Local Surplus							23	12	19	7	32	5	83	10	129	332																		
22 Traditional Aruban Hhok																	88	49	10		55													
23 Metropolitan Aruban Hhok																	41	122	207		350													
24 Migrant Households																	22	12	3		19													
25 Expatriate Households																	7	22	37		95													
26 Firms																				151	86													
27 Government																	10	15	21	4														
28 Household Capital																						1	16	0	8	138								
29 Firms Capital																							68	−2	16									
30 Government Capital																										101	−2							
31 Stayover Tourists																																		
32 Cruise Ships																																		
33 Imports Goods/Services	1997	2017																				11	47	13	25		9				96	10		
34 Overseas Finance																						−6	68	−2	16		−2							
EXPENDITURES	2023	2067	100	47	80		200	123	112	28	76	22	446	308	732	757	168	221	277	155	604	242	785	71	173	239	298	95	416	298	571	38	639	1069
RECEIPTS	2023	2068	100	47	80		200	123	112	28	76	22	446	309	734	759	168	220	275	159	624	242	785	71	173	237	298	76	417	298	572	39	639	1051

Notes: Data are from various sources and years. The matrix has been scaled and balanced (see text). Amounts are shown to nearest AFI million (1990)

247

how changes in the income of any other actor will eventually affect all other actors. This is the basis of the calculations considered later.

The following provides brief details on sources of data and how the cultural accounts were assembled and reconciled, and indicates how the items related to the earlier discussion.

The Community Sector

Following the divisions explained earlier, the population is divided into four groups: traditional Aruban, metropolitan Aruban, migrant, and expatriate. Proportionately, these groups comprise about 35%, 40%, 20%, and 5% of the population.[18] Even though the boundaries between the groups are diffuse, it is possible to establish a consistent quantification of their situation from the available data (UNESCO 1989). It should be said that since there were inconsistencies across these statistics, in establishing the table it was necessary to rely also on the judgment of officials concerned with their collection (United Nations 1994), and on ethnographic studies (Green 1973; Latham 1984; Razak 1995). The significant point about the table is that the income sources and consumption propensities vary across groups in distinctive ways; for example, expatriates and wealthy Arubans spend proportionately more money abroad (the bottom row in their expenditure column), are more involved in entrepreneurial activity (the intersection of the production columns and the household rows), derive income from higher status jobs (the intersection of the factor columns and the household rows), and so on. Because of the networking within each subgroup, there are self-reinforcing expenditure flows for each population (Cole 1993).

The Domestic Production and Public Sectors

The construction of the interindustry component of this matrix will not be described in detail since this has been reported elsewhere and similar procedures are used fairly widely (Cole et al. 1983). One great advantage in modeling island economies (compared to regions of metropolitan countries) is that data on cross-border flows of population, commodities, and finance are available. The table was developed initially at the one-digit level from a survey of firms subdivided by size with partial company accounts for principal businesses such as the main hotels, the oil refinery and larger transshipment operations, using the standards of contemporary input–output model construction approximated to a "full survey" extended input–output model.[19] Evident here are variations in purchasing of different commodities locally and overseas, the varied skill mix in employment, and the high gross surplus in commerce and service activities (seen in the intersection of the local production columns and the factor rows).

The Tourism Sector

The tourism sector is treated as clusters of similar activities at a meso-level of aggregation. As indicated earlier, tourism in Aruba is expanding very rapidly. From 1986 to 1990 the average annual growth rate of tourist arrivals in Aruba was 24% (compared to 8.5% in the Caribbean as a whole). The industry comprises a range of hotels with an emphasis on high-rise and low-rise hotels, timeshare apartments, and a number of smaller condominium complexes. Income from tourism in 1990 was at least AFl 373 million (excluding time share), and hotel employment alone stood at 4,000 (out of a total labor force of around 27,000). The sector also involves a variety of shopping plazas, casinos (mostly linked to hotels) and other entertainment, eating, and sightseeing facilities providing another 3,000 jobs (CEP 1991). The data on income and expenditures used for the tourism network also comes from a number of sources and has been scaled into the CAM as described above.[20] Again, these data show distinctive payment structures, especially in terms of imports and payments overseas, and that most of their income is from visitors to the island. The tourist sector in Aruba displays a marked cultural division of labor, evident, for example, in the ethnicity of front desk and kitchen employees (Latham 1984), arising from the desire to impress a distinctive Aruban image on visitors (Spinrad 1981).

Physical and Environmental Sectors

The extension of input–output tables to include ecological variables has been pioneered by several authors, notably Isard (1972), Leontief (1970), Leontief and Carter (1976), and most recently by Duchin and Lange (1994). Replicating this transforms the CAM into an EcoCAM. When activities have a significant monetary component, or feedback income to enhance multiplier-type effects, then it is necessary for them to be made explicit within the matrix. For this reason, commercial water and fuel are detailed in the Aruba matrix. In other cases, a satellite table of empirically derived coefficients are appended to the input–output table in a manner similar to that used for labor and capital coefficients (e.g., Bartelmus et al. 1991). These include industry and pollutant-specific coefficients representing the level of physical emissions, or the cost of curtailing emissions, or the physical flows associated with monetary transactions in the social accounts.

The Fuel–Electricity–Water Network

The most detailed sectors in the matrix are the so-called lifeline sectors. In view of their criticality to the economy and environment, the water, electricity, and fuel sectors are elaborated at the level of individual businesses and operations, and endogenized in the accounts. The way these activities are linked together and to the rest of the economy is shown schematically in Figure 11.4.

Oil is imported into Aruba by the Wickland transshipment terminal and a partially reopened oil refinery operated by Coastal. Both are located in San Nicolas at the extreme east of the island on the Lago site. Fuel oil is piped from Coastal to Water and Electricity (WEB) which is located on the central southern coast of Aruba at Balashi. WEB coproduces electricity and water, the latter through distillation from sea water. In the matrix, WEB is treated as a vertically integrated corporation (i.e., providing its own intermediate inputs) with coproduction costs allocated between production of water and electricity. Electricity and water are sold directly to Wickland and Coastal by WEB, who is contracted to purchase any excess from Coastal's own generator (CEP 1991). WEB distributes directly to residences, hotels, and commercial users via separate pipelines. Electricity is distributed to other users by a separate company, ELMAR.[21] One important aspect of Aruba's water supply associated with the island's cultural division of labor is that the rain water cisterns are still found at about 10% of rural dwellings, but only 2% of urban dwellings. Although these are noncommercial, they offer the prospect of a backup supply in short-term emergencies, in addition to the water tanks mounted on several hills at strategic points around the island (Cole 1995).

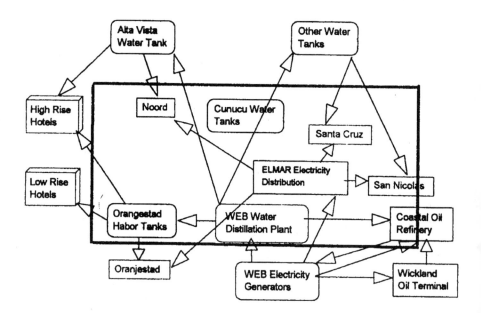

Figure 11.4. Linkage in the Aruba fuel and water lifeline system

Physical Land Constraints

Table 11.5 includes the physical land use, water, fuel, and yields of waste and toxins. In Aruba there are clear limits to the amount of land available. Partly because of the Dutch heritage (and Holland's continuing influence in the island), there is the possibility of rather useful data covering items such as land use by type – residential, commercial, agricultural, and so on – as well as specific uses such as beachfront and scenic areas. The amount of land used by the main activities varies considerably; for example, a conventional hotel resort has 125 units per hectare, about twice that of an enclave resort. Nonbulk industry situates 25 units per hectare (PlanD2 1980). In practice different lifestyles demand quite contrasting amounts of land. In Aruba there are on average 12 dwellings per hectare, but traditional cunucu houses (essentially small holdings) occupy far more, as do the second home ranchos of urban Arubans. Land required for public access, such as roads, airports, and harbors, depends on the level of activity and income, for example, from car ownership or tourism. Again these data do not appear in the matrix, but in making calculations the demand for land arising from a particular pattern of change is compared with the amount that is currently made available. (In some cases marginal coefficients are required since the intensity of use of existing sites may increase. For example, the maximum plot size allocated by the government for dwellings has been recently halved.)

Toxins and Bulk Waste

There are relatively few data on toxic emissions in Aruba, although for several local industries such as food and aloe processing, timber yards, and paint manufacture, these may be approximated by industry-specific data for similar technologies in other countries (e.g., Floyd 1994). There are also preliminary data on the amount of bulk waste (garbage) produced by various households and businesses in Aruba (Boerwinkel 1995). However, the core difficulty in this kind of analysis is tracing the physical, nonlinear, and combinatorial consequences of emissions (e.g., Hanemann 1995). The goal is to systematically extend the physical emissions in the direction advocated by the modified SNA for integrated environmental and economic accounting (Bartelmus, Stahmer, and van Tongere 1991), but to focus on specific issues and to incorporate the variability across economic cultures on both the supply and demand sides of the accounts. The coefficients for labor, waste, land, water, and energy are shown in Table 11.5. These are used in the calculations presented next.

Table 11.5. Environmental Satellite Table for the Aruba Cultural Accounts

SECTOR or ACTIVITY	OUTPUT Total AFl million	Work year/AFlm Jobs/O	Waste lb/AFlm TR/O	Land km2/AFlm Area/O	Water m3/AFlm Vol/O	Energy Btu/AFlm E/O
Wickland Terminal	2023	0.1	3.7	0.002	0.001	0.002
Coastal Refinery	2068	0.1	18.6	0.002	0.002	0.001
WEB-Electric	100	2.2	9.3	0.030	0.000	0.673
WEB-Water	47	2.6	4.6	0.086	0.000	0.868
ELMAR	80	1.5	2.3	0.050	0.012	0.846
Transport-Telecom	0	0.0	0.0	0.000	0.000	0.000
HighRise Hotels	200	11.9	1.1	0.050	0.025	0.047
LowRise Hotels	123	12.8	1.0	0.041	0.017	0.043
Tourist Shops	112	6.7	0.7	0.089	0.001	0.019
Bars/Cafes	28	7.7	0.7	0.142	0.037	0.004
Casino	76	10.8	0.9	0.013	0.013	0.039
Taxi/Tours	22	10.2	1.0	0.048	0.000	0.000
Industry/Agriculture	448	1.7	1.8	0.000	0.002	0.005
Construction	309	14.2	5.0	0.016	0.000	0.000
Other Commerce	734	6.4	5.0	0.027	0.005	0.017
Other Services	759	8.7	5.0	0.013	0.001	0.007
Labor (low education)	168					
Labor (middle education)	220					
Labor (high education)	275					
Depreciation	159					
Local Surplus	624					
Traditional Aruban Hholds	242	0.0	10.0	0.144	0.016	0.026
Metropolitan Aruban Hholds	785	2.0	5.0	0.025	0.021	0.029
Migrant Households	71	0.0	5.0	0.141	0.014	0.022
Expatriate Households	173	2.0	5.0	0.087	0.017	0.023
Firms	237	0.0	0.0	0.000	0.000	0.000
Government	298	22.2	5.0	0.017	0.003	0.006
Household Capital	76					
Firms Capital	417					
Government Capital	39					
Stayover Tourists	672					
Cruise Ships	11					
Imports Goods/Services	5096					
Overseas Finance	1051					

Note: These are author's working estimates based on various sources.

TOWARD SUSTAINABLE DEVELOPMENT

The first part of this chapter indicated how historical changes in Aruba have led to the present configuration of cultures, economy, and society. The same forces that shaped the island's economy and social structures shape the imported tropes (or constructs) that today compete to determine present-day Aruban attitudes toward, and treatment of, the natural environment. These related directly to the categories of economic culture used in the CAM, and play into the political dynamics. They are now discussed in more detail as a precursor to considering alternative strategies to achieve sustainable development.

Traditional

The first trope concerns the myth versus the reality of the traditional lifestyle. Despite popular images that traditional people live in harmony with nature, the historic reality in Aruba was a hard fight against nature, clearing small holdings of unwanted cacti and thorny shrubs, clearing fields of sharp stones, and constantly rebuilding walls to defend against marauding goats, and parsimonious use only of limited resources such as water. Traditionally, Arubans used tank and sewage water on their crops and left the native species to fend for themselves. Today, while many Arubans would claim a strong emotional link to this land, with its tall cacti, divi-divi trees, rocky outcrops, and desert vistas as an aspect of their belongingness to the island (Razak 1995), they nevertheless still appear to treat this nature as an enemy to be defeated. With modern construction equipment, such as bulldozers, for construction of new hotels, homes, and the inevitable shopping plazas, the odds have shifted in their favor. Moreover, while traditional household and farm refuse dumped in the cunucu eventually biodegraded or was eaten by goats, modern waste, including old cars, bottles, and refrigerators, remains for decades.

Metropolitan

In the last decades younger more educated Arubans have moved to urban jobs and homes, and increasingly have sought a consumerist lifestyle. Historically this desire was driven by the affluent lifestyles of American oil workers and other expatriates. More recently it is fueled by Venezuelan and American tourists and fantasy television, and returning Aruban migrants. A rising income has enabled upper income Arubans to increase consumption dramatically, and in an ersatz manner to hark back to their traditional roots. They are setting up second homes on the island – either refurbished traditional family homes or new homes built in the traditional style in previously lightly settled parts of the island. Rather than grow traditional species, they favor planting palm trees and other nonnative species. Thus, in competing ways, both traditional and modern lifestyles (or metropolitan Arubans) are placing an increasing burden on the natural environment through increased demand for land and water, and the production of waste.

Migrants and Expatriates

The rising number of temporary migrant and expatriate workers strains these same ecological variables. While the incomes of expatriates are typically higher than Arubans, they tend to live in the urban centers around Oranjestad and San Nicolas or in nearby enclaves, realizing their own (socially constructed) image of the tropical paradise. Most poor migrants, including an estimated 7,000 of whom are illegal, are obliged to live in relatively squalid parts of these towns, as well as the hastily constructed annexes to Aruban households. Many come from wretched urban areas around the Caribbean, and often seem even less caring of the environment, and are less well served by the island's garbage collection. The influx of so many non-Arubans is prompting a popular reaction against further expansion of tourism, much to the consternation of the industry and its supporters. Both expatriates and migrants see the island as a place to get rich quick and then leave, and have relatively little interest in the long-run future of the island (an attitude which is reinforced by the government's decision to prevent their permanent settlement by limiting work permits to one year).

The pressure on land and other resources is compounded because, while the former refinery was located at the southeast end of the island in San Nicolas, the tourist strip is predominantly to the northwest of the capital Oranjestad, and the greatest pressure for land is at that end of the island, around the old settlement of Noord. Historically, because of the close-knit character of the rural communities, it has proved difficult, even for some longtime immigrants to settle at this end of the island, so there has been a considerable increase in commuting along the length of the island.

Tourism and Business

Another imported trope comes from the demands of the international tourist industry, as the major hotels, international airlines, and tour operators attempt to lock the island into a standardized package of beaches and palm trees. Aruba is well-endowed with beaches, but palm trees are not native to the island and demand copious amounts of water. Because the island is so small, the expansion of tourism in Aruba has placed new demands on access to land, beaches, drinking and garden water, and the disposal of solid wastes. For example, the Hyatt hotel agreed to locate on the island only on condition that a full-size golf course be established. Not only does this literal greening of the island place incredible new demands on the water supply, it also has resulted in a formerly publicly-accessible wilderness being fenced off and appropriated for an expensive residential development. Although the new development may be a wonderful place to live, it is tragic in the context of a disappearing ecosystem. The fragility of this style of development in Aruba is demonstrated by the decay of the former oil refinery colony after only a few years of abandonment. The insistence of the tour operators to improve visual amenity has forced the authorities to reduce the level of litter and nonaesthetic waste, and groups of school children spend their summers cleaning beaches and other tourist sites. Because of the importance of the tourism industry to Aruba, all political parties are hostage to its dictates. In small vulnerable economies, tourism and other businesses insist on rapid payback on investments rather than focus on longer-term issues. Although this may appear to be a shortsighted strategy, it is based on a quite rational expectation given the island's history – that in the medium-run there is likely to be another dramatic and unpredictable change.

Environmentalism

The last trope arises mainly with Arubans educated in Holland during the environmentalist era of the 1960s, many of whom are now in civil service positions in Aruba, and are determined to rescue native flora and fauna beyond the bird sanctuary and natural park[22] (e.g., van Aller et al. 1994; Boerwinkel 1995). With Dutch encouragement, there have been several relatively unsuccessful efforts to revegetate parts of the island and encourage citizens to plant native trees. This ambition somewhat feeds the desire of most Arubans to create a distinctive national identity as a counter to the rising tide of immigrants, in part through identification with their native flora and fauna. Not entirely synergistic here is that almost daily they see that traditional recreation areas where they have camped, the wilderness where they have hunted iguana and rabbits, and the beaches where they have fished, dwindle. This loss is made more apparent because the very smallness of the island has allowed urban Arubans to retain regular links with the land, for example, regularly visiting relatives in the cunucu. But while, in the face of the evident surge of development across the island, the environmental movements on the island are finding a voice, this nevertheless remains the weakest force in Aruba's environmental future.

APPLICATIONS OF THE MODEL

The EcoCAM might help to inform the issues raised in this chapter in several ways. In effect, the matrix becomes the empirical core of a variety of applications related to economic and other developments in Aruba, and to apply the model directly within the evolving dialogue just described. This last section summarizes the methodology and findings of four kinds of applications. In each case there is an effort to use the model as a practical tool to address current development and ecological concerns.

The first and most tractable application is to assess the income effects of the prevailing economic structure in Aruba, for example, how the changing structure of the economy or the introduction of a new business activity impacts on other firms and households, or how networking activities influence the distribution of income among the population. This is the most common use of a social accounting model. The second is to explore the vulnerability of the island to specific short-term natural and economic events such as hurricanes, the loss of major businesses, or the vulnerability of environmental support systems such as fuel or water (for example, as a consequence of an oil spillage). As emphasized by the last discussion, one important aspect of establishing more respectful attitudes for the long run is to reduce the uncertainty and vulnerability in everyday life. Through the island's Calamity Preparedness Committee, Aruban institutions are becoming more sensitized to these issues. A third and more experimental application extends this discursive framework to a wider national debate in Aruba using the matrix as part of an effort to design ecologically sustainable futures (i.e., in the direction advocated by Duchin 1994). A last and yet more elaborate use would integrate the matrix with a long-run simulation model, linked to an appropriate geographic information system, noting that environmental issues in Aruba, as elsewhere, have a strong temporal and spatial component.[23] Examples of how the EcoCAM is being used for these four applications are discussed below.

Community-Based Development

The earlier discussion showed how the cultural division of labor in Aruba cuts across technology, sectors, and populations in relatively well-defined ways. Thus, given a particular change in the economy it will differentially impact on the various populations. In some cases, reinforcing circular flows of income arise within a given community. In particular, an entrepreneur from a particular group will employ workers from that group, and both will tend to purchase goods from the same group. In some cases this is a matter of spatial proximity, in other cases it arises from social preference or kinship (e.g., Olson 1971; van der Berge 1981). Clearly, such mechanisms can be used to target economic development towards particular populations, making use of specific multiplier processes within the island's economy (e.g., Adelman, Taylor, and Vogel 1988).[24]

The organization of homes and other construction among traditional Arubans provides one example. In this case, the present style of development in Aruba undermines the networking that has been a core economic activity within the Aruban culture. Because Aruban construction activities are often organized on a semiformal basis, they cannot compete in the construction of high-rise hotels and condominiums, and large-scale public buildings and infrastructure. A similar situation arises in the provision of food and other commodities for hotels; the volume and uniform quality required forces hotels to import most produce. It is apparent that cooperative arrangements to share equipment among builders, to adopt a policy of smaller-scale and alternative tourism development, to pool and grade local produce and manufactured products would help to reverse this situation and to slow the erosion of the traditional income and lifestyle. All of these actions would have an impact on the environmental health of the island and the viability of community structures. That it might be possible, in principle, to double the share of income to the traditional community from development projects is demonstrated by Cole (1993). However, whether such arrangements could work in practice depends on several social and political considerations made evident by the earlier discussion. Thus, in this case the matrix can be used to demonstrate possibilities, but ethnographic analysis is required to determine the modus operandi or viability of such proposals.

Reducing Short-Run Vulnerability

An example of the second use, elaborated by Cole (1995), is to assess the risk value of specific components of the lifeline system in Aruba, such as backup storage tanks. This is done, assuming a variety of contingencies suggested by the Aruba Calamity Committee. For example, it is assumed that a serious rupture resulting in several days loss of water supply occurs in the main pipeline from Oranjestad to Palm Beach, cutting the strip off from the Balashi plant and the Harbor tanks. In this case, the Alta Vista tank (shown in Figure 11.4) is assumed to become the fallback supply for the hotels. The *value* of the tank for this purpose can then be assessed by asking how much economic loss is averted by its presence.[25]

The most common method used in cost–benefit analysis is to weigh economic losses to the various interest groups uniformly, for example, by minimizing the loss to domestic value added, or that part of value added that is retained on the island, within specified constraints – in this case the total cutback in water supply.[26] Depending on the priorities for the allocation of cutback impacts, there can be quite contrasting outcomes. This is seen from Table 11.6 which summarizes the consequences of applying different priorities.

(a) Shows a uniform five-day cutback when all activities lose publicly supplied water for the same period;
(b) Favors the tourism sector;
(c) Favors local businesses; while
(d) Favors all households,
(e) Favors rural households, and
(f) Favors different communities and households.

The last item attempts to balance several needs. The columns show the weightings and calculated income to each sector when these are used to minimize the weighted welfare loss from a fixed loss of public water supply. Comparing the losses in (a) against those in (f) suggests that activities could gain from a managed response to emergencies.

The calculations behind Table 11.6 suggest a number of specific ways of managing a breakdown in water supply in Aruba through reallocation of water supply, and that major economic loss might be avoided if the burden of water shortage was passed to households. The prevalence of many household reservoirs in rural areas in Aruba suggests these could be used for emergency supplies in rural areas. The calculations show that reducing noneconomic hardship depends on the balance of essential versus discretionary water usage by households. Again, this strategy for assuring a minimum supply could only be effective as a means of reducing life-threatening hardship if it took account of the social networks on the island and the varying degrees of access between the island's different communities. Since the events considered often go beyond the direct experience of participants, an indirect means of ascertaining trade-offs through model simulations can help to reveal preferences and value contingencies (e.g., van der Veen et al. 1995).

Table 11.6. Impact of Alternative Allocations of Water Supply on Communities in Aruba

CRITERIA / Water Loss (Constrain)	(a) UNIFORM ALLOCATI Schedule Loss AFlm ******		(b) FAVOR TOURISM SECTOR Weight Schedu Loss AFlm ******			(c) FAVOR LOCAL ECONOMY Weight Schedu Loss AFlm			(d) FAVOR ALL HOUSEHOLD Weight Schedu Loss AFlm			(e) FAVOR RURAL HOUSEHO Weight Schedu Loss AFlm			(f) WEIGHTED INTERESTS Weight Schedu Loss AFlm		
All Lifelines	5.0	53.4		2.2	21.1		1.9	20.2		2.2	22.7		2.2	24.1	2	2.2	22.1
Tourism Sector	5.0	6.8	1	0.6	0.2		1.6	0.8		1.7	1.6		1.7	2.4	2	1.8	1.3
All Other Sectors	5.0	44.5	1	1.1	4.8	1	0.3	1.5		3.4	24.2		4.5	40.9	1	2.2	15.2
Wages		11.8			1.1			0.6			4.4			8.5			3.0
Margins		12.1			1.2			0.5			5.5			11.1			3.5
All Households	5.0	23.4		6.3	2.2		6.3	1.1	1	5.1	9.6		5.5	18.7		5.7	6.3
Rural	5.0	4.3		7.0	0.4		7.0	0.2		5.7	1.7	1	4.2	3.2	2	4.9	1.2
Urban	5.0	14.7		6.0	1.4		6.0	0.7		6.0	6.1		6.0	12.0	1	6.0	4.0
Local Value Added		26.7			2.6			1.4			11.0			21.8			7.3
Government	5.0	6.5		0.1	0.5		0.1	0.3		0.1	2.5		0.1	4.3		0.1	1.5
Objective Function	None		Minimize Income Loss			Minimize Income Loss			Minimize Weighted Welfare Loss			Minimize Weighted Welfare Loss			Minimize Weighted Welfare Loss		

For a complex society, such as Aruba, there may be no other way.[27] People will say whether an outcome is acceptable, but not why, and it is not unusual for participants to veto specific outcomes without specifying their precise reasons. When many of the population are quite vulnerable to fluctuations in economic conditions, and their survival rests on social networks, much defensive activity is covert. So long as a situation of high short-run uncertainty prevails, there is unlikely to be serious discussion of the longer term. It should be said that one reason for using the model in the context of policy issues, such as the threat of lost business from hurricanes, that are of direct concern to island government via the Aruba Calamity Committee (ACC) and the private sector via the Aruba Hotel and Tourism Association (AHATA), is to increase confidence that the model may be applicable to other considerations, such as those discussed next.

The Implications of Alternative Lifestyles

Most notions of sustainability refer to the longer run, and are based on variants of economic, ecological, and intergenerational constructs (Munasinghe and McNealy 1992). In Aruba, one way in which the trade-offs between these constructs are played out is through the dialogue between tradition and modernity. An effort has begun to use the cultural accounts to address this issue using a method similar to that described above, and to provide a simple framework based on the cultural accounts that may be used to demonstrate the implications of the various alternatives in a public forum (Aruba Today 1995).

For this, it has been useful to describe possible outcomes for the Aruban lifestyle as comprising a mix of existing ways of life of the Traditional and Metropolitan Arubans – thus, outcomes represent the share of different components of the traditional and modern in the present Aruban lifestyles. The proportions may be adjusted to reflect changes, as may be the land and waste coefficients associated with each. In the example shown, the high/low forecasts of the hotels and the oil industry are combined with national labor supply growth and GNP targets, and matched to specified waste and land constraints. In the illustration given in Table 11.7 the lifestyle target tritely comprises two parts tradition to one part modernity, but could be elaborated up to the limits of data or imagination. Various welfare goals are then optimized to meet the forecasts, targets, priorities, and constraints set for the other variables. In the example shown the target for value added and employment, and the upper limit on the levels of pollutants, and all available land (i.e., in this case newly zoned land) are met, but constraints on water and energy production are not. Through discussion of many such examples, it is hoped that the framework might contribute to a discussion of alternative priorities and lifestyles, and debates within the Aruban community.[28]

Table 11.7 The Impact of Lifestyles on Welfare and Environmental Variables

CRITERIA	Welfare Weighting	Income Change	Employment Coeff	Employment Amount	Waste/Pollutants Coeff	Waste/Pollutants Amount	Land Coeff	Land Amount	Water Coeff	Water Amount	Fuel Coeff	Fuel Amount
All Lifetimes		344	0	77	11	3768	0.004	1.4	0.002	0.5	0.038	13.2
WEB-Water		6.5									0.868	
Tourism Sector		147.9	11	1569	1	140	0.048	7.2	0.016	2.4	0.035	5.2
All Other Sectors		177.7	7	1297	4	777	0.014	2.4	0.003	0.5	0.009	1.6
Wages		76.6										
All Households		137.1							0.019		0.027	
Traditional	10	27.3	2	169	10	273	0.127	3.5	0.016	0.4	0.026	0.7
Metropolitan	5	84.6			5	423	0.022	1.9	0.021	1.8	0.029	2.4
Migrant		7.5			5	38	0.124	0.9	0.014	0.1	0.022	0.2
Expatriate		17.7	2	35	5	88	0.076	1.3	0.017	0.3	0.023	0.4
Local Value Added		154.8										
Government		38.4	22	852	5	192	0.015	0.6	0.015	0.6		

GOALS	Welfare	Income Value added	Employment	Waste/Pollutants	Land	Water	Fuel
Constraints/Targets	Maximize	≥ 150	= 4000	< 6700	< 20	< 7	< 30
Priority (Weight)	1	1	1	100	100	10	10
Current Results	696	165	4000	5700	19	6	24
Weighted Contribution	696	0	0		4	1	2
Consolidated Welfare	704						

Note: Some income items are mutually exclusive, so that not all variables are included simultaneously. Items in bold are directly affected by the optimization

260

Regional Implications of Population Trends

Present trends in Aruba suggest a greatly increased population (see Figure 11.2). While this national trend is a matter of common concern to both Arubans and immigrants (but for different reasons), the implications for specific communities and for the natural environment in different parts of the island are far more acute. To assess the implications of present trends, a temporal spatial model has been developed to illustrate the likely geographic trends in commercial and residential development across the island. This model is partially linked to a version of the cultural accounts and the satellite table.[29] Trend forecasts or suggested alternatives are used as the basis for projections which are then distributed across the various regions of the island. The map in Figure 11.5a shows the expected distribution of population (by census tract in the year 2005) should present trend continue. The trends suggest that there will be a great increase in population densities in existing settlements and a steady in-filling between them. Moreover, the map suggests that there will be increasing pressure to develop the remaining wilderness regions, such as the National Park which is home to a variety of protected species (STINAPA 1982). Again, the aim here is to introduce such simulations into a participatory public debate.

This census tract-level model has been extended so as to explore the implications of achieving targets for income and employment in the face of local constraints on emissions, resource use (e.g., water), and wildlife preservation. One of the major considerations in constructing integrated models is that, in general, individual firms, ethnic populations, particular wildlife species, or environment characteristics dominate any specific location – typically a subcensus tract block, land parcel, or residential address (United Nations 1994). To address these location-specific interrelationships it is necessary to have a level of geographic description that matches the present (and potential future) variations of the natural and human geography of the island.[30] The possibilities for this depend on available data and legal restrictions on its public use. Both these issues are in flux in Aruba, and their resolution depends on the political and cultural factors discussed earlier. The compromise adopted is to use a cellular spatial description that reduces data from population census and remote surveys, and distributes them across a common grid (Engelen et al. 1994). A smaller grid allows more specific details for residential areas, business zones, and local environmental concerns to be portrayed without being unacceptably explicit about individual firms or neighborhoods. Figure 11.5b shows the spatial distribution of populations in relation to the industrial that might arise from the patterns of land use interpolated from the high growth population scenario. Insofar as these activities are also responsible for the highest levels of toxic emissions, this allows us to correlate the proximity of environmental hazards

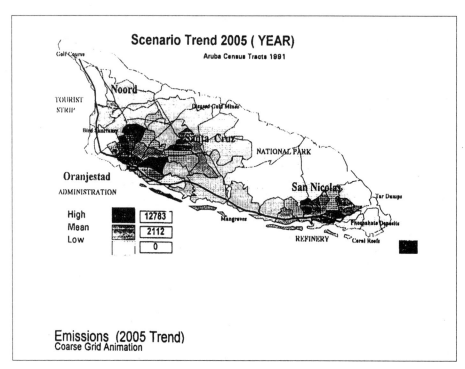

Figure 11.5a. The land use implications of demographic trend

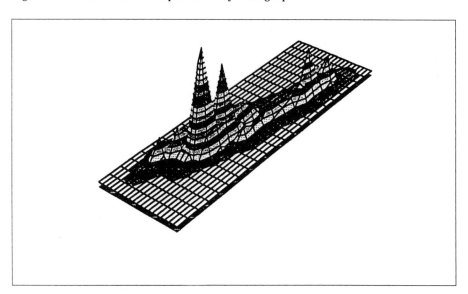

Figure 11.5b. The spatial distribution of populations compared to industrial sources
of emissions

and populations, especially the inequitable impacts for poor and minority communities (Glickman 1994; Bowen et al. 1995).

CONCLUSIONS

This chapter describes an effort to develop a cultural accounting matrix for the small Caribbean island nation of Aruba that can be used for economic and environmental analysis. This empirical exercise must be backed up by historical and ethnographic analysis if the model is to contribute to an understanding of the possibilities for sustainable development. The introduction places this work in the context of Duchin's (1994) call for a revised agenda for ecological economics to research specific situations and strategies for sustainable development in a concrete manner. In attempting to construct new classifications based on the "economic culture" of the several populations in one small community, and to introduce the model into an ongoing debate within that community, this chapter exposes several empirical and practical considerations. This includes the nature of the interface between ecological economic modeling and public policy in complex societies where a diversity of economic cultures compete to determine the ecological future of the community. Complex and contradictory social processes of small island politics easily can frustrate such an exercise. Through the various examples, the chapter illustrates that short-run considerations such as economic or natural disasters must be dealt with since they can inhibit aspirations for longer-run sustainable development. It also demonstrates some of the compromises in terms of detail and modeling sophistication that might be required.

For reasons of space, the presentation here is necessarily illustrative of the issues and methods, but attempts to explain the main components of the work. Although the focus of the chapter is one small island, some of the findings may be more generally applicable. It is evident that historic economic, cultural, and environmental change manifest themselves in an especially acute way in small islands, but this is true also of any small community in a metropolitan nation, unless they are well cushioned by their membership in a wider community. In this sense the problems for islands that come from size (rather than remoteness) may be transferred to larger nations. As an object of research, therefore, they can provide useful insights into interface between global ecological and economic change in general.

ACKNOWLEDGMENTS

This work was supported in part by the National Center for Earthquake Engineering Research (NCEER) under NSF Master Contract BCS90-25010 and NYSSTF Grant Number NEC-91029. This support and the cooperation of the Aruba Calamity Committee and FUNDINI is gratefully acknowledged.

FOOTNOTES

1. A draft version of this paper was presented at a Technical Session on "Ecology and Economy in the Caribbean," Third International Meeting of the International Society for Ecological Economics, San Jose, Costa Rica, October 24–28, 1994. A revised version was presented in the session on "Resources, Environment, and Development in the Caribbean," Caribbean Studies Association Twentieth Annual Conference, May 22–26, 1995, Willemstad, Curacao, Netherlands, Antilles, "International Development in the Caribbean: Acting upon Changing Structures."

2. Several recent works explore the concept of sustainable development for the Caribbean islands (e.g., Albuquerque and McElroy 1992; Griffith and Ashe 1993; Ragster and Gardner 1993; Barker and McGreggor 1995). Similarly, ecologists are still seeking to define the concept at a subnational level (e.g. Hardy and Lloyd 1995).

3. The overarching framework used by this author has evolved from a futurist and public policy perspective that identifies culture as the defining variable in the economy–ecology relationship (Cole 1990, 1995).

4. At a finer geographic scale variables become more discrete. Indeed, many ecological associations can only be analyzed at this level without risk of falling into false associations as a result of inappropriate areal unit aggregation (e.g., Fotheringham and Rogerson 1994).

5. Small countries pose a special problem for development economists. Kuznets (1969), for example, observed that small countries are under a great handicap in the task of economic growth. This is still a matter of debate, especially for small island nations new to independence. On balance there is no consensus as to whether the disadvantages in economies of scale, distance from markets, and vulnerability to fluctuations can be compensated for by flexibility, openness, and competitiveness.

6. Here too, it is sensible to recognize the merit in the empirical critiques of positivist approaches to social analysis that argue, in particular, that since no absolute grounds exist for asserting the validity of mathematical logic, alternative epistemologies cannot be assumed to be inferior in pursuit of truth about reality (e.g., Godel 1962), and so cannot comprehend subjective differences between groups and individuals.

7. This analysis draws on the primary history of Aruba (Hartog 1958) and sources given in the text. More recent information comes from various government, agency, and press reports gathered over 14 years of research in Aruba. Especially useful are the annual reports of the Aruban Investment Bank (1995) and the Central Bank of Aruba (1990), and the publications of STINAPA (e.g., Aruba Foundation for Nature and Parks 1982) and Foundation for Investigation and Information (FUNDINI; e.g., van Aller 1994), and the resources of the Bibliotek Nationale. The islands of the Netherlands Antilles vary in their economies, cultures, and physical environments. One persistent problem in researching Aruba is that studies and data for the Netherlands Antilles are weighted to the largest island, Curaçao. This is true even of post-status aparte writings that refer specifically to ecological conditions (e.g., Sampson 1989).

8. Levy in the Daily Mail (1993) reported that the island has "billions in laundered money." While the proximity of the island to South America and its history as a smuggling community make some links to international crime inevitable, the broad claim that Aruba is becoming "a private island ruled by the powerful crime syndicate" is generally rebutted by the Aruban government. Certainly, by most standards, Aruba is peaceable and relatively crime free (AIB 1995).

9. It should be said that the notion of "nativeness" in Aruba is complex, but is typically claimed by people with ancestors arriving before the arrival of the oil refinery (e.g., Razak 1995).

10. Recognizing that the pattern of economic and social development in any country is the consequence of various interactions between the different resources, technology, and people involved in the process of change, and reflects the fundamental motivation, incentives, and

attitudes of the society, Ward (1977) recommended the construction of social accounts with distinctive taxonomies. This observation is probably nowhere more true than in small isolated societies (e.g., Pyatt and Roe 1977; Adelman, Taylor, and Vogel 1988; Cole 1993).

11. While this approach clearly draws on the structuralist anthropology tradition of Furnival (1948), Herskovits (1961), Clarke (1984), and Glazier (1985), it is also informed by ethnographic studies such as Razak (1995).

12. For example, Kalm (1974) observed that in Aruba most food is retailed by Chinese and most luxury consumer items by Eastern European Jews. The rural Aruban community was organized along family lines; until recently it centered on particular barrios or town sectors.

13. It should be appreciated here that some of these issues and variables are very sensitive, and in some circumstances are practically inadmissible. For example, during the preparation of the Aruba independence plan the author was advised not to discuss regional or ethnic differences on the island (Cole 1986).

14. While even today over 40% of rural homes have a rain tank, less than 2% of modern urban or rural homes have a tank (from 1991 Census data).

15. Commercial development is relatively unconstrained by either party. The plan for reopening the refinery received little evaluation despite the fact that Lago left 800,000 m^3 of waste. Neither did the new golf course which uses 2,500 m^3/day of water, about half the partially treated water that was formerly used by the bird sanctuary and agriculture (Boerwinkel 1995). Residential development is slowed mainly by the archaic and convoluted system for zoning and approving building permits.

16. Other versions of these accounts have been subdivided into the four main geographic regions of the island, and into large and small-scale enterprises and have been presented elsewhere (NCEER 1993).

17. A second table showing the amount of labor by occupation, region, and cultural group, and ownership size of firm, region, and cultural group has also been constructed (this is not shown in the table). Aggregation of these last data provide the labor- and capital-output coefficients associated with each industry.

18. A variety of empirical sources are used, including census data on household income and occupation by sector and birthplace, ethnicity, household expenditure surveys, the historical records of the Chamber of Commerce on the ownership and valuation of businesses by sector and nationality, as well as cross-linkages between families and cultural groups, public sector employment and allocation of public resources, and tax records (UNESCO 1989).

19. A small number of entries were imputed from the other Caribbean islands, and not all the data used were surveyed in a single year. This was scaled using a multiproportional RAS procedure (see Cole et al. 1983) to include the new data on the cultural division of labor and adjust the overall level of activity to national income and production accounts (NIPA) for 1990, in turn constructed from various data from Central Bank of Aruba, World Bank, IMF and Aruban Development Plan (1990), and the Aruba Capital Expenditure Plan (CEP 1991). These national income and product accounts first were organized into a small matrix in a manner similar to that described by Hanson and Robinson (1989). Additional information on value added wages by sector, imports, and exports, and public sector activity were then used to scale individual activities and transactions to 1990 levels.

20. The gross data on tourism revenues comes from the Central Bank (1990) and CEP (1991). Details of the allocation of tourist and hotel expenditures between activities come from Spinard (1981), Latham (1984) and more recent publications of the Aruba Tourism Board. Again the data in the SAM are preliminary, but offer a fair impression of the island's tourist industry. In principle, the available data allow some individual hotels to be described in the matrix in a similar fashion to WEB and ELMAR in the lifelines sectors. The division into high and low-rise hotels follows Spinard (1981) and differentiates between the class of hotel (high-rise tending to be larger and more luxurious).

21. This network has been quantified from company reports and data in the Capital Expenditure Program (CEP 1991). It should be noted that since that time Coastal has absorbed Wickland, and the WEB is undergoing privatization.
22. To the extent that these Arubans are often descendants of more recent immigrants, they belong to an "outsider" group and have had less influence within the political system.
23. The state of the art in applying sophisticated schemes (e.g., Costanza et al. 1993) here appears to be that such models are useful to demonstrate possible outcomes and contingencies, but are not reliable for detailed policy-making.
24. Multipliers are the ratio of the total economy-wide impact of changes on the level of a given activity to the original impact. These are obtained by inverting the EcoCAM coefficients matrix. Total impact coefficients are simply the ratio between the level in a given activity (e.g., household income) arising from a unit change in another activity (e.g., the level of tourism). Both may be calculated in several ways, most common are Type I or Type II multipliers (e.g., Miller and Blair 1985; Stevens and Lahr 1988). However, some earlier work on the present project comparing actual and forecast shifts in employment in Aruba during the years 1980–1990 suggests that a time-lagged method is likely to give better results (Cole 1988; NCEER 1993). In a rapidly changing economy, the table needs to be updated at regular intervals, using an appropriate scaling method (e.g., Cole 1992).
25. Input–output analysis is increasingly used for just this kind of impact analysis (West and Lenze 1993; Cole 1995). By combining proposals and forecasts for the various sectors a scenario may be set up and the total impact calculated. Since the changes in output are also associated with labor and waste coefficients, changes in these variables may also be calculated. Moreover, within the technological possibilities of the supply system an optimal allocation of cutbacks may be designed so as to reduce the impact on selected groups or interests, or to develop a cost–benefit schedule that balances several interests.
26. This is done subject to constraints such as upper limits based on industry and other assessments. Then it is evident that noneconomic factors are implicitly included. This is equally the case when the future income expectations of the various actors are discounted to their present values at different rates. Thus even this approach should be considered to be a multi-criteria assessment (MCA) in the sense of van der Veen et al. (1994), rather than a cost–benefit analysis.
27. There are well-known practical and philosophical difficulties in balancing economic and noneconomic utilities across competing interest groups (e.g., Hanemann 1995). Arguably, from a public policy perspective what matters most is that the final outcomes proposed can be understood by the various parties, and are acceptable to them, and that the outcomes are readily predicted. The preferred use of the model here is to use it to illustrate outcomes and let their acceptability determine the weights. Once such trade-offs have been ascertained for several events, or negotiated across interests groups, the same mix of trade-offs can be adapted to hypothesize their response to other events.
28. In some cases, environmental concerns are not central, but the consequences for environment can be assessed. For example, because the model includes a target for employment, it can be used to explore both sides of the immigration coin, not the least the very contentious issue of how Aruban living standards might be affected by legislation to reduce immigration.
29. For this the accounts are revised into a four-region input–output model based on Noord et al. (NCEER 1993).
30. Geographic Information Systems (GIS) in particular provide data structures to link disparate coordinate and attribute data by generating a probabilistic spatial distribution database, and providing the empirical framework for more detailed microsimulation (e.g., Spiekermann and Wegener 1994).

REFERENCES

Adelman, I., S. Taylor, and S. Vogel. 1988. Life in a Mexican village: A SAM perspective. *Journal of Development Studies* 25(1):5–24.

Albuquerque, K. and J. McElroy. 1992. Caribbean tourism styles and sustainable strategies. *Environment Management* 16(5):619–632.

Aruba Today. 1995. FUNDINI to present Lectures on Aruba's identity and development. August 14.

Aruban Investment Bank (AIB). 1995. Economic Memorandum, Oranjestad.

Aysan, Y., A. Coburn, and R. Spence. 1989. Turning Short-term Recovery into Long-Term Protection, mimeo, Reconstruction after Earthquakes, An International Agenda to Achieve Safer Settlements in the 1990s. Buffalo: National Center for Earthquake Engineering Research.

Barker, D. and D. McGreggor. 1995. *Environment and Development in the Caribbean*. Mona: University of the West Indies Press.

Bartelmus, P., C. Stahmer, and J. van Tongere. 1991. Integrated environmental and economic accounting: Framework for an SNA satellite system. *The Review of Income and Wealth* 37(2):111–147.

Benedict, B. 1978. Sociological characteristics of small territories. In *The Social Anthropology of Complex Societies,* ed. M. Banton. London: Tavistock.

Boerwinkel, D. 1995. Small Islands, Big Problems: Aruba, the Environment and International Relations, mimeo, Caribbean Studies Association. Curaçao, May.

Bowen, W., M. Salling, K. Haynes, and E. Cyran. 1995. Towards environmental justice: Spatial equity in Ohio and Cleveland. *Annals of the Association of American Geographers* 85(3).

Capital Expenditure Plan (CEP). 1991. Capital Expenditure Plan 1991–1995. Oranjestad: Department of Economic Affairs.

Central Bank of Aruba. 1990. Annual Report, Oranjestad.

Clarke, C. 1984. Pluralism and plural societies: Caribbean perspectives. In *Geography and Ethnic Pluralism,* eds. C. Clarke, D. Ley, and C. Peach et al. London: George, Allen and Unwin.

Cohen, A. 1985. *The Symbolic Construction of Identity. London:* Routeledge.

Cole, S. 1985. Paradise lost? Rediscovering tradition in Aruba. *Caribbean Review* 14(3):22–43.

Cole, S. 1986. The tragedy of Aruba: Lessons for small island development. *Antillien Review* 5(2):9–14.

Cole, S. 1988, The delayed impacts of plant closures. In a reformulated Leontief Model. *Proceedings of the Regional Science Association* 65:135–149.

Cole, S. 1990. Cultural diversity and sustainable futures. *Futures* December:1044–2015.

Cole, S. 1992. A Lagrangian derivation of a general multi-proportional scaling algorithm. *Regional Science and Urban Economics* 22:291–297.

Cole, S. 1993. Cultural accounting for small economies. *Regional Studies* 27(2):121–136.

Cole, S. 1994. Contending voices: Futures, culture, and development. *Futures* 27(4):473–481.

Cole, S. 1995. Lifelines and livelihood: A social accounting matrix approach to calamity preparedness. *Journal of Contingencies and Crisis Management* 3(4).

Cole, S., H. Opdam, B. van Veen, and R. Zambrano. 1983. A Social Accounting Matrix for Aruba, mimeo, ITEO/DECO, Oranjestad.

Costanza, R. et al. 1993. Modeling complex economic–ecological systems: Towards an evolutionary, dynamic understanding of people and nature. *Bioscience* 43(8):545–555.

Cvejanovich, G. 1985. Future Aruba: Can it make it alone? *Caribbean Review* 14:3.

Duchin, F. 1994. Ecological economics: The second stage. In *Getting Down to Earth: Practical Applications of Ecological Economics,* eds. R. Costanza, O. Segura, and J. Martinez-Alier. Covelo, CA: Island Press.

Duchin, F. 1995. Livelihood and Economic Development, mimeo. August, Institute for Economic Analysis, New York.

Duchin, F. and G.-M. Lange. 1994. *Ecological Economics, Technological Change, and the Future of the Environment. Institute for Economic Analysis.* New York: New York University.

Engelen, G., I. Uljee, S. Wargies, and R. White. 1994. *A Modeling Framework to Explore Impacts of Climate Change, Research Institute for Knowledge Systems.* Belgium: Maastricht.

Floyd, J. 1994. *Estimating Future Waste Remediation Costs in LDCs, North American Regional Science Association.* Ontario: Niagara Falls.

Fotheringham, S. and P. Rogerson. 1994. *Spatial Analysis and GIS.* London: Taylor and Francis.

Furnival, J. 1948. *Colonial Policy and Practice: A Comparative Study of Burma and the Netherlands Antilles.* Cambridge: Cambridge University Press.

Glazier, S. 1985. *Caribbean Ethnicity Revisited.* New York: Gordon and Breach.

Glickman, T. 1994. Measuring environmental equity with Geographical Information Systems. *Resources* 93:281–301.

Godel, K. 1962. *On Formally Undecidable Propositions of Principa Mathematica and Related Systems.* London: Oliver and Boyd.

Green, V. 1973. *Migrants in Aruba: Inter-ethnic Integration.* Assen: Van Gorcum.

Griffith, M. and J. Ashe. 1993. Sustainable Development in Small Island States, Technical Meeting for Global Conference on Sustainable Development. Port of Spain, May.

Hanemann, W. 1995. Improving environmental policy: Are markets the solution? *Contemporary Economic Policy* 13(1):74–82

Hanson, K. and S. Robinson. 1989. *Data, linkages, and models.* Washington DC: U.S. Department of Agriculture.

Hardy, S. and G. Lloyd. 1995. An impossible dream? Sustainable regional economic and environmental development. *Regional Studies* 28(8):773–780.

Hartog, J. 1958. Aruba – Past and Present. Original Dutch Van Dorp, Aruba. English Translation De Wit, Aruba, 1961.

Henry, R. 1989. Inequality in plural societies: An exploration. *Social and Economic Studies* 38:2.

Herskovits, M. 1961. Economic change and cultural dynamics. In *Traditions, Values, and Socio-Economic Development,* eds. R. Braibanti and J. Spengler. London: Cambridge University Press.

Hoetink, H. 1967. *The Two Variants of Caribbean Race Relations: A Contribution to the Sociology of Segmented Societies. Institute of Race Relations,* Oxford University Press.

Isard, W. 1972. *Ecological–Economic Analysis.* New York: Collier Macmillian Free Press.

Jones, B. 1982. Planning for Reconstruction of Earthquake Stricken Communities, PRC-US Joint Workshop, Beijing.

Kalm, F. 1974. *The dispersive and reintegrating nature in society: Aruba, Netherlands Antilles, unpublished thesis.* New York: City University.

Latham, E. 1984. Direct and Indirect Impacts of Tourism on the Population of Aruba. Mimeo, National Library of Aruba.

Leontief, W. 1970. Environmental repercussions and economic structures: An input–output approach. *Review of Economics and Statistics* 52:262–271.

Leontief, W. and A. Carter. 1976. *The Future of the World Economy.* New York: United Nations.

Levy, G. 1993. How the Mafia moved into paradise. *Daily Mail* March 13, p. 60.

Miller, R. and P. Blair. 1985. *Input–Output Analysis. Foundations and Extensions.* New Jersey: Prentice Hall.

Morrison, W. 1994. Data and modeling. In United Nations op cit, 197–231.

Munasinghe, M. 1993. Environmental Economics and Sustainable Development, World Bank Environment Paper No 3, IBRD, Washington DC.

Munasinghe, M. and J. McNealy. 1992. Key Concepts and Terminology of Sustainable Development, UNU Conference on Sustainability, June, Washington DC.

NCEER. 1993. A Social Accounting Matrix Approach to Disaster Preparedness and Recovery Planning. National Center for Earthquake Engineering Research, NCEER 92-0002, Buffalo.

Olson, M. 1971. *The Logic of Collective Action.* Cambridge: Harvard University Press.

PlanD2. 1980. *Aruba Spatial Development Plan 1981–1990. Fudashion Desaroyo Planea.* Aruba: Oranjestad.

Pyatt, G. and A. Roe. 1977. *Social Accounting Matrices for Development Planning with Special Reference to Sri Lanka.* London: Cambridge University Press and Washington DC: World Bank.

Ragster, L. and K. Gardner. 1993. Environmental Conservation Policies and Cooperation in the Caribbean. INVESP Regional Project.

Razak, V. 1995. Land, Economy and Culture in Aruba, ISEE Conference, mimeo, Costa Rica, October, 1994, revised as Culture under Construction: The Future of Aruban Identity. *Futures* (May):Special issue on Anthropological Perspectives on the Future of Culture and Society.

Sampson, M. 1989. *The Netherlands Antilles, Urbanization, Planning and Development in the Caribbean,* ed. R. Potter. London and New York: Mansell.

Sedoc-Dahlberg, B. 1989. *The Dutch Caribbean: Prospects for Democracy.* London: Gordon and Breach.

Spiekerman, K. and M. Wegener. 1994. Microsimulation and GIS: Prospects and First Experience, Third International Conference on Computers and Urban Planning and Management, Atlanta, Georgia, July.

Spinard, B. 1981. *The Aruba Tourism Plan.* Oranjestad: DECO.

Strathern, M. 1995. Future kinship and the study of culture. *Futures* 27(4):423–436.

Stevens, B. and M. Lahr. 1988. Regional economic multipliers: Definition, measurement and application. *Economic Development Quarterly* 2(1):88–96.

STINAPA. 1982. Wildlife in Aruba, STINAPA, Seroe Colorado, Aruba.

Stone, R. 1973. A system of social matrices. *Review of Income and Wealth* 19(2):143–166.

UNESCO. 1989. A Pilot Cultural Accounting Matrix. Bureau of Policy and Studies, UNESCO, Paris, BEP/GPI/SOC 1989.

United Nations. 1994. Planning for Sustainable Development: Guidelines for Developing Countries. Department for Development Support and Management, DDDSMS/DEPSD, New York.

van Aller, R. et al. 1994. The Future Status of Aruba and the Netherlands Antilles, FUNDINI, Aruba, VAD.

van der Berge, P. 1981. *The Ethnic Phenomenon.* New York: Elsevier.

van der Veen, A. et al. 1995. Cost–benefit analysis and multi-criteria analysis. *Journal of Coastal Engineering.*

Verton, P. 1973. Kiezers en Politieke Partijen in de Nederlandse Antillen, de Witt, Aruba.

Ward, M. 1977. The extension of the UN SNA supply-disposition table for development policy analysis. *Review of Income and Wealth* September:237–258.

West, C. and D. Lenze. 1993. Modeling Natural Disaster and Recovery: An Impact Assessment of Regional Data and Impact Methodology in the Context of Hurricane Andrew. Bureau of Business and Economic Research. Gainesville, University of Florida.

Wever, O. 1970. Proceedings of the First Aruban and Antillean Congress on Alcoholism, Aruba, Vad.

12 SUSTAINABILITY AND RANGELAND MANAGEMENT

Jaap Arntzen
Department of Environmental Science
University of Botswana
Gaborone, Botswana

INTRODUCTION

Few subjects have been so extensively researched and are yet so poorly understood as rangeland management. This observation by Dasmann, Milton, and Freeman (1973) still largely holds true today. Rangeland dynamics and use were frequently oversimplified. As a result, degradation is progressing and sustainable rangeland management remains in most cases a mirage. This adversely affected rural development, particularly in largely pastoral societies. Therefore, this chapter examines the following questions.

1. What is rangeland degradation and to what extent does it occur?
2. What explanations do current theories offer for changes in rangelands?
3. How can the concept of sustainable development be used for the analysis of rangeland changes? What are key elements and interventions?

The concept of sustainable development offers a suitable analytical framework because it does justice to the complexities of inter-resource and intersectoral dynamics governing rangelands. The well-known WCED definition suffices for our purposes.

Development that meets the need of the present generation without jeopardizing the ability to meet the demands of future generations.

Desertification assessments cannot be compared because the description of desertification has frequently changed, causing considerable confusion among policy-makers and researchers, and limiting the comparability of individual studies. The present definitio n – adopted in 1992 at UNCED and used in the Convention to Combat Desertification – equates desertification with degrada-

270

tion and stresses both physical and human causes (and the synergy between both) (Cardy 1993):

> Land degradation in arid, semiarid and subhumid areas resulting from various factors including climatic variations and human activities.

Other definitions of desertification try to separate physical and human causes of degradation or they restrict the term degradation for certain elements of desertification. For example, Abel and Blaikie (1990) reserve desertification for effectively irreversible decreases in land productivity. There are at least two problems with this definition. First, the majority of rangeland users are poor. All productivity losses imply income and subsistence losses, enhancing their poverty and reducing their livelihood security. Reversing productivity losses does not offer the immediate help that is needed. Secondly, what is *effectively irreversible* is determined by the local context. Even though it may be technically possible to rehabilitate rangelands, the costs are very high. Therefore, effective irreversibility can be seen as a function of affordability related to the macroeconomic condition of a particular country as well as the socioeconomic conditions of the rangeland users.

Briefly, the chapter has the following structure. After reviewing two rangeland theories, key elements of a sustainable rangeland theory are discussed. This includes a brief assessment of the main features and dynamics of southern African rangelands. Subsequently, three major issues are discussed in more detail: comparative advantages, multiple rangeland use, and the role of people's participation. The chapter concludes with a brief summary and some recommendations.

THEORIES OF RANGELAND DEGRADATION

Two theories on rangeland degradation are discussed here (Sandford 1983; Behnke and Scoones 1993). The traditional rangeland theory aims to maintain an equilibrium between the carrying capacity (the number of livestock that can be sustained by the range resource) and stocking rate (the number of livestock per rangeland unit; labeled exploitation level in Figure 12.1) in order to stay near the climax situation of rangelands. The carrying capacity fluctuates within a limited margin. For example, the carrying capacity for eastern Botswana is given as 12–16 ha per livestock unit (Field 1978). Sandford (1983) labels this a conservative stocking strategy. The rangeland problem emanates from the combination of soaring livestock numbers without an increase in available rangeland or intensification of livestock management. If the stocking rate exceeds the carrying capacity, the land productivity will drop sooner or later, reducing the actual carrying capacity and requiring a drop in livestock numbers. If such a drop is not forthcoming, a downward spiral of resource productivity and income losses is likely to result. The reduced resource productivity is associated with the process of so-called bush encroachment, which has the following features:

- Disappearance of the per-annual grasses in favor of less palatable annual grasses
- Reduction of the grass cover and an increase in woody biomass
- Increased runoff and soil erosion

The process of rangeland degradation and productivity losses is summarized in Figure 12.1, which depicts the potential rangeland conditions ranging from under to over utilization. Progression of the stage of under utilization (A) to over utilization with degradation (D) has been common during this century. Situation D shows degradation together with a decrease in livestock numbers following increased mortality and decreased calving rates. Situation (B) is the *ideal* for livestock managers.

Doubts about the theory's validity started to emerge after countries remained at stage C without apparent adverse impact on the livestock sector (sector D). Little empirical evidence was found to suggest that bush encroachment inevitably led to soil erosion and loss of livestock productivity. More specific points of criticism include:

- Practical and theoretical difficulties in calculating carrying capacity figures. Highly variable rainfall may lead to enormous fluctuations in the carrying capacity. Most empirical calculations omit important productivity determinants such as browse, soil conditions, and the slope.
- Practical difficulties in calculating stocking rates. Livestock is mobile in search of grass and water. Consequently, stocking rates fluctuate in time.
- Figure 12.1 assumes constant management practices. In practice, management may change in time, and there are management differences among livestock owners.
- The theory is sectoral (i.e., restricted to livestock production). Consequently, changes in non-livestock activities are treated as exogenous. This is particularly unacceptable for communal rangelands which are used for a variety of activities.

In response to the above criticism, Sandford (1983) and later Behnke and Scoones (1993) developed a new rangeland theory. The central assumption is that rainfall fluctuations are a more important determinant of the vegetation than stocking rates. Instead of the expected dramatic collapse in livestock productivity envisaged by the traditional theory (stage D), smaller but more frequent die-offs occur during droughts. This corroborates empirical evidence of many countries. On the positive side, livestock numbers quickly recover after droughts. Rather than the equilibrium situation of Figure 12.1, rangelands and livestock are constantly in disequilibrium following rainfall fluctuations as depicted in Figure 12.2. During droughts, rangeland productivity and livestock

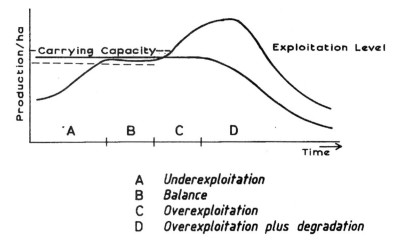

A   *Underexploitation*
B   *Balance*
C   *Overexploitation*
D   *Overexploitation plus degradation*

Figure 12.1. Trends in stocking rates and carrying capacity according to the traditional rangeland theory

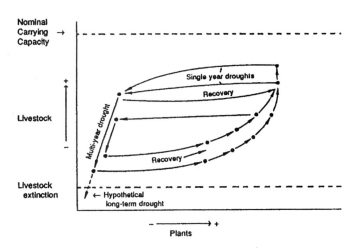

Source: Behnke and Scoones (1993).

Figure 12.2. Turkana plant–livestock interactions under the influence of frequent drought perturbations

numbers decline; during wetter periods, rangeland productivity and livestock numbers are increasing. Generally, rangeland resilience is substantial and the contraction process during droughts therefore does not constitute desertification as defined by Abel and Blaikie (1990). The greater the climatic variability, the greater the rangeland resilience. Vegetation changes are widespread, but this does not permanently affect land productivity.

According to this theory, higher stocking rates make economic sense because the total productivity per hectare will increase, even though individual animals may be in poorer condition. Therefore, so-called opportunistic stocking strategies are favored whereby the stocking rates exceed the carrying capacity during wet years. The costs of this strategy (i.e., increased mortality during droughts) are outweighed by the benefits during the good years (Sandford 1983). While vegetation changes in rangeland associated with bush encroachment adversely affect the condition (and value) of individual animals, total productivity per hectare is higher than under conservative stocking strategies because of the large number of animals. Given the climatic uncertainties and risks, it is argued that increasing livestock numbers and high stocking rates – checked by sales or die-offs during recurrent droughts – are the highest-yielding management strategy. According to this theory, livestock owners seek not only meat as an output, but seek a variety of outputs such as milk, meat, draught power, savings and payments for social obligations.

Vegetation changes do not necessarily mean degradation for all resource users. What constitutes negative vegetation changes for one user may be positive or harmless to another one. Unlike the traditional theory, the modern one does not generate a single management rule. Instead, management advice is linked to different management strategies employed by livestock holders. Generally, the importance of continuous adaptability to changing climatic and range conditions is emphasized. Furthermore, livestock mobility is emphasized as a survival strategy (Figure 12.2). Consequently, fencing and ranching are considered poor solutions to rangeland problems.

The modern theory still needs considerable elaboration before it offers an alternative theory. There is considerable uncertainty about a number of key issues.

The regeneration process of rangelands. Rangeland resilience is considerable, but it is as yet unclear how this works. For example, how long do seeds survive in the soil? Which types of grass are most resilient? To answer such questions, a more detailed study of rangeland resilience is required.

The browsing process.   Browsing is important to cattle and other animals, but there is no information on important questions such as: to what extent do cattle, smallstock, and wildlife browse, and what is the impact of their diet on their performance? How do grazing/browsing patterns change during droughts and what are the impacts on the animals and range? A grazing/browsing analysis is needed for cattle, smallstock, and the main wildlife species.

The linkage between soil cover and erosion. How does the soil retention capacity of perennial grasses compare with that of shrubs and annual grasses?

The modern theory has a better grasp of the livestock complexities and dynamics, but there are two concerns which cast doubts on its future relevance. The first concern regards the mobility potential. The importance of animal mobility is widely recognized. However, empirical evidence shows that the mobility potential is rapidly decreasing with mounting pressure on rangelands. The second concern is that the theory remains restricted to the livestock sector, and nonetheless concludes that vegetation changes do not lead to soil and productivity losses.

> Changes in rangeland such as species composition, reversible or otherwise, will not matter to land users provided the output of livestock products is not reduced. (Abel and Blaikie 1990).

What about the people who do not keep livestock (e.g., close to 50% in Botswana)? Moreover, the long-term sustainability perspectives are not clearly incorporated in the new rangeland theory. Even if it were true that present livestock productivity per hectare would increase in the short-term, this may not be the case in the long term. A World Bank evaluation of agricultural projects found that adverse environmental impacts mostly appear in the long term (World Bank 1988).

There is conflicting evidence as to the applicability of the two theories in southern Africa. Until recently, most studies automatically and uncritically applied the traditional theory. The conclusion was that most southern African rangelands were heavily overstocked. For example, Namibia experiences overstocking (Adams and Devitt 1992), Lesotho is overstocked by a factor of four (Swallow and Brocken 1987), and Botswana's stocking rates exceed the carrying capacity in most districts (Arntzen 1990). Kwazulu-Natal in South Africa and Zimbabwe also report widespread overstocking (Tapson 1991; Blaikie 1982). Recently, studies based on the modern theory have become more common in response to the continued growth of livestock numbers, which is only interrupted by recurrent droughts.

Bush encroachment is observed throughout the region's rangelands, both in communal and private rangelands. In Zimbabwe, livestock production leads to more rapid vegetation changes than wildlife. This is mainly caused by the higher livestock stocking rates (Muir 1993). The associated vegetation changes include the following.

- Replacement of perennial grasses by annuals; this leaves the soils more exposed during the dry season. Annual grasses are considered less resilient than perennials (Abel and Blaikie 1990), probably because of the effectiveness of seed storage. At the same time, annual grasses are not necessarily inferior fodder.
- Increase in woody biomass, particularly shrubs. Usually, the species variety is reduced because of the dominance of invading species.
- Reduced herbal cover and increased barren soil due to a reduction in grass cover. If this persists for some time, risks of soil erosion increase.

It appears, however, that bush encroachment is not a function of stocking rates alone; global warming could be a contributing factor. The vegetation is found to be more resilient than previously assumed. Vegetation recovers relatively quickly after droughts or when grazing pressure is reduced.

Few rangeland studies assess erosion or soil productivity. Soil erosion is negatively correlated to herbal cover. Therefore, if the vegetation changes last for a long time, soil erosion is more likely to result. The risk is particularly high in hilly and mountainous areas such as Lesotho and Swaziland. Through modeling exercises for an area in eastern Botswana, Byot (1991) concluded that soil erosion does occur, but it will not significantly affect livestock productivity in the next 400 years.[1] In Botswana's Boteti region on the edge of the Kalahari sandveld, livestock grazing caused vegetation changes, barren soils, and widespread loss of 2–3 cm of topsoil (Arntzen et al. 1994). There was no evidence of a decline in herd performance or animal condition, but according to the local population, the area's productivity for wildlife and useful plants was rapidly declining. Because of its mountainous nature and the livestock sector, erosion hazards are high and erosion is widespread in Lesotho. According to the modern theory, soil erosion and productivity losses only occur around watering points – the sacrifice zone (Perkins and Thomas 1993).

In Zimbabwe, vegetation changes through grazing had a negative impact on livestock performance (calving rates and average animal conditions). In Swaziland, high stocking rates are held responsible for lower calving rates and increased mortality (Fowler 1981). In Botswana, a switch has occurred from cattle to smallstock over the last decade. This probably reflects deteriorating rangeland conditions and cattle performance providing comparative advantage to smallstock (e.g., Namibia and Lesotho already have more smallstock than cattle). The switch also reflects resource access difficulties for small cattle owners, which forces them out of the cattle business.

ELEMENTS OF A SUSTAINABLE RANGELAND MODEL

The starting point of a sustainable rangeland model is fundamentally different from the theories discussed above. It lies in the recognition that rangelands are simultaneously used for many purposes and that they involve dynamic processes between renewable and nonrenewable resources. Most southern African rangelands share some common changes, albeit with significant spatial differences.

a. Increase in domesticated animals. Initially, cattle numbers increased rapidly; more recently, smallstock is rapidly increasing because of environmental and social reasons.
b. Decline in wildlife numbers and species outside Parks and Reserves.
c. Bush encroachment with an increase in shrubs and a decline in grass and soil cover.
d. Decline in biodiversity.

Using sustainable development as analytical framework, questions arise concerning the following.

- *Dynamics of resource exploitation.* Which resources are critical and for which purposes? The answer is likely to be related to income level and activity pattern.
- *Number of rangeland users.* How many people depend on communal rangelands and how many on private rangelands? Population pressure on communal rangelands is particularly high in countries with large tracts of private rangeland such as Namibia, South Africa and Zimbabwe.
- *Effectiveness of institutional structures and management.* What is the role of traditional and modern institutions and how effective are policies and instruments being used? Which incentives and disincentives exist for sustainable rangeland management. For example, in Botswana private ranchers can externalize degradation impacts onto communal areas because they have dual access to private and communal land.
- *Technology, investments, and management techniques.* For example, appropriate technologies.

Table 12.1 shows the various uses of southern African rangelands. A distinction is being made between primary and secondary forms of rangeland use. These terms are slightly misleading as the primary use differs among households. In the past, some rangelands were primarily used for livestock and others without permanent water by wildlife. With the development of groundwater technology, livestock has become the primary form of rangeland use in most areas with the exception of rangeland specially earmarked for wildlife such as parks, reserves, and so on. Note that there is an important difference between private and communal rangelands. The former are mostly used for a single purpose and product (i.e., cattle and beef).[2] The latter have a more varied use which offers a much broader range of products. Consequently, changes in communal rangelands are likely to have diverse impacts which transcend the livestock sector. For example, rangeland changes may affect cultivation if animal draught power becomes a constraint. Changes may also affect gatherers of food and medicinal plants, or families, who derive subsistence from wildlife. Note too, that livestock in communal areas is frequently used for nonconsumptive purposes (e.g., draught power, savings, etc.). In contrast to private ranches, livestock is seen as a capital asset rather than a source of income (Barret 1992).

Table 12.1. A Typology of Rangeland Use

	Primary Use	Secondary Use
Communal Rangelands	livestock holding meat, milk, draught power, cultural functions, savings	wildlife (viewing and hunting); veld products such as thatching grass, edible plants, wood
Private Rangelands	livestock ranching (meat); some game ranching (hunting, viewing)	negligible

The second element of the starting point concerned the key rangeland resources and their interactions. What the key resources are depend on the use and user; they are summarized in Table 12.2. Clearly, virtually all animals, plants, and trees are important resources in addition to water. In other words, the biodiversity of rangelands needs to be preserved in order to retain their value to the categories of users. Sustainable productivity assessment should take into account all uses of all key resources. Data must be obtained about the regeneration capacity of each resource, and the impact of each use on its key resources and other uses plus resources. This requires a comprehensive analysis. In this way, opportunities for multiple rangeland use can be assessed as well as externalities between different uses. There are indications that cattle production has adverse impacts on vegetation diversity and wildlife (e.g., Arntzen et al. 1994), but further research is needed to probe this in detail and to assess whether this leads to a reduction in total land productivity or not.

A common oversight in rangeland discussions is the sustainability of water supply. This issue arose with the switch in the livestock, and more recently wildlife, sector from surface water (renewable) to groundwater (only partly renewable) sources during this century. The borehole technology in southern Africa has greatly reduced water constraints for those livestock owners, who can afford it. Although groundwater use by the livestock sector itself may not exceed the recharge, the consumption of other economic sectors is rapidly increasing over the last decades and may in the end affect the water supply to the livestock sector.

Table 12.2. Key Rangeland Resources

Rangeland Use	Key Resources
cattle production	grass (R), water (PR), browse (R)
smallstock production	browse (R), water (PR), grass (R)
wildlife production	wildlife (R)
gathering of plants and wood	vegetation (R)

Notes: R denotes a renewable resource; PR denotes a partly renewable resource. Livestock uses surface and groundwater; part of the latter is fossil and nonrenewable.

Having outlined some key issues with respect to sustainable rangeland management above, what guidelines can be derived for rangeland management? The following have been adapted to rangeland conditions from the general literature.

- The consumption of renewable resources (grass, water, plants, and trees) should not exceed their regeneration capacity.
- The partly renewable resource of water should be consumed with care. Sole dependence on fossil groundwater should be avoided. Rangeland should be managed so as to maximize the recharge opportunities through maintenance of a proper vegetation cover.
- Biodiversity must be maintained. This will benefit forms of multiple use of rangeland use over single use.
- Poverty alleviation will contribute to sustainable rangeland management.

Under mounting rangeland pressure, three areas of particular concern emerge. First, it becomes imperative to identify the comparative ecological and socioeconomic advantages of each rangeland use and to assess opportunities for compatible multiple uses. Such judgments can be based on value and damage estimates of rangelands. Second, popular participation and decentralization are seen as instrumental in reviving active rangeland management. In private rangelands, management is determined by the owner. In communal rangelands, traditional management has been gradually eroded during this century, but was unfortunately not replaced with an effective new management system. Consequently, communal rangelands may suffer from open access, particularly in the vicinity of villages. Third, it is important to evaluate the impacts of traditionally used economic instruments on rangelands, and to identify possibilities to enhance the contribution to sustainable rangeland management. Now each concern will be discussed in more detail.

COMPARATIVE ADVANTAGES

Sustainable development combines resource conservation and income generation. Therefore, in order to analyze the sustainability of rangeland management, we examine both ecological and economic comparative advantages. An activity has a comparative ecological advantage when the local environment is most suitable for that particular activity. In comparison to other parts of the world, Africa in general and southern Africa in particular are well-endowed with wildlife, although the resources are in decline. The region has a great variety and large numbers of wildlife. Governments and most of the public has only recently started to appreciate the development potential of wildlife. An activity is considered to have a comparative socioeconomic advantage when it is most suitable for the local population. For example, local people may lack the means to keep cattle, but primarily depend on smallstock and wildlife instead. In that event, wildlife would have a comparative socioeconomic advantage. Comparative ecological and socioeconomic advantages do not necessarily concur; in practice, trade-offs may be necessary, and a compromise between both may have to be reached on activity development. In development planning, the application of the concept of comparative ecological advantages has often been restricted to the agricultural sector, comparing the merits of crop and livestock production. The general wisdom has been that in semiarid areas, livestock production is more productive than crop production. In addition, the drier the areas are, the more suitable they are believed to be for smallstock and/or wildlife.

Socioeconomic comparative advantages are rarely explicitly considered in development planning. Considerable differences exist between countries, but it is fair to say that cattle production is usually more suitable for the middle to high-income groups; goats and wildlife utilization are more important for the low income groups as they require less investments.

Above we briefly touched on the dynamics of comparative advantages. Changes may be natural or human-induced. Comparative ecological advantages change with the state of the environment and technology. For example, groundwater technology has opened large parts of southern African rangelands for livestock. Vegetation changes, natural or human-induced, may alter the suitability of rangelands for specific purposes. During this century important changes occurred in favor of livestock production primarily as a result of two factors.

1. *Groundwater development.* Increased access to this resource has opened up previously inaccessible rangelands to livestock.

2. *Generous financial support to the livestock sector.* This was justified on the grounds of comparative advantages over crop production without a proper comparison with wildlife utilization.

Both factors have led to an expansion of the livestock sector deep into marginal land without adequate assessment of the ecological (can the natural resource base be sustained?) and socioeconomic (does the activity generate income to the local population?) sustainability. For example, livestock expansion into western Botswana is only feasible for the high income groups, and probably adversely affects local incomes. Another important change has been the general reduction in wildlife numbers and diversity due to the expanding human influence sphere. In this respect, the ecological advantage of the region has eroded substantially.

In the future, comparative advantages are likely to change further because of:

- *Land degradation.* Which alters the vegetation and possibly the land productivity.
- *Global climatic change.* Which will lead to higher temperatures, increased evapotranspiration and more extreme events. It is unclear what will happen to precipitation. For large parts of southern Africa, this may favor smallstock and small wildlife species over cattle and large wildlife species (Arntzen and Ringrose 1995).
- *Cuts in livestock subsidies.* Governments are likely to reduce these because of the World Trade Agreement and government deficits.
- *Reduction of wildlife habitat and numbers.* Outside protected areas, this has generally been the trend, but obviously people and policies can control this development.
- *Poverty.* Parts of the rural population are likely to become impoverished.

Further research is needed to assess which sector will be favored because of these changes. To enhance sustainable development planning should preempt the possible impacts of changing comparative advantages. Obviously, it does not make sense to boost wildlife or livestock production now if such activities would become uneconomic in future.

The impacts of vegetation changes on comparative advantages are illustrated in Figure 12.3. The production opportunity curve indicates the maximum production which can be obtained from two inputs, (i.e., grass and browsing). The isoquant represents different input combinations with the same level of output. The optimal production level and combination input is found at the point where the isoquant touches the production opportunity curve.

Initially, the analysis is restricted to three species (cattle, smallstock, and wildlife) and two input factors (i.e., grass and browse). In extreme cases, the vegetation could be almost 100% grass or 100% browse. In reality, the vegetation of most rangelands will be somewhere between both extremes. Their position can be indicated through the production opportunity curve AB (Figure 12.3). The requirements for different production levels can be summarized in sets of isoquants for each species. The optimal production level and input combination is indicated by the point where the isoquant touches AB. This point differs between cattle, goats, and wildlife, depending on their forage habits. The isoquants for cattle, smallstock, and wildlife differ because of different foraging habits. Browsers, such as goats, may have isoquants like GG, relying mostly on browse and some grass. Cattle may have isoquants such as CC, indicative of the fact that they graze more than they browse. The isoquants for wildlife (WW) are species-dependent because of their varying forage habits: some are primarily browsers, others grazers. Bush encroachment, resulting from high stocking rates, is associated with reduced grazing and increased woody biomass. This may lead to a new production opportunity curve with more browsing and less grass, and offers an explanation for the switch toward smallstock in the region. Cattle will probably increase their browsing, especially during droughts. This implies a movement along the line AB without adverse impacts on cattle productivity. However, grass and browse are not perfect substitutes, and the larger the vegetation changes are the more likely it

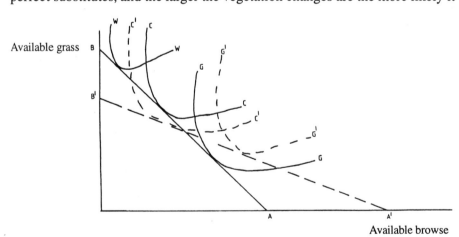

Key: AB and A'B': production opportunity curves.
CC, GG, WW: isoquants for cattle, goats, and wildlife respectively.

Figure 12.3. Production opportunity curves and animal production

is that cattle conditions will be adversely affected. The new production opportunity curve A'B' would apply. In this case, the maximum livestock production would be lower (at the intersection of A'B' and C'C'). The production decline may manifest itself in poorer cattle quality and/or declining numbers. The line A'B' offers the potential for a higher production of browsers as a higher isoquant G'G' can be achieved. As bush encroachment is most severe around water sources and slowly declines with increasing distance from the water source, one may argue that goats should be kept in the vicinity of the water source and cattle should forage further away.

The framework identifies a number of important research areas. For example, research should estimate the exact shape and slope of the production opportunity curve and the isoquants. This requires better knowledge about the forage habits and the impacts on animal performance.

MULTIPLE RANGELAND USE

In terms of multiple use, the degree of complementation and compatibility of activities needs to be assessed. In most cases, there is direct competition for water, but complementation may exist with respect to fodder patterns. For example, browsers could easily complement animals, which primarily graze without causing additional pressure and competition. Unfortunately, information is still far from perfect. Traditionally, it has been assumed that wildlife and cattle were incompatible. Recent evidence shows that there is some complementation with proper management. Cattle is adversely affecting gathering, but again, there may be scope for complementation with proper management.

In order to weigh and compare different types of rangeland use, the total economic value of rangelands has to be estimated. In Table 12.3 a framework for the estimation of the total economic value of rangelands is given. The use of such a framework will lead to a more comprehensive valuation of rangeland. In doing so, it may:

- Provide more incentives for proper rangeland management;
- Identify opportunities for multiple rangeland use; and
- Bring government policies more in line with the comparative advantage of each activity (e.g., reduced beef support).

As the use and function of rangeland vary widely, the value composition and total value of rangeland must be determined on a case-by-case base. The total value is likely to fluctuate substantially. No comprehensive rangeland valuations exist for the region. In Namibia, the costs of communal rangeland degradation are crudely estimated at approximately 100 million Namibian dollars per annum (Quan, Burton, and Conroy 1994). This estimate is restricted to

Table 12.3. Total Economic Value of Rangelands

Value	Usage	Users	Possible Valuation Methods
Direct Use	cattle-consumptive beef, cattle noncon-sumptive: draught power milk, dung, livelihood security	cattle-owner	method varies per output. Examples: corrected market prices for beef; replacement value for draught power
	smallstock-consumptive: meat smallstock-non consumptive: milk, drug, security	small stock owners	method varies per output (cf. cattle)
	useful plants	potentially the entire local population	corrected market prices; replacement value; health improvement
	wildlife: consumptive wildlife: nonconsumptive	usually permit holders + government	income generation
	wood	potentially the entire local population	replacement value; income generation; im-proved living conditions
Indirect Use Value	water retention capacity	local population	value of water storage capacity; replacement value
	Carbon dioxide sink function	biosphere	Examples: replacement value; willingness-to-pay
	biodiversity/gene pool	biosphere	Examples: lost income opportunities: willingness to-pay
Option Value	present non-cattle holders	reduced chances to start livestock farming	foregone future income opportunities
Extension Value		(world) population	willingness-to-pay

certain users costs such as loss of draught power and loss of milk. Market prices and replacement costs are used to estimate the losses. Bush encroach-ment also causes damage to the private livestock sector. Bush encroachment is estimated to cause a loss in meat production of some 100 million Namibian dollars per annum over the last decades (Quan, Burton, and Conroy 1994). In Zimbabwe, in-depth studies show that rangeland degradation on commercial farms leads to beef losses, but no quantification is given (Muir 1993). For other countries no detailed damage estimates are available. We conclude that rangelands are not valued or are undervalued for three reasons.

1. Restriction to one sector only, usually livestock. As a result, values derived from other sectors and external costs imposed on these sectors are discarded. Examples of external impacts are given in Table 12.4. A sectoral orientation would lead to serious underestimates. There is some evidence that wildlife utilization may yield higher per hectare returns than livestock production in marginal areas (Martin 1993).
2. Restriction to certain livestock outputs. Many studies of communal rangelands erroneously measure livestock output in terms of meat production, either per producer or per hectare. This causes an undervaluation of communal area productivity. If all outputs are included, communal area livestock rearing achieves a higher total productivity per hectare than the private ranches (Barret 1992).
3. Restriction to users value and users costs only. As a result, important other aspects of rangelands are left out. Particularly in communal rangelands, valuation should be based on the concepts of total economic value and costing on the marginal opportunity costs (Perrings et al. 1987). The valuation method must also be determined per case study.

Table 12.4. External Costs of Rangeland Uses

From: On:	Cattle	Wildlife	Useful Plants and Wood
Cattle	poorer livestock performance	predation	
Wildlife	reduced habitat; marketing constraints		
Useful Plants and Wood	plants: species and number decline wood: species decline but biomass increase	unknown, but probably varied	
Others	decline in groundwater recharge; reduced CO_2 sink; loss of biodiversity; adverse distributional impacts	probably a moderate influence on vegetation and watering	risk of loss of biodiversity

POPULAR PARTICIPATION AND DECENTRALIZATION

The vastness of the rangeland resources, considerable variations in local environmental conditions, and the limited implementation capacity of governments offer sound reasons for decentralized rangeland management. And yet over the last two decades we have witnessed a common trend towards centralization with central government taking over management responsibilities of local authorities. As a result, communal rangelands suffer from overcrowding and open access, particularly in the vicinity of settlements; only remnants of common property management remain. At the moment, local institutions are often consulted, but in most cases do not really participate in policy development and implementation. Increased popular participation must be based on understanding peoples' income generating and resource use strategies and constraints. In southern Africa, experiences with community-based rangeland management are limited, but they are increasing and some are promising. Below, some experiences are summarized.

In Botswana, so-called communal grazing cells were planned to improve range and livestock management. The cells were in fact replicas of commercial ranches in communal areas. It proved very difficult to find communities and places for pilot projects. The program and operational cells were a failure. Sweet (1987) advances the following reasons: farmers do not perceive overgrazing as their most urgent problem; they are unwilling to reduce stock numbers; governments' extension support is poor; communities are unable to form effective groups; farmers are reluctant to hand over control over their cattle to a group; and finally, farmers are reluctant to pay grazing fees. These reasons do not reveal more fundamental weaknesses, to explain the lack of community cooperation. Grazing cells were essentially a top-down approach. Communities only became involved during the implementation, not in the design phase. Therefore, the cells failed to appreciate the fundamental differences between communal and private livestock production (Table 12.1). In addition, communities pointed out that there was no space for the cells without adversely affecting nonscheme members. Finally, the scheme was sectoral and aimed at increasing beef production only, neglecting other key outputs of cattle and other uses of rangelands. The lessons learned have led to a new approach to establish bottom-up grazing associations in each district. It is too early to evaluate the results.

In Lesotho, grazing associations have been formed with exclusive grazing rights. These associations appear to have been reasonably successful because the benefits of joining the association (i.e., exclusive grazing rights) outweighed the costs (a modest grazing fee). However, this has been achieved with external costs (i.e., higher stocking rates outside the associations' areas). The heterogeneity of the community must be taken into account during the establishment of new associations. Households differ in terms of wealth and livestock dependence and this impacts on their attitude toward and role in grazing associations (Lawry 1987).

Zimbabwe's Communal Areas Management Program for Indigenous Resources (CAMPFIRE) has the broadest scope and is most promising (Child and Peterson 1991; Murphree 1991). CAMPFIRE aims to increase the rural incomes from wildlife[3] utilization in communal areas, and at the same time to ensure wildlife conservation. The program is based on the following assumptions.

- Local people presently consider wildlife as a nuisance instead of a resource;
- Present numbers and diversity of wildlife in southern Africa cannot survive in parks and reserves; and
- Wildlife utilization in semiarid rangeland is at least a valuable supplementary source of income.

Projects are ongoing in 12 communal areas covering 15,500 km^2 (Muir 1993). The key element of the program is resource management decentralization. Central government delegates the wildlife management authority to District Councils, which in turn delegate responsibilities to communities. District Councils and local communities become responsible for wildlife management and the related benefits and costs. The government annually sets wildlife quotas for each project area based on wildlife counts. Subsequently, councils and communities propose annual plans for the utilization and management of wildlife. In essence, communities choose to exploit wildlife themselves or to transfer the rights to safari companies.[4] The guidelines for revenue distribution reserves 35% of the total revenues for resource management. Total income has been 11.5 million Zimbabwean dollars in the period 1989 to 1992. The primary source of revenues is safari hunting (90%); elephants and buffalo bring in most revenues (82% of total). It is not exactly known which percentage of the household income wildlife revenues constitute. The current consensus is that wildlife is able to supplement but not replace income from crop production and cattle. In addition to the generated income, the program has led to a decline in poaching and to a more positive attitude towards wildlife. However, the CITES ban on ivory trade has led to a drop of revenues of 20% (Bond 1994).

Preliminary program evaluation has identified some key factors contributing to the achievements so far (Child and Peterson 1991; Murombedzi 1991; Murphree 1991).

- *The resource choice was good.* Wildlife is particularly suitable for community management because of its high value and the absence of individual resource ownership. It is a relatively new sector without vested interests;

- *Distribution of the revenues.* Benefits accrue to the producers in proportion to their production. Villages which make better use of their resources benefit more;
- *Destination of the revenues by the communities.* A mixture of supplements of individual household income supplements – proportional to their contribution – and financing of community projects seems to give the best incentives;
- *Decentralization of resource access and management.* However, wildlife is highly mobile, and projects must clearly delineate the land boundaries and the resource responsibilities; and
- *Development of local expertise.* Communities must invest in skills for effective wildlife management and group management.

Areas of current concern are:

- *The role of councils.* CAMPFIRE revenues are important income sources of some councils, hence councils may wish to remain involved for financial reasons.
- *Economic viability.* Some projects had heavy overhead and low net revenues, adversely affecting peoples' attitude towards the project and the long-term sustainability of the project.
- *Sustainability of the wildlife resource.* Given the heavy reliance on consumptive wildlife use, excessive hunting may occur. Therefore, quotas must be carefully set and adhered to. This is presently the case as wildlife numbers are stabilizing in the CAMPFIRE areas. However, the prospects of wildlife in communal areas is determined by other factors, many of which are beyond the control of the local communities. Here lies a major long-term concern.

The CAMPFIRE experience shows that community management is a process, which has to evolve gradually when there are no existing local resource management groups. Once groups are effective, the program could exert a positive influence on development in general (an important positive externality of the program). The CAMPFIRE projects suggest that multiple use of communal areas are most productive.

CONCLUSIONS

Current theories of rangeland management do not sufficiently address the issue of sustainable rangeland management. This is a severe limitation. Communal rangelands in southern Africa are used for at least three purposes (livestock, wildlife, and gathering) and provide a range of products. Although the new rangeland theory deals better with the rangeland dynamics and complexities, it fails to look beyond the boundaries of the livestock sector. In this respect, the theory strengthens the livestock bias in government policies and trade-offs between livestock on the one hand and wildlife utilization and gathering on the other hand are not considered. Key issues for sustainable rangeland management include comparative ecological and socioeconomic advantages (and changes therein), opportunities for multiple rangeland uses and popular participation. I recommended that government policies and research should adopt a holistic approach, incorporating all rangeland uses and all key resources.

ACKNOWLEDGMENTS

This chapter is based on research carried out under the CREED program. It is primarily based on a paper, "Revaluation of Communal Rangelands: the Southern Africa Experience," presented to the ISEE conference in Costa Rica. The section on comparative advantages is based on a paper, "Cattle and Wildlife: Alternative or Supplementary Forms of Rangeland Use?" presented at the SADC-ELMS seminar on Applied Techniques in Conservation and Land Management in Gaborone, Botswana. I am grateful to the editors for their comments on an earlier draft.

FOOTNOTES

1. This may be different on shallow soils and around boreholes (Byot 1991).
2. Recently, private ranches have diversified into wildlife either as a supplement or replacement of cattle because of the higher returns from wildlife in semiarid areas.
3. The program covers, in principle, all natural resources. For practical purposes, a start has been made with wildlife.
4. When safari companies are brought in, community returns are maximized by auctioning the wildlife rights.

REFERENCES

Abel, N. O. J. and P. M. Blaikie. 1990. Land Degradation, Stocking Rates and Conservation Policies in the Communal Rangelands of Botswana and Zimbabwe. London: ODI Pastoral Development Network Paper 29a.

Adams, M. E. and P. Devitt. 1992. Grappling with Land Reform in Pastoral Namibia. London: ODI Pastoral Development Network 32a.

Arntzen, J. W. 1990. Economic policies and rangeland degradation in Botswana. *Journal of International Development* 4:471–499.

Arntzen, J. W., R. Chanda, Musisi-Nkambwe, C. vanderPost, R. Ringrose, and F. Sefe. 1994. Desertification and Possible Solutions in the Mid-Boteti Region: A Case Study for the INCD. Botswana: Ministry of Agriculture.

Arntzen, J. W., and R. Ringrose. 1995. Possible Impacts of Climate Change on Southern African Rangelands. Harare: WWF/Climate research unit workshop.

Barret, J. C. 1989. Tsetse Control, Land use and Livestock in the Development of the Zambezi Valley: Some Policy Considerations. Addis Ababa: ALPAN Network Paper 19.

Barret, J. C. 1992. The Economic Role of Cattle in Communal Farming Systems in Zimbabwe. London: ODI Pastoral Network Paper 32b.

Behnke, R. H. and I. Scoones. 1993. Rethinking Range Ecology: Implications for Rangeland Management in Africa. London: IIED/ODI paper No. 33.

Blaikie, M. J. 1982. Improved Productivity from Livestock Production in the Communal Areas of Zimbabwe. Harare: Working Paper 2/82, Department of Land Management, University of Zimbabwe.

Byot, Y. 1991. How long can livestock production be sustained in the hardveld of Botswana. *Pedologie* 2:133–147.

Cardy, F. 1993. Desertification: A fresh approach. *Desertification Control Bulletin* 22:4–8.

Child, B. and J. H. Peterson. 1991. *CAMPFIRE in Rural Development: The Beitbridge Experience*. Harare: CASS/UZ and Department of National Parks.

Dasmann, R. F., J. P. Milton, and P. H. Freeman. 1973. *Ecological Principles for Economic Development*. London: John Wiley and Sons.

Field, D. 1978. *Rangeland Management Handbook for Botswana*. Gaborone: Ministry of Agriculture.

Fowler, M. 1981. Overgrazing in Swaziland: A Review of the Technical Efficiency of the Swaziland Herd. London: ODI Pastoral Development Network Paper 12d.

Lawry, S. W. 1987. Communal Grazing and Range Management: The Case of Grazing Associations in Lesotho. Addis Ababa: ALPAN Network Paper 13, ILCA.

Martin, R. B. 1993. *Should Wildlife Pay Its Way?* Harare: Department of National Parks.

Muir, K. 1993. Economic Policy, Wildlife and Cattle Management in Zimbabwe and Their Environmental Implications. Washington: AFTEN, World Bank.

Murombedzi, J. 1991. Decentralising Common Property Resources Management: A Case Study of the Nyaminyami District Council of Zimbabwe's Wildlife Management Programme. London: Dryland Networks Programme Paper 30. IIED.

Murphree, M. W. 1991. *Communities as Institutions for Resource Management*. Harare: Centre for Applied Social Studies.

Perkins, J. S. and D. S. G. Thomas. 1993. Spreading deserts or spatially confined environmental impacts? Land degradation in the Kalahari desert of Botswana. *Land Degradation and Rehabilitation* 4:179–194.

Perrings, C., J. B. Opschoor, J. W. Arntzen, A. Gilbert, and D. W. Pearce. 1987. Economics for Sustainable Development: A Case Study of Botswana. Gaborone: Technical Report prepared for Botswana's National Conservation Strategy.

Sandford, S. 1983. *Management of Pastoral Development in the Third World*. London/Chicester: ODI and Wiley and Sons.

Swallow, B. M. and R. F. Brokken. 1987. Cattle Marketing Policy in Lesotho. Addis Ababa: ALPAN Network paper 14. ILCA.

Sweet, R. J. 1987. The Communal Grazing Cell Experience. London: ODI Pastoral Development Network Paper 23b.

Tapson, D. R. 1991. The Overstocking and Offtake Controversy Reexamined for the Case of Kwazulu. London: ODI Pastoral Development Network Paper 31a.

World Bank. 1988. *Sustainable Resource Management in Agriculture and Rural Development Project: A Review of Policies, Procedures and Results*. Washington DC.

Quan, J., D. Burton, and C. Conroy. 1994. A Preliminary Assessment of the Economic Impact of Desertification in Namibia. Windhoek.

13 VALUING ECOSYSTEM CHANGE: THEORY AND MEASUREMENT

Susan Kask
Department of Economics and Finance
Western Carolina University
Cullowhee, North Carolina

Jason Shogren
Economics and Finance Department
University of Wyoming
Laramie, Wyoming

Pete Morton
Department of Biological Sciences
University of Denver
Denver, Colorado

INTRODUCTION

The valuation of an ecosystem versus the valuation of its parts (such as timber, genetic resources, and recreational activities) is becoming increasingly important as resource management agencies move to a more holistic management approach, and the need to include environmental resources into our national income accounts becomes more pressing. These changes suggest the need for a more holistic valuation approach than is presently found in the literature. Such an approach must account for the varied and wide-ranging flow of direct and indirect services to economic systems provided by ecosystems (e.g., basic life support, filtration of nonpoint sources of pollution from urban and rural runoff, maintenance of gaseous composition in the atmosphere, regulation of the hydrological cycle, pollination of crops, control of potential pests, generation and maintenance of soils, and biodiversity).

Both the theoretical basis and the measurement of ecosystem values pose challenges for economists. For example, familiarity with the good (value formation and preference formation), definition of the good, embedding, and surrogate valuation. In addition, problems with measurement procedures occur such as those associated with using the hypothetical market approach, the difficulty of defining the good, or defining a private proxy. (Crocker and Shogren 1991a, 1991b; Desvousges et al. 1992; Navrud 1992; Arrow et al. 1993; Hanley and Splash 1993). Further development of the theoretical foundation for consumer valuation of ecosystems may provide useful insights for addressing these problems. Moreover, further development of the tools available may address some of the measurement problems. This chapter presents a theoretical framework for analyzing consumer ecosystem values, discusses the issues surrounding measurement, and presents a proposed valuation approach that may address these issues. This proposed approach combines a laboratory procedure with the hypothetical market approach to capture the best aspects of both, a broad base and laboratory learning. We call this combined approach CVM-X.

WHY VALUE AN ECOSYSTEM?

What is an ecosystem? As defined by E. O. Wilson (1992) an ecosystem is the grouping of "organisms living in a particular environment, such as a lake or a forest, and the physical part of the environment that impinges on them." Wilson defines ecosystem services as the role of organisms in providing a healthy environment for humans. Are these the only services humans may value? In addition to the life support and a healthy environment, an ecosystem provides inputs for the production of both market and nonmarket goods and activities (e.g., timber for wood products, genetic material for development of pharmaceutical products, fish and wildlife for fishing and hunting, or an attractive environment for hiking), and it provides aesthetic services (e.g., beautiful views or a variety of species). Given this simplified view of ecosystem services, humans may value an ecosystem directly for its contribution to the provision of life support and aesthetic services and indirectly through the goods and services it produces.

Is it necessary to value an ecosystem as a whole, or can we infer value to the whole system from the value of its outputs? Much of the valuation literature for environmental goods has focused on consumer values for changing recreational activities, or on changes in environmental quality such as air or water pollution. These values have often focused on one aspect of these changes, such as a change in recreational values from reduced water quality or health values from improvements in air quality. Can we use these values to infer a total value for the ecosystem, or do we need new measures? Is the total value of an ecosystem reflected in the value of its outputs? For example, is the value of the Grand Canyon reflected in the value of a recreation day? Or is the value of the Costa Rican Dry Forest reflected in the value of the timber? If we consider the ecosystem an input to these goods, and these goods are the highest valued use for the ecosystem, and markets work efficiently when allocating the ecosystem between these goods and others, then yes, the value of timber or recreation days will reflect the value of the ecosystem used to produce them. However, these assumptions do not hold due to the nonrival and nonexclusive nature of an ecosystem.

This nonrival, nonexclusive nature of an ecosystem prevents markets from pricing and allocating it efficiently. An ecosystem is nonrival in that once it is protected, it is protected for everyone, and it is nonexclusive in that it is difficult to divide up and sell the ecosystem in a market since it is difficult to exclude a consumer from consumption of the ecosystem. As a result, an ecosystem as a whole has no value reflected by market prices. In contrast, the commodity resources of the ecosystem are valued on the market, and the supply and demand for these commodities reflect the relative scarcity of them alone. Therefore, there is pressure to harvest the commodity goods at the expense of the ecosystem and other services it provides leading to a potential misallocation of resources. Our challenge is to determine the value of an ecosystem from the many goods and services it supplies, not only from one. Given a change in an ecosystem, how can we determine the benefits from improvement or losses from degradation? The model below illustrates just such a valuation approach.

A BASIC MODEL

Given the various ways an individual may value an ecosystem (i.e., the indirect value through market and nonmarket goods and services and direct values), a household production framework best captures both avenues for value. To maintain simplicity we initially define an individual's utility function as a function of a single household service (z) and a single ecosystem characteristic (e). The household service could be an activity such as maintaining good health, leisure activities, meal production, family activities, and so on.

$$\mu = \mu(z,e), \tag{13.1}$$

where z is represented by a household production function

$$z = z(x,e). \tag{13.2}$$

The production of services in the household depends on both the good the consumer purchases (x) and the ecosystem characteristic (e). For example, a fishing rod is a market good (x) that combined with a clear river (e) together produce the fishing activity defined as the fish caught per hour (z). For a household service we expect $\partial z \partial e \geq 0$ (i.e., an improvement in the ecosystem characteristic may not affect production of the household service, or it may affect the household service positively). In addition, $\partial z \partial x > 0$. Furthermore, good x and the ecosystem characteristic may be either substitutes or complements (i.e., $\partial x/\partial e < 0$, or $\partial x/\partial e > 0$. The fishing example above is a case where x and e are complements. They may be substitutes in a case such as sea fishing where sonar technology is a substitute for a high quality fishery.[1]

The individual maximizes utility subject to a budget constraint: $p \bullet x = M$. Where p is the price of x and M is income. The ecosystem is assumed to have no prices; it is a free good to the consumer. Solving the consumer's maximization problem for x^* the Langrangian and first order conditions are:

$$L = \mu \, (z \, (x,e),e) + \lambda \, (M - px) \tag{13.3}$$

$$\frac{\partial L}{\partial x} = \frac{\partial \mu}{\partial z} \frac{\partial z}{\partial x} - \lambda p = 0 \tag{13.4}$$

$$\frac{\partial L}{\partial \lambda} = M - px = 0 \tag{13.5}$$

Substituting x^*, the demand expression, into the utility function we get the following indirect utility function.

$$\mu = v \, (M,p,e). \tag{13.6}$$

Setting the total differential of this expression equal to zero and assuming prices do not change, we get:

$$du = \frac{\partial v}{\partial M} dM + \frac{\partial v}{\partial e} de = 0. \tag{13.7}$$

Rearranging the above equation we get the equation below.

$$\frac{dM}{de} = - \frac{\dfrac{\partial v}{\partial e}}{\dfrac{\partial v}{\partial M}}. \tag{13.8}$$

The denominator, $\partial v/ \partial M$, is equal to λ, the marginal utility of income, and from the first order conditions above we find λ is equal to the marginal utility of good (x) per dollar spent on that good, therefore, the denominator of equation (8) is described below.

$$\lambda = \frac{\dfrac{\partial u}{\partial z} \dfrac{\partial z}{\partial x}}{p}. \tag{13.9}$$

Furthermore, the numerator, $\partial v/\partial e$, is the partial derivative of the indirect utility function with respect to e.

$$\frac{\partial v}{\partial e} = \frac{\partial u}{\partial z}\frac{\partial z}{\partial e} + \frac{\partial u}{\partial e}, \tag{13.10}$$

and

$$\frac{\partial z}{\partial e} = \frac{\partial z}{\partial x}\frac{\partial x}{\partial e} + \frac{\partial z}{\partial e}. \tag{13.11}$$

Substituting these expressions and equation (9) into equation (8) we get the marginal value of a change in an ecosystem characteristic.

$$MV_e = -\frac{\partial v/\partial e}{\partial v/\partial M} = -\frac{\frac{\partial u}{\partial z}\left(\frac{\partial z}{\partial e} + \frac{\partial z}{\partial x}\frac{\partial x}{\partial e}\right) + \frac{\partial u}{\partial e}}{\frac{\frac{\partial u}{\partial z}\frac{\partial z}{\partial x}}{p}}. \tag{13.12}$$

This result suggests consumers choose the marginal value of a change in e by balancing the marginal utility from a change in e and the marginal utility per dollar spent on x. Note the three sources of marginal utility from e. The numerator represents the indirect value through z and x, and the direct value.

The model is easily generalized to m household services in vector Z, n goods in vector X, and r ecosystem characteristics in vector, E. The result follows.

$$MV_{e_i} = -\frac{\partial v/\partial e_i}{\partial v/\partial M} = -\frac{\sum\limits_{k=1}^{m}\frac{\partial u}{\partial z_k}\left(\frac{\partial z_k}{\partial e_i} + \sum\limits_{j=1}^{n}\frac{\partial z_k}{\partial x_j}\frac{\partial x_j}{\partial e_i}\right) + \frac{\partial u}{\partial e_i}}{\sum\limits_{k=1}^{m}\sum\limits_{j=1}^{n}\frac{\frac{\partial u}{\partial z_k}\frac{\partial z_k}{\partial x_j}}{p_j}}. \tag{13.13}$$

The marginal valuation of a change in an ecosystem characteristic, e_i, includes the value of the characteristic in relation to all the z's and x's relevant to that ecosystem characteristic, thus this result gives the holistic approach proposed above. Extending the model to include the potential interaction between ecosystem characteristics would add additional interactive terms to the numerator in equation (13.13) above.

An alternative specification for the consumer's value can be expressed as a compensating surplus (CS) where the CS is the solution to:

$$v(M, P, E^0) = v(M - CS, P, E^1),$$ (13.14)

or the equivalent surplus (ES), where the ES is the solution to Equation (15).

$$v(M + ES, P, E^0) = v(M, P, E^1).$$ (13.15)

Surplus measures are used since the change in the ecosystem characteristic is a change in the quantity of the resource, and the consumer cannot adjust the quantity of the resource to satisfy the optimizing conditions (Freeman 1993). The model presented above does not account for the uncertain nature of ecosystem services. Ecosystem services come from natural systems which may be cyclical or changing, thus posing uncertainties in the availability of services to the economy. Furthermore, a full understanding of the impact of human activities on natural systems remains to be achieved. Thus, two dimensions of uncertainty surround the valuation process, uncertainty in the availability of an ecosystem service (good weather for agriculture or recreational activities) and in our understanding of ecosystem change itself (global warming). The model also does not address the temporal and spatial aspects related to consumption of ecosystem services. Extending the model to include these issues is an important next step for understanding ecosystem valuation.

MEASURING ECOSYSTEM VALUES: ISSUES

Although the value of ecosystem services may be reflected in various market (housing) and nonmarket (hunting) goods and services, it is unlikely the value of the ecosystem itself can be determined from the value of any particular market good. Therefore, ecosystem valuation must use a hypothetical method for valuation.

The contingent valuation method (CVM) directly elicits value by constructing a hypothetical market for a nonmarket good through the use of a survey. The market creates an opportunity for an individual to reveal his willingness-to-pay (WTP) or willingness-to-accept (WTA) for a change in the level of the good. The market is constructed so that features of actual markets and institutions are used to describe what the good is, how it will be changed, who will change it, how long the change will occur, and who will pay for the change. The major advantage of CVM is its flexibility to construct a market where no market currently exists. But flexibility is also the major weakness of CVM, as it allows ample opportunity for misperception. A researcher can specify a hypothetical good and elicit a value, but a respondent may perceive the good quite differently when providing his actual value. Other problems with the

CVM approach are discussed later in this chapter. The CVM-X may ameliorate these problems since it uses a combination CVM survey and the experimental lab approach.

Ecosystem valuation is particularly plagued with problems in study design because of the difficulty in defining the good and the respondents' familiarity with the good. Furthermore, the potential for dynamic inconsistency, and the need to address additional questions of market context (i.e., how the good will be changed, who changes it, how long and who pays) also become difficult with ecosystem valuation. These issues and the CVM-X approach are discussed below.

Defining the Good: The Ecosystem Characteristics

The first and foremost problem of ecosystem valuation comes from defining the good. A poorly defined good can lead to a variety of problems associated with scenario mis-specification. These include mis-specification with respect to the theoretical basis of value, or with the respondents' inability to understand the scenario presented (Mitchell and Carson 1989).

The model above provides some useful insights into defining the good. For example, the value of a change in an ecosystem characteristic comes from the impact of the characteristic change on the consumption of the market good (x), the ability of the consumer to pursue household activities (z), and directly from the utility function. The analyst must therefore define the vector of ecosystem characteristics (E) so they are relevant to the consumer's household production function (Z) and utility function (u). An example clarifies the importance of this task. The U.S. Environmental Protection Agency (USEPA) Environmental Monitoring and Assessment Program (EMAP) forest resource group uses a set of ecological indicators to measure the status and trends of forest environmental quality (USEPA 1993). These indicators are based upon scientific goals of quantifying and measuring the degree of ecological/biological response, the magnitude of stress on a forest, various habitat characteristics, and the degree of exposure to stressors. These goals are related to environmental values of ecological integrity, extent, and aesthetics. Based on these values and goals, the forest resource group uses several categories of indicators: vegetative quality, nutrient balance, soil productivity, contaminants, biodiversity, and landscape characterization. Within each of these categories there is a set of indicators such as ozone concentration, songbird population levels, fire occurrence, lichen biomonitoring, and so on. These indicators are based on scientific goals and values and may or may not be relevant to society's interests and concerns about the forest. For example, songbird populations may be very relevant to society's bird watching or forest experience activities (i.e., the z's), however, lichen biomonitoring may not have much meaning or value to the public unless it is related to some socially valued activity (z_k) or can be directly included in the utility function.

Herriges and Shogren (1993) used water quality characteristics to elicit farmers' opinions about water pollution. They used four characteristics: fish caught per hour, lake depth, lake bottom muck, and water clarity. All are measurable and related to activities or objectives the farmers may have regarding the lake. For example, lake depth can affect swimming, fishing, and recreational boating, and water clarity may affect swimming and fishing enjoyment. These lake quality characteristics are scientifically useful and measurable, and they are relevant to the fisherman, boaters, swimmers, walkers, bird watchers and farmers regarding their lake activities. These characteristics do not assume the same behavioral characteristics for each person; instead each has their own interpretation of the quality of the lake for swimming and boating. This allows variation across activity functions (z's) and allows analysts to elicit a surface of attitudes for the set of ecosystem characteristics (e's). The striking difference between these two sets of characteristics, the forest group e's and the Herriges–Shogren e's, is the social relevance of the latter. These characteristics can be used by the respondents to make judgments about the condition of the lake in relation to their preferences for the lake. The social relevance, or the relevance of the e's to the household production function (z) is critical for the success of ecosystem valuation.

Other analysts have defined particular ecosystem characteristics. Examples include Weitzman (1993) and Solow, Polansky, and Broadus (1993) which both provide measures of biodiversity. In each paper, the authors investigate the applicability of using a species distance measure for analyzing conservation policy for the case of crane conservation. This work, however, represents only one example of an ecosystem characteristic which may be applicable for the vector E.

Where should the vector E come from? From both the scientific and economic communities. Criteria for evaluating and selecting ecosystem characteristics is significantly different from that used for solely scientifically based ecological indicators. Ecological indicators should be sensitive to stress, respond to stress in a predictable way, be easy and economical to measure, be relevant to goals of investigation, and apply to single species or management goals as was the case with the EMAP forest indicators. However, ecosystem characteristics used for valuation should have properties such as completeness, be operational, measurable, separable, nonredundant, and have a minimum size (Keeney and Raiffa 1976). In addition, the characteristics must be policy and socially relevant. A beneficial but not required property is transferability. The environmental economics literature includes many studies that use some measure of environmental quality or quantity that is related to consumer production of household activities. Analysts can begin with these measures to develop the vector of ecosystem services required for valuation. A sample listing of ecosystem goods and services (Z and X) and potential ecosystem characteristics (E) are given in the appendix. If we can overcome the problem of defining the good for valuation, we must then face a variety of other problems with measurement.[2]

Preference and Values

Recent papers that define a rigorous and workable economic definition of ecosystem characteristics are conspicuous for their lack of a value dimension. A probable reason for this neglect is the difficulty in assigning economic value to goods that people are unfamiliar with and never directly use. How can we attach an economic value to the mere existence of an environmental good when our preferences for the good are ambiguous or underdeveloped? Three questions of preference and value need to be addressed in the design of an economic valuation study: 1) Do specific values act as surrogate preferences for general environmental preferences (i.e., can respondents distinguish between E^0 and E^1)? 2) How does the lack of familiarity with a good affect valuation (i.e., does the respondent understand what the E vector is); and 3) How does the dynamic inconsistency that is predicted to occur with variation in access to ecosystem changes, either temporally or spatially, affect value estimates? We consider each question below.

Surrogate Preferences

Following Krutilla (1967), economic value can be grouped into three broad categories – use values, potential demand values, and existence value. Total value is the idea that consumers have both use and nonuse values for an environmental resource. Use value is straightforward – the economic value of current use. But a nonuse value is more problematic and controversial. Option price is the economic value of future use of a resource, while existence value is the value of its mere existence with no plans to ever use it. As academicians debated the theoretical justification, the United States District of Columbia Court of Appeals ruled in 1989 that nonuse value constitutes a valid representation of economic value. In *Ohio versus U.S. Department of the Interior*, 800f.2d432, the court stated that "option and existence values may represent 'passive use' but they nonetheless reflect utility derived by humans from a resource and thus prima facie ought to be included in a damage assessment." Nonuse values have been recognized further in the Exxon Valdez case where the court accepted high estimations of nonuse values. Finally, the view that nonuse values are bona fide was also supported by a panel of economists (including two Nobel Prize winners) convened to evaluate contingent valuation (Arrow et al. 1993).

But there is an opposing view that nonuse value does not really measure total value, rather it is a surrogate measure of general preferences towards the environment (i.e., a "warm glow" effect). Eliciting nonmarket values with a contingent valuation survey provides the opportunity for a respondent to state his or her general preference toward the environment and not for the specific ecosystem or ecosystem service in question. This is probably the first, if not only, occasion he or she has been asked to reveal a public opinion on the environment. Therefore, the value revealed may reflect the warm glow of contributing to save the general environment rather than the specific service in question. For example, Crocker and Shogren (1991a) find mixed evidence of surrogate bidding for atmospheric visibility in Oregon. They observed no significant difference in values for improved visibility in one specific mountain location as compared to the value for statewide improvements. In addition, Arrow et al. (1993) note that the bimodal distribution of value estimates in many CVM studies – zero or a positive value around $30 to $50 – suggests that these values may serve a function similar to charitable contributions. Not only does the respondent want to support a worthy cause, but he or she also receives a warm glow from donating to the cause.

The recent debate between Kahneman and Knetsch (1991) and Smith (1992) further illustrates the issue. Kahneman and Knetsch observed that the average WTP to clean up one lake in Ontario was not significantly greater than the WTP to clean up all the provincial lakes. They cite this as evidence that individuals are not responding to the good, but rather to the idea of contributing to environmental preservation in general – the warm glow effect. Smith questioned this view, arguing that incremental WTP should decline with the amount of the good already available, and as such the evidence is consistent with economic theory. But other reports such as Desvousges et al. (1992) support the warm glow argument finding evidence the average WTP to prevent 2,000 birds from dying in oil-filled ponds was not significantly different than the value to prevent 20,000 or 200,000 birds from dying. While accepting the argument that WTP for additional protection probably does decline, Arrow et al. (1993) note that the drop to zero "is hard to explain as the expression of a consistent, rational set of choices."

Separating total value from warm glows presents a challenge to the nonmarket valuation of ecosystems. Total values are more accurately estimated for well-defined areas and well-specified resources. But a piecemeal resource-by-resource approach will overestimate economic value because it does not address substitution possibilities across the set of resources. For example, if we value ten resources across the Appalachian region, then the summed values of the ten studies for each resource will exceed the value of one study over the ten resources. But as we move towards one comprehensive valuation study, we increase the likelihood of warm glows as the resources become less tangible and more symbolic. Considering ecosystem size and the numerous services available from ecosystems, ecosystem valuation requires a study design that includes well-defined substitution possibilities and checks for internal consistency.

UNFAMILIARITY AND PREFERENCE LEARNING

Even if we get beyond warm glows and elicit meaningful values for an ecosystem, we must still appreciate that many individuals are simply unfamiliar with most of the services and functions that ecosystems provide. As an example, a survey of Scottish citizens revealed that over 70% of the respondents were completely unfamiliar with the meaning of ecosystems and biodiversity (Hanley and Splash 1993). Such levels of unfamiliarity are of concern if consumer sovereignty is to command respect in resource policy questions.

The question of unfamiliarity is central to understanding the values estimated with nonmarket valuation. Standard guidelines suggest that nonmarket valuation is more reliable if the respondent is familiar with the good. The individual who is familiar with the good will be better able to value changes in its provision. For example, most U.S. respondents would be familiar with the bald eagle and may be able to provide a dollar value for an increased population of the species. But for many other environmental assets, such as wetland filtration, most respondents may be unfamiliar with the actual services provided. What does value mean when an individual is unfamiliar with the asset they are asked to value? Consider two approaches to this question – value formation and preference learning.

Hoehn and Randall (1987) define value formation as the process of an individual attaching a dollar value to his resource preferences, given that he completely understands his relative ranking of the resource relative to other resources. That is, an individual knows that he prefers improved environmental quality to a new toaster, but has not attached a monetary value to that preference. Value formation is affected by the time and resource constraints inherent in any decision to allocate a resource. Time and resource constraints inhibit the individual's ability to comprehend the complex services provided by the resource, thereby making the service appear unfamiliar. Hoehn and Randall examine how values are formed by comparing the values obtained under the ideal consumer problem to the values obtained given time and resource constraints. They argue that imperfect communication can cause an individual to undervalue the service relative to the same measure of value formed under ideal circumstances. This undervaluation problem can be alleviated if more time and decision resources are devoted to the value formation process.

Figure 13.1 illustrates the value formation issue. The revealed value is presented on the vertical axis, while time to learn is represented on the horizontal

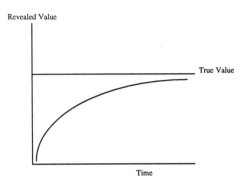

Figure 13.1. Revealed value relative to true value given time to learn

axis. Note that as time to learn about the good is constrained, the value of the respondent is low relative to his or her true value. The individual did not have enough time to accurately translate his or her preferences into a monetary value. But as the time to form a value is increased, the individual has more opportunity to translate preferences into a monetary manifestation, and therefore his revealed value will approach his true value from below.

But the value formation argument presumes the individual understands his initial preferences for resources. In short, the argument assumes the individual's sense of well-being is static and invariant and that he suffers no doubt about the preferences for any outcome. This follows the standard view that preferences for goods are fixed and the changes in demand for an ecosystem service must occur because of changes in shadow prices, household technology, or resource constraints. Thus, demand changes cannot arise because the individual does not understand how an unfamiliar service affects his overall satisfaction, or because of changes in preferences.

But there are numerous applications involving environmental resources with which respondents are unfamiliar. Frequently, the respondent has little day-to-day contact with the service, or if he does, he may view his efforts to alter these experiences as futile, and therefore, has devoted little effort to understanding how these services affect his well-being. If this is the case, the individual may well need to form conjectures and accumulate experience with the resource in order to more accurately assess his relative preference for the resource. Crocker and Shogren (1991b) demonstrate that if an individual does not know his preferences for a resource, his revealed value will exceed the true value when he does know his preferences. The individual is willing to pay extra to acquire information about the potential value the resource may provide in the future. In contrast to value formation, this result suggests that an individual will overvalue an unfamiliar asset. In addition, overvaluation decreases as the individual becomes more familiar with the service. Figure 13.2 shows that as time increases, the revealed value approaches the true value from above.

We have two effects that work in opposite directions; value formation implies undervaluation, while preference learning implies overvaluation. This suggests that when valuing nonmarket goods, such as an ecosystem, analysts need some protocol that accurately specifies the degree of value formation and preference learning occurring, thus determining whether we have an over or underestimate of value. If such a protocol can be defined, we can compare an individual's value when his situation (time and resource decision constraints) and his preference knowledge change simultaneously or sequentially. Otherwise, estimates of value for an ecosystem will be misspecified.

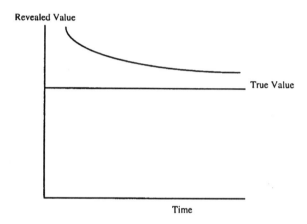

Figure 13.2. Revealed value relative to true value given time to learn

DYNAMIC INCONSISTENCY

Crocker and Shogren (1993) explore how an individual's marginal rate of time preference is affected by the access conditions to an ecosystem. They develop a model that suggests an individual will value avoiding delayed access to an ecosystem more than securing extended access, given that time and money are complements. The disparity in values results in a fundamental dynamic inconsistency – a low marginal rate of time preference to avoid delayed access and a high rate to acquire extended access. Using a contingent valuation approach, they find that behavior is partially consistent with this hypothesis, and that marginal rates of time preference are highly situation and individual-specific.

These results illustrate an internal inconsistency in two commonly held presumptions on preferences: an individual has an invariant rate of time preference and he equally values a gain or loss from the status quo endowment of resources. Crocker and Shogren (1993) show that if an individual has an invariant marginal rate of time preference, his value of a gain versus a loss must differ. Alternatively, if the individual values a gain and loss equally, his implied marginal rate of time preference must differ.

To illustrate, suppose an individual reveals that he is willing to pay \$100 to secure a status quo level of access to an ecosystem. Let R be the individual's WTP, R = \$100. He is then given the opportunity to change his bid given a change in the temporal conditions of access – either a ten-year extension of access or a ten-year delay in access. Using standard discount formulae, the equations for his WTP for extended access, (R_e), and delayed access, (R_d), are

$$R_e = R \left[((1 + r)^{10} - 1)/r (1 + r)1^{10} \right] \tag{13.16}$$

and

$$R_d = R / (1 + r)^{10} \tag{13.17}$$

where *r* is the individual's discount rate. Suppose the individual decides not to change his or her bid of \$100 for either the delayed or extended access, R = R_e = R_d = \$100. By equations (13.16) and (13.17), the implied discount rate is infinite for the extended access, while the implied rate is zero for the delayed access. The change in value from the status quo is identical, but the implied discount rate is infinitely different. Now we can reverse the scenario. Assume the individual's change in value is still zero for the extension, but decreases by \$100 for the delay. The implied discount rate is now infinite for both cases, even though the change in values is different. These examples work just as well for intermediate values, not just the extremes we have used here. Given the existence of such dynamic inconsistencies, how the temporal access conditions are defined must be carefully considered in any study design for valuing ecosystems.

Market Context

Designing the market context, such as how will the good be changed, who will change it, how long the change will occur, and who will pay for the change, is an important part of study design for a hypothetical valuation procedure. These questions refer to the description of the policy objectives and proposed policy solutions. Policy objectives such as promoting ecosystems for sustainable development need to be plausible, clearly stated, and likely achieved by the policy solutions proposed.

Proposed policy solutions revolve around two basic economic concepts: changing either constraints or incentives. First consider constraints. Using the U.S. Appalachian region as an example, people in this region face a set of constraints that inhibit their opportunities to adjust to new policy initiatives. Constraints include income, time, information, technology, and access to markets. One way to overcome the threats to an ecosystem is to alter these constraints, thereby providing a larger and more varied set of opportunities. For example, relaxing legal constraints that allow citizens to take action for an ecosystem gives them an incentive to learn more about the ecosystem and to participate in the policy process, thus increasing their access to the market.

Policies can also attempt to change behavior using economic incentives either by increasing the benefits of preservation or the costs of ecosystem alteration. Increasing the benefits of preservation can occur by giving the local population property rights to the stream of economic benefits gained from ecosystems. This allocation of rights increases the private benefits of habitat conservation so that they approach the social benefits of conservation. A longterm investment in an ecosystem results in benefits associated with excludable nonconsumptive use values, as well as those associated with the steady stream of consumptive use benefits issuing from a sustainable harvest of surrounding areas. In addition to refocusing those who would overuse the protected areas, enlisting the help of the locals removes their support and tolerance of overusers. An alternative is to remove any perverse incentives which already exist and increase the benefit of ecosystem destruction. For example, subsidies for land purchases where agricultural land receives a higher price than forested land increases the incentive to cut down the trees and begin cropping.

Increasing the costs of ecosystem destruction is potentially more difficult. This implies a strict monitoring and enforcement scheme that raises the expected penalty from the overuse of the protected area. Locals can be motivated to exclude themselves from the protected area or buffer zones if it becomes unprofitable to stay; the marginal benefits are outweighed by the new higher marginal costs. The question becomes: does the government have the resources to set up an effective monitoring system that will deter entry and overuse? In most countries where ecosystems are currently being promoted, the answer is generally, no. The vast expanses and multitude of access areas implies that increased enforcement is probably not possible.

Policy objectives and solutions need to be clearly specified when valuing a nonmarket good. If we consider the valuation of the Appalachian regional ecosystem as an example, we might consider the policy objective to be to establish a sustainable human and natural ecosystem in areas of the Appalachian region where ecosystems are threatened. The goal could be to encourage sustainable natural resource management through an institutional framework of incentives and revenue generation and expenditure, on the assumption that this will lead to increased ecosystem stability and conservation. Policy solutions might include:

1. To establish an association to manage protected areas with sufficient authority and capabilities to perform their management function;
2. To establish and operate an ecosystem information service to provide data;

3. To implement management plans in several protected areas that balance the need for economic growth with conservation;
4. To facilitate local environmental initiatives by strengthening regulatory incentives, and fostering participation with local groups; and
5. To generate revenue expenditure, and resource pricing through improved natural forest management, and the establishment of a Regional Environmental Endowment Fund (REEF) as a sustainable source of financing for environmental initiatives. Such a scenario description could be used to present the policy approach for ecosystem valuation.

Given a market context, definition of the good, and addressing the problems of familiarity and dynamic inconsistency we can design a survey instrument to elicit values for ecosystem values. Utilizing the CVM-X approach below provides additional avenues for addressing the various biases occurring with CVM.

MEASURING ECOSYSTEM VALUES: CVM-X

Experimental lab markets are a relatively new approach for directly valuing a nonmarket asset. Experimental markets are real markets selling real goods to real people, but within a highly stylized context. Experimental markets can elicit values over several levels of market experience by developing and testing auctions with repeated market experience and information. Lab experiments can isolate and control how different auctions and market settings affect values in a setting of replication and repetition. Experiments with repeated market experience provide a well-defined incentive structure that allows a person to learn that honest revelation of his or her true preferences is his or her best strategy. The relative ability to isolate and control potential problems such as surrogate bidding elevate experimental markets as a viable alternative to standard nonmarket valuation methods. The experimental approach can serve as both a complement and substitute for CVM surveys. The lab work can complement CVM surveys by providing an opportunity for extensive pretesting of the CVM market design; substitution occurs when the lab auctions a service that can actually be bought and sold, but is currently not on the market.

Experimental markets can be used to guide environmental policy. Experiments motivated by the questions of policy-makers can provide insight into how a proposed change in incentives or benefits will affect behavior. By supplying information on the behavioral link between incentives, values, and choice, experimental markets can influence how environmental policy is made and evaluated. Since the lab environment differs from the natural environment by necessity, experiments should be viewed as a dress rehearsal and not the play itself. Experimental markets do not generally dictate policy, rather they are used to improve our understanding of the underlying assumptions and incentives that drive behavioral responses to policy.

Experiments have been promoted as an ex ante means to strengthen the contingent valuation of nonmarket goods (see Coursey and Schulze 1986). The idea is to go into the lab prior to the CVM survey and observe how bidding behavior is affected by alternative incentive compatible auctions and repeated market experience. This is a valuable approach, however, experiments can also be used ex post as well. For lack of a better name, call this proposed ex post procedure CVM-X. There are four steps to CVM-X. First, after testing and revising the questionnaire, run the CVM survey and elicit hypothetical or real bids for the good in question. Second, bring subsamples of the CVM respondents into the lab to determine how their initial CVM bids are affected by a lab environment with real goods, real money, repeated market experience, and alternative demand revealing auctions. Third, apply appropriate statistical analysis to predict the final experienced bids (X) based on the initial hypothetical bids and other socioeconomic characteristics. Finally, adjust the bids of the CVM respondents who did not participate in the lab experiments for the learning and market experience effects revealed by the subsample. The CVM-X procedure could prove a cost-effective tool to combine the strength of CVM and the lab, increasing survey accuracy and broadening the scope of nonmarket valuation in the lab.

Following the work of Bohm (1972), Coursey, Hovis, and Schulze (1987), and Shogren et al. (1994), the value of an ecosystem, such as the Appalachian region, could be elicited in a lab environment using the REEF. The experimental market could elicit the measures of value for alternative donations to conservation programs promoted by the REEF. Furthermore, additional experiments to evaluate how subjects respond to changes in the experimental design features and to determine if there is a pattern of surrogate bidding in the elicited values could be done. All experiments use real money, real auctions, repeated opportunities in the auction market, and full information on the probability and severity of the ecosystem changes.

The general experiment would follow a two-stage procedure. First, after subjects fill out a questionnaire on general knowledge of ecosystems, a five-trial pretest using a good such as a lottery will be used to acquaint the subjects with the Vickrey auction (a sealed bid, second price auction where the highest bidder secures the 100% risk reduction and pays the highest losing bid; Vickrey 1961). The Vickrey auction has been promoted as a possible elicitation device for contingent valuation because of its well-known preference-revealing properties.

The second stage elicits an actual contribution scheme where the REEF is introduced and described to the subjects. Ten trials of the Vickrey auction are used to elicit naive bids. The bids are naive in that the monitor does not provide information on the nature of the Appalachian ecosystem; only the individual's subjective perception and the second highest bid are available to guide bidding. After trial ten, the monitor provides information about ecosystems, and ten more trials will be run to elicit informed bids.

Experiments should explore at least four key patterns of behavior. First, they should test for surrogate bidding. Kahneman (1986) argued that surrogate bidding exists if the value measures for the specific aspects of ecosystems act as ersatz measures for general environmental preferences. If surrogate bidding prevails, then values for specific goods cannot be relied on as accurate indicators of preference. Surrogate bidding is tested by comparing the value estimates from each specific good with the value estimate from a description that combines all the goods.

Second, the experimental design should explore the question of unfamiliarity that is central to understanding the value of ecosystems. Unfamiliarity decreases the reliability of the value estimates. Respondents who are unfamiliar with ecosystems will be less able to value changes in its provision. For example, although most U.S. respondents are familiar with the bald eagle, and may be able to value an increased level of the species, respondents will likely be unfamiliar with the actual services provided by ecosystems. What do value measures mean when an individual is unfamiliar with the asset they are being asked to value? If this is the case, then the respondent may well want to form conjectures and accumulate experience with ecosystems in order to more accurately assess how it enters into his preferences. If a respondent does not know his preferences for ecosystems, his WTP for a given quantity will exceed the value occurring if he does know his preferences (i.e., the respondent is willing to pay extra to acquire information about the potential utility value an asset may provide in the future; a respondent will overvalue an unfamiliar asset). In addition, the overvaluation of the asset will decrease as the individual becomes more familiar with the asset. The valuation experiment requires an explicit protocol specifying the time and resource decision constraints, and the knowledge of respondents; otherwise, estimates of value for ecosystems are inherently biased.

Third, psychologists have observed that an individual's valuation of a good can be influenced by alternative ways of representing a good including both the definition of good and market context (e.g., Tversky and Kahneman 1981). In the case of the risk of ecosystem loss, this evidence suggests that how the risk is reduced may affect the value an individual assigns to private and collective forms of protection. Individuals can reduce the expected damages of an environmental risk by employing self-protection or self-insurance, either privately or collectively. Understanding how the chosen risk reduction mechanism affects value is important for public policy (Shogren and Crocker 1991). Self-protection reduces the probability of the loss, while self-insurance reduces its severity (Ehrlich and Becker 1972).

Finally, examining the robustness of the value estimates to changes in the design of the experimental auction markets by considering alternative auction procedures is an important part of any valuation design.

CONCLUSIONS

The valuation of an ecosystem has been discussed in the preceding pages. The discussion addressed both the theoretical basis and the measurement issues surrounding ecosystem values. Familiarity with the good (value formation and preference formation), definition of the good, embedding, and surrogate valuation were discussed. In addition, problems with measurement procedures such as those associated with using the hypothetical market approach and the difficulty of defining the good were discussed. Further development of the theoretical foundation, however, is warranted as several issues were not addressed. This chapter also proposes a valuation procedure, CVM-X, which is an experimental laboratory procedure combined with the CVM approach.

ACKNOWLEDGMENTS

The authors wish to thank the editors and F. Craig Conley for their valuable comments. In addition, Jay Shogren wishes to acknowledge that this work draws from earlier work done with Tom Crocker. All errors and omissions, however, remain the responsibility of the authors.

FOOTNOTES

1. The relationship between x and e is important if the demand for c is estimated from the demand for x.
2. EMAP currently has a study underway defining socioecological indicators which may very well serve the purpose of the ecosystem characteristics needed for ecosystem valuation.

REFERENCES

Arrow, K., R. Solow, P. Portney, E. Leamer, R. Radner, and H. Schuman. 1993. Report of the NOAA Panel on Contingent Valuation. Mimeo. Washington DC: Resources for the Future.

Bohm, P. 1972. Estimating demand for public goods: An experiment. *European Economic Review* 3:111–130.

Coursey, D. L. and W. D. Shulze. 1986. The application of laboratory experimental economics to the contingent valuation of public goods. *Public Choice* 49:47–68.

Coursey, D. L., J. Hovis, and W. D. Schulze. 1987. The disparity between willingness to accept and willingness to pay measures of value. *Quarterly Journal of Economics* 102:679–90.

Crocker, T. and J. Shogren. 1991a. Ex-ante valuation of atmospheric visibility. *Applied Economics* 23:143–151.

Crocker, T. and J. Shogren. 1991b. Preference learning and contingent valuation methods. In *Environmental Policy and the Economy,* eds. F. Dietz, R. van der Ploeg, and J. van der Straaten. Amsterdam: North-Holland.

Crocker, T. and J. Shogren. 1993. Dynamic inconsistency in valuing environmental goods. *Ecological Economics* 7:239–254.

Desvousges, W., F. R. Johnson, R. Dunford, K. Boyle, S. Hudson, and K. Wilson. 1992. *Measuring Natural Resource Damages with Contingent Valuation: Tests of Validity and Reliability.* NC: Research Triangle Institute.

Ehrlich, I., and G. S. Becker. 1972. Market insurance, self-insurance, and self-protection. *Journal of Political Economy* 80:623–648.

Freeman, A. M. 1993. *The Measurement of Environmental and Resource Values: Theory and Method.* Washington DC: Resources for the Future.

Hanley, N. and C. Splash. 1993. The Value of Biodiversity in British Forests. Report to the Scottish Forestry Commission, University of Stirling, Scotland.

Herriges, J. and J. Shogren. 1993. Valuing Water Quality Through Ecological Indicators: The Case of Storm Lake. Mimeo. Iowa State University, Ames, Iowa.

Hoehn, J. and A. Randall. 1987. A satisfactory benefit cost indicator from contingent valuation. *Journal of Environmental Economics and Management* 14:226–247.

Kahneman, D. D. 1986. Comments. In *Valuing Environmental Goods: An Assessment of the Contingent Valuation Method,* eds. R. G. Cummings et al. Totowa NJ: Rowman and Allenheld.

Kahneman, D. and J. Knetsch. 1991. Valuing public goods: The purchase of moral satisfaction. *Journal of Environmental Economics and Management* 22:57–70.

Keeney, R. L. and H. Raiffa. 1976. *Decision with Multiple Objectives: Preferences and Value Tradeoffs.* New York: John Wiley & Sons.

Krutilla, J. 1967. Conservation reconsidered. *American Economic Review* 57:787–796.

Mitchell, R. C. and R. T. Carson. 1989. *Using Surveys to Value Public Goods: The Contingent Valuation Method.* Washington DC: Resources for the Future.

Navrud, S. ed. 1992. *Pricing the European Environment.* Oslo: Scandanavian University Press.

Shogren, J. and T. Crocker. 1991. Risk, self-protection, and ex-ante economic value. *Journal of Environmental Economics and Management* 20:1–15.

Shogren, J., S. Shin, D. Hayes, and J. Kliebenstein. 1994. Resolving differences in willingness to pay and willingness to accept. *American Economic Review* 84:255–270.

Smith, V. K. 1992. Arbitrary values, good causes, and premature verdicts. *Journal of Environmental Economics and Management* 22:71–89.

Solow, A., S. Polansky, and J. Broadus. 1993. On the measurement of biological diversity. *Journal of Environmental Economics and Management* 24:60–68.

Tversky, A. and D. D. Kahneman. 1981. The framing decisions and the psychology of choice. *Science* 211:453–458.

USEPA. 1993. EMAP Monitor. USEPA 620/N-92/001. Washington DC. February 1993.

Vickrey, W. 1961. Counterspeculation auctions and competitive sealed tenders. *Journal of Finance* 16:8–37.

Weitzman, M. 1993. What to preserve? An application of diversity theory to crane conversation. *Quarterly Journal of Economics* 108:157–184.

Wilson, E. O. 1992. *The Diversity of Life.* Cambridge: Harvard University Press.

APPENDIX

Ecosystem Goods and Services (Z, X)

Life support/quality of life/health

clean water	waste disposal
clean air	soil quality
climate moderation	flood control

Scenic Beauty

Aesthetics

Recreation

hiking	picnicking
hunting	camping
fishing	riding horses
driving	biking
bird watching	off-road driving

Forest products

timber pulp and wood
non-timber (plant and animal) products

Existence values

all life is valuable

Scientific and education

understand nature
pharmaceutical

OTHER_____   _____

List of Potential Socially Relevant Ecosystem Characteristics (E)

A. NUMBER OF NATIVE SPECIES
B. NUMBER OF ALIEN SPECIES—(e.g., kudzu)
C. NUMBER OF ENDEMIC SPECIES—species that only occur in the Southern Appalachians
D. NUMBER OF GLOBALLY RARE SPECIES—fewer than 100 known occurances worldwide
E. NUMBER OF THREATENED OR ENDANGERED SPECIES
F. NUMBER OF BIG GAME SPECIES—(e.g., deer, bear)
G. NUMBER OF SMALL GAME SPECIES—(e.g., squirrels, turkey)
H. NUMBER OF NONGAME SPECIES—(e.g., salamanders)
I. POPULATION OF NEOTROPICAL BIRDS
J. TIMBER VOLUME CUT (TOTAL)
K. TIMBER VOLUME CUT – Even-Aged Management (e.g., clearcutting)
L. TIMBER VOLUME CUT – Uneven-Aged Management (e.g., selective harvest)
M. TIMBER VOLUME CUT FOR PULPWOOD
N. TIMBER VOLUME CUT FOR SAWTIMBER
O. TIMBER VOLUME CUT FOR FIREWOOD

P.   JOBS IN THE TIMBER INDUSTRY
Q.   POUNDS OF NONTIMBER RESOURCES HARVESTED – (e.g., Ginseng)
R.   INCOME EARNED FROM THE HARVEST OF NONTIMBER RESOURCES
S.   INCOME EARNED FROM THE HARVEST OF TIMBER RESOURCES
T.   MEDICINAL PRODUCTS
U.   MILES OF VISIBILITY
V.   ACRES FORESTED – NATURAL/UNMANAGED FORESTS
W.   ACRES FORESTED – PLANTATION/MANAGED FORESTS
X.   ACRES IN TIMBER PRODUCTION (PUBLIC)
Y.   ACRES IN WILDERNESS AREAS
Z.   ACRES OF OLD GROWTH FORESTS
AA. ACRES IN ROADLESS AREAS
BB. ACRES PROTECTED FROM LOGGING
CC. ACRES DESIGNATED TO WILDLIFE CORRIDORS
DD. ACRES IN BIODIVERSITY RESERVE WHERE NATURAL DISTUR-
     BANCES ARE ALLOWED TO OCCUR
EE. ACRES IN BIODIVERSITY WHERE NATURAL DISTURBANCES ARE
     SUPPRESSED
FF. ACRES IN LAND TRUST/CONSERVATION EASEMENTS
GG. ACRES IN RESEARCH NATURAL AREAS
HH. ACRES IN ECOSYSTEM MANAGEMENT DEMONSTRATION PROJECTS
II. ACRES DEVELOPED (HOMES, CONDOS, PARKING LOTS, ETC.)
JJ. CHANGE IN HUMAN POPULATION OF THE ECOSYSTEM
KK. HOUSING STARTS IN THE ECOSYSTEM
LL. EMPLOYMENT CONSIDERATIONS
MM. MILES OF NEW ROAD CONSTRUCTION
NN. MILES OF ROAD WIDENING/IMPROVEMENT
OO. MILES OF ROAD CLOSED
PP. MILES OF ROAD OBLITERATED
QQ. MILES OF HIKING TRAILS MAINTAINED
RR. NUMBER (SUPPLY) OF DEVELOPED CAMPSITES
SS. NUMBER OF BACKCOUNTRY CAMPSITES
TT. MILES OF BIKING TRAILS
UU. NUMBER OF PICNIC AREAS
VV. NUMBER OF SELF-GUIDED NATURE TRAILS
WW. NUMBER OF GUIDED NATURE TRAILS
XX. FISH CAUGHT
YY. NATIVE FISH CAUGHT
ZZ. STOCKED FISH CAUGHT
AAA. GAME HUNTED
BBB. TROPHY-QUALITY GAME CAPTURED
CCC. RECREATION VISITS
DDD. RECREATION VISITS WHERE CONGESTION/CROWDING OCCURS
EEE. RECREATION VISITS WITH NO CONGESTION/CROWDING

PART IV

INSTITUTIONAL SCALE

14 STRATEGIC PLANNING FOR SUSTAINABLE DEVELOPMENT IN INDONESIA USING NATURAL RESOURCE ACCOUNTS

Glenn-Marie Lange
Institute for Economic Analysis
New York University
New York, New York

INTRODUCTION

Too often economic development and natural resource conservation have been viewed as separate objectives, if not conflicting ones. Natural resource accounts (NRAs) are a new tool designed to help achieve the combined objectives of economic development and natural resource conservation by linking economic activities with their use of the natural resource base. NRAs are constructed initially in physical units as stock and flow accounts which, in the framework proposed by the UN (1993) for NRAs as a set of satellite accounts to the System of National Accounts SNA), may also be at least partly compiled in monetary terms through the application of valuation techniques to the physical accounts.[1]

Stock accounts for natural resources include entries for levels of stocks and changes in the stocks showing the depletion and degradation of stocks, and changes in estimated reserves. There are also entries for the revaluation of stocks compiled in monetary terms and estimation of resource rents. (Since the work in Indonesia discussed in this chapter did not require compilation of stock accounts, these accounts are not discussed here further.) The flow accounts are similar in structure to the input–output table of the SNA; for each sector and for households, the flow accounts record the use of resources in production and the discharge of waste materials or other impact on the environment (see Table 14.1). The physical flow accounts of NRAs have a basis in the materials balance approach of Ayres (1978). NRAs differ from materials balances in that NRAs do not account for all the transformations of materials through different production processes. Furthermore, NRAs use industry as the unit of classification in order to link the information with economic accounts of the

315

SNA whereas materials balances typically trace the flow of materials at the more desegregated level of processes.

The primary advantage of NRAs is the comprehensive framework it provides for integrating environmental and resource concerns with economic accounts. This makes NRAs especially useful for understanding the environmental implications of economic activities where complex trade-offs need to be evaluated from an economic perspective. With its framework determined in large part by the framework and concepts of economic accounts, NRAs are less satisfactory for portraying complex ecological processes and feedback loops which ecologists and environmental scientists need for environmental management. For example, the spatial and temporal characteristics of economic accounts are often not those most suitable to understanding natural phenomena.

Table 14.1. Example of the Physical Flow Accounts of Natural Resource Accounts

	Rice	Livestock	Food Processing	Construction	Household
WATER (000's of m^3)					
Uptake: ground water					
Uptake: surface water					
Water discharge					
Discharge of Pollutants (tons)					
Biological oxygen Demand					
Chemical oxygen Demand					
LAND (000's of ha)					
Land type 1					
Land type 2					
•					
•					
•					
Soil erosion (tons)					
FORESTS (various units)					
Timber					
Fuelwood					
Medicines					
Other food products					
Other products					
•					
•					
•					

Note: Entries along the rows represent the amount of resources used as inputs by each of the economic activities listed across the columns or the levels of emission of pollutants or other environmental degradation caused by the economic activities in a given year. The economic sectors correspond to a hypothetical classification of industry or activity accounts in the SNA.

Despite the growing recognition of the importance of NRAs, there is uncertainty among policy-makers about how to use NRAs effectively. There are three types of policy applications for NRAs.

1. *Provide an improved indicator of macroeconomic performance,* Environmentally-adjusted Domestic Product (EDP). EDP attempts to adjust GDP (or NDP) for degradation of natural capital and thus provide a more accurate indicator of whether we are "living off our (produced plus natural) capital." It is calculated by estimating the net physical degradation and depletion of every environmental and natural resource, estimating a monetary value for this degradation, and subtracting this number from GDP.

2. *Monitor the state of the environment and economy through specific environmental and natural resource variables.* NRAs provide a framework for monitoring specific resource variables such as soil erosion, water pollution, and losses of biological diversity and linking these variables to economic activities.

3. *Policy analysis and planning.* NRAs can provide the environmental and natural resource input to economic tools and models for analysis at the regional and national levels, or for sectoral and project management. Examples of policy applications include the modeling of the distributional effects of alternative natural resource policies, or the links between trade, natural resource policies, and the state of the environment. Economic tools include cost–benefit analyses, operations research models, input–output and social accounting matrix models, and general equilibrium models.

Of the three applications for NRAs, the calculation of EDP is the most well known (e.g., Repetto et al. 1989; Hueting 1991; Hueting, Bosch, and de Boo 1992). A single-valued indicator of sustainability like EDP has a very strong appeal to a number of people such as Daly (1994), but the construction of this index number faces major conceptual and methodological problems, especially when attempting to include non-marketed resources (see Lange and Duchin 1994 for discussion of these issues). More importantly, it is of limited policy usefulness. While drawing attention to the urgency of environmental problems, EDP itself provides no guidance about what actions are needed to achieve sustainable development. For this reason, the UN does not recommend constructing NRAs solely to calculate EDP, a common practice in earlier NRAs studies (Bartelmus and van Tongeren 1994).

The applications of NRAs for monitoring and policy analysis are less well known. While these applications offer much more to the policy analyst concerned with sustainable development, they are also a more ambitious undertaking than the construction of EDP. The use of NRAs for policy analysis and planning requires the identification of possible development strategies and construction of an ecological–economic model to evaluate these strategies. Experience in different countries has shown that effective use of NRAs for this purpose poses a number of institutional and technical challenges, especially in developing countries where experienced professional staff are often in short supply (Lange 1993, 1994).

Worldwide, relatively few NRAs have been constructed and even fewer used for analysis. Not surprisingly, the most extensive use of NRAs is made in the country which has compiled NRAs the longest, Norway. Alfsen (1994) describes five recent analyses carried out by government agencies in Norway which focus on energy use and air pollution using a general equilibrium model. Other applications, based on static input–output models include de Boer, de Haan, and Voogt (1994) for the Netherlands (air and water pollution); de los Angelos, Peskin, and Bennagen (1994) for the Philippines (air and water pollution); and Deardon, Lonergan, and Ruitenbeek (1994) for Thailand (water pollution and land use). Additional analyses with NRAs are underway in both the Netherlands and the Philippines.

The limited number of examples, especially in developing countries, for interested countries to draw on increases the challenge to potential users of NRAs. This chapter provides a concrete example of how NRAs can be used for policy analysis at the national and sectoral levels, based on a study undertaken for Indonesia's Planning Ministry. NRAs were constructed and incorporated as the environmental module in an ecological-economic model in order to calculate the demand on the natural resource base of Indonesia's second Long-term Development Plan (1994–2018). In particular, the analysis sought to anticipate emerging conflicts between economic development and sustainable resource management, and to identify the kinds of technological changes that might make it possible to achieve Indonesia's development objectives within the constraints posed by the natural resource base.

The chapter begins with a discussion of Indonesia's planning process, its long-term development strategy, and the ways in which the environment plays a critical role in its development objectives. The next section describes the framework for the NRAs and the ecological-economic model and database constructed for the study. This is followed by a description of the construction of NRAs' flow accounts for the historical years, 1985 and 1990. For the future, four alternative scenarios are analyzed with the model based on alternative technologies which might be adopted in each sector described in terms of sectoral input structures including resource requirements. Next I present the assumptions about future production practices. Finally, the results of the analysis are presented in terms of NRAs calculated by the model for 2020 under two alternative development scenarios and policy implications of these NRAs. This chapter summarizes extensive work that has been carried out over several years by a team of researchers; for additional detail, the reader is referred to a series of (unpublished) reports and working papers (Duchin and Lange 1992, 1993; Duchin, Hamilton, and Lange 1993).

THE PLANNING PROCESS IN INDONESIA

For more than 25 years, Indonesia's Planning Ministry (Bappenas) has constructed medium-term (5-year) and long-term (25-year) Development Plans to help define its economic objectives and to guide government and private sector action to achieve those objectives. The Development Plans combine elements of macroeconomic planning, target setting for some sectors (e.g., rice, petroleum), and strategic planning. In the period covered by the first long-term Development Plan (1970–1994), Indonesia achieved impressive economic growth and reduction of poverty as well as specific objectives such as rice self-sufficiency and the initiation of industrialization. These achievements were based mainly on its natural resources – oil, agriculture, and forestry (World Bank 1994).

The second long-term Development Plan, covering the period 1994–2018, seeks continued growth, higher rates of employment in the formal sector, and improvements in economic equity. It emphasizes industrialization and substantially reduced dependence on oil revenues (indeed, Indonesia is likely to become a net importer of oil over this time period). The Plan recognizes the importance of environmental considerations: expansion of industry will depend on sustainable management of land, forests, and water, and the serious deterioration of the environment which accompanied the rapid economic growth of the past 25 years needs to be halted, if not reversed.

Over the next 25 years, economic growth will intensify competition for land. Some of the most fertile rice land is being converted for residential, industrial, and commercial use, especially land near urban areas. Forests and coastal wetlands are being converted to agriculture production. While Indonesia has abundant water resources, there are large seasonal variations in water availability and it is already in short supply in some areas. Water pollution and air pollution have become a major threat both to human health and welfare and to industrial productivity in urban areas. Increasing urbanization of the population and the continued concentration of industry in urban areas over the next 25 years make dealing with these problems a priority.

Conflict over resource use and the deterioration of the environment may force Indonesia to make some difficult decisions concerning trade-offs between economic growth and the possible exhaustion or serious degradation of its natural resources. However, through the use of more efficient and cleaner technologies, Indonesia may be able to achieve substantial economic growth without sacrificing its natural capital.

The second long-term Development Plan is, naturally, a very broad planning document that addresses many economic and social issues, not just the environment. Given the continued importance of the natural resource base in Indonesia's economy, however, the environmental aspects held a prominent place in the analysis. In addition to assessing the overall impact on the environment of Indonesia's development over the next 25 years, several issues were identified for close attention and are discussed in this chapter, including the following.

- *Food Self-sufficiency.* As incomes increase, the average diet can be expected to include more meat, fruit, and vegetables. Increases in livestock production require a great deal of land, either directly, if livestock is raised on rangeland, or indirectly, to provide the feed if livestock is raised on feedlots. Rice, the staple crop of Indonesia, is extremely water-intensive, accounting for 90% of current water use. Even moderate increases in production would require large amounts of water and some increase in land area at a time when the most fertile rice-growing land is being lost to urban expansion.
- *Forestry and the Paper Industry.* Indonesia has a strong comparative advantage in producing forest products. Consequently, a reasonable development strategy would focus on expansion of the wood processing industries, especially pulp, paper, and wood products. However, Indonesia's forests, which are not always managed sustainably, are barely able to meet current levels of demand. The scale of operation of wood-using industries over the next 25 years is likely to place demands on Indonesia's forestry sector which would decimate its forests. How much wood would be required in the future? Would existing forests be able to meet the demand, especially if a large expansion in the pulp and paper industry is planned? What combination of revised management techniques, including plantation forests, might be needed? Where would land be found for expanded forestry? What would be the cost of this new approach to forestry and what policy changes might be needed to implement it?
- *Water and Air Pollution.* The provision of clean water for household use and for industry is also a major objective over the next 25 years. Mistrust of municipal water supply has led many private citizens to establish their own wells for domestic consumption, but the extraction of groundwater in cities like Jakarta has resulted in salt water intrusion. With little treatment of waste water from industry and households, water pollution has

become a serious problem. Indonesia also has serious air quality problems which have been associated with health problems (World Bank 1994). However, measures to control emissions have yet to be introduced. Will the levels of pollution expected in the future warrant speedy introduction of pollution control measures?

STRUCTURE OF THE NATURAL RESOURCE ACCOUNTS, THE ECOLOGICAL–ECONOMIC MODELING FRAMEWORK, AND THE DATABASE

The issues raised by Indonesia's development strategy require an analytical approach that is multisectoral and cumulative; the former in order to identify spillover or intersectoral effects and the potential conflict for resources or inconsistencies among sectoral objectives, and the latter in order to keep track of the cumulative, economy-wide environmental degradation and demands on the resource base. The analytical framework chosen to analyze these issues was a 30-sector, dynamic input–output (IO) model of the economy with an environmental module. The model is dynamic in the sense that investment is endogenous, determined by expected growth in each sector's output, the technologies in use (the sectoral capital stock requirements), and sectoral rates of capacity utilization. The mathematical model, data requirements, and sectoral classification system are given in the Appendix.

The model covers the period 1985–2020, roughly the 25 years of the Long-term Development Plan (1994–2018) and the historical period ten years prior to the plan. Modeling the historical period allowed testing of model performance against the historical record. The economic database for 1985, the base year, was constructed from official statistics, notably the 1985 IO table supplemented by information about sectoral capital stock and employment. The environmental module in the base year was constructed from the NRAs compiled for this study; no official NRAs were available at the time. Construction of the future database will be discussed later.

The development strategies and environmental constraints determined the kinds of variables to be included in the NRAs: land suitable for different crops, forests, and water. Factors affecting the quality of land and water were also included: soil erosion and three types of water pollution, biological oxygen demand (BOD), chemical oxygen demand (COD), and suspended solids. In addition, three types of emissions were included, carbon dioxide (CO_2), sulfur dioxide (SO_2), and nitrogen oxide (NO_x). Given the time constraints of the study, environmental variables were restricted to those for which data could be readily obtained or estimated. Consequently, some important environmental variables could not be included at this time, for example, water-borne wastes of households or the emission into the atmosphere of particulates.

The economic sectors includes six agricultural sectors, nine manufacturing sectors, seven energy sectors (in order to calculate air pollution; fuel-wood could not be included at this time), eight service sectors, as well as detailed components of final demand. Additional sectoral detail was developed in the course of the sectoral case studies (described below) when needed. For example, the forestry sector was disaggregated into natural forests and plantation forests.

The second Long-term Development Plan is a largely descriptive document. For analysis, the objectives of the plan had to be quantified in terms of the model parameters and database. Six different scenarios were constructed to describe alternative development paths Indonesia might take. The six scenarios were based on combinations of two alternative GDP growth targets, moderate (about 5% per year) and high (about 7% per year), and three alternative sets of assumptions about technological change, which reflected progressively stronger approaches to environmental protection and conservation of resources. Scenario S1 represents a continuation of present trends towards more efficient use of resources and environmental protection, S2 includes much stronger resource conservation measures, and S3 adds to the projections of S2 assumptions about the use of clean coal combustion technology in the Electricity sector. (Since S3 differed only marginally from S2, it is not discussed further in this chapter.) The scenarios about the future were represented in the model and database by alternative projections about sector-specific changes in production technology and associated resource input requirements per unit of output. These projections are discussed later.

CONSTRUCTION OF NRAS FOR 1985 AND INCORPORATION OF NRAS INTO THE ECOLOGICAL–ECONOMIC MODEL

Much of the literature about NRAs stresses the conceptual similarity between NRAs and economic accounts, and between natural capital and produced capital. However, there is no commensurable unit for the two kinds of accounts, or even for the different variables within the NRAs. While market prices can be used to measure virtually all economic transactions, there are only limited markets for environmental resources. The consequences of this difference are discussed in (Lange and Duchin 1994). In operationalizing NRAs, there is also an essential difference between data about the environment and economic data, which affects the collection of environmental data. In principle, virtually all transactions for the national accounts can be directly observed and measured. The compilation of economic data relies on an establishment's records of how much electricity, paper, and so on is purchased or sold in a given year. Similarly, use of marketed natural resources can be accounted for in NRAs. However, some environmental data cannot be directly observed or measured.

Estimates for nonmarketed resource use like fuel-wood, soil erosion, water and air pollution are based on a range of different methods (see UN 1984 for detailed discussion of this issue). Surveys may be used to establish average water use or fuel-wood use by different types of households in a given area. Soil erosion or air pollution may be estimated by a combination of the empirical measurements and scientific modeling. Standards and guidelines for estimating these data for the NRAs have not yet been established.

In compiling the NRAs for Indonesia for historical years, a combination of observed and estimated data were used, some obtained from official sources, others estimated by researchers during the course of the study. The study often relied on ad hoc data obtained from special studies and reports, data that were sometimes incomplete or inconsistent with each other in terms of classifications, units of measurement, and so on. A large part of the effort of the research team went into making as consistent as possible the data obtained from different sources. Where comprehensive data for all sectors of the economy were not available, efforts focused on obtaining data about the most important sectors. This ensured that the results obtained from the model were of the right order of magnitude. The data used to compile accounts are described briefly below. For some variables, data were available for both 1985 and 1990; in many cases, data for 1990 were not available and the model was used to estimate that portion of the 1990 accounts. The sources for the data are fully described in Duchin, Hamilton, and Lange (1993) and associated working papers. The NRAs compiled for 1985 and 1990 are shown in Tables 14.2a and 14.2b.

Land

Sectoral accounts for land were derived from official records of the amount of agricultural and forest land use in 1985 and 1990. Land under cultivation for each crop was associated with the corresponding agricultural sector in the NRAs, and land for production forests was assigned to the forest products sector. No land use was recorded for livestock since the animals, mainly chickens, are either raised along with other crops and require no additional land, or are raised intensively in factory-style feedlots which require very little land. Land use for other purposes, notably human settlements, industry, and roads and other infrastructure, was not included since it accounts for a very small share of total land use. Information about the annual amount of soil erosion was obtained from studies which measured on-farm erosion occurring on sample farms and used these measurements to estimate soil erosion on all farms, adjusting for different characteristics which affect soil erosion (vegetative cover, farm management, slope characteristics of rainfall, etc.).

Table 14.2a. Natural Resource Accounts for Indonesia in 1985

A. 1985

		Air Pollution			Water				Land		
	Sector	CO_2 10^3 t	SO_2 10^3 t	NO_x 10^3 t	Water Uptake 10^6 m³	BOD 10^3 t	COD 10^3 t	Susp. Solids 10^3 t	Land Use 10^6 ha	Soil Erosion 10^6 t	Sector
Agriculture											
1	Rice	18	0.0	0.1	363,251	0	0	0	7.8	0	1
2	Other Food Crops	133	0.0	1.1					6.2	170	2
3	Other Agr. Crops	126	0.2	7.7					10.0	62	3
4	Livestock	134	0.2	7.2	4	na	na	na			4
5	Forest Products		0.2	7.8					36.2	79	5
5.1	Natural Forests								34.8	79	5.1
5.2	Plantations								1.4	0	5.2
6	Fisheries	273	0.3	16.0							6
Mining											
7	Coal	92	2.7	0.6							7
8	Crude Oil	3,865	46.2	26.9							8
9	Natural Gas	1,597	0.3	15.3							9
10	Other Mining	267	7.2	1.0							10
Manufactur-ing											
11	Food and Tobacco	352	9.4	1.3	124	24	35	59			11
12	Wood Products	256	6.9	0.9							12
13	Pulp and Paper	53	1.4	0.2	164	43	142	49			13
14	Fertilizer	1,717	10.0	14.3							14
15	Chemicals	244	7.0	1.5	1	0	0	0			15
16	Cement	509	13.9	2.3							16
17	Other Manufact.	1,033	27.1	4.0							17
18	Petrol. Refining	908	11.9	5.7	339	68	271	339			18
19	LNG	283	2.1	2.0							19
Utilities											
20	Electricity	3,132	102.2	41.6							20
21	Gas Utilities	285	6.9	1.3							21
22	Water Utilities	40	0.3	0.1							22
Services											
23	Construction	6,582	43.2	23.7							23
24	Trade	624	4.0	2.3							24
25	Rest. and Hotels	580	3.6	2.2							25
26	Transp & Comm.	4,772	67.5	303.0							26
27	Business Services	101	0.6	0.4							27
28	Public Admin.	0	0.0	0.0							28
29	Services	363	2.1	1.4							29
30	Unspecified	14	0.1	0.1							30
Households	Households	5,807	5.5	116.2	8,757	na	na	na	na		
Total		34,157	383.0	608.2	372,640	135	449	448	60.2	311	

324

Table 14.2b. Natural Resource Accounts for Indonesia in 1990

			Air Pollution			Water				Land		
	Sector	Sector	CO_2 10³t	SO_2 10³t	NO_x 10³t	Water Uptake 10⁶m³	BOD 10³t	COD 10³t	Susp. Solids 10³t	Land Use 10⁶ha	Soil Erosion 10⁶t	Sector
Agriculture	1	Rice	21	0.0	0.1	392,298	0	0	0	8.3	0	1
	2	Other Food Crops	162	0.0	1.2					7.6	208	2
	3	Other Agr. Crops	173	0.2	9.4					10.8	67	3
	4	Livestock	210	0.2	10.0	5	na	na	na			4
	5	Forest Products		0.3	12.3							5
	5.1	Natural Forests								49.4	109	5.1
	5.2	Plantations								47.9	109	5.2
	6	Fisheries	401	0.5	23.4					1.5	0	6
Mining	7	Coal	116	3.4	0.8							7
	8	Crude Oil	4,230	50.6	29.4							8
	9	Natural Gas	2,183	0.4	20.9							9
	10	Other Mining	200	5.4	0.7							10
Manufacturing	11	Food and Tobacco	431	11.5	1.6	152	30	43	73			11
	12	Wood Products	589	15.8	2.1							12
	13	Pulp and Paper	57	1.5	0.2	177	47	155	54			13
	14	Fertilizer	1,962	11.4	16.3							14
	15	Chemicals	71	2.0	0.4	1	0	0	0			15
	16	Cement	442	12.1	2.0							16
	17	Other Manufact.	455	11.9	1.7							17
	18	Petrol. Refining	1,004	13.2	6.3	149	30	119	149			18
	19	LNG	443	3.3	3.1							19
Utilities	20	Electricity	3,629	118.4	48.2							20
	21	Gas Utilities	335	8.0	1.5							21
	22	Water Utilities	53	0.3	0.2							22
Services	23	Construction	6,156	40.4	22.1							23
	24	Trade	724	4.6	2.7							24
	25	Rest. and Hotels	755	4.7	2.8							25
	26	Transp & Comm.	6,088	86.1	386.5							26
	27	Business Services	130	0.8	0.5							27
	28	Public Admin.	0	0.0	0.0							28
	29	Services	465	2.7	1.8							29
	30	Unspecified	3	0.0	0.0							30
Households		Households	7,589	7.1	151.8	9,744	na	na	na			
Total			339,078	416.9	760.4	402,526	107	317	276	76.1	384	

Source: Air pollution, Tables D4 and D5; Water, Tables D8 and D9; Land, Tables 3.7, 3.8, 3.9, and text pp. 29 (Duchin, Hamilton, and Lange 1993).

Water Use and Water Pollution

Information about water use by major sectors in 1985 and 1990 was obtained from official statistics for agriculture, households, and several industries, supplemented by information developed in sectoral case studies. Official statistics about water use were compiled from administrative records of purchases of water and surveys of households and industries which provide their own water. The latter is especially important because metered delivery of water accounts for only a part of total water use; it is common for industry and households in urban as well as rural areas to supply their own water from privately owned wells.

Outside of agriculture, comprehensive information about water use by the 30 sectors of the model was not available so this study focused on water use by agriculture, several manufacturing sectors, and households. The manufacturing sectors – food processing, pulp and paper, chemicals, and other manufacturing – were chosen on the basis of their overall importance to the study and their importance as sources of water pollution. Since water use by industry is quite small relative to agriculture (rice accounts for nearly 90% of all water used), estimates of total water use are not much affected by the omission of water requirements for other sectors.

No economy-wide estimates of water pollution by sector were available so these were estimated in the following manner. First, researchers reviewed technical studies to determine the pollution parameters (tons of pollutant per unit of sectoral output) for individual companies in each of the major water-using sectors. The company-specific parameters were then generalized for an entire sector based on experts' judgment about how representative the individual companies were. The annual level of pollution for a sector was calculated by multiplying the sector pollution parameter by sectoral output. Since accounting for all forms of water pollution was beyond the scope of this study we concentrated on types of water pollution for which information was readily available – biological oxygen demand (BOD), chemical oxygen demand (COD), and suspended solids.

Air Pollution

The NRAs created for this study include three types of air emissions: carbon dioxide, sulfur dioxide and nitrogen oxide. These pollutants[2] were chosen both because of their serious environmental impacts and because most of the technical parameters required to estimate these pollutants were available from a previous study (Duchin and Lange 1994). There are no comprehensive estimates of the annual levels of air pollution emitted by each sector, though some information about concentrations of various air pollutants is available for selected locations within Indonesia.

Carbon dioxide is important because of its contribution to global climate change. Sulfur and nitrogen can have serious impacts on human and ecosystem health. Other air pollutants affect global climate and local health; unfortunately they could not be included at this time given the constraints of the study. All three pollutants included in this study are determined by a relatively small number of technical factors mainly associated with the combustion of fossil fuels (emissions from other sources are relatively minor and were not included in the model). The emission of carbon dioxide is directly related to the carbon content of each type of fuel (coal, oil, natural gas); the emission of sulfur oxides is directly related to the sulfur content of each fuel burned; the emission of nitrogen oxides is a more complex phenomena based on fuel type and the conditions of combustion, especially the temperature of combustion.

For each of the pollutants, an emission parameter is developed for each fuel input in each sector (three types of fuel for each of 30 sectors plus households and government for a total of 96 emission parameters for each pollutant). Each type of pollution is calculated in two steps: first, pollution resulting from the use of each fuel in a sector is calculated by multiplying each sector's fuel input coefficient by the emission parameter for that fuel and by sectoral output. Then total pollution associated with each sector is calculated by summing pollution over the three types of fuel.

Incorporating NRAs Into a Model: From Flows to Model Parameters

The NRAs provide information only about the state of the environment in a given year: the levels of environmental and natural resource variables. To anticipate the state of the environment in a future year, a matrix of parameters are required as input to ecological-economic models: environmental inputs and impacts per unit of sectoral output. For some environmental variables, such as the air pollution variables, the NRAs in the base year were constructed by first deriving a sectoral parameter. These parameters can be incorporated directly in the ecological–economic model for the base year. Parameters for other variables, like land use, must be calculated by dividing the level of that variable in the base year NRAs by sectoral output in that year.

Naturally, as production technology changes in the future the environmental and natural resource parameters will also change. For example, water use per unit of output in the rice sector is projected to decline significantly as the irrigation infrastructure is modified and farm management improves. The projection of these parameters for the future associated with projected production technologies is an important component of the sectoral case studies used to build scenarios about the future and is discussed in the next section.

PROJECTING THE DATABASE ABOUT THE FUTURE: SECTORAL CASE STUDIES

The impact of the economy on the environment will depend in part upon the technologies in use in each sector so the alternative scenarios previously described focused on projecting the methods of production that each sector might use in the future. To quantify these alternative technologies, individual case studies were carried out for 15 sectors of the economy (listed in Table 14.3) as well as for the labor, capital, and energy requirements in all 30 sectors. The sectoral case studies reflect the views of engineers, scientists, managers, and sector experts based on reviews of the literature and interviews.

The assumptions about future production techniques are described and quantified for each sector in terms of changes to intermediate, labor, and capital input requirements per unit of output, as well as to the matrix of environmental inputs and discharges per unit of output (in contrast to the common use of IO models based on a constant-coefficients, no-technological change assumption). In addition, projections were made for final demand, excluding investment which is calculated by the model. For the sake of brevity, the description of sectoral case studies provided in the rest of this section is limited to the assumptions about the most important environmental elements. (For a more detailed discussion, see Duchin 1993.)

Table 14.3. List of Sectoral Case Studies

Sector Code	Name	Sector Code	Name
1	Rice	2	Other Food Crops
3	Estate Crops	4	Livestock
5	Forest Products	11	Food, Beverage, Tobacco
13	Pulp and Paper	15	Chemicals
16	Cement	17.2	Textiles, Leather, Apparel
17.5	Iron and Steel	20	Electric Power
26	Transport Services		
	Household Energy Use		
	Industrial Energy Conservation		

Agriculture

Increases in yields (greater under S2 than S1), reducing land requirements per unit of output are projected for all agricultural sectors due to improved seed varieties or cultivars and improved farm management. For rice, greater multiple cropping is projected which further increases annual yields and reduces land requirements. The farming techniques currently used for other food crops result in serious soil erosion which undermines the potential gains in yields from improved cultivars by reducing soil fertility. Under S2, soil conservation measures are introduced to preserve soil fertility. In total, land requirements per unit of output in rice decrease by 35% under S1, and 56% under S2; for other food crops the land requirements drop 29% and 24% under S1 and S2, respectively. The slightly higher land requirements under S2 reflect soil conservation measures. The land input for estate crops declines 46% under both scenarios.

Water use in rice production is also projected to decline significantly. Presently accounting for 90% of Indonesia's water use, rice is estimated to require only 25% of the water it actually draws through the irrigation system, and improvements in water efficiency are needed if rice production is to expand in the future. Modification of the irrigation infrastructure to allow greater control of the flow of water and to reduce water leakage and losses reduce water requirements per unit of output by 63% under S1, and 73% under S2.

Forestry

It was clear from earlier analysis (Duchin and Lange 1992) that the natural production forests would not be able to satisfy Indonesia's domestic demand for wood products in the near future, even without an expansion of the pulp and paper sector. The sustainable yields of natural forests may already be declining due to poor management practices which cause extensive deforestation and soil erosion. The study now focused on the extent to which plantation forests would need to supplement wood products from natural forests, and on what measures would be required to manage natural forests sustainably, preventing, or at least reducing, further losses.

It has been widely recognized that plantation forests will be needed to satisfy the demand for wood in the future. Plantation forests on a 15-year cycle are projected to account for 40% of log production under S1, and 68% under S2. The study assumes that they will be established on already degraded land not suitable for other crops and, consequently, will not compete with agriculture for land. Some soil erosion will occur when the plantations are first established, but erosion is expected to be negligible thereafter. Changes in methods of road building, felling, and transportation of timber from natural forests are introduced to reduce soil erosion and deforestation. The net impact of plantation forestry and improved practices in natural forests is to reduce land requirements per unit of forestry output by 35%, soil erosion by 80%, and deforestation by 65% under S1. The figures under S2 are 60%, 92%, and 81%. While in many sectors projected technological changes either reduce costs or increase them only slightly because many inputs to production are reduced, that is not the case in forestry. In contrast to forestry operations in already existing natural production forests where no costs are incurred to establish the forest, plantation forestry requires much more intensive management and is considerably more expensive.

Manufacturing, Transportation, and Electricity

Projections for manufacturing include increases in energy efficiency, reduction in water requirements, and the introduction of measures to reduce the emission of water pollutants in line with current or likely future regulations. In some sectors the energy mix will change; coal, gas, or purchased electricity will substitute for oil, presently the most widely used energy source. An improvement in the fuel efficiency of motor vehicles (but not other forms of transportation) is projected in the transportation sector, 25% under S1 and 50% under S2. In contrast to water pollution, the government currently has no policies mandating measures to control air pollution. Consequently, no air pollution control technologies, such as catalytic converters for motor vehicles, are assumed in the scenarios.

In the future, production of electricity is characterized by a reduction in transmission and distribution losses, an improvement in thermal conversion efficiency, and a shift in the fuel mix. Under S1, oil, the fuel most commonly used at this time, is largely replaced by coal and gas. Under S2, gas is burned in highly efficient combined cycle generators and provides a greater share of fuel used by electricity than coal.

All other sectors not subject to case studies are projected to improve energy efficiency between 1985 and 2020 by an average of 20% through a variety of means from simple improvements in energy use such as regular tune-ups, to more complex methods like waste heat recovery and cogeneration of electricity.

Household Energy Use

Households accounted for 20% of fuel consumption in 1985 (not counting noncommercial fuels like fuel-wood). In the future, energy use is likely to increase due to population and income growth. In addition, more people will substitute cleaner and more convenient commercial fuels and electricity for noncommercial fuels. Extensive rural electrification is planned over the next 30 years. At the same time, households will increase the shares of natural gas and coal (mostly in briquette form), reducing the share in fuel consumption of petroleum, currently the most widely used commercial fuel.

Moderating this trend towards increasing energy use are substantial improvements in energy efficiency of goods used by households. Motor vehicle fuel efficiency increases 25% under S1 and 50% under S2. Electrical appliances are 10% more efficient under S1 and 25% under S2. Even with these efficiency gains, households are projected to use more than 20 times the electricity used in 1985 under S1 and 15 times the 1985 level under S2. Fossil fuel use increases more than fourfold under S1 and just under threefold under S2.

RESULTS AND POLICY IMPLICATIONS

The results indicate that to some extent conflicts between economic growth and conservation and sustainable use of resources can be reconciled through the use of appropriate technology. In other instances, development objectives will need to be modified or reconsidered and some issues not currently included in the Development Plan, such as air pollution, may need to be addressed. Even with fairly strong assumptions about improvements in technology (S2), a rapid rate of economic growth (7%) cannot be sustained over the next 25 years.[3] Moderate rates of economic growth (5%) are feasible, but only with the introduction of strong measures to conserve resources and protect the environment in some sectors; improvements likely to occur under "business as usual" practices (S1) are not sufficient.

The results of the model concerning resource use and the environment are presented in Tables 14.4 and 14.5 by the NRAs calculated for 2020 under two alternative scenarios, S1 and S2 under the moderate growth path. Since these tables report the levels of resource use and environmental impact, methods to interpret the NRAs in policy terms are needed. Such methods include both physical standards or indicators and economic valuation techniques for assessing costs and benefits. Physical indicators were compiled to assess first of all whether the resource demands of economic growth are within the physical supply constraints (see Table 14.6). (In later work we will turn to costs, prices, and income effects of alternative development scenarios.) The results for land are given as a ratio of the total land required for each agricultural sector and forestry to the supply of land suitable for that activity, based on a classification of land area in Indonesia according to five categories of crop suitability. For other variables, the figures are reported as a ratio of the value in 2020 to the value for 1985. Detailed results and policy implications are discussed below.

Agriculture

With projected gains in yields and in water efficiency, rice self-sufficiency will be possible, especially since expansion of rice output need only keep pace with the slowly growing population. Land required in 2020 under S1 is only 2% more than supply and under S2 it is considerably less than supply. In 2020, rice still uses most of the water in the economy, but it is much less than the amount of water used in 1985. However, these changes will require substantial improvements in the efficiency of irrigation and incentives for farmers to change their behavior regarding water use, such as appropriate water pricing. In addition, since rice land on Java is steadily being lost to urban encroachment, much of the land for rice production in the future will be located on other islands such as Irian Jaya. Incentives will be required for extensive cultivation on this distant island which was the target of a controversial transmigration program in

Table 14.4. Natural Resource Accounts for Indonesia in 2020 Under Alternative, Moderate Economic Growth Scenarios

Sector	Air CO₂ 10^3 t	Air SO₂ 10^3 t	Air NOₓ 10^3 t	Water Uptake 10^6 m³	Water BOD 10^3 t	Water COD 10^3 t	Water Susp. Solids 10^3 t	Land Use 10^6 ha	Land Soil Erosion 10^6 t	Sector
Agriculture										
1 Rice	2	0.0	0.1	112,255	0	0	0	9	0	1
2 Other Food Crops	43	0.1	2.5					10	440	2
3 Other Agr. Crops	637	0.8	37.0					27	180	3
4 Livestock	1,048	1.3	60.6	24	na	na	na			4
5 Forest Products	694	0.8	40.5							5
5.1 Natural Forest								109	64	5.1
5.2 Plantation								106	64	5.2
6 Fisheries	1,563	1.9	91.4					3	0	6
Mining										
7 Coal	3,898	115.0	26.4							7
8 Crude Oil	6,855	82.0	47.7							8
9 Natural Gas	14,092	2.8	135.0							9
10 Other Mining	978	26.5	3.6							10
Manufacturing										
11 Food and Tobacco	1,034	27.4	3.9	121	6	9	8			11
12 Wood Products	1,377	36.9	5.0							12
13 Pulp and Paper	876	25.9	6.5	429	76	299	25			13
14 Fertilizer	6,092	31.0	51.7							14
15 Chemicals	2,717	79.0	18.1	19	0	0	0			15
16 Cement	2,437	72.2	17.8							16
17 Other Manufact.	1,736	44.8	6.9							17
18 Petrol. Refining	2,893	39.2	18.4	688	55	220	172			18
19 LNG	3,301	25.9	23.4							19
Utilities										
20 Electricity	18,445	314.5	299.2							20
21 Gas Utilities	2,266	53.5	10.5							21
22 Water Utilities	244	1.6	0.9							22
Services										
23 Construction	26,409	173.3	94.9							23
24 Trade	2,900	18.4	10.8							24
25 Rest. and Hotels	2,557	16.0	9.6							25
26 Transp & Comm.	22,251	314.4	1,412.1							26
27 Business Services	559	3.4	2.2							27
28 Public Admin.	0	0.0	0.0							28
29 Services	2,091	12.2	8.3							29
30 Unspecified	20	0.1	0.1							30
Households	41,328	446.0	534.6	18,494i	na	na	na			
Total	171,343	1,966.9	2,979.7	132,030	138	528	205	264	684	

Source: Duchin, Hamilton, and Lange 1993.

Table 14.5. *Natural Resource Accounts for Indonesia in 2020 Under Scenario 2 with Moderate Economic Growth*

		Air			Water				Land		
Sector	Sector	CO₂ 10³ t	SO₂ 10³ t	NOₓ 10³ t	Water Uptake 10⁶ m³	BOD 10³ t	COD 10³ t	Susp. Solids 10³ t	Land Use 10⁶ ha	Soil Erosion 10³ t	Sector
Agriculture 1	Rice	2	0.0	0.1	81,476	0	0	0	6	0	1
2	Other Food Crops	43	0.1	2.5					11	200	2
3	Other Agr. Crops	619	0.8	36.0					27	180	3
4	Livestock	1,045	1.3	60.4	24	na	na	na			4
5	Forest Products	689	0.8	40.2							5
	5.1 Natural Forest								62	35	
	5.2 Plantation								58	35	
6	Fisheries	1,562	1.9	91.3					4	0	6
Mining 7	Coal	2,999	88.5	20.3							7
8	Crude Oil	6,075	72.7	42.3							8
9	Natural Gas	13,777	2.7	132.0							9
10	Other Mining	898	24.3	3.3							10
Manufactur-ing 11	Food and Tobacco	1,033	27.3	3.9	121	6	9	8			11
12	Wood Products	1,370	36.7	5.0							12
13	Pulp and Paper	854	25.2	6.3	418	74	291	24			13
14	Fertilizer	5,739	29.2	48.7							14
15	Chemicals	2,535	73.7	16.9	18	0	0	0			15
16	Cement	2,350	69.7	17.2							16
17	Other Manufact.	966	24.9	3.8							17
18	Petrol. Refining	2,356	31.9	15.0	383	31	123	96			18
19	LNG	3,298	25.9	23.3							19
Utilities 20	Electricity	12,770	183.1	212.2							20
21	Gas Utilities	2,425	57.2	11.3							21
22	Water Utilities	242	1.6	0.9							22
Services 23	Construction	26,187	171.9	94.1							23
24	Trade	2,808	17.8	10.4							24
25	Rest. and Hotels	2,542	15.9	9.5							25
26	Transp & Comm.	17,509	247.3	1,110.6							26
27	Business Services	552	3.3	2.1							27
28	Public Admin.	0	0.0	0.0							28
29	Services	2,072	12.1	8.2							29
30	Unspecified	4	0.0	0.0							30
Households	Households	27,817	321.4	328.4	18,494	na	na	na			
Total		143,139	1,568.8	2,356.4	100,934	111	423	128	168	415	

Source: Duchin, Hamilton, and Lange (1993).

Table 14.6. Resource Demands and Constraints in 2020 Under Alternative, Moderate Economic Growth Scenarios

Sector	Land available (10⁶ ha)	Ratio of land required to land available in 2020	
		S1	S2
1 Rice	8.3	1.02	0.70
2 Other Food Crops	9.8	1.06	1.13
3 Other Agr Crops	19.6	1.37	1.37
4 Livestock			
5 Forest Products			
Natural Forests	61.0	1.74	0.94
Plantation	19.8	0.13	0.22

1990 Levels

Water	Water: 10⁶m³ Pollution: 103 t	Ratio of 2020 to 1990 Levels	
Total water			
Uptake	402,526	0.33	0.25
Total BOD	107	1.29	1.04
Total COD	317	1.67	1.33
Total Suspended	276	0.74	0.46
Air Pollution			
Total CO_2	39,078	4.4	3.7
Total SO_2	417	4.7	3.8
Total NO_x	760	3.9	3.1

Source: Tables 14.2, 14.3, and 14.4 and Duchin, Hamilton, and Lange (1993).

the past. In the absence of such changes, the required land and water inputs will far outstrip supply, cutting into land and water needed for other activities or requiring a reconsideration of the policy of rice self-sufficiency.

Other food crops face tight land constraints, despite projected increases in yields, in part because of the rapid growth of output associated with rising incomes and improved diet. The expected increase in meat in the diet will require a substantial increase in livestock production. Land requirements exceed supply under both scenarios. Under the more realistic scenario, S2, in which soil conservation measures necessary to maintain improvements in yields are undertaken, land requirements are 18% higher than supply in 2020.

In the first Long-term Development Plan, a large share of the resources of the Ministry of Agriculture and Ministry of Public Works was devoted to rice in order to achieve rice self-sufficiency. In the future, the Ministries will need to shift their attention increasingly to non-rice crops, especially to deal with the problem of soil erosion. Even under optimistic assumptions about what can be achieved with new crop strains and improved management, Indonesia will probably have to consider importing some of its food. The results in Tables 14.4, 14.5, and 14.6 already reflect an increase in imports for this sector but land requirements still exceed supply. The level of imports for other food crops may need to be even higher than that included in the model's macroeconomic projections.

Land required for estate crops exceeds supply by 37%. All the significant crops in this sector are important export commodities except for coconuts which form a major part of the Indonesian diet. A more detailed analysis than was possible in this study is needed to develop a strategy for this sector. Projections of exports from this sector and self sufficiency in coconuts may need to be reconsidered in view of the land constraint

Forestry

Under scenario S1, based on current forest management practices and establishment of plantation forests to meet a third of the timber needs, the area of natural forests would have to expand from the current level of 61 million ha to over 100 million by 2020. Since this expansion is not possible, the consequence is likely to be the devastation of Indonesia's remaining natural forests. Under S2, large-scale plantation forests are rapidly expanded and meet up to two-thirds of the timber demand which allows the existing production forests to be managed sustainably. However, in order for the expansion of plantations not to conflict with goals for agriculture, these plantations must be established on degraded lands and not on land suitable for food crop or estate crops. While food and estate crops are expected to face a shortage of suitable land, there is no shortage in the supply of degraded lands for plantation forests; even under S2, plantation forests would use only 22% of available land. Since these two sectors already need land in excess of supply, incentives would have to be designed carefully to ensure that plantations are established on these lands.

Plantation forests and improved management of natural forests also require significant increases in labor and capital inputs per unit of output. Preliminary calculations indicate that the costs of timber from plantation forests will be roughly 50% greater than timber from natural forests. Fee and pricing policies may need to be reviewed to provide incentives for the establishment of the more expensive plantation forests.

Water and Air Pollution

Using currently available technologies, control of water pollution from industrial sources can be achieved by 2020 with the measures projected under S2, though additional measures will probably be required to alleviate local water pollution problems. Suspended solids are substantially reduced under both scenarios. BOD increases very little under S2 (4%) despite rapid growth of polluting industries over the period from 1990 to 2020. COD is not significantly reduced, mainly because the expansion of the pulp and paper industry outweighs the effects of pollution control measures. Additional measures may be required in specific sectors, such as pulp and paper. As with all pollution regulation, strong enforcement by the government will be required.

All forms of air pollution increase substantially between 1990 and 2020, 300% to nearly 500% depending upon the pollutant and the scenario. Since no pollution control measures are projected for the future, air pollution is directly related to the growth of polluting sectors. The most polluting sectors – households, transportation, and electricity – are among the fastest growing sectors. Air pollution is closely linked with combustion of fossil fuels so the only moderating factor in the growth of air pollution results from gains in energy efficiency which are not sufficient to offset the effects of sectoral growth.

The sectoral distribution of carbon emissions (see Table 14.7) does not change significantly between 1990 and 2020 for most sectors except services whose share declines mainly due to increased energy efficiency in transportation, and households where the increase in use of energy outweighs efficiency gains increasing its share. Emissions of sulfur are influenced by the changing fuel mix: the increased use in electric utilities of gas and relatively low sulfur coal instead of relatively high sulfur petroleum products reduces its share of sulfur emissions. The increased use of coal by households instead of relatively clean petroleum products increases its share of sulfur emissions. The distribution of nitrogen emissions does not change very much. Substantial additional measures could be introduced to reduce pollution, for example, higher standards for appliance energy efficiency, improvement of public transportation, reduction in the sulfur content of diesel fuel, and the use of catalytic converters for motor vehicles. Postcombustion pollution control equipment could be introduced for electricity as well as cleaner, more advanced combustion technologies.

Standards for water pollutants and other air pollutants are usually set in terms of concentration levels because it is the local concentration rather than the total level of emissions that has a potentially negative impact. While the economy-wide model used in this study does not include a mechanism for determining the geographical distribution of pollution, we can, nevertheless, make the following observations.

- Most of Indonesia's industry, population, and motor vehicles – the main sources of pollution – are located on Java and are expected to be concentrated there in the future despite efforts to disperse activities on other islands. Consequently, any increases in economy-wide pollution is expected to increase the concentration of pollutants on Java.

- Current concentrations of pollutants are already considered harmful to human health in many parts of Java (see World Bank 1994). Any increases in pollution will result in worsening of health on Java. While it is likely that other areas will also suffer, projections of the geographic distribution of pollution will be required in order to identify these areas.

- By omitting other types of pollution, for example, water-borne wastes of households, atmospheric emissions of particulates, and lead, the results shown here understate of the extent of the pollution problem and threats to human health.

CONCLUSIONS

Few policy decisions are, or should be, based solely on economic criteria. A primary purpose for economic analysis, including the one described in this chapter, is to promote dialogue among decision makers about development objectives and the best means to achieve them. This study, along with others similar in spirit such as World Bank (1994), has helped to increase the dialogue about Indonesia's Long Term Development Plan. For example, in response to projected massive increases in air pollution, the government of Indonesia is now considering the introduction of measures to control air pollution. In addition, food self-sufficiency is no longer taken for granted.

From the policy perspective, the work reported here could be extended in a number of directions that would be useful to planners in Indonesia. One direction would be to go more deeply into some of the issues addressed here, such as forestry management. Another would be to include a broader range of environmental issues. Examples of other issues which could be explored include the estimation of costs and benefits and the income effects of natural resource policies, an assessment of environmental impacts in different regions of Indonesia, or an assessment of the impact of trade policies.

The analysis reported in this chapter emphasizes a technological perspective on the environmental implications of alternative development paths. Indeed, one of the great strengths of the analytical approach used in this study is its explicit and realistic representation of alternative technologies in each sector. However, significant changes in government policy will be needed to bring about the adoption of new technologies and practices required for sustainability. For example, enforcement of existing regulations for water pollution and forestry management needs to be strengthened; agricultural research and support needs to be redirected towards crops other than rice; and new, politically

Table 14.7. Distribution of Air Pollutant Emissions by Sector in 1985 and 2020 (in %)

1985	CO_2	SO_2	NO_x
Agriculture	2	0	7
Mining	17	14	7
Manufacturing	14	20	4
Utilities	10	30	7
Services	37	33	55
Households	19	2	20
TOTAL	100	100	100
Thousands of tons	39,078	417	760

2020 Under Scenario 1, Moderate Economic Growth

	CO_2	SO_2	NO_x
Agriculture	2	0	8
Mining	15	12	7
Manufacturing	13	19	5
Utilities	12	19	10
Services	33	27	52
Households	24	23	18
TOTAL	100	100	100
Thousands of tons	171,343	1,967	2,980
Agriculture	3	0	10
Mining	17	12	8
Manufacturing	14	22	6
Utilities	11	15	10
Services	36	30	52
Households	19	20	14
TOTAL	100	100	100
Thousands of tons	143,139	1,569	2,356

Note: Figures may not sum to 100 due to rounding.

Source: Tables 14.2, 14.4, and 14.5.

sensitive policies will need to be introduced, such as pricing water used in agriculture. While many of these changes have been identified in this chapter, their full political and social implications represent another important dimension which needs to be considered in assessing the feasibility of a development path.

The success of this and other NRAs demonstration projects in Indonesia is reflected in the decision by the government of Indonesia to institutionalize the compilation of NRAs. Indonesia is currently in the process of adding the capacity to compile NRAs on a regular basis to the data collection activities of the Central Bureau of Statistics. This will improve the quality and consistency of the NRAs database considerably and guarantee that they will be updated and available for policy-makers in a timely fashion.

In addition to providing useful recommendations to the Indonesian Ministry of Planning, I hope that the study reported in this chapter can serve a larger purpose. Statistical offices and potential users of NRAs are naturally skeptical about constructing NRAs until their usefulness can be demonstrated. By providing a clear demonstration of how NRAs can be used with analytical models to address development policy issues, this study may encourage other countries to compile NRAs and to introduce them into their policy-making processes.

More generally, this chapter adds to the small, but growing body of empirical literature helping to define and improve NRAs. The framework and concepts used for NRAs will evolve as the System of National Accounts did: through the interaction over several decades between those who compile the accounts and those who use them. Because the strengths and weaknesses of NRAs are often revealed through attempts to use them, public discussion of the applications of NRAs plays a critical role in their development as a more effective policy tool. This is especially important for an information system like NRAs which brings together information from very different disciplines, the social sciences and the natural sciences.

FOOTNOTES

1. In contrast to the UN system for NRAs, the two countries with the most well-established program for NRAs, Norway and the Netherlands, compile only physical stock and flow accounts (see Alfsen, Bye, and Lorentson 1987; de Haan, Keuning, and Bosch 1993; Keuning 1992, 1993).
2. Unlike oxides of sulfur and nitrogen, atmospheric carbon is not always considered a pollutant in the normal sense of the word. Carbon is referred to as a pollutant in this chapter in order to facilitate simultaneous discussion of all three types of atmospheric emissions.
3. The high economic growth scenarios did not appear feasible in terms of natural resources, labor, and capital requirements. The results are not reported here.

REFERENCES

Alfsen, K. 1994. Natural Resource Accounting and Analysis in Norway. Paper presented at the Third International Conference of the International Society for Ecological Economics, October 24–29, 1994, San Jose, Costa Rica.

Alfsen, K., T. Bye, and L. Lorentson. 1987. *Natural Resource Accounting and Analysis, The Norwegian Experience, 1978–1986.* Oslo: Central Bureau of Statistics of Norway.

Ayres, R. 1978. *Resources, Environment, and Economics: Applications of the Materials/Energy Balance Principle.* New York: Wiley and Co.

Bartelmus, P. and J. van Tongeren. 1994. Environmental Accounting: An Operational Perspective. UN Department for Economic and Social Information and Policy Analysis Working Paper Series No. 1.

Daly, H. 1994. Fostering environmentally-sustainable development: Four parting suggestions for the World Bank. *Ecological Economics* 10(3):183–188.

Deardon, P., S. Lonergan, and J. Ruitenbeek. 1994. An Ecological Economic Study of the Chao Phraya River Basin, Thailand. Report prepared for the Canadian International Development Agency.

de Boer, B., M. de Haan, and M. Voogt. 1994. What Would Net Domestic Product Have Been in an Environmentally Sustainable Economy? Occasional Paper NA/67 for the National Accounts Research Division, Central Bureau of Statistics, The Netherlands.

de Haan, M., S. Keuning, and P. Bosch. 1993. Integrating Indicators in a National Accounting Matrix Including Environmental Accounts (NAMEA), Netherlands Central Bureau of Statistics, No. NA–060.

de los Angelos, M., H. Peskin, and M. Bennagen. 1994. Managing pollution in the Philippines: insights from environmental and natural resource accounting. Paper presented at the Third International Conference of the International Society for Ecological Economics, October 24-29, 1994, San Jose, Costa Rica.

Duchin, F., C. Hamilton, and G. Lange. June 1993. Environment and Development in Indonesia: An Input–Output Analysis of Natural Resource Issues. Final report prepared for BAPPENAS (Indonesian Ministry of Planning) and Natural Resources Management Project, USAID.

Duchin, F. and G. Lange. March 1992. Input–Output Modeling: Development and the Environment in Indonesia. Final report to EPSS for CIDA.

Duchin, F. and G. Lange. August 1993. Development and the Environment in Indonesia. Final report to EPSS for CIDA.

Duchin, F. and G. Lange. 1994. *The Future of the Environment: Ecological Economics and Technological Change.* New York and Oxford: Oxford University Press.

Duchin, F. and D. Szyld. 1985. A dynamic input–output model with assured positive output. *Metroeconomica* 37:269–282.

Hueting, R. 1991. Correcting national income for environmental losses: A practical solution for a theoretical dilemma. In *Ecological Economics: The Science and Management of Sustainability,* ed. R. Costanza. New York: Columbia University Press.

Hueting, R., P. Bosch, and B. de Boo. 1992. *Methodology for the Calculation of Income.* Gland, Switzerland: Worldwide Fund for Nature.

Keuning, S. 1992. National Accounts and the Environment: The Case for a Systems Approach. Occasional Paper NA/53 for the National Accounts Research Division, Central Bureau of Statistics, The Netherlands.

Keuning, S. 1993. An information system for environmental indicators in relation to the national accounts. In W. de Vries, G. den Bakker, M. Gircour, S. Keuning, and A. Lenson eds., *The Value Added of National Accounting.* Voorburg: Netherlands Central Bureau of Statistics.

Lange, G. August 1993. The Use of Natural Resource Accounts for Integrated Natural Resource Management in Botswana. Report to USAID, Bureau for Africa.

Lange, G. 1994. Natural resource accounting in Africa: Integrating environmental and economic objectives in natural resource management. Paper presented at Conference on Natural Resources and Environmental Policy in Africa sponsored by the USAID, Bureau for Africa in Banjul, The Gambia, January 18–22, 1994.

Lange, G. and F. Duchin. 1994. Integrated Environmental-Economic Accounting and Natural Resource Management in Africa. Paper prepared for USAID, Bureau for Africa.

Leontief, W. and F. Duchin. 1986. *The Future Impact of Automation on Workers.* New York: Oxford University Press.

Repetto, R. et al. 1989. *Wasting Assets: Natural Resources in the National Income Accounts.* Washington, DC: World Resources Institute.

United Nations. 1984. A Framework for the Development of Environment Statistics. Statistical Papers, Series M, No. 78. New York: The United Nations.

United Nations. 1993. Integrated Environmental and Economic Accounting, Interim Version. Studies in Methods, Handbook of National Accounting, Series F, No. 61. New York: United Nations.

World Bank. 1994. Indonesia Environment and Development: Challenges for the Future. Washington, DC: World Bank Report No. 12083–IND The Dynamic Input–Output Model.

APPENDIX

The dynamic input–output model used to carry out the analysis extends the model developed by Duchin and Szyld (1985) and first implemented in Leontief and Duchin (1986) to include an environmental module. It is dynamic because investment is made endogenous. Investment takes place both for replacement of used up capital stock and for expansion. Expansion investment occurs only when there is unused capacity; it is determined by expected growth in each sector's output, the technologies in use (the B matrices), and rates of capacity utilization. The mechanism is based on the well-known accelerator principle.

This description includes a list of the variables and parameters comprising the database. All the parameters need to be projected for future years. Generally y and δ are exogenous variables while c, c^*, o, and x are endogenous. The model calculates the levels of sectoral production and investment given the technical coefficients and final demand (excluding investment).

Employment requirements by level of education of worker (equation 14.5) and natural resource use and emissions (equation 14.6) are determined by a separate set of calculations after the physical model is solved. Equation (14.6) for environmental variables is only a schematic representation since not all calculations were made directly on a per-unit-of-output basis. Soil erosion was estimated by multiplying the erosion coefficient by total land use in a sector (the product of the land requirement coefficient and sectoral output). Air emissions were calculated by multiplying fuel-specific emission parameters to the amount of fossil fuel used in a sector (the product of energy input coefficients and sectoral output).

Definition of Variables and Parameters

$c(t)$	capacity at beginning of period t
$c^*(t+\tau)$	capacity planned in period t for t+ τ where τ is the maximum number of periods lag between delivery of a capital good and its use in production
$o(t+\tau)$	increase in capacity, if any, planned in period t for t+τ
R	matrix of requirements for replacement of existing capacity
δ_i	maximum admissible annual rate of expansion of capacity for sector i

A, x, y   defined as usual (A is the matrix of current account require-
                ments per unit of output, x is the vector of outputs, and y is
                the vector of deliveries to final users)
B τ (t)   matrix of those capital requirements per unit increase in out-
                put that need to be produced in period t for first use in period
                t+ τ
L   matrix of labor requirements per unit of output by educational
                category and by sector
e   vector of labor requirements by educational category
N   matrix of natural resource inputs or emissions per unit of
                sectoral output
m   vector of natural resource inputs and emissions

Initial Conditions

$c(t_0)$

$c^*(t), t = t_0+1, ...,t_0 + t -1$

$x(t), t = t_0 - \tau,...,t_0-1$

The initial conditions are completed by computing o and then c, according to
the equations below for

$t = t_0 +1,...,t_0 + \tau -1$

Model

For $t = t_0,...,T$

$$c^*(t+\tau) = \min \left[1+\delta_p \frac{x_i(t-1) + x_i(t-2)}{x_i(t-2) + x_i(t-3)} \right]^{\tau+1} \cdot x_i(t-1) \qquad (14.1)$$

$$ \qquad (14.2)$$

$$o(t+\tau) = \max [0, c^*(t+\tau) - c(t+\tau-1)]$$

$$c(t+\tau) = c(t+\tau-1) + o(t+\tau) \qquad (14.3)$$

$$[I - A(t) - R + (t)]x(t) = \sum_{\theta=1}^{\tau} B^{\theta}(t) o(t+\theta) + y(t). \tag{14.4}$$

$$L(t)\, x(t) = e(t) \tag{14.5}$$

$$N(t)\, x(t) = m(t) \tag{14.6}$$

Sectoral Classification

1	Rice (Paddy)	16	Cement
2	Other Food Crops	17	Other Manufacturing
3	Other Agricultural Crops	18	Petroleum Refining
4	Livestock	19	LNG
5	Forest Products	20	Electricity
6	Fisheries	21	Gas Utilities
7	Coal	22	Water Utilities
8	Crude Oil	23	Construction
9	Natural Gas	24	Trade
10	Other Mining	25	Restaurants and Hotels
11	Food and Tobacco	26	Transportation & Comm.
12	Wood Products	27	Business Services
13	Pulp and Paper	28	Public Administration
14	Fertilizer	29	Services
15	Chemicals	30	Unspecified

15 LIMITED KNOWLEDGE AND THE PRECAUTIONARY PRINCIPLE: ON THE FEASIBILITY OF ENVIRONMENTAL POLICIES

Friedrich Hinterberger
Division for Material Flows and Structural Change
Wuppertal Institute for Climate, Environment, and Energy
Wuppertal, Germany

Gerhard Wegner
Faculty of Economics
University of Witten
Herdecke, Germany

INTRODUCTION

Since the early days of ecological economics Funtowicz and Ravetz have claimed the need for post-normal science. Facing the threats of global environmental disruption, "scientists now tackle problems introduced through policy issues where, typically, facts are uncertain, values in dispute, stakes high, and decisions urgent. ... On the basis of such uncertain inputs, decisions must be made, under somewhat urgent conditions" (Funtowicz and Ravetz 1991). The environmental problems we are facing today provoke some new dimensions of complexity that are a challenge for economic policy as well as for the theory of environmental policy. Therefore a new type of policy is needed in which a precautionary principle is included as a part of the strategy. In this chapter we will deal with an isomorphy concerning interventions into open natural and societal systems. This isomorphy highlights one aspect of successful environmental policy. The ecosphere as well as the market system are evolutionary open systems which: 1) cannot be steered according to well-defined outcomes; 2) are able to absorb exogenous shocks without destroying the internal order, but only to a limited extent, resulting in 3) the need for a precautionary principle if interventions are undertaken. The degree of mutual interference between natural and societal systems should be kept within bounds. With respect for the economy we draw our arguments from a tradition of theory of economic policy that suggests being careful with regard to the limited capacities of political steering. The German liberal tradition of economic policy has been warning us for several decades not to be too optimistic regarding the ability of policy measures to achieve certain goals (Eucken 1967[1959]; Streit 1991). The core of this argument is that there are knowledge problems that make the outcome of interventions uncertain elaboration of this view from an advanced market process view (see Wegner 1996). This matches the arguments of many ecological economists who claim limited knowledge regarding the behavior of ecological systems. Unintended effects arise in the context of virtually every human interference with nature.

Nevertheless, limited knowledge is not a sufficient argument for refraining from intervention at all. In the first sections of this chapter the main arguments raised by the German liberal school are presented. To our knowledge, they have not been discussed in connection with ecological economics so far. Later we will show how one can deal with knowledge problems in a way that can increase the chances for environmental policy to be successful. Instead of attempting a precise steering of the socioeconomic development towards an ecological and economic optimum, we introduce a general guideline for economic activities: the overall reduction of material input to all economic activities. Such a precautionary strategy will be suggested as a way of protecting socioeconomic development from both socioeconomic and ecological disruption.

THE LIBERAL CRITICISM OF EPHEMERAL INTERVENTIONS

Within the liberal tradition of economic policy theories, interventions into market processes have often been a goal of criticism. The genealogy of these criticisms includes names such as Mises, Robbins, Eucken, and Hayek.[1] Although these authors rarely denied the necessity of some correction of economic outcomes concerning income distribution or market performance in general, they strongly argued against an unbounded interventionist state. Especially the German ordoliberal school, represented by Walter Eucken, argued in favor of market allocation corrections but at the same time looked for principles to restrain the interventionist state. The manifold and well-received arguments against the interventionist state can be condensed to the limited capacity of complex socioeconomic systems to absorb and deal with exogenous shocks. We briefly summarize the main arguments in this chapter. As we have learned from experiences with numerous cases of market regulations, interventions normally produce at least some unintended results in terms of allocational distortion. Often, the correction of such unintended results induced by a former intervention sets a dynamic of interventions in motion (Mises 1976 [1929]). Meanwhile economic history offers many examples of such "spirals of interventions." If, for example, the government endeavors to fix incomes in agricultural markets – as is still the case in the European Union's agricultural policy – resources will be shifted from unregulated to regulated branches. As a consequence, an excess supply is induced, which stimulates further interventions in order to regulate market supply. If the government tries to establish some environmental quality standards by stipulating and enforcing best technologies to firms, the incentive to improve these technologies will (unintentionally) be low. In similar cases, Mises (1976[1929]) developed a general critique of interventionist economic policy, which was continued by the ordoliberal school; the latter has exerted quite a substantial influence on practical economic policy in the early postwar period in Germany.[2] In order to avoid unintended side effects on the economic order, the liberal tradition of economics recommended interventions into market only in exceptional cases, which should supplement the working principles of a market order instead of dominating it. Political interventions should be part of the ingredients of a mixed economy, in which markets are the main device of the economic order. This normative a priori covers the whole range of interventions that have direct as well as indirect impacts on market outcomes and range from direct price controls to more indirect instruments like non-price regulations, standards, and so on.

Furthermore, interventions into markets are ephemeral: they are characterized by short-term revisions and would themselves emerge as a source of destabilization of market allocation. Long-term economic planning by individual agents will be impaired, if the cases for interventions are not confined to an easily comprehensible and stable set. If one takes into account that market data (such as prices, consumer preferences, and techniques) are likely to change in a disruptive way, economic planning will be aggravated in a twofold manner: first, by fluctuating market data and second, by ephemeral interventions which would turn out to be an additional source of destabilization. In the latter case, economic agents are compelled to speculate on political decisions instead of speculating on gainful market conditions. Their entrepreneurial efforts are misdirected and the capacity of market agents to react flexibly on changes in market data are reduced. This disturbs (Eucken 1967 [1959]), if not destroys (Hayek 1969), the working principles of a market order.

As a consequence, political interventions should be chosen with circumspection, restricted to a clearly defined set of cases and stabilized as to their intensity. This is the core of Eucken's "principle of a constant economic policy." For example, he pleaded for a constant tax scheme instead of short-term variations in taxes in order to stabilize expectations of economic agents (Eucken 1967 [1959]). It should be noted that the arguments mentioned above, to some degree, contrast with the market failure approach derived from neoclassical theory. Within the latter the state is not only allowed, but obliged to intervene in every case in which it can be shown that markets do not reach a Pareto-optimal situation. In fact, it has been pointed out that the market failure approach can be interpreted as a special form of interventionism (Riese 1988; Streit 1991; Cordato 1992): by comparing Pareto-efficient states with actual market outcomes, market failure would easily turn out to be the normal and not the exceptional case. Especially with regard to external effects it seems obvious that a large number of economic activities affect the utility/cost level of other agents positively as well as negatively. If theory fails to differentiate between external effects relevant to policy on the one hand and external effects irrelevant to policy on the other, a detailed system of Pigovian taxes would have to be installed (Cordato 1992). In this view, the notion of market failure requires a careful reinterpretation if it is to be useful for political purposes at all. Such a reinterpretation should go beyond the usual classifications of policies as being first-best, second-best, third-best, and so on.

It should be mentioned that attempts have been made to reduce the interventionist bias of the market failure approach. Inefficient market outcomes might be explained by transaction costs that prevent agents from exhausting gains from trade privately and does not necessarily indicate a case for intervention. On the other hand, interventions are costly themselves (Le Grand 1991) and gains from an allocational improvement might not offset these administrative costs.[3] In the light of such insights the market failure approach has undergone some refinements (Demsetz 1969). Nevertheless, the approach still justifies interventions provided that allocational distortions exist. Few economists have gone as far as Hayek, who never tired to argue that evolutionary (spontaneous) market processes fail to meet the criteria of welfare economics (Hayek 1969); the latter would necessarily misdirect economic policy and prepare a "road into the interventionist state." The new Austrian school of economics has stressed this point by looking for some refined criteria of interventions (Streit 1991; Wegner 1991; Cordato 1992).

WHY ENVIRONMENTAL POLICY CAN BE EPHEMERAL

In view of the spirit of liberal criticism against political interventions, environmental policy seems to be a likely target. At first glance the nature of environmental policy issues conflicts with the criteria raised by the liberal or Austrian school. Due to the character of environmental issues as they have been experienced in the past decades, environmental policy can easily take the form of interventionism. Environmental policy is exposed to dimensions of uncertainty that make a form of intervention that is likely to stabilize private expectations very difficult (no matter whether politicians possess a preference for interventionism or not). Later we discuss a possible way out of this dilemma. First we want to highlight three dimensions of knowledge problems that every environmental politician has to tackle.

1. Due to a lack of full insight into the complexity of ecological systems, we are (and always will be) unable to draft a comprehensive list of all economic activities contributing to the deterioration of the ecosphere. In their records of environmental politics in the Netherlands, Dietz and van der Straaten (1992) illustrated the emergence of many new environmental goals over the past decades. SO_2 was followed by NO_x, CFCs, and CO_2 as the main targets for emission control. Extrapolating from our experience we can exclude the possibility of obtaining full information on the most relevant ecological impacts in the future. This is not surprising, if we take into account the complex character of the ecosphere, in which cause–effect relationships depend heavily on time paths and singular antecedent conditions. Hence, every reaction of the ecosphere to human interference has to be experienced anew and will be impossible to predict. Knowledge of environmental deterioration is therefore necessarily limited and subject to change. One consequence of better environmental monitoring will be that we will have to reckon with a growing list of environmental damage; on the other hand, it may be doubtful whether earlier damages can be cut back sufficiently to disappear from the political agenda. Hence, the list of environmental goals is likely to become longer in the future. [4]

2. New knowledge about the environmental impacts caused by economic activity may lead to the revision of environmental goals. As the example of CO_2 pollution has shown, the former priority of abating toxic chemical substances into the ecosphere can be downgraded somewhat. Chemical substances such as CO_2, which only ten years ago was regarded as harmless, are receiving much attention now, since it has become obvious that they cause irreversible ecological effects. In other words, the ranking of the most damaging activities ("absolute protection goals" as labeled in the German Environmental Policy) might change over time.

3. A third problem of environmental policy, however, differs quite substantially from other realms in economic policy. As we have experienced in the debate over nuclear power, it is quite risky to base political decisions exclusively on knowledge that is presently valid from a scientific point of view. The well-known argument of the supporters of nuclear power emphasized the harmless effects of low radiation according to a particular state of knowledge; at the same time opponents of nuclear power claimed a potential danger, which, in combination with irreversible effects, could not be accepted; nevertheless such arguments were criticized as being irrational, because the danger could not be proven at that moment. Therefore the notion of a rational decision must be reflected upon long-term consequences: To some degree it might be rational to base

present decisions on presumed environmental consequences which might turn out to be real in the light of a future state of knowledge. In other words, it may be rational to speculate on the progress of ecological knowledge. If we agree with this argument in general, another problem arises in connection with the collective character of political decisions. Unlike private investment decisions which are normally based on subjective views and beliefs, collective decisions require a certain degree of congruence among the subjective views of the citizens in order to form a decision. In this context the question arises: How much information should be regarded as sufficient to define an environmental issue? If we decide on defining such an issue at an early stage when only flimsy conjectures are available, the reputation of ecological policy might sooner or later be undermined, as former goal definitions are revealed as misconceptions. What is needed is some appreciation of the present state of ecological knowledge, which stops short of being objectively valid, but which is generally accepted as a basis of political decisions nevertheless. In any case, the possibility of a revision has to be anticipated.

In summary, due to our limited knowledge, at least three aspects will characterize environmental policy in the long-run:

- The list of environmental issues will increase;
- The priorities between single issues are open to change; and
- Sometimes environmental goals are ill-founded.

If we take only these three aspects of the nature of environmental problems into consideration, we may apply what we stated earlier for general economic policy. If environmental policy reacts to single issues, it may lead to an unbounded interventionist state, assuming that the political sphere is willing to run environmental policy (i.e., vested interests will push environmental issues onto the political agenda). Not only will the number of environmental issues increase; but there will also be a need for quick adjustment in the light of the latest news of damage cases. Essentially, the set of an environmental agenda items must be preliminary.

But if this holds true, environmental policy will have negative effects on the functioning of an economic order. At first glance, there seems to be little hope of reconciling requirements of environmental policy with Eucken's principle of a constant economic policy.[5] The ephemeral character of environmental interventions seems to be unavoidable. This interim result motivates our further investigation. A solution to the problems sketched above is likely to be found, if the following question can be answered: is it possible to define one single long-term goal in environmental policy which provides a sufficient basis and is likely to withstand short-term revisions?

The following discussions deal with this problem. We realize that an unbounded interventionist state will sooner or later impair the reputation of environmental policy in general, because of its interfering economic decisions. The main idea in the following should be seen in light of setting constant goals in the realm of environmental policy. We shall consider how to bundle the growing variety of environmental standards and how to substitute them into a single long-term goal. Such an ersatz goal would provide a stable framework for private decisions and hopefully avoid the problem delineated above. Instead of adapting their plans time and again to a changing set of standards and goals, private agents would be offered a long-term orientation. In this way the unavoidably destabilizing effects of an ephemeral environmental policy could effectively be absorbed.

WHY EPHEMERAL POLICIES ARE ALSO ECOLOGICALLY FLAWED

Although the widespread discussion of environmental issues started with a look at the global limits to growth, environmental policy of the 1960s through the early 1980s was mainly concerned with single pollutants such as asbestos, lead, dioxin, or SO_2. In many cases, we remember these issues in connection with certain events widely reported in the media, such as Seveso or the forest dieback. We do not mean to imply that all the programs aimed at controlling anthropogenic pollutants, such as chemicals legislation, were not successful with regard to their specific goals. Some parts of the world have recently indeed become cleaner and healthier, such as, for example, the water quality of most European rivers and lakes as well as the air quality in many industrial zones. Policies that prevent humans from health damages, such as the banning of dioxins or DDT, are necessary but not sufficient to prevent global environmental disruption. Until now, environmental policy has tried to react to certain disturbances in an ephemeral way. But the ecological limits to such an approach become more and more obvious. Some 100,000 chemicals are on the market today and every year a great number of additional ones is invented. Traditional environmental policy, such as chemicals legislation, is able to deal only with some of them, given the necessary laboratory, administrative, and political capacity. Regulatory measures tend to specify concrete scientifically and administratively operationalized rules of conduct with regard to the setting of norms and standards, exemptions, and tolerances. To make them operational it is also necessary to specify the administrative controls and punishments for violators (Schmidt-Bleek 1994).

Since the mid-1980s, global effects of economic activities have appeared on the agenda. But again policy focused on single substances, such as greenhouse gases. A policy that refers only to particular cases risks disturbing ecological equilibria in other parts of the system. These considerations lead us to a similar principle as presented earlier from purely economic arguments. We need general principles according to which interventions into open complex natural systems can be reduced. Besides the availability of resources and the danger coming from hazardous emissions and wastes, it is the carrying capacity of ecosystems and the complexity of global fluxes such as the carbon or water cycle that complicates the identification of the environmental impact potential. The intensity of anthropogenic material flows forces dynamic natural systems to reactions that endanger the stability of ecological equilibria. Historical evidence shows that these material flows are ever increasing. Since material resources are an unavoidable basis of every production process, economic activities will always interfere with natural processes, as long as we produce and consume. The more primary materials are moved by humans, the greater the risk of detrimental effects. Moreover, the total amount of emissions and waste (output) can only be reduced by a reduction of the material input (from nature) to the economy. According to the first law of thermodynamics, material inputs can only be transformed into outputs and stocks. From the point of view of ecological distortion, there seems to be hardly any difference between the two categories. They represent rather a social (i.e., anthropogenic) conceptualization: we consider what is useful for humans; the rest is waste to reside in the technosphere. But, as we have argued in our preceding section, not only emissions and wastes harm the environment.

Every extraction of resources changes the environment. Some of these changes may lead to new equilibria that are much less favorable for us, the humans, than others; and in the end such changes may even threaten human life on earth. Although open, complex ecological equilibria are quite robust with respect to exogenous shocks imposed by anthropogenic activities, but there are limits to this buffering capacity. Unfortunately these limits are very difficult to determine in advance. There have, of course, always been changes in the natural composition of the ecosphere. It seems to be mainly the high velocity of changes induced by humans with their technological abilities that drive ecological systems into a situation far removed from that in which humans became evolutionarily viable (see Hinterberger 1994; Schmidt-Bleek 1994; Hinterberger and Köhn 1996). Another result of this is that environmental policy can never repair ecological damages. Experience, knowledge and the newly emerging theories of complex phenomena inform us about the fundamental impossibility of fully predicting natural changes with regard to their intensity, place and timing as well as of the consequences of these disturbances.

Every movement of material, be it the extraction of gold, coal, sand or gravel, a redirection of soil water, or air, induces changes in the ecological equilibria.

We summarize our arguments in Figure 15.1. For the sake of the argument we assume that environmental damage can be measured by one single parameter. Any environmental policy that refers to perceived ecological damage (curve II) faces at least two shortcomings. It falls short of the actual ecological damage (curve I) which is partially hidden behind a veil of ecological ignorance, and, maybe more importantly, it is only oriented in the past with no chance to integrate future changes, be they real changes or only changes in perception. This is not only economically flawed, as we argued in the preceding sections. It is also ecologically wrong to base environmental policies on single substances and perceived environmental deteriorations, which can therefore not provide a sound basis for environmental goals. Whether such goals would correspond to individual evaluation or not, any policy oriented toward known damage will necessarily lag behind actual damage, which is to a considerable extent uncertain at every moment in time. Political instruments of every kind would only be directed to damages of the recent past that are better known.

Figure 15.2 presents this in analogy to Figure 15.1. Again, curve I represents the actual ecological damage, which is unknown in advance and only

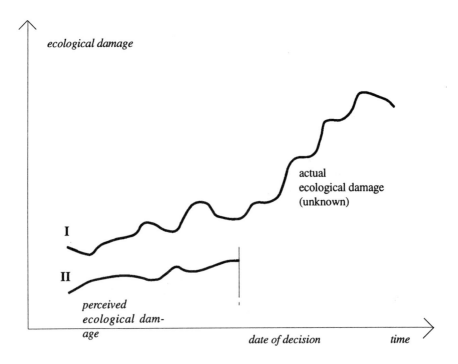

Figure 15.1. Actual and perceived ecological damages

partially perceived in the present (curve II). Yet, in order to get a long-term orientation we propose to align political instruments with the material flow curve (curve III). Such a reorientation would supercede the set of numerous and scattered ecological damages and would handle the lack of knowledge about their concrete shape.

In this section we present the principle of dematerialization along these lines before we ask whether such a policy would be compatible with the reduction of policy intervention in open complex economic systems.

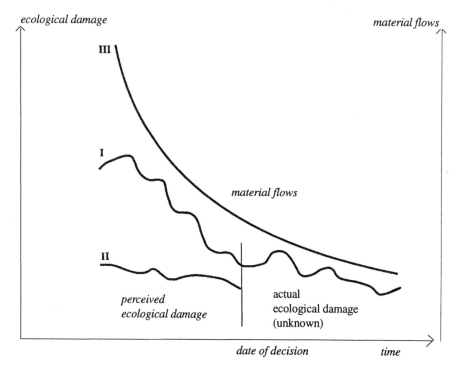

Figure 15.2. Actual and perceived ecological damages

DEMATERIALIZATION: A NEW WAY OF LOOKING AT ENVIRONMENTAL ISSUES

It follows from our considerations in the last section that as a general rule for a nonephemeral environmental policy, the global reduction of material flows would be a reasonable candidate for a generalized goal in environmental policy. Such a suggestion was made at the Wuppertal Institute by Schmidt-Bleek (1993a, 1993b, 1994). His starting point was to use the sum of human-induced material flows from ecosphere to technosphere as a simple measure to estimate the environmental impact potential of economic activities. These material inputs should be reduced by about 50% over the next 50 years (The Factor Ten Club 1994). Taking into account the differences in both current resource use and economic dynamics between the northern and the southern hemisphere, it follows that industrialized countries should take a much higher share. A factor ten reduction of material flows in northern countries is therefore widely discussed today in NGOs, governments and private enterprises.[6]

In order to derive working principles for an environmental policy as well as for individual economic actions from this general principle, it is necessary to provide an exact rule of how to calculate material flows. This has been done in the Handbook for Material Intensity Analysis (MAIA Handbook). The material input (MI) includes all materials displaced by humans, such as overburden, minerals, ores, oil, water, air, biomass, and so on that are needed in the life-cycle of a product or service. All materials used for production (natural materials needed for energy production, for auxiliary material production, infrastructures, transportation, factories, and other common goods in the product line) are added up, yielding the material input from nature to the industrial world. The units of MI are tons. In principle, all products can be analyzed with a view to their material intensity through the whole life cycle. The same calculation has to be done during usage, disposal or recycling phases. The total MI of the analyzed product results in an "ecological rucksack," which consists of the materials used directly or indirectly during the life cycle.[7] Waste flows per second are not accounted for in this approach, since they are outputs, not inputs (counting of waste flows would result in a double-counting). As for material streams of secondary materials, only the natural materials used for the secondary processing are counted (again, to avoid double-counting). A second effect of this calculation method is the incentive it provides for preferring secondary materials in the production systems in cases where MI can be reduced. This means that only the low-MI processing of used materials can reduce the material intensity of the different production systems (see Liedtke, Manstein, and Merten 1994 for more details). Here we can only give some examples: the production of one kw/hr of electricity in Germany induces on the average 4.7 kg abiotic material, 83 kg of water, and 0.6 kg of air. For a German citizen this means that his or her direct and indirect electricity consumption alone adds up to 27 tons of material, 482 tons of water, and 3.5 tons of air per capita per year! Attempts have also been made to calculate material flows for the German economy as a whole and to ascertain how the material flows are distributed among various industries as well as the role of imports and exports. In total, every German statistically induces about 70 tons of material flows world wide – not including water and air, which is about 1.3 kg per DM income (see Behrensmeier and Bringezu 1995).

CONCLUSION: AN ECONOMIC FOUNDATION OF DEMATERIALIZATION

Taking our earlier considerations into account, an environmental policy needs general objectives that can be kept constant in the longer run even if new knowledge arises about environmental deterioration. Since the material input (MI) is a general measure of the environmental impact potential, it could also provide a general objective for an environmental policy. The material productivity of an economy would increase if goods and services would be produced with less material input (technical or intrasectoral change), and if less material intensive industries increase their share in an economy (structural or intersectoral change). Dematerialization as a long-term goal will also turn out to be a challenge for economic agents. Hence, to reach a dematerialization by a factor of 10 over the next 50 years, or 4.5% per annum, it will be necessary to strengthen an economy's innovative capacity. This includes not only technical innovations but also organizational and social innovations. Nevertheless, general rules of conduct allow for a greater variety of potential innovation than the well-specified command and control system of traditional environmental regulation. Under current socioeconomic conditions, economic agents seem to have only few incentives to do so. Therefore the dematerialization principle should be implemented as a general rule for environmental policy. Under such a regime, various specific instruments, such as materials taxes or material input certificates (tradable permits) can be discussed.[8]

We argue that in the realm of environmental policy, a need for a long term goal does exist. As far as we can see, this need has not been carefully taken into account by the standard theory of environmental policy. The same applies a fortiori for practical environmental policy. In practice, politicians have been constructing a tight network of regulations that are setting standards for well-defined single environmental issues (for example SO_2 standards, No_x standards, standards defining water quality, radiological protection, etc.). In the absence of a guiding principle an increase in the number of regulations is likely to occur. Obviously, the standard theory in environmental economics, while criticizing the political measures, is not well prepared to define limits for the amount of environmental goals. The main point of standard theory emphasizes that measures should be chosen from a welfare point of view, implicitly admitting that a huge amount of efficient measures (for example, a network of Pigovian taxes) is likely to be well absorbed by the economic system. (The New Austrian criticism of the theory of market failure stresses the point that interventionism can paradoxically be justified from that perspective.) Adherents of first–best solutions provided that informational questions can be solved – have strong arguments in favor of constructing a tight network of single environmental taxes in order to set incentives for a reduction in well-specified economic activities causing environmental damage. Even if the requirements of efficiency are lowered – as is the case in alternative versions of second best approaches – political measures are bound to single environmental issues. As the amount of these issues increase, the number of single, separate policy measures would have to be increased as well. This is what we expect against the background of a still unfinished agenda in environmental policy. To avoid such consequences, guiding principles directed to a long-term goal have to be developed according to a precautionary principle.

ACKNOWLEDGMENTS

The authors are grateful to Alicia Bárcena, Peter Boettke, Reuben Deumling, Israel Kirzner, Fred Luks, Mario Rizzo, Thomas Sikor, Udo Simonis, Steven Viederman, Maria Welfens, and the editors of this volume for helpful discussions on an earlier paper from which this chapter evolved.

FOOTNOTES

1. See Mises (1976 [1929]); Eucken (1967 [1959]); Hayek (1969) and Robbins (1978).
2. Interestingly enough Dorner (1992) investigates some "spirals of interventions" from a psychological perspective. Experiments with complex systems simulated by computers showed how individuals tend to react to short-term bottlenecks and, unintentionally, produce bottlenecks in the future.
3. See Demsetz (1969), for a textbook version of these arguments see Streit (1991) and Fritsch Wein, and Ewers (1993).
4. Some of what appears on the political agenda might in fact only be due to better environmental monitoring and a better understanding of ecological systems. On the other hand, most of the main ecological problems of the past decades came on the agenda through activities of environmentalists and the media and not as a result of scientific examination of ecological relationships.
5. Obviously these arguments apply especially to the second best approach as developed by Baumol and Oates (1971). Nevertheless, we cannot see how the problems which cause destabilizing effects within the economic order can be escaped if we base environmental policy on a rigorous individualistic approach, be it a system of Pigovian taxes or a system of newly created property rights; for a detailed discussion of this point see Wegner (1994).
6. See, for example, studies like "Sustainable Europe" (Friends of the Earth Europe 1995), or "Zukunftsfhiges Deutschland" (BUND and Misereor 1996), the declarations of the international "Factor 10 Club," the National Environmental Plan of Austria (Österreichische Bundesregierung 1995) and publications of the World Business Council for Sustainable Development (WBCSD).
7. In principle, the MAIA methodology allows us also to disaggregate material input according to various qualitative parts. It would also be possible to weigh water differently from air or biotic resources. This in turn would require good reasons for such weighing factors differing from those employed now (equating all materials). The rationale behind the aggregation of various qualities is that we lack sufficient information to argue the extent some material inputs are more harmful to the environment than others.
8. See Wegner (1994, 1995) and Hinterberger, Luks, and Stewen (1996) for a more detailed discussion.

REFERENCES

Baumol, W. J. and W. E. Oates. 1971. The use of standards and prices for protection of the environment. *The Swedish Journal of Economics* 73:42–54.

Behrensmeier, R. and St. Bringezu. 1995. Zur Methodik der volkswirtschaftlichen Material-Intensitäts-Analyse: Ein quantitativer vergleich des Umweltverbrauchs der bundesdeutschen Produktionssektoren. Wuppertal Papers.

BUND and Misereor (eds). 1996. Zukunftsfhiges Deutschland. Ein beitrag zu einer global nachhaltigen Entwicklung. Berlin: Birkhäuser.

Cordato, R. E. 1992. *Welfare Economics and Externalities in an Open Ended Universe: A Modern Austrian Perspective,* eds. Boston et al. Kluwer Academic Publishers.

Demsetz, H. 1969. Information and Efficiency—Another Viewpoint. *Journal of Law and Economics* 7:1–22.

Dietz, F. J. and J. van der Straaten. 1992. Rethinking environmental economics: Missing links between economic theory and environmental policy. *Journal of Economic Issues* 26:27–51.

Dorner, D. 1992. *Die Logik des Mißlingens. Strategisches Denken in komplexen Situationen.* Hamburg: Rowohlt.

Eucken, W. 1967 [1959]. *Grundsätze der Wirtschaftspolitik.* Hamburg: Rowohlt.

The Factor Ten Club. 1994. *Carnoules Declaration.* Wuppertal: Wuppertal Institute.

Friends of the Earth Europe. 1994. *Towards a Sustainable Europe.* The Study.

Fritsch, M., T. Wein and H. J. Ewers. 1993. *Marktversagen und Wirtschaftspolitik. Mikroökonomische Grundlagen staatlichen Handelns.* Munchen: Vahlen.

Funtowicz, S. O., and J. R. Ravetz. 1991. A new scientific methodology for global environmental issues. In *Ecological Economics,* ed. R. Costanza. New York: Columbia University Press.

Le Grand, J. 1991. The theory of government failure. *British Journal of Political Science* 21:423–442.

Liedtke, C., C. Manstein, and T. Merten. 1994. MIPS, resource management and sustainable development. In Proceedings of the International ASM Conference "The Recycling of Metals." Amsterdam.

Hayek, F. A. V. 1969. Grundsatze einer liberalen Gesellschaftsordnung. In *Freiburger Studien,* Tubingen: Paul Siebeck.

Hinterberger, F. 1994. Biological, cultural, and economic evolution and the economy–ecology relationship. In *Toward Sustainable Development,* eds. J. van der Straaten and J. van den Bergh. Washington DC: Island Press.

Hinterberger, F. and J. Köhn. 1996. Hierarchy and Velocity of Systems. What Makes a Development Sustainable. Paper prepared for the Ecological Summit. Copenhagen.

Hinterberger, F., F. Luks and M. Stewen. 1996. *Ökologische Wirtschftspolitik. Zwischen Ökodiktatur und Umweltkatastrophe.* Berlin: Birkhäuser.

Mises, L. 1976 [1929]. *Kritik des Interventionismus.* Darmstadt: Wissenschaftliche Buchgesellschaft.

Österreichische Bundesregierung. 1995. *Nationaler Umweltplan.* Wien.

Riese, H. 1988. Wider den Dezisionismus der Theorie der Wirtschaftspolitik. In *Politische Ökonomie heute,* ed. W. Vogt. Regensburg: Transfer-Verlag.

Robbins, L. 1978. *The Theory of Economic Policy.* London, Basingstoke: MacMillan.

Schmidt-Bleek F. 1993a. MIPS: A universal ecological measure? *Fresenius Environmental Bulletin* 2:306–311.

Schmidt-Bleek F. 1993b. MIPS re-visited. *Fresenius Environmental Bulletin* 2:407–412.

Schmidt-Bleek F. 1994. Wieviel Umwelt braucht der Mensch? MIPS—Das Maß fur Ökologisches Wirtschaften. Berlin: Birkhäuser.

Streit, M. E. 1991. *Theorie der Wirtschaftspolitik.* Dusseldorf: Werner Verlag.

Wegner, G. 1991. *Wohlfahrtsaspekte evolutorischen Marktgeschehens. Neoklassisches Fortschrittsverstandnis und Innovationspolitik aus ordnungstheoretischer Sicht.* Tubingen: Paul Siebeck.

Wegner, G. 1994. *Marktkonforme Umweltpolitik zwischen Dezisionismus und Selbststeuerung.* Tubingen: Paul Siebeck

Wegner, G. 1996. *Wirtschaftspolitik zwischen Selbsteund Fremdsteuerung—ein neuer Ansatz.* Baden-Baden: Nomos.

16 DEVELOPING COUNTRIES' PRIMARY EXPORTS AND THE INTERNALIZATION OF ENVIRONMENTAL EXTERNALITIES

Henk Kox
Department of Economics and Econometrics
Free University
Amsterdam, The Netherlands

INTRODUCTION

Many developing countries, particularly the least developed among them, are still largely dependent on the export of a few primary commodities. Although production of these export commodities often causes considerable environmental externalities, governments have little maneuvering space with regard to the incorporation of these externalities in commodity export prices. This chapter analyzes why this is the case, and describes a possible new form of international environmental cooperation to deal with the problems at hand: International Commodity-Related Environmental Agreements (ICREAs).

First, I describe the role of primary commodity exports in developing country trade, and analyze the margins for individual countries to influence the world market price of their main export commodities. Next, I summarize the evidence on environmental externalities in primary commodity production of less developed countries (LDCs) and the rather scanty empirical data on the magnitude of these externalities. I discuss the problems governments of developing countries face when they would subject their primary producers to a strict polluter-pays policy. Subsequently, I examine whether or not these internalization problems should be regarded as purely domestic issues for the individual countries. I also discuss how ICREAs can operate as instruments for temporarily relieving the income effects of an internalization policy with regard to primary export commodities. After briefly discussing some operational issues of ICREAs, I then close with concluding remarks.

DEVELOPING COUNTRIES AND PRIMARY COMMODITY EXPORTS

Traditionally, the composition of developing country exports differed sharply from that of the developed countries. The former were primarily commodity exporters while the latter exported industrial goods. This stereotypical image is becoming a bit inadequate. Fast industrialization over the past two decades has led to higher shares of manufactured goods in the export of most LDCs. Many middle-income countries, particularly in Asia, have thus succeeded in diversifying the commodity composition of their merchandise exports. Nevertheless, the pervasiveness of this tendency is often exaggerated. Primary commodities (i.e., unprocessed food commodities, agricultural raw materials, metals, minerals, and fuels), still form the main export component for a vast majority of LDCs. The countries in sub-Saharan Africa and in Latin America remain dependent on primary commodity exports for roughly two-thirds of their exports. For the low-income countries (excluding India and China) and the middle-income countries, primary commodities still represent more than 50% of exports (Table 16.1).

Table 16.1. Primary Commodity Share in Merchandise Exports (%)

Country Group	1970	1992
By Geographical Criteria:		
Sub-Saharan African countries	83	76
Latin America and Caribbean	88	62
East Asia and Pacific	67	26
By Income Criteria:		
Low-income countries	73	38
Low-income countries excl. India and China	87	61
Middle-income countries	73	51
High-income countries	27	18

Source: World Bank (1994).

Alternative sources of export earnings are not readily available in many LDCs. Commodity exports are often highly concentrated in a few commodities. In the period 1987–1989 a group of 76 LDCs averaged a dependence on three or less primary commodities for more than half their export earnings (UNCTAD 1992).

The direct contribution of primary exports to Gross National Product (GNP) averages about 20% in sub-Saharan Africa, and 8% in the countries of South and Central America. Being a major source of foreign currency these exports create several positive domestic externalities, form an important employment sector, and often are one of the main sources of government revenue. These exports enable the import of foreign inputs which are essential for domestic production, investment, and productivity improvement. Export growth tends to create an outward shift of the domestic production possibilities frontier. Some primary export sectors like mining have a potential for scale economies and learning effects,[1] which can spill over to other sectors of the domestic economy.

PRIMARY COMMODITY PRODUCTION AND ENVIRONMENTAL EXTERNALITIES

In August 1995 after a large leakage of wastewater containing cyanide from a gold mine in Guyana into the country's largest river, fish were killed over a large distance and the region was declared an environmental disaster zone for the foreseeable future. An identical, smaller leakage had occurred a few months earlier in the same mine. These incidents illustrate the ecological risks of certain mining and ore concentration methods. Causality relations between environmental degradation and commodity production are seldom straightforward and always have a stochastic character. Large-scale, spatially concentrated production such as many like mining projects may entail spectacular pollution risks. This should, however, not blind us to the possibility that the cumulative effect of some production practices applied by spatially dispersed small farmers is equally damaging for the environment. The types of environmental impact studies needed are those that distinguish between general environmental characteristics of the production of certain commodities, area-specific effects, producer-specific characteristics, and effects which occur only when particular production technologies are applied. Environmental impact assessment studies for particular commodities are still rather scarce. Most of them focus on large (infrastructural) projects and particular regions. A few attempts have been made to construct a more or less comprehensive picture of the environmental impact of particular primary commodities.[2]

Few studies quantify the magnitude of environmental externalities and real resource costs of commodity production in LDCs. Cotton is one of the crops with the highest pesticide use intensity, and an overall bad environmental record. After including yield effects, cotton production costs per unit may rise 15% to 32% or even more compared to current standard production costs, when the environmental production externalities are to be effectively abated (de Vries 1995). Khalid et al. (1995) estimated that a 10% reduction of pesticide use in Malaysian cocoa cultivation would result in a 15% increase in production costs, mainly in the form of higher labor costs. Blunden (1985) estimated some 10% additional costs for avoiding water pollution in the extraction of nonferrous metals in Canada. A similar figure was found for the costs of reducing harmful exhaust gas emissions in a Chilean copper smelter (de Vries and Leliveld 1995). Several empirical studies quantify the costs of deforestation and soil erosion in semiarid regions, though multicausality often makes it difficult to identify the costs caused by commodity production.[3] Further circumstantial evidence can be derived from estimates of the overall economic importance of environmental degradation in commodity-producing LDCs. Table 16.2 summarizes the results of a number of available studies. Pearce and Warford (1993) estimate that annual gross environmental damage in poor developing countries may be around 10% of GDP and above. Even though the empirical basis for this generalization is still weak, we conclude here that the environmental externalities due to production of primary commodities are often of a nontrivial magnitude.

Table 16.2. Estimates of Environmental Damage in Selected LDCs, Various Years[*]

Country and Year	Form of Ecological Damage	Annual Costs as a % of GDP
Burkina Faso 1988	Crop, livestock and fuelwood losses from land degradation	8.8
Costa Rica 1989	Deforestation	7.7
Ethiopia 1983	Effects of deforestation on the supply of fuelwood and crop output	6.0–9.0
Indonesia 1984	Soil erosion and deforestation	4.0
Madagascar 1988	Land burning and erosion	5.0–15.0
Malawi 1988	Lost crop production from soil erosion	1.6–10.9
Malawi 1988	Costs of deforestation	1.2–4.3
Mali 1988	On-site soil erosion losses	0.4
Mexico 1985	Natural resource depletion, deforestation, land degradation	6.0–13.0[**]
Nigeria 1989	Soil degradation, deforestation, water pollution, other erosion	17.4
Papua, New Guinea	Deforestation, soil erosion, water pollution	7.0–10.0

Notes:
* The estimates use different techniques and vary in the quality of underlying research.
** Percentage of Net Domestic Product.
Sources: Pearce and Warford (1993); van Tongeren et al. (1993).

PERSPECTIVES FOR INTERNALIZATION OF ENVIRONMENTAL EXTERNALITIES BY INDIVIDUAL LDC EXPORTERS

In a document on proper pricing methods for natural resources the OECD Secretariat suggests the use of the user pays principle: "The price for the use of a resource should be the full long-run marginal costs of using that resource including the external costs associated with its development and any resultant pollution prevention and control activities" (Dommen 1993). The existence of negative environmental externalities in commodity production implies that cost prices of producers are lower than they should be. In competitive markets this means that sales prices will be too low as well. Consumers therefore do not pay the full resource price. They receive a hidden welfare transfer, paid for by environmental degradation in the production region. The domestic allocation of production and consumption is suboptimal from the point of view of Pareto efficiency, and should be corrected by public intervention. The 1992 UNCED summit, at which many developing countries were also represented, adopted the widely publicized Rio Declaration for future environmental policy. In careful wording this declaration calls upon countries to apply the polluter pays principle (PPP), as a guiding principle for their environmental policies: "National authorities should endeavor to promote the internalization of environmental costs and the use of economic instruments, taking into account the approach that the polluter should, in principle, bear the cost of pollution, with due regard to the public interest and without distorting international trade and investment" (UNCED 1992, Principle 16). Governments have a whole array of measures (legal regulation and economic incentives) at their disposal to achieve that environmental externalities get incorporated in domestic costs and prices.

The development of an environmental policy on the basis of the PPP is not a free lunch. An implementation apparatus has to be built up, complete with monitoring and enforcement instruments. The policy also affects relative prices, so that the country's consumption package, regional production patterns, and economic structure may have to adjust. International competitiveness issues are at stake in affected sectors producing internationally traded goods.[4] These factors explain why environmental policies in OECD countries do not systematically apply PPP in all relevant areas. In developing countries the internalization of environmental costs through PPP is still in its very infancy (e.g., Biggs 1993). Primary exports sectors in developing countries have only scarcely been confronted with polluter pays measures.

Let us consider in more detail why internalization tends to be problematic. We suppose that a PPP policy is considered, and that its impact is a substantial increase in cost price for the commodity producers, and certainly so in the short-term. What happens now? Two cases must be discerned. The first one concerns commodities which are nontradable (i.e., their price is relatively independent from the world market price). This is the case for many indigenous food commodities (yams, cassava, and perishable fruits). Producers can pass on the additional costs to the domestic consumers. Some sales volume may be lost depending on the price elasticity of domestic demand, but usually this constraint is not overly restrictive. Internalization therefore tends to be relatively easy for nontradable commodities.

The more interesting case, however, which applies to all export commodities, is when the commodity is tradable, meaning that its price is largely determined by the world market. Whether a commodity-exporting country *(i)* can pass on a domestic price increase (due to PPP) to the foreign consumers depends on several factors.

- *The country's international market share (s_i).* The higher its market share, the higher its degree of market power, the more likely it is that a country is able to effectively raise its export supply price.
- *The share of the commodity export in the country's total exports (v_i).* The higher the export dependency rate is, the riskier it is to take unilateral steps. Country *i* could more easily accept the risk that the international market doesn't swallow the higher export supply price when its v_i is low. So, the "passing on capacity" is inversely related to the export dependency factor.
- *The overall price elasticity of demand for the export commodity (e_d).* This partly determines how a price increase (due to internalization) would work out on export earnings. For all ($e_d > -1$), price increases result in higher export earnings.
- *The structure and intensity of competition in the international commodity market.* When some or all ($n - 1$) competing export countries step up their export volumes after a price increase, their supply reaction could prevent a unilateral internalization step by country *i*. This factor is captured by the price elasticity of export supply of the other export countries ($e'_{s,n=i}$). If this is above unity for at least some international competitors with a considerable joint market share, it negatively affects the "passing on capacity" of country *i*.

The two latter factors together constitute the price elasticity of demand for the individual export country. Now, if C_{ji} represents the "passing on capacity" of country *i* for commodity *j* we can summarize the aforementioned factors in a functional form.

$$C_{ji} = f(s_{ji}, v_{ji} e_{dj}, e_{sj,n=i})$$

Large exporters may successfully pass on internalized environmental costs, but they must be careful. A price rise may fire back in the form of a lower export demand. Furthermore, if they increase the world market price, other exporters will benefit as well, thus receiving a windfall profit. This will invoke additional supply from their side, so that in the end the large country loses market share. Small exporting countries are totally unable to pass on their domestic cost increase to foreign consumers. Their export producers experience a drop in profit margins, and the PPP policy works out as an implicit tax on output.[5] Export production of the commodity becomes less attractive. When alternatives are available, they switch to other products (not necessarily export products) or just stop producing, re-enter subsistence activities, or in the case of small farmers, sell their labor power in the local labor market. In any case a drop in export earnings from the original export commodity follows.

This chapter subsequently reviews the empirical importance of the four aforementioned factors for LDC primary commodity exports, starting with the economic weight of the commodity exports in terms of export shares and the country's international market shares.

Export Shares and International Market Shares

For 22 LDC primary export commodities we considered those cases where either a LDC's share in the international market was above 1%, or where the country depended on more than 1% of its export of this very commodity. This resulted in 415 country-commodity cases. The export and market shares are averages for the period 1985–1987. The source of the data is World Bank (1993). For a first impression, the selected country-commodity cases have been plotted in Figure 16.1. Most asterisks gravitate toward the lower left corner.

The results can be discussed more easily when the cases are split up into six subsets characterized by different export positions. The boundaries of the subsets are somewhat arbitrary, and at a less aggregate, more commodity-specific level they should be adapted to the structure of individual markets. Nevertheless, for an overall picture (allowing some fuzziness on the borders) the subsets reflect major differences between the 415 country-commodity cases. We discuss the perspectives for unilateral internalization attempts (for the moment disregarding the effects of the price elasticity of demand) for these six cases.

A. *Small international market share (< 10%) and tiny export share (≤ 2%): 118 cases.* Because these exporters are small players in the world market, unilateral internalization attempts are unlikely to influence the world market price, and therefore result in lower profit margins for domestic producers. The relative importance of these exports is small, however, so that governments could perhaps afford to risk losing some of these exports, certainly when the environmental benefits of internalization are valued high.

B. *Large international market share (10%) and tiny domestic export share (2%):* 9 cases. These are cases with good perspectives for unilateral in-

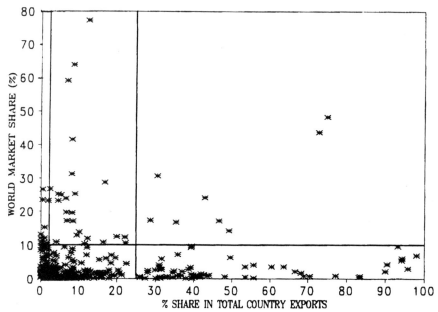

Figure 16.1. Scatter diagram of LDC export dependency ratios and international market shares for 22 selected primary commodities (415 country-commodity cases, 1985–1987)

ternalization actions. These countries are major players in the world market. Not coincidentally, eight out of these nine cases regard large countries like Brazil (tobacco, groundnut oil, tin), China (tea, jute), and Indonesia (tin). Their internalization attempt may affect the world market price, but in case it did not work this would only affect a small section of the country's export.

C. *Small market shares (< 10%) intermediate export dependency 2–25%):* 191 cases. These exporters cannot but act as price takers, unless they would produce world market specialities. The export stakes are high and these governments will not easily embark on unilateral internalization attempts.

D. *Small market share (< 10%), high export dependency (>25%):* 63 cases. These export countries find themselves in the very weakest position. They are price takers, and they are in no position to experiment with internalization measures, when the latter could endanger large sections of their exports and, hence, their import capacity.

E. *Large market share (> 10%), intermediate export dependency (2–25%):* 26 cases. Their internalization measures are likely to increase the world market price. Hence, unilateral internalization steps may pass on the additional costs to foreign consumers, unless demand reactions (intercommodity substitution, price elasticity) would form a problem.

F. *Large market share (> 10%), high export dependency (> 25%):* 8 cases. The high market share puts the exporter in a good position to take unilateral steps, but the stakes are very high for the domestic economy. No risks can be afforded. Governments will perform a close examination of potential reactions by international competitors and importers (inter-commodity substitution, price elasticity). This subset includes, for instance, Cuban sugar, Guinean bauxite, and Chilean copper.

In, at most, 43 country-commodity cases (B, E, F), or 10% of the total, a government could expect that its export producers can successfully pass on environmental policy compliance costs to foreign consumers. Table 16.3 presents more detailed data for 22commodities, using the same subsets as in Figure 16.1.

Table16.3. LDC Export Dependency and Market Shares for 22 Major Primary Export Commodities Sectoral Disaggregation of the 415 Country-commodity Case Studies of Figure 16.1*

Commodity	Subset A	Subset B	Subset C	Subset D	Subset E	Subset F	Total
Bananas	1	0	0	0	3	1	12
Bauxite	2	0	2	1	1	1	7
Cocoa	6	0	10	1	0	2	19
Coffee	3	0	21	13	1	1	39
Copper	2	0	5	3	0	1	11
Cotton	13	0	14	5	0	0	32
Fisheries	4	0	30	6	0	0	40
Groundnuts	5	1	2	0	0	0	8
Groundnut oil	3	1	2	0	1	0	7
Iron ore	0	0	4	2	1	0	7
Manganese	5	0	0	0	1	0	6
Natural rubber	3	0	3	0	3	0	9
Oilseed cake/meal	10	0	1	0	2	0	13
Palm oil	2	0	2	0	1	0	5
Petroleum	1	0	6	17	0	0	24
Phosphate rock	2	0	2	1	2	0	7
Sugar	3	0	14	5	0	1	23
Tea	4	1	4	0	2	1	12
Timber	2	0	19	3	1	0	25
Tin	4	2	2	0	1	0	9
Tobacco	8	1	3	1	0	0	13
Zinc	4	0	2	0	1	0	7
Other commodities	31	3	36	5	5	0	80
Total	118	9	191	63	26	8	415

Note: * The boundaries of the subsets are described in the text with regard to Figure 16.1.
Source: World Bank (1993).

Elasticity of World Demand

Suppose the world market price is indeed increased to such an extent that additional environmental costs can be passed on to foreign consumers. Would this not mean that the exporting countries "shoot themselves in the foot," because the higher price results in a large demand fall? With a given supply curve the share of internalized costs borne by consumers is higher the more inelastic the demand curve is (and the lower the elasticity of intercommodity substitution is). Econometric research in primary commodity markets generally finds very low price elasticities for world import demand and for the import demand of developed countries.[6] Price elasticities in the long and medium term are significantly less than one, often between 0.10 and 0.35. For nonagricultural commodities the elasticity tends to be somewhat higher, namely in the range between 0.40 and 0.60, but these values still imply that export countries gain from a price rise. Hence, demand elasticity in most cases forms no impediment to the internalization of environmental costs in world market prices.

Competition from Other Export Countries

For unilateral internalization attempts to succeed it is crucial to know how other exporting countries will react. What really needs to be known is what the price elasticity of commodity demand for the individual export country is. No empirical estimates for this variable were found. Most exporting LDCs show self-restraint in applying unilateral price rises and merely act as price-takers. Hence, the price elasticity of demand for the individual export country remains latent and is difficult to perceive. But its empirical significance can be derived another way. If in a competitive world market for a homogeneous commodity country i unilaterally increases its export supply price, this initially curtails supply, however small this effect may be. A small price reaction will occur. If competing countries react to this small price increase by vigorously stepping up their exports, the result will be that the market share of the internalizing country erodes and/or that the terms of trade gain is eroded by additional supply. Importers can satisfy their demand for the commodity at a price that is still below the supply price of country i. Disregarding the existence of large international stocks, the individual price elasticity of demand for country i depends on:

a. The sourcing flexibility of the importers,[7] and
b. The eagerness with which other exporters take over another country's market share.

The latter is measured by the price elasticities of supply of competitor countries (or if that is not available, the price elasticity of world export supply). If these elasticities are more than unity for at least some competing exporters, the latter are inclined to take over the market share of country i. Commodity market studies found above unity price elasticities of supply in several primary commodity markets.[8] Therefore, individual countries in many cases find themselves confronted with a highly price-elastic demand for their primary exports.

Here I take a closer look at the possibilities for individual LDCs to internalize environmental externalities in the price of their export commodities, and thus to pass on the real resource costs of these commodities to foreign consumers. It appears that in 90% of all considered country-commodity cases the country only has a negligible influence on the world market price. Exports are large enough to influence the world price in only 10% of the considered cases. But even here the possibility for successfully passing on the real resource costs is diminished considerably by supply reactions of other countries, and by the possibilities of intercommodity substitution available to importing countries.

A very interesting case study stems from Malaysia where in the mid-1980s domestic palm oil mills were confronted with increasingly tough anti-water pollution measures. Malaysian palm oil exports, one of the "E cases" in Figure 16.1, form over two-thirds percent of world exports. However, palm oil competes with many other edible oils so that substitution elasticities are high. The massive effluent problems caused by the industry have been successfully reduced due to the measures. The cost of this operation has mainly been borne by Malaysia's primary producers, the farmers and estates who grow the oil palm fresh fruit bunches. These producers suffered a more than 40% income loss. Compared to other segments of the Malaysian palm oil sector, the primary producers had the lowest price elasticity of supply, so that most of the PPP burden was shifted to their shoulders. In the end, hardly any of the increased production costs were passed on to foreign consumers in the form of a higher supply price (Khalid and Braden 1993). So, even a large international market share may not be sufficient to shelter a country against the competitive forces in the world market. Disaggregated data (cf. Table 16.3) suggest that in less than 20 country-commodity cases (i.e., 4%) opportunities exist for unilaterally passing on domestic price increases to international commodity prices.[9]

After considering four crucial factors on which the "passing-on" capacity depends we can conclude that in the overwhelming majority of cases the trade-off is between domestic environmental quality and export earnings. For some 118 cases (28% of total) the trade-off need not be too harsh because only a small part of the country's exports is at stake, but for others the export loss may be prohibitive. The prime cause is not the demand reaction by import countries, but rather the competitive nature of most primary commodity markets. Other exporting countries (often LDCs) tend to be free riders for each others' unilateral internalization attempts.

INCOME AND FOREIGN EXCHANGE EFFECTS

When only a single country faces the virtual impossibility to pass on the real resource costs of production to foreign consumers, one could say, "It is a pity for the country, but apparently its natural environment is unfit for the production of the commodity involved." For that country the dilemma is a domestic trade-off between purely domestic preferences which should be left entirely to domestic government. A few qualifications have to be added with regard to this choice, because income effects and foreign exchange effects may give rise to unexpected consequences.

If unilateral internalization policy works out as a tax on exports, the reaction of producers depends on the presence of income alternatives. When the producers have no income alternatives available for the lost export production, they may even produce more export commodities to compensate for the income effect, thus aggravating the environmental impact.[10] Small farmers in LDCs hardly have access to formal credit due to information asymmetries and adverse selection (cf. Hoff and Stiglitz 1993), and hence cannot use this for overcoming temporary income problems. Producers, because they have to satisfy current consumption needs, may increase the implicit discount rate with which they value the future benefits of environmental resources. More consumption of open access natural resources like fuel-wood can be the consequence. They may seek off-farm employment to maintain household income levels. Less household labor time is available for environmentally important activities with long-term payoffs, like terracing and other erosion abatement works, maintenance of irrigation and drainage systems, tree planting, and maintenance of the nutrient status of the soil. On-farm labor allocation shifts toward labor with short-term payoffs like weeding and harvesting. These reactions have repeatedly been reported in the comparable situation that world market price levels depress producer incomes (e.g., Dommen 1992; Akande 1993; May, Vegro, and Menezes 1993).

For the country as a whole, a similar income effect occurs when there are no alternatives for the lost foreign exchange earnings. Many LDCs find their economic growth bound by a foreign exchange constraint (e.g., Bacha 1990; Taylor 1993). Their import capacity and debt-servicing capacity are limited by export earnings.[11] Export growth tends to induce dynamic externalities in the form of an outward shifting of the country's production possibilities frontier. But the opposite occurs with shrinking exports and a binding foreign exchange constraint. The impossibility of importing essential foreign inputs paralyzes several domestic activities and thus causes a cascade of economic consequences. The negative income effect is then larger than the amount of lost export earnings. Because in many LDCs exports are a significant source of tax revenue, lower export earnings limit the financial margin for further development of an environmental policy.

DOMESTIC ISSUE OR CAUSE FOR INTERNATIONAL CONCERN?

A rationally acting LDC government will take the aforementioned income and foreign exchange constraints into account when it designs its domestic internalization policy.[12] This implies that all relevant costs and benefits are considered. The efficiency of such a policy cannot be improved upon by international intervention. International intervention would add additional costs and, therefore, inefficiencies. The picture changes, however, when there are transborder externalities, switching costs, or international capital market imperfections. If these conditions occur, national policy decisions are likely to produce allocation patterns that are not efficient from an international point of view.

Transborder externalities occur when an activity causes costs or benefits beyond the border of the country in which the activity takes place. We discern five main types of transborder externalities caused by the production of primary export commodities.

- So far we have considered the case of a single export country being unable to pass on the real resource costs of production to importing countries. The empirical data given before make it plausible that many export countries in a particular market face the same problem. This indicates that a form of international market failure must be involved. By not internalizing environmental costs, each exporting country contributes to the persistence of a too-low international price and thus imposes a welfare loss on other commodity-exporting countries. For each of them this welfare loss is a reciprocal transborder externality. International coordination among exporting countries can here improve on the laissez-faire scenario (noncooperative Nash solution). By coordination the exporting countries can surmount the underlying first-mover and free rider problems.
- Transborder pollution and depletion of internationally shared natural resources (e.g., rivers, aquifers) form two obvious cases of border-crossing impacts. Less obvious is the case of primary production that negatively affects biodiversity, for instance the cutting of tropical rainforests for agricultural purposes or large-scale killings of animals that harm agricultural crops. Production countries tend to entrench themselves behind the national sovereignty argument. In recent years this line of defense has started to erode, however. This is exemplified by the CITES treaty on trade in endangered species and several other international environmental agreements.
- At first sight many ecological side-effects of commodity production seem to affect only the production region or, at most, the production country. But choosing the proper observation period is essential for an adequate

assessment. Since the world is an almost closed ecological system, accumulation of local damage can easily have border-crossing consequences. All issues now being recognized as transborder or global externalities initially started as isolated, local forms of environmental degradation. This holds true for the use of ozone-depleting gases, carbon-dioxide emissions, extinction of species, genetic erosion, disappearance of tropical rainforests, pollution of oceans, pollution of outer space, and several other issues. The accumulation of local environmental disarrangements can cause disproportionately large consequences for the Earth's ecological system. The biophysical relations in ecosystems often are nonlinear in character, and to a large extent still unknown.[13] Hence, there is reason to expect that many of the ecological side-effects of commodity production that are now considered local will turn out to be international externalities, once considered in a proper time frame. Since as yet we have no instruments to decide which ecological side-effects will eventually appear to have been transborder in nature, it would be beneficial to future generations if the precautionary principle is applied much wider than it is currently. done. It is beyond doubt that feedback loops exist between the abundance of environmental resources and world commodity prices. This is illustrated by the sharp price increases of tropical timber and many sea fish varieties over the last two decades. Commodity-importing countries may be better off facing a moderate import cost increase now instead of huge cost increases in the future. Supporting a switch to best-practice, most environment-friendly production methods in commodity-producing LDCs may turn out to be a wise policy, though it does not maximize current welfare.

- A rapidly emerging issue is psychological transborder externalities. Country B's inhabitants may appreciate natural values (e.g., natural species, forests, or landscapes) in country A. There can be several motives for this. They may appreciate particular natural resources from the point of view of option and bequest values to future generations, or they may attach an intrinsic, nonuse value to nature itself in the ecosystem concerned.[14] If commodity production in country A causes proved effects on these natural values in country A, B's inhabitants may regard these impacts as psychological externalities, even without physical flows taking place to country B. The elusive character of psychological externalities is a fertile soil for trouble. Microeconomic theory offers no reason why psychological spillovers should not be treated on the same footing as physical transborder effects. The mere fact that the environmental developments in country A form part of the preferences of country B's inhabitants makes the transboundary effect economically relevant. Countries severely disagree on the question of whether or not psychological spillover effects can be regarded as a justified basis for intercountry policy reactions. Governments of Malaysia and Indonesia, for instance, have vocally protested against the use of such arguments in the context of international negotiations on tropical timber and rainforest conservation. The same issue played a background role in the U.S.–Mexican tuna/dolphin trade conflict. Whatever the outcome of such debates is,[15] one may expect that the increasing economic integration of national economies offers more and more scope for exerting policy pressure, and for negotiating package agreements that include physical as well as psychological transborder externalities. Rather than protesting against the use of the psychological externality argument, commodity-exporting LDCs had better tag price on such international concerns, place the issue in the context of international services trade, and derive financial transfers from it.

- A last form of transborder externalities is the indirect economic effects of environmental degradation due to commodity production. If ecological degradation is driven beyond local regenerative capacities this may endanger the very livelihoods of people living there, resulting in international migration flows and in the necessity of international poverty relief. The expectation of such economic transborder effects offers a motive for international cooperation in an early phase.

When transborder externalities exist—and they are likely to exist—a trade-off between purely national preferences no longer generates allocative decisions that are also rational from an international perspective.

Switching costs are implementation and adjustment costs that accompany an internalization policy. A switch to environmentally less-damaging production methods or to export products which are more adapted to the country's environmental resources brings about switching costs for the public sector (e.g., infrastructural investment, extension services, tax structure) and for the private producers (e.g., investment requirements, learning-curve inefficiencies, recurrent costs, employment). The costs can be such that governments are deterred from pursuing their first choice. Commodity-exporting countries are thus kept in environmentally damaging export specialization patterns which they would be keen to give up. From an international perspective the adjustment costs retard or even inhibit the reallocation of production to those countries whose environmental resources are best fit for a particular primary commodity, and, hence, produce suboptimal outcomes.

The effect of switching costs is aggravated when international capital market imperfections exist. To finance the switching costs, producers and their governments need access to additional financing resources. Since many LDC governments already wrestle with fiscal deficits and ongoing fiscal adjustment, the switching costs create an additional government demand at the capital market. Domestic financial markets are often shallow.[16] To avoid crowding out domestic private companies, governments turn to international capital markets. However, existing foreign debts and prior debt-servicing problems create great reluctance in international banks and in international bond markets to make further financial commitments in commodity-exporting LDCs. Information asymmetries like moral hazard problems and adverse selection has led to credit rationing behavior by international lenders. Such capital market imperfections make it difficult to surmount the switching costs problem. Suboptimal international production patterns are the result. International coordination is required to cure such capital market imperfections.

The conclusion here is that several certainly not unlikely conditions may occur which make nationally-determined environmental policy decisions suboptimal from the point of view of international welfare maximization. International intervention could then generate Pareto improvements across countries. Intergovernmental agreements substitute for the lack of supranational regulatory authorities. International cooperation makes it possible to reach policy decisions that consider all relevant costs and benefits. Moreover, by invalidating real and imaginary "beggar-thy-neighbor" arguments it will also facilitate domestic political compromising with regard to environmental issues vis-à-vis commodity export sectors.

INTERNATIONAL COMMODITY-RELATED ENVIRONMENTAL AGREEMENTS (ICREAS)

Several forms of international cooperation can be conceived of for dealing with the aforementioned problems, including commodity-specific instruments (cf. Kox and Linnemann 1994) and more issue-specific instruments (e.g., for dealing with international credit rationing for commodity-dependent LDCs). The rest of this chapter will be devoted to the potential contribution of a new instrument to regulate the issues at hand, namely International Commodity-Related Environmental Agreements (ICREAs).

ICREAs are voluntary agreements between countries to regulate particular aspects of the internalization of commodity-specific environmental externalities.[17] They are designed as cooperative solutions to achieve internalization of environmental externalities in the price of internationally-traded primary commodities. Like most other international environmental instruments they can only complement and certainly not substitute for environmental policy by governments of commodity-producing countries. ICREAs fully respect the sovereignty of governments in exporting countries while offering them possibilities to reconcile environmental targets with their macroeconomic constraints. Although priority ranking can be subject to negotiation, the basic objectives of this type of agreement are to:

- Temporarily relieve the income effects and foreign exchange effects caused by the introduction of domestic internalization programs;
- Effectuate natural resource pricing for internationally traded primary commodities by improving the operation of markets;
- Bring about a transition process toward ecologically sound production methods;
- Support governments of the poorer LDCs in shaping an ecological policy toward the commodity export sector; and
- Contribute to export diversification programs in LDCs where natural preconditions are not fit for producing the commodity in an environmentally sound way, but where switching costs and a lack of alternative foreign exchange sources would otherwise impede the diversification process.

The eventual form of an ICREA must be adapted to the market situation, production conditions, and production costs structures for the commodity concerned. Two basic variants will be mentioned here. The first one is a standard-setting variant. It is an agreement between countries to apply common standards with regard to production technology. The second variant is a transfer ICREA with a financial compensation mechanism. It operates through a compensation fund formed by contributions from importing countries. Both types of agreements are created for a particular time period that is sufficiently long for the majority of LDC exporters to adopt environmental policies and switch to environmentally preferable production methods. By adopting and supporting international ecolabel systems for sustainably produced commodities the ICREAs can improve the operation of commodity markets and thus create a basis for subsequent national policy measures. After the agreements expire market forces can again take over. In some cases it may be necessary to maintain some form of international monitoring to avoid backsliding to old practices.

In a standard-setting agreement exporting countries agree to certain technology-related environmental standards for a specific commodity over an agreed-upon transition period. By doing so, they can avoid undercutting each other's prices through a continued use of cheaper but environmentally damaging production methods. An example would be an agreement to ban a particular damaging production method, or an agreement to apply common minimum norms for environmental quality in production regions. The coordinated introduction of alternative but more expensive new production methods and a ban on damaging but cheaper methods will, all other things equal, result in a price increase.[18] Exporting countries can create a cartel-like agreement in which the cooperation of importing countries is not required. However, if the cartel coalition is unstable or if important export countries stay outside the cartel, participation of major importing countries helps to suppress free ridership among exporters.

The transfer variant achieves full resource pricing (user pays) in a more direct and more flexible way. A compensation fund is created from financial contributions by importing countries. The annual contribution of the importing countries is proportional to their net import volume of the commodity and their per capita income level. The exporting LDCs may draw on this fund for financing projects and programs that improve the environmental record of the commodity involved. Drawing rights on the fund can be made proportional to export volumes. Countries may use the funds differently according to their natural preconditions and environmental policy priorities. While one country uses funds for abating or avoiding erosion problems caused by production of the commodity, another country may prefer to use the funds for stimulating the use of production methods that result in less water pollution. Funds should only be used for the commodity involved and funding must fit a commonly agreed mandate. Some follow-up monitoring is necessary to secure that proper use is made of the funds. Repeated abuse should result in exclusion from further funds, or even in trade sanctions by importing countries.

The magnitude of the ICREA fund can be derived by taking incremental costs in a reference country as a starting point, or more simply by a rule of thumb method, say 3%–10% of a trend price. How the import countries collect their contribution for the compensation fund is up to them. Several forms are possible that differ in the degree to which they effectuate the user pays principle: a levy on domestic commodity use, contribution from general tax receipts, or even an import levy (provided this is made consistent with GATT/WTO obligations).

Operational Issues

A major operational issue concerns the degree of country participation. Without sufficient participation this type of agreement will not succeed in finding a way out from the international free ridership problem. The ICREA is an agreement between sovereign governments. Hence, positive incentives rather than negative sanctions should encourage participation. Free ridership by exporting or importing countries can be handled by transfer ICREAs in the following way. For exporting countries the financial transfers are the most important incentive for participation. Importing countries can provide a further incentive by levying the ICREA charge on all their imports (i.e., without discriminating for country of origin). This removes a possible incentive for price undercutting by nonparticipating export countries. To secure participation by the environmentally most disadvantaged countries such as those countries who stand to lose most export earnings by internalization policy, side payments from the fund will be necessary (e.g., for export diversification out of this commodity). Nonparticipation by import countries is discouraged when the export countries charge a higher price for nonparticipating import countries, with the differential being channelled back to the ICREA fund. Parallel markets between nonparticipating import and export countries can only be abated with political pressure and possibly with financial pressure and/or trade sanctions.[19] Positive incentives are much more preferable, however.

Participation by importing countries would not only substantiate the promises made in the Rio Declaration to which most of them subscribed; the existence of transborder externalities, certainly in a long-term view, makes it a matter of enlightened self-interest to participate. A further motive for them to cooperate is the desire to avoid the use of environmental policy as a strategic instrument in international trade competition.[20]

The appropriateness and efficiency of ICREAs depends on a number of critical conditions. Causality links between commodity production and the occurrence of negative environmental impacts must be well-established. The occurrence of these environmental problems must be sufficiently general in major export countries. Furthermore, domestic government policy should not form the main cause (incentive) for the negative environmental consequences of commodity production. Technological alternatives for current polluting or resource depleting production methods must be available, either in the form of process improvements or in the form of "after-process" neutralization measures. Moreover, implementation of the alternative technologies must have a more than trivial consequence for unit costs or government budgets.[21]

Simulation studies (Karp et al. 1994; Kox 1994) are useful means to further specify the conditions in which introduction of ICREAs is feasible and efficient. The feasibility of an ICREA for a particular commodity can only be established by in-depth studies. Khalid et al. (1995) studied the feasibility of an ICREA for cocoa. As 90% of world cocoa producers are small farmers, national institutions like extension services, cocoa research institutes, cocoa marketing boards, and agricultural departments play major roles in formulating and implementing domestic policies with regard to cocoa. These institutes undertake research and development to adapt cultivation practices to local circumstances, disseminate knowledge on new technologies, supply inputs, and provide extension services to smallholders. If the international cocoa price would rise through a coordinated approach, the additional costs of environmentally superior technologies could be passed on to the importing countries. The financial transfers of a cocoa ICREA can strengthen the exporting countries' institutional infrastructure for the promotion of environmentally sustainable production methods. The possibilities of an ICREA for raw cotton were investigated by de Vries (1995). Although cotton is an agricultural crop with severe negative environmental externalities in most export countries, it was found that an ICREA for cotton is unlikely to be successful because of the relatively small part of LDC exports in world cotton consumption, the large share of domestic cotton consumption in major LDCs, and the fact that most cotton is exported in processed form. De Vries and Leliveld (1995) investigated the potential for an ICREA for copper. They found a combination of a standard-setting ICREA and a transfer ICREA to be instrumental for achieving environmental upgrading of LDC copper mines. Ecological standards for copper mining in an OECD country could be taken as a basis. Financial transfers offset the concomitant income and foreign exchange effect in LDCs.

CONCLUDING REMARKS

The 1992 UNCED summit in Rio de Janeiro called for a worldwide application of the polluter-pays principle as a central guideline for the internalization of environmental costs. This chapter argued that developing countries will not easily follow this recommendation for their major source of foreign exchange earnings, the export of primary commodities. Given the virtual impossibility of most countries to influence the world commodity price, unilateral internalization measures work out as a tax on exports. The concomitant income and foreign exchange effects create a difficult trade-off between domestic environmental quality and export earnings. Without a concerted international endeavor it is unlikely that international commodity prices will ever reflect the real natural resource costs of their production. The presence of recurrent transborder externalities, adjustment costs, and international capital market imperfections render the resulting international production allocation inefficient. Exporting countries stand to gain from a joint approach to suppress free rider behavior with regard to each other's internalization attempts. The presence of transborder externalities and the existence of feedback loops between environmental quality and commodity prices make participation by the importing countries a matter of enlightened self-interest. This chapter described the potential of a new type of international environmental agreement, International Commodity-Related Environmental Agreements, to deal with the issues at stake. These institutions enable LDC governments to implement now, rather than in the far future, the necessary environmental policies.

ACKNOWLEDGMENTS

I would like to thank Jeroen van den Bergh and Jan van der Straaten for their useful comments on this chapter.

FOOTNOTES

1. Higher output of these export sectors combined with greater exposure to world markets strengthens the opportunities to observe and adopt new technologies and to acquire better knowledge about foreign consumer preferences. A massive literature exists on the static and dynamic advantages of exports for LDCs (cf. Bhagwati 1989; Pack 1989).
2. One of them is a series of studies undertaken by UNCTAD on the ecological footprint of rice, cocoa and cacao (UNCTAD 1993a). Conway and Pretty (1991) give a broad assessment of the relation between agriculture and pollution. Warhurst (1993) reviews much of the literature on the impact of mining on the LDC environment. Kox, van der Tak and de Vries (1993) sketch 18 environmental commodity profiles. Panayotou and Ashton (1992) assess the ecological impacts of tropical timber trade. Further surveys of the relevant literature can be found in Proops et al. (1993), Pearce and Warford (1993), and Kox (1994).
3. On the costs of deforestation, see Repetto et al. (1987) on Indonesia, WRI (1990) on Costa Rica, and Paris and Ruzicka (1991) on the Philippines. On soil erosion in African regions see Bishop and Allen (1989), Mortimore (1989), and Magrath and Arens (1989).
4. The OECD PPP guidelines were meant to prevent a broad-scale application of subsidies and tax exemptions for pollution control. This preoccupation is reflected in the name of the original guidelines, Guiding Principles Concerning the International Economic Aspects of Environmental Policies (OECD 1972, 1975).
5. The negative trade effects of unilateral environmental policy in small open economies have since been documented in trade literature (e.g., Grubel 1976; Siebert 1977).
6. More details on empirical estimates can be found in Kox (1994) and Repetto (1994). The latter regards the inelastic demand as a success condition for export taxes reflecting the production-related costs of pollution abatement and natural resource preservation.
7. Primary commodities offer few opportunities for product differentiation, because apart from some product grades most commodities are traded as bulk goods. Given the homogeneity of most LDC primary export commodities, importing countries switch easily between import sources.
8. The long-term price elasticity of tin supply (worldwide, weighted) amounted to 1.07 according to estimates by Tan (1987), while it amounted to 1.25 and 1.34 for Thailand and Bolivia. The long-term cotton acreage elasticity with respect to price changes amounted to 1.80 for developed countries and 0.44 for LDC exporters (Thigpen 1978). In a more recent study, the long-run price elasticity of cotton supply was estimated at 1.40 for Argentina and 2.46 for Australia (Coleman and Thigpen 1991). The long-term elasticity of world soy bean production with respect to the world market price amounted to 2.75 over the period 1961–1977 (Augusto and Pollak 1981). The short-run elasticity of new tea plantings with regard to prices was estimated at approximately 0.5 in India and Kenya, but between 1.5 and 2.0 in Sri Lanka and Malawi (Akiyama and Trivedi 1987). The long-term elasticity of jute acreage in India amounted to 1.07 according to estimates of Thigpen and Akiyama (1986). The long-run elasticity of coffee supply was estimated at 1.10 for Brazil and 1.05 for Indonesia (Akiyama and Duncan 1982a). For cocoa and rubber the supply elasticities were sometimes found to be below unity, hinting at a less sharp international competition intensity (e.g., Lopriore and Burger 1992). However, other research for cocoa found several regions with long-run supply elasticities above unity (Askari and Cummings 1976). Apart from price elasticity of supply, another indicator of competition intensity is the supply elasticity with respect to idle capacity. The elasticity of primary copper supply with respect to mine capacity over the period 1964–1983 was estimated to be 1.20 for Chile and 1.10 for Peru (Tan 1987).
9. Rubber, groundnuts, groundnut oil, cocoa, tin, palm oil, bauxite, copper, oilseed cake/meal, bananas, phosphate rock, and sugar appear to be the markets in which a few countries could perhaps influence world market prices. However, when one accounts for intercommodity substitution, palm oil, groundnut oil, sugar, and oilseed cake/meal drop from this subset.

from this subset. Seventeen promising cases remain: cocoa from Côte d'Ivoire and Ghana; manganese ore from Gabon; phosphate rock from Morocco and Jordan; jute from Bangladesh and China; tin from Brazil and Malaysia; rubber from Malaysia, Indonesia and Thailand; tea from India, China, Sri Lanka and Kenya; and iron ore from Brazil. If there is no short-term alternative export supply from other countries, the aforementioned nine countries are in a good position to influence the international market price by their unilateral actions.

10. The relevance of this mechanism is illustrated by the following observation of UNCTAD: "Over the last two decades, the traditional structural problems faced by commodity producers and exporters, such as price and earnings instability and relatively slow growth in demand, have been exacerbated by rapidly increasing supplies. The latter stem from increased productivity and the emergence of new and efficient producers, coupled with the inability of inefficient ones to diversify into other economic activities. This has been the case, in particular, for cocoa, vegetable oils and bauxite. For a wide range of commodities exported by developing countries, the expansion in supply has also reflected the pressure to increase exports resulting from the need to service large foreign debts" (UNCTAD 1993b).

11. Kox (1994) shows that in the early 1990s developing countries with a high dependency on primary exports systematically had a higher debt service ratio, debt-to-export ratio, and a higher incidence of debt restructuring. Debt servicing problems due to a lack of foreign exchange damage a country's international credit reputation, resulting in international credit rationing or higher cost of international credit.

12. The development of a consistent environmental policy requires that the incentives created by other government policies are also subjected to an audit. It is well-documented (e.g., World Bank 1992) that other policy areas, like those to enhance agricultural productivity, create disincentives for environmental protection, or worse, stimulate environmental degradation by producers. Input subsidies like those on agrochemicals (pesticides and fertilizers), irrigation water and energy may lower the private marginal costs of these inputs below the appropriate social marginal costs. Linking land ownership titles to deforestation and land clearance, as practiced in several LDCs, gives a wrong incentive to producers. Governments should first screen their own policy consistency before jumping into incremental policy measures.

13. For example, see Hannon (1991), Cleveland (1987), van den Bergh (1991), Beanlands (1995) and other contributions in Munasinghe and Shearer (1995).

14. The latter motive, also labeled "existence value," is sometimes wrongly considered nonanthropocentric. Any valuation represents an instrumental judgment, even if one values nature for the sake of nature itself. The latter case is the attachment of a nonuse value.

15. In international trade policy the unwarranted use of psychological externality arguments is kept in check with a material injury test and proportional response test. In the GATT/WTO treaties, for example, a material injury test has been developed in the context of regulations on antidumping and countervailing duties. It gives procedural criteria to establish the extent of injury created by imports of allegedly dumped or subsidized import goods. The procedure would most likely sift out psychological spillovers as nonactionable. U.S. trade legislation also uses a material injury test, which defines material injury as "harm which is not inconsequential, immaterial, or unimportant" (Jackson 1992).

16. Emerging capital markets tend not to be found in developing countries highly dependent on primary commodity exports.

17. International Commodity-Related Environmental Agreements (ICREAs) must be clearly distinguished from "old-style" international commodity agreements. The latter is aimed at commodity price stabilization, which is not an objective of ICREAs, even though a stable and rewarding commodity price would probably facilitate the introduction of environmentally sound production methods (Kox 1991).

18. To avoid an additional supply and a subsequent price fall, it can be necessary to supplement the ICREA with a temporary agreement on production quantities.

19. The use of trade sanctions against free riders in the context of international environmental agreements (IEAs) is subject of intensive debate within the WTO. Some IEAs, like the Montreal protocol, the CITES treaty and the Basel Agreement, contain trade sanctions against free riders. The crucial issue is that trade-affecting environmental measures should not be used to cover up "ordinary" trade protectionism and should not affect international trade in an unnecessarily restrictive way. A central message from the UNCED conference in Rio was that trade and environment policies should be mutually supportive. Agenda 21 explicitly stated that the accomplishment of "an open, equitable, secure, nondiscriminatory and predictable multilateral trading system" would represent a large step in this direction.

20. Participation in ICREAs is probably more effective than crusades against so-called environmental dumping (i.e., the use of deliberately lower environmental standards as a competition instrument). Different costs of complying with environmental standards may reflect different natural preconditions for the production of certain goods or different environmental preferences in the country of origin. Hence, it is bizarre to use trade measures in order to equalize environmental compliance costs.

21. If the increases in operational and investment costs are small, the producers themselves could probably easily absorb the income effect of a unilateral internalization policy. No international coordination would be required in principle.

REFERENCES

Akande, S. O. 1993. The Effects of Producing and Processing Cocoa on the Environment: A Case Study of Nigeria. UNCTAD/COM/23. Geneva: UNCTAD.

Akiyama, T. and R. C. Duncan. 1982a. Analysis of the World Coffee Market. World Bank Staff Working Paper #7. Washington DC: World Bank.

Akiyama, T. and P. K. Trivedi. 1987. A New Global Tea Model: Specification, Estimation and Simulation. Staff Working Paper #7. Washington DC: World Bank.

Askari, H. and J. T. Cummings. 1976. Agricultural Supply Response—A Survey of the Econometric Supply Response. New York: Praeger.

Augusto, S. and P. Pollak. 1981. Structure and prospects of the world fats and oils economy. In World Bank Commodity Models, Volume I. World Bank Staff Commodity Working Papers #6. Washington DC: World Bank.

Bacha, E. L. 1990. A three-gap model of foreign transfers and the GDP growth rate in developing countries. *Journal of Development Studies* 32:279–296.

Beanlands, G. 1995. Cumulative effects and sustainable development. In *Defining and Measuring Sustainability—The Biophysical Foundations*, eds. M. Munasinghe and W. Shearer. Washington DC: United Nations University / World Bank.

Bhagwati, J. N. 1989. Outward orientation. In *Handbook of Development Economics, Volume II*, eds. H. B. Chenery and T. N. Srinivasan. Amsterdam: North-Holland.

Biggs, G. 1993. Application of the polluter-pays principle in Latin America. In *Fair Principles For Sustainable Development: Essays on Environmental Policy and Developing Countries*, ed. E. Dommen. Aldershot: Edward Elgar.

Bishop, J. and J. Allen. 1989. The On-Site Costs of Soil Erosion In Mali. Environment Department Working Paper No. 21. Washington DC: World Bank .

Blunden, J. 1985. *Mineral Resources and Their Management.* London: Longman.

Cleveland, C. J. 1987. Biophysical economics: Historical perspective and historical research trends. *Ecological Modelling* 38:47–73.

Coleman, J. and M. Thigpen. 1991. An Econometric Model of the World Cotton and Non-Cellulosic Fibers Market. World Bank Staff Working Paper #25. Washington DC: World Bank.

de Vries, A. P. M. 1995. An International Commodity Related Environmental Agreement for Cotton: An Appraisal. ICREA Project. Amsterdam: Economics Department, Free University.

de Vries, A. P. M. and A. Leliveld. 1995. An International Commodity-Related Environmental Agreement for Copper: An Appraisal. ICREA Project. Amsterdam: Economics Department, Free University.

Dommen, A. J. 1992. Physical and Economic Interactions in African Traditional Agriculture: Implications for Resource Conservation, UNCTAD/COM/10. Geneva: UNCTAD.

Dommen, E. ed. 1993. *Fair Principles for Sustainable Development: Essays on Environmental Policy and Developing Countries.* Aldershot: Edward Elgar.

Grubel, H. G. 1976. Some effects of environmental controls on international trade: The Heckscher-Ohlin model. In *Studies In International Environmental Economics,* ed. I. Walter. New York: J. Wiley and Sons.

Hannon, B. 1991. Accounting in ecological systems. In *Ecological Economics: The Science and Management of Sustainability,* ed. R. Costanza. New York: Columbia University Press.

Hoff, K. and J. E. Stiglitz. 1993. Imperfect information and rural credit markets: Puzzles and policy perspectives. In *The Economics of Rural Organization: Theory, Practice And Policy,* eds. K. Hoff, A. Braverman and J. E. Stiglitz. Oxford: Oxford University Press.

Jackson, J. H. 1992. *The World Trading System—Law and Policy of International Economic Relations.* Cambridge MA: The MIT Press.

Karp, L. et al. 1994. Internationalization of Environmental Costs and International Trade. Mimeo Paper. Department of Agricultural and Resource Economics. University of California, Berkeley.

Khalid, A. R. and J .B. Braden. 1993. Welfare effects of environmental regulation in an open economy: The case of Malaysian palm oil. *Journal of Agricultural Economics* 44:25–38.

Khalid, A. R., S. Mad Nasir, S. Ahmad, and H. Siti Aishah. 1995. Case Study on the Appropriateness and Feasibility of an International Commodity-Related Environmental Agreement for Cocoa. Universiti Pertanian Malaysia/ICREA Project Free University, Serdang, Amsterdam.

Kox, H. L. M. 1991. Integration of environmental externalities in international commodity agreements. *World Development* 19:933–943.

Kox, H. 1994. International Commodity-Related Environmental Agreements: Background and Design, Working Paper. Amsterdam: Economics Department, Free University.

Kox, H. and H. Linnemann. 1994. International commodity-related environmental agreements as instruments for promoting sustainable production of primary export commodities. In *Sustainable Resource Management and Resource Use: Policy Questions and Research Needs,* eds. F. Duijnhouwer, G. van der Meer, and H. Verbruggen. Rijswijk: RMNO.

Kox, H., C., van der Tak, and H. de Vries. 1993. Preconditions for International Commodity-Related Environmental Agreements—Results of a Pre-Feasibility Study. Working Paper ICREA Project. Amsterdam: Economics Department, Free University.

Lopriore, M. and K. Burger. 1992. An Annual Model of the World Cocoa Market. Paper Presented at Seminar on Commodity Analysis (Jakarta 15–27 June). ESI. Amsterdam.

Magrath, W. and P. Arens. 1989. *The Costs of Soil Erosion on Java—A Natural Resource Accounting Approach.* Washington DC: World Resources Institute.

May, P. H., C. L. Vegro, and J. A. Menezes. 1993. Coffee and Cocoa Production and Processing in Brazil. UNCTAD/COM/17. Geneva: UNCTAD.

Mortimore, M. 1989. *Adapting to Drought: Farmers, Famines and Desertification in West Africa.* Cambridge: Cambridge University Press.

Munasinghe, M. and W. Shearer. eds. 1995. *Defining and Measuring Sustainability—The Biophysical Foundations.* United Nations University/World Bank. Washington DC: World Bank.

OECD. 1972. *Guiding Principles Concerning the International Economic Aspects of Environmental Policies.* Paris: OECD.

OECD. 1975. *The Polluter Pays Principle: Definition, Analysis, Implementation.* Paris: OECD.

Pack, H. 1989. Industrialization and trade. In *Handbook of Development Economics,* Volume II, eds. H. B. Chenery and T. N. Srinivasan. Amsterdam: North-Holland.

Panayotou, Th. and P. S. Ashton. 1992. *Not by Timber Alone—Economics and Ecology for Sustaining Tropical Forests.* Washington DC: Island Press.

Paris, R. and I. Ruzicka. 1991. Barking up the Wrong Tree: The Role of Rent Appropriation in Tropical Forest Management. Environment Office Discussion Paper. Manilla: Asian Development Bank.

Pearce, D. W. and J. J. Warford. 1993. *World Without End: Economics, Environment and Sustainable Development.* Oxford: World Bank/Oxford University Press.

Proops, J., P. Steele, E. Ozdemiroglu, and D. Pearce. 1993. The Internalization of Environmental Costs and Resource Values: A Conceptual Study. CSERGE/EFTEC. London.

Repetto, R. 1994. Trade and Sustainable Development. Environment and Trade Series # 1. Geneva: UNEP.

Repetto, R. et al. 1987. *Natural Resource Accounting for Indonesia.* Washington DC: World Resources Institute.

Siebert, H. 1977. Environmental quality and the gains from trade. *Kyklos* 30:657–673.

Tan, C. S. 1987. An Econometric Analysis of the World Copper Market. World Bank Staff Working Paper #20. Washington DC: World Bank.

Taylor, L. 1993. The rocky road to reform: Trade industrial, financial and agricultural strategies. *World Development* 21:577–590.

Thigpen, M. E. 1978. International Cotton Market Prospects. World Bank Commodity Paper Series #2. Washington DC: World Bank.

Thigpen, M. and T. Akiyama. 1986. Prospects for the World Jute Industry. World Bank Staff Commodity Working Paper #14. Washington DC: World Bank.

UNCED. 1992. *Agenda 21: The United Nations Programme of Action from Rio.* New York: United Nations.

UNCTAD. 1992. UNCTAD VIII – Analytical Report by the UNCTAD Secretariat to the Conference. New York: United Nations.

UNCTAD. 1993a. Experience Concerning Environmental Effects of Commodity Production and Processing: Synthesis of Case Studies on Cocoa, Coffee and Rice. Report by the Secretariat. TD/B/CN.1/15. Geneva: UNCTAD

UNCTAD. 1993b. Trade and Development Report 1993. New York: United Nations.

van den Bergh, J. C. J. M. 1991. *Dynamic Models for Sustainable Development.* Amsterdam: Thesis Publishers and Tinbergen Institute.

van Tongeren, J. et al. 1993. Integrated environmental and economic accounting: A case study for Mexico. In *Environmental Economics and Natural Resource Management in Developing Countries,* ed. M. Munasinghe. Washington DC: CIDIE/World Bank.

Warhurst, A. 1993. Environmental degradation from mining and mineral processing. In Developing Countries: Corporate Responses and National Policies. OECD Development Centre. Paris: OECD.

World Bank. 1992. *World Development Report 1992: Development and the Environment.* Oxford: Oxford University Press.

World Bank. 1993. *Commodity Trade and Price Trends 1989–1991.* Washington DC: World Bank.

World Bank. 1994. *World Development Report 1994: Infrastructure for Development.* Oxford: Oxford University Press.

World Resources Institute (WRI). 1990. *Costs of Resource Degradation in Costa Rica.* Washington DC: World Resources Institute.

INDEX